# LIVING WITHOUT
# RESERVATIONS

*a journey by land and sea
in search of happiness*

# BARBARA ELAINE SINGER

Published in the United States of America by:
Hear Me Roar Press
www.BarbaraElaineSinger.com

ISBN: 978-0-9843254-1-2

Book and cover design by Darlene and Dan Swanson of Van-garde Imagery, Inc.

# Acknowledgements

Thanks to Debby Campbell for being by my side during all of my years of transition. I am so glad you got Parker, your happy ending. Thanks to Megan, Jennifer, Christy and Patti for responding to all my emails with silly questions and doubts, and to Risa for your meticulous read-through. Thank goodness you can't sleep and I was able to give you something to do in the middle of the night.

Thanks to my Dad and Pete for being such good sports by letting me share their trips. Thanks to Buddy, Paola and Eduardo who opened their homes to a woman who didn't ask any of the normal questions.

To Brittany, I love you for sticking with your mom when I didn't always behave the way you wished I would. Thank you for putting your flair and creativity into designing the cover.

And to Giuseppe, my happy ending and new beginning. Without your strong belief in my story, this book would never exist.

Go confidently in the direction of your dreams.
Live the life you have imagined.

Henry David Thoreau

# Chapter One

## Driving Home from Atlanta
## May 2006

I slide behind the wheel of a borrowed silver Honda. It is a beautiful sunny Monday morning and I have seven hours of solitary driving in front of me.

I just kissed the cheek of my sleeping daughter and grabbed my carry-on-only size suitcase and blow up mattress bag as I snuck quietly from her apartment, trying not to wake her and her roommate. My only child is successfully set up in her first apartment; she is a third-year college student. Just four days ago Brittany, Seth (her high school sweetheart and fellow Emory student), and I headed out of Orlando at o-dark-hundred with the car packed to the gills with everything we could think of to outfit her newly rented apartment.

We did the *Design on a Dime* reality TV show in two days, but in real life. Brittany's room turned out adorable, serene yet hip. She had a vision, walked into Home Depot and within thirty seconds of scanning the millions of colors of paint, picked out Durango Blue. Armed with a brush, a roller and a tray, we were ready to transform her empty slate into a vision of deep smoky blue walls, white platform bed, and black accessories. The centerpiece of the room is an Andy Warhol style black and white Audrey Hepburn piece of art for over the bed.

Now I head for home, just me and the road. In typical Barbara Singer style, I have a plethora of books on tape planned out to the minute so that I won't waste any time. Making the best use of every minute of my life has been my driving force for the past forty-four years.

After an hour or two or three, the quiet monotone hum of the road gets to me. What am I going back to? What am I doing? What am I going to do with the second half of my life? I am going back to no job, no husband, no family and a one-bedroom garage apartment that houses the remnants of a life I no longer have.

How can this be? I am a girl who did everything right! I contributed the maximum to my 401K, I was a good wife and devoted mother. I had lots of friends, fought my way through college and taught myself how to behave in the world of the "haves". I learned how to be successful, had a big, beautifully decorated pool home in the suburbs, and won many sales achievement rewards and trips. I stayed thin, ran an efficient household and in my spare time, finished two Ironman competitions and three marathons.

But now it is all gone. I am an empty slate just like Brittany's bedroom, except I don't have a vision of what should come next. I am a girl who has had every second of my life planned since I can remember. I had the one-year plan, the three-year plan, even the five- year plan. I had a list of the 100 things I wanted to do. I had a list of places I wanted to go; I even had a list of things I didn't want to do. I knew every event going on in town, but I couldn't wait for Brittany to grow up so I could do something else.

Maybe my mother was right. "Stop being in such a hurry," she would say. "You will run out of things to do and places to see." This was mind-blowing to me. There is a whole world out there to be conquered. Run out of things to do, please! But now, here I sit driving along without a plan, no list, nothing.

What do I really want to do this summer, this year, for the rest of my life?

If money were no object, what would I be? Probably a travel buddy where I would take people on the trips of their dreams using my travel experience, or maybe an Italian tour operator, a travel writer or a personal coach. The thought of throwing myself into a new job in the same field has zero appeal. Maybe I'll move to an island, or as I have always dreamed, move to Italy. I am just too tired. When I had obstacles, I could overcome them, but now without hurdles, I cannot see the road. Given the option to choose anything, I can't decide what to do next.

What do I really want to do this summer?

I am enjoying this driving thing, hours of scenery just passing by; me and the highway. I have always wanted to drive across the United States in an RV. Tom, my former fiancé, and I had always planned on taking such a trip, but we never got around to it. Now, on this day, I do have the time. My dad has a camper just sitting in the driveway at his home in Pennsylvania. I am sure he would let me borrow it. Why not? It would give me some time to think.

I look at the clock. It's noon on a Monday; I will never get him on the phone. Surely he is not home and he never answers his cell phone. I dial anyway, thinking I'll leave a message.

To my surprise, he answers the phone. "Hey Dad, I was thinking of doing a little driving trip this summer and want to see if I can borrow your RV," I ask.

"Well, where are you going?"

"I am thinking of Montana, Wyoming, Colorado, and Washington. You know, places I have never been, hit all the big national parks." I explain.

"I see," he says, "Well, when do you want to do this?"

"Right now," I say firmly, "I can be in Pennsylvania in a few days, then I'll hit the road for a month or two. I want to be back for Mom's seventieth birthday party on July 28th. So, can I borrow your camper?"

"No."

"No! What do you mean no?" I say, stunned.

"I won't loan it to you, but I will go with you," he says.

"You will? I am talking about going next week, Dad."

"I know. Would you consider driving to Alaska?" he asks.

"Alaska—you can't drive to Alaska, can you?" I respond. "I thought you have to cruise there."

"Well, it is far, but we can do it."

I have never been there and I have always wanted to go, so why not? Within three minutes, we have a plan. My dad and I are driving to Alaska in a camper. I will fly to Pennsylvania, we will leave right away, and be back for the birthday party.

I call my girlfriends to tell them the news and, and of course, the phone lines are burning up. What are you going to do with your apartment? What about your car? Who's going to take care of your rental properties? I hadn't thought of any of this, and yet I was completely unconcerned and 100 percent certain that it didn't even matter.

Within three days I rent my completely furnished apartment to my girlfriend who is building a new home and needs a temporary place. I loan my car to my friend with five children who loves driving my two-seater BMW convertible—this, of course, in exchange for gas money—and find a reluctant volunteer to check the mail at the first of the month and deposit the rent checks. The rest I can manage from the road. I buy an airline ticket. And just like that, it is done.

In a matter of ten days, I go from leaving a job without a clue of what to do next, to embarking on a journey. . . . I send an email blast and it goes like this:

I have news. I am driving across the United States in an RV to Alaska with my Dad. On June first, I am flying to PA then we're off to Montana, Wyoming, Idaho, Washington, Alaska and back.

I have sublet my apartment and car for the summer. I have lost my mind and found my soul. I am completely out of control and couldn't be less afraid and more happy. I am in the right place at the right time and I am eager and open to see what comes next. I know, you are saying, "I thought she had her mid-life crisis a few years ago?" The saga continues!

Barbara

And the responses I got were amazing. My email struck a cord.

*I'm so glad Dad has a travel partner this summer. I think you will make a good team. Thanks for helping fulfill his lifelong dream of traveling to Alaska. Sharon*

*Go for it Barbara, life should be gulped not sipped. Keep in touch. All the best, David.*

*You have lost your mind . . . good for you . . . wish I could lose mine! Glenda*

*You go girl and have the time of your life! Cherish the time with your Dad & be safe. Best Wishes, Kim*

*Tickled for you!!!! Follow your heart and soul! Great stuff. Robin*

*Perfect!!!!! Enjoy and congratulations. "No risk no gains." Jake*

*You are my hero!!!! Have a blast and keep us
posted along the way. xxoo Susan*

*I got cold chills reading your email.
You are sooooo on the right track. David*

*You're a mess!  and I can't wait to
hear all about it :-) Thearon*

*Sweeeet, have fun and don't look back.  Peter*

Lewis and Clark
Me and Dad
Barbara and Clarence

# Chapter 2

*Leaving*
*May 2006*

My ride drops me at curbside check-in for my early morning flight. The pile of luggage being unloaded is mind-boggling to me. I have traveled all over the world and as a rule, don't check luggage unless I'm skiing or traveling for two weeks or more. I hate waiting for the bags at the airport and have terrible luck. But this time, I have packed two huge cases, a carry-on and, of course, my shoulder bag. I have more than I will need for the trip. One case is filled with just reading materials, travel guides, a fat journal, books on tape and electronics, including my laptop. I packed for months, not a few weeks. Looking at this pile of luggage, I realize I am not coming back. I can't go on this way. I am in love with a man whose life I cannot live in; I have to get away and make a clean start. Am I running away from or running to? I have waited my whole life to make decisions with just myself in mind. Now, here it is. I am running *to*, yes, I must believe I am running *to*. Be Brave.

Goodbye is much harder than I thought it would be. My heart is pounding. My ride pulls away from the curb and I wait in line for the skycap. Big dark sunglasses hide the tears washing my carefully applied make-up down my cheeks. I can barely speak by the time it is my turn at the check-in counter. It feels so permanent.

"Where are you going?" the skycap asks.

Good question, I say to myself. I don't know. Wherever the wind blows. No, I am going in search of it. I want to go to that place I know. I want to go to that place that makes my heart sing. That place where I can be who I really am and where I can slow down enough to hear what I need. Is that a place or a level of consciousness? I just know that I need to make a change, and that is really what this summer is all about.

"I am going to Philadelphia," I announce. I am going home to where I grew up; to where my seven brothers and sisters live with their families and where my parents are. I moved away right after college and only went back over the years to visit. I am the only one who moved away. The black sheep.

"You can go, Gate 59. Here are your boarding documents." The agent instructs.

I am doing my best to remain composed and hold back the flood of emotions that has caught me off guard. Get to the gate and find a quiet spot and you will be fine, I tell myself. You are running to, not running from. I round the corner and head for the security check, but I am stopped by a huge line.

I have time, but desperately want to find a quiet place to regain my composure. Instead, I wait. People are looking at me with my big dark sunglasses still on. Keeping my head down, I squirm and tap my foot. Can they tell I am crying? I try to hide behind my long blonde hair that is hanging down around my face. I am wearing a brightly colored chartreuse and pink floral jacket, white pants and heels. I always dress up to travel. I have been rewarded handsomely in my lifetime by looking the part. I am really feeling like I am in a fish bowl. People are staring at me. Breathe, just breathe. I am sure it is the sunglasses, but I can't take them off right now.

After an eternity of waiting, the security officer reviews my documents. Holding up the photo ID, he asks me to remove my sunglasses, which I do. My eyes are red and watery. He tells me he is sorry for making me do this, but it is just his job. I nod understandingly because I can't speak. I hear the lady next to me whisper to her friend, "She is not someone famous, she is crying." On any other day, that would have made me laugh out loud, but not today. Today I am holding on to every shred of courage I have. Be brave. Just get to the gate.

As I get on the plane, I repeat my new mantra again and again. *I am open and eager to see what comes next. I am in the right place at the right time. Life is meant to be fun and I am willing to enjoy it.*

The man sitting next to me is trying to be pleasant, but I can do nothing but weep. I am so embarrassed that I try to sink down into the seat and just disappear, but there is nowhere to go, nowhere to hide. I don't want anyone to know that I am struggling. I try to hold back the tears, but they just keep coming. He hands me his napkin and asks if there is anything he can do.

Everyone asks that same question. "Is there anything I can do?" Oh how

I wish there were. Make the sorrow go away. Make the ache in my heart stop for just one day or just one minute. I feel like I am being punished for bad choices I have made and then, in the next moment of consciousness, I know that that is completely untrue. I am traveling down an unfamiliar path. Change is scary. After all the years of self help, motivation and personal development books I have read, I know intellectually what is happening, yet I never imagined it would be so emotionally difficult. I am way outside of my comfort zone. Nothing is the way it used to be. I am operating without a plan, going on the fly. Some days there are moments of total clarity when I know I am doing exactly what I should be, and I am not scared for a second. And other days, I am totally gripped with fear that is completely paralyzing. I couldn't make a decision if my life depended on it.

This trip is exactly what I need to do. It is an adventure of a lifetime. This is what I have always dreamed about doing. I am driving across the United States in an RV, even though it is with my dad—not Tom; he is gone. Better yet, this is my dad's lifelong dream. I get the chance to take my dad to Alaska. I wish this made me happy, but the pain in my heart hurts too much to leave room for anything else.

How I wish this trip were with Tom. Oh, how I miss him. How did things go so desperately wrong? Thinking back, I know I was living the American Dream, and yet I didn't want it. I had it all—life in the suburbs with the perfect home, a boat on the lake, a well-adjusted, bright daughter in private school, a loyal husband with a secure job and the time and energy to pursue my interests. To put the icing on the cake, I had a dream job as membership director of a private club that allowed me to socialize among the Who's Who of Orlando. I hosted parties, attended wine tastings, and was involved in the community. Our club was wildly successful, partly due to my efforts and those of Debby, my partner in the membership department. We had a huge quota and knocked it out of the park year after year.

On the outside I had it all, but underneath something was stirring. Something just wasn't quite right. For years, I dismissed it. My first priority has always been my daughter. I took motherhood very seriously and made sure she had a stable home life. I needed to stay still so she could grow. There was no doubt, though, that when she went off to college, things would change. I wanted to move, live different places and experience different lifestyles. Perhaps I would live a season on an island, live a season on a boat, live a season in Italy, and live a season in Aspen. I'd give up the treadmill of sales in corporate America and give up the American Dream for freedom. I wanted to stop living for the future and live only for today.

My then husband, Gary, said he bought into my dream, yet as time went by, I learned it was more a mild accommodation than a belief that it would really happen. He was as steady and predictable as the rising sun. Taking a risk was not for him. This lifestyle would take enormous leaps of faith over and over again. It was not something he could stomach. He was raised in a fear-based home by a father who was a former World War II soldier and an engineer. Gary was taught to look for problems, not to just wing it. We had always treated each other with true respect. We didn't argue. Things had settled into a routine. There was plenty for everything.

I pursued my interests, worked, traveled, competed in triathlons and so on. We worked hard and lived below our means. We saved our money for retirement. The harder I worked and the more money I made, the more complicated life got. It was a never-ending search for tax write-offs and second businesses, and being a landlord while investing in real estate. The hamster wheel just kept going faster and faster. The more I accumulated, the more it weighed me down. I wasn't even interested in accumulating stuff, I was interested in financial freedom. It got to the point that I just wanted to get Brittany graduated from high school and off to college so I could do something else. I knew in my heart that working this way for twenty more years until retirement was never going to happen.

I didn't think that Gary and I would stay together after Brittany moved away, but I certainly didn't think it would end the way it did.

# Chapter 3

*Four Years ago*
*February 2002*

When I wake up, I have no idea how today will change my life. I am no one special. I am just a girl. I don't understand the power I have.

Tonight is a big event. The club is booked for a private event, which is notable because we are celebrating the 30th anniversary of the club's inception by Frank Hubert, our founding father. The entire place is booked; there will be no member dining—a necessary evil, but always unpopular with the members.

I bring my dress to change in to rather than driving home to the suburbs in traffic and back again, which would take an eternity. I put on my conservative evening suit, check myself out in the mirror of the athletic club, and with a slight nod of approval I head for the hotel lounge across the street. I have two hours to kill and I think I will see if any displaced club members have landed next door.

I walk into the lounge of the Westin Grand Bohemian with an air of confidence. I know this town inside and out. I know everyone and they know me. After years of working as the membership director of the most prestigious club in Orlando, I can walk into any room and know more than half of the people in it. I walk up to the bar and see a familiar face. Tom Ison, a fixture at the club, gives me an enthusiastic hello. I have seen and greeted Mr. Ison many times at the club, but have never really talked to him. Tonight would be different.

"Let me buy you a drink," he says.

"No, I can't stay. I must go next door for the big celebration."

"Oh, that's why the club is closed," he comments.

"Yes, you didn't know? I am sorry about that," I apologize.

"It's okay. I just came across the street. This place is really nice," he says.

"I rarely come here myself, but it does feel good," I comment.

"Please have a seat. I feel really uncomfortable sitting while such a beautiful lady is standing," he says.

"Really, it's okay. I can only stay for a minute," I explain.

"I think it is so great for Orlando to finally have a five-star hotel downtown. This is a good thing," he says.

"What can I get the lady to drink?" the bartender asks.

"Nothing really, I'm not staying."

"Please. I insist that you at least sit down. I would like to buy you a glass of wine. Would you please allow me to do that?" he says.

"Since you insist, I'll have a Kendall Jackson Chardonnay. Thank you Mr. Ison."

"Hey, we are not in the club. I think it's okay for you to call me Tom."

We talk about everything and nothing. Time passes without my once giving it a thought.

"Are you hungry?" he asks.

"Yes, I am starving," I answer.

"Let's go to Hue. It's a trendy new place down the street," he suggests.

"I would love to," I say. "I am starving."

I am starving. Do I really have any idea what I am saying? What am I feeling? What am I about to do? Even today, with 20/20 hindsight, I cannot or choose not to see what was right in front of my very eyes. I am being pulled by such an incredible power. I feel no real concern about not being at the club. I know I'm supposed to be somewhere else, but it doesn't seem important. Being in that moment completely eclipsed every concern I should have had.

After our snack of Asian shrimp—ironically my daughter's favorite—he holds the door for me as I sink into his low riding corvette. "I need to close up the restaurant. Would you like to go with me?" Tom asks.

"Yes," I tell him. Not having a clue of when or how far away this closing is to take place, and definitely not knowing that I am changing my life forever. I'm totally unaware that from this moment when I say that one simple word, "yes," my life will never be the same.

What I do know for sure, is that I am completely at ease with this stranger. My shoulders have come down at least four inches. The intensity in my entire body has backed down a few octaves. I am so relaxed. I have spoken with this man many times, but I can assure you that I never heard a word he said, not that he didn't say anything important before, I just simply never actually heard a word. But I am listening now. I am hanging on his every word. And he is ever so entertaining. He is charming, charismatic and oh, so attractive. We ride on the highway for what seams like an eternity and like a flash at the same time.

Once at his restaurant, a big black dog greets our car as we pull up. "That's Debo," Tom says, "He won't hurt you."

Tommy, Jr. opens my car door. Introductions are made. I pretend not to notice the silent nod of approval between father and son. I am dressed in a perfectly tailored black Armani suit with a light blue blouse and vintage jewelry. The exact same thing I would wear to his funeral. Tommy is happy for his Dad.

Tom openly introduces me around the bar to his people: the regulars, the newcomers, the drunks, and the nobodies. He is obviously loved and adored. He is in his element.

"Let's take a drink to the pier," he suggests.

"The pier?" I ask. "Where is that?"

"Down by the water, you can see the moonlight much better from there. Bobby, how about a Corona and Crown Royal for us?" he tells the bartender. "It's a beautiful night to be on the water." We walk down to the pier. Tom fumbles with the wad of keys on his ring. After a few minutes of silliness, Tommy comes to the rescue.

"Dad, what are you doing?"

"I want to show Barbara the pier bar."

"Here, then let me open it for you," Tommy says.

Inside, it is a throwback to another era. All kinds of artifacts hang from the walls and the ceilings. It is filled with remnants of a life Tom no longer has. I do not know this man. I do not know his path or his pain or his future, but I do know for sure that I am profoundly connected to him right now and forever.

Tom flips on the stereo and without skipping a beat, we dance as though we've danced a thousand dances. He spins and turns me with complete authority. I am not a dancer, but tonight I am putty in his hands. We are great together. I am laughing and twirling. I do not recognize this girl whose head is thrown back with laughter and whose silly giggles can be heard across the parking lot of Lake Susan Lodge.

Eventually we land on tattered boat seats ripped from an old vessel. They are propped up against the side of the pier. My knees scrape as I straddle Tom. We are enveloped in passion and I don't know or care where I am or who may be watching. He is kissing my lips, my face, my neck. Goosebumps run rampant all over my body. I want him. I want him right now. I want him more than I want to breathe. I want his body all over mine. He obliges and takes me right there on the pier. He sends me out there to a place I do not know. I do not know who I am and if I do, I do not care. I do not know this man, yet I've known this man for a thousand years. I am home. I do know this place. I have longed for it. I will never leave.

Later we drive to Tom's house and it's obvious that he is not expecting a visitor. No one has come here in quite some time. It doesn't matter. We could be in a palace or a prison, and it wouldn't matter because neither of us would notice. Tom takes my hand and leads me into the hallway that is filled with photos of his pride and joy, Tommy Jr, and Kelly, his beloved daughter who was killed in a car accident six years ago. A piece of Tom died that night; he would never be the same. He was supposed to live on through her, but it was not meant to be. I do not know the pain of having someone you love die. I have no clue of what is to come.

There is no carpet on the hallway floor, only bare concrete and thin strips of wood that line the edges of the narrow passage, a remodeling job that never got finished. Tom points carefully to each photograph, explaining to me every scene and every event. Pride and passion fill his voice. Oh how he wants them to be little again, so he can protect them. But this is now, and no matter how rich or powerful he is, he cannot keep them from harm. He cannot undo life's cruel reality. All he has are his memories.

We talk, we laugh, and we cry. We stay up all night. I never look at my watch. All concept of time and place is lost. I never think to call anyone. I am home. There is no one to call or to tell. I have no idea of the mayhem that my being *missing* is creating.

At 6:30 a.m., I open my eyes to a dreamy morning. I look at the twenty-year-old wallpaper on the bedroom walls. I turn my head to look into the eyes of my bed partner. He hasn't closed his for a moment all night. It feels like I am in a time warp. I know where I am, but I feel strange—like I have gone to another realm, and it is a place I have been to before, and oh how I have missed it. I am warmed and loved and home. It's like part of my brain is turned off and I only feel bliss. I am not supposed to be here. Where is my mind? I should be panicked, but I am not. What I have done is unthinkable, but it doesn't feel like me.

"I am not going to miss one minute of this, Babe," Tom says.

"I think I should make a phone call," I tell him. He nods. I am not shaken. I am not stirred. I am freakishly calm.

I call my husband of nine years and he shouts back to me in the phone, "Oh my God, she is alive. Oh, thank God you are alive. Are you okay? Where are you? Let me come get you. Oh, my God. Thank God you are alive!"

My mother is visiting from Pennsylvania. My sixteen-year-old daughter has spent the night in the police department with my husband. I have no idea of the sheer panic I have created.

I am officially a missing person. My photo will be splashed across the local TV news at 7:00 a.m. Have you seen this missing ordinary suburban devoted wife and mother? Missing and presumed kidnapped.

Gary, Brittany, and the police have watched the surveillance tape from the security office of my building. They saw me walk out at five o'clock yesterday evening and my car was still parked in the garage where I left it Friday morning. I had no idea that Brittany was summoned home from her overnight birthday party with the dreadful news that her mother hadn't come home from work, and the worst was feared. I had no idea that she was taken into the restroom by a female detective to be interrogated as to my relationship with my husband. Did we fight? Did he ever threaten me? Did we have a violent relationship? Would he harm me? Do you have any idea where your mother can possibly be?

Gary works for the TV news station. He knows all too well how these missing person stories turn out. He insisted that the private club where I work was searched from top to bottom and inside-out. He was sure I had been attacked, brutally raped and dismembered, and left for dead in a broom closet somewhere. They called everyone who may have had a clue as to where I was. No one knew. I did not have a history of not showing up. I just wasn't that kind of girl.

I finish the call. Completely calm, I get dressed and Tom drives me to my car. I don't know where my mind is; I should be completely unglued at what I have done and what I am going home to, but I am not. It's like I am watching someone else's life. It is in slow motion and surreal. It is lightly raining. Once back at the parking garage, Tom carries an umbrella over my head and walks me to my car. It is surrounded by orange cones. Two policemen are waiting for me.

"Are you Barbara Singer?"

"Yes, I am," I answer.

"May we see some ID? Are you ok? Are you here on your own free will? Who is this man? Did he harm or threaten you in any way?"

"This is Tom Ison and no, he did not harm me in any way."

"Just sign this form, Miss, and you can be on your way."

"Thank you," I tell the officer.

The drive home is long and slow. I don't feel normal at all. I know what I have done is completely wrong. What am I going to tell my family? I feel like I am floating between two worlds. I am not on the ground. I am doing the motions, but my emotions are completely altered. I know what I am doing, but I feel completely disconnected.

I walk into the front door of my home and my daughter runs into my arms and sobs in waves of violent torrents. She clings to me as I feel her wet tears roll down my cheeks and onto my chest. "Where were you? Why didn't you call? How could you do this to me?"

Beyond my daughter stands my husband and my mother, both clearly scared out of their minds. I don't know what to say. I had an explanation, but nothing I can say will make any sense. No reason is good enough to make their pain acceptable.

All I could offer was a superficial fraction of the truth: I hadn't eaten all day and had had too much to drink, so a member volunteered to drive me home and I fell asleep. He couldn't wake me, so he let me sleep and I called when I woke up in the morning.

Lame, I know. Even *I* can't get my head around the truth, much less articulate it in words. It is my state of mind that I can't get right. What really happened last night? It is like I opened the door to another world where everything was completely normal and wonderful, like that was my life. I felt like I was home. Then in an instant I knew where my real home was and now I am stuck in the middle.

# Chapter 4

*Remembering Pennsylvania*
*June 2006*

My flight lands and my sister, Linda, picks me up as she has done many times. I spend the first night at her house. She is married with three boys, one graduating from high school this year, and twins who are just starting high school. She is a CPA by trade, but being a mother is the job she cherishes.

My sisters are all great mothers and homemakers. Being a mother is truly honored and valued in my family. I see them running their households very similarly to the way we were raised. They clip coupons. They hang clothing out on the line to dry. They shuffle their children's schedules like professional card dealers in Las Vegas. They have jobs too, but they clearly put their children and families first. I especially admire the way they talk to their children. I listen to real conversations going on between them. What the children say is truly heard. My nieces and nephews are expressive and have lots to talk about. It is beautifully choreographed, this big family dynamic.

The landscape in the Amish country of Pennsylvania is an endless expanse of deep green rolling hills and fields, expertly planted so the corn rows grow straight into the horizon. The red barns, silos, dairy cows in the pasture and roadside vegetable stands embrace me like familiar old friends.

Why did I want to get away from this place so bad? It is absolutely beautiful—small town living and family all around. No, no, that's not what I wanted. I wanted college and a career; I wanted to go and seek my fortune. Oh, I did all right. Places to go, people to see. Give me a goal and I would make a plan and make it work. Year after year, I climbed and succeeded, only to discover that when I got to the top of the ladder, it was propped up against the wrong building. Some people call it a mid-life crisis, I choose to think of it as a midlife wake-up call. I have had other wake-up calls. I believe that death is a wake-up call for the living. It's a reminder that we don't have unlimited time.

With my family background as a standard, I took motherhood very seriously—looking back now, perhaps too seriously. I love my daughter, and she is a source of endless pride for me. I am a ferocious lioness when it comes to my cub. Opportunities and education are my primary focus so that Brittany has all she needs to grow up as a strong, independent member of society. She is a smart girl with a good heart and is wise beyond her years.

⚜

Brittany is missing the family campout this year, but I am enjoying it before Dad and I head out on our adventure. Every year on the same weekend, my family gets together for a two-day campout at this old-time amusement park in the mountains not too far from our home. With a standing reservation for eight sites, we take over the place. There are ten people in my immediate family, most are married and all have children. Give or take a few, depending on schedules, there are about thirty-five of us. The comings and goings are comical. Meal times are even more amazing. Everyone brings food and cooking apparatuses. The amount of camping gear, cookware, clothing, lawn chairs and so on borders on the ridiculous. The SUV's, trailers, and campers are lined up. A gigantic circus-like tent is erected smack in the middle of the ring of campsites. With Dad being the ringmaster, the only thing missing is an elephant.

It is great fun, this big family commotion; never a dull moment. My nieces and nephews play made-up games, riding their bicycles through the camp and around the fire ring, all the while chatting excitedly and singing silly songs. My favorite scene is my three little nieces, all about the same height, walking arm in arm in their little jeans with the cutest bubble butts; one with short blonde hair, one brown, and the third with braided pigtails hanging way down her back. They walk in uniform stride as one unit. Oh, to be little again and pretend my bike is Tonka, my horse. I remember being eight years old.

The amusement park is only open in the summertime. The air is filled with smells of food, children laughing, and the wonderful sound of the Wurlitzer pipe organ. The park has a whole collection of them, so at practically every turn the old-time music drifts over us, but we have come to ride the roller coaster. I love roller coasters—the rush, the anticipation, and the free fall. Knobbles has one of the best. I have ridden many and always look forward to riding this one. Dad loves the roller coaster too. We ride it three times in a row.

Flushed and exhilarated, I suggest we eat a funnel cake, a kind of deep-fried dough sprinkled with confectioner's sugar, another thing unique to Pennsylvania Dutch Country. It reminds me of my childhood. I am happy here.

After a day of eating, sitting, and chatting around the campfire, I decide I must get some exercise. Running shoes on, I head for the top of the campground. My sister Doris, also a runner, said to go left down the hill. As I round the turn, there stretching out before me is corn, rows and rows of corn. I have not run along corn rows since high school field hockey practice. The air smells so good. I love how organized and perfectly spaced the rows are with brown tilled soil in between row after row of green corn only about one foot high. At the bottom of the slope is another lovely reminder of my hometown, a red covered bridge. Once on the bridge I walk, taking time to read the messages left there by lovers. Kissing bridges is what we call them. No one can see you steal a quick kiss while you are passing through.

I spend my first night in the camper with Dad, and I am cold. I remember being little and being cold. To save money, we didn't heat the upstairs of our home until it was time to go to bed, then we would turn the radiators on, open the bedroom doors and let the heat rise. We would lay our pillows on top of the radiators to warm them, brush our teeth first, then quickly change into our pajamas, grab our warm pillows and lay back-to-back. We had two double beds, so four girls slept in one room. My two older sisters had a room and my two brothers shared the forth bedroom.

I have long forgotten what it is like to be cold. Even when we moved into our new house when I was sixteen-years-old, it too was cold. That time, Dad installed an alternative heating source, a combination of wood and solar. It didn't work well. The first winter we froze. I can remember waking up and seeing my breath while I was still in bed. My sister said her perfume turned to ice while still in the bottle.

If I am this cold in Pennsylvania in May, I can't imagine how cold I will be in Alaska. I definitely didn't bring enough warm clothing. Dad insists it will be a 100 degrees in Alaska. "The summers are warm there," he says. "You'll see." Still, I go by my sister's house and borrow long pants, a heavy jacket, and long underwear. Little do I know that for six weeks, I would take them off, only long enough to wash them.

# Chapter 5

*April in Paris*
*April 2002*

Just one month after meeting Tom, I am off to Paris with my friend Debby. This trip was supposed to happen last year at this time, but it wasn't meant to be. Debby and I work together and have the closest friendship two people possibly can. She knows me better than I know myself and has listened to my ramblings, readings, theories, heartaches, parenting woes, wishes, and wants—on and on for hours.

When I came to work at the Citrus Club, she had already been there for ten years and had lots of partners in the membership office. I would be her last. When I first got to know and love Debby, she had dated Glenn for several years and they were married for eight, but had no children. She was the party girl, Miller Lite was her language and everyone knew she liked to have a good time. She was the sweetest, most accepting, fun loving, driven girl I had ever met, and did I mention, wise too? I, on the other hand, was a mother and took my job very seriously. I was sophisticated—I knew about wine, food, and had traveled the world. I was proper, and had a different belief system than most of the people I knew. I thought of ideas, read, and learned concepts and dreamed of accomplishing things that my other co-workers couldn't accept, but not Debby—she got me and I got her.

Our trip was delayed by a year because Debby and Glenn adopted a baby boy, Parker. He came into their lives suddenly, just two weeks before we were supposed to leave for Paris last year at this time. She held the sweet little newborn in her arms and said, "I don't know how to tell you this, Barbara, but I can't go to Paris."

"I know," I said. That decision was made the minute we knew the baby was coming home with them. There was no way she could leave this wonderful new bundle of joy to play tourist. "Paris will always be there and last time I checked, they have spring every year. We'll go another time."

Debby didn't have a passport when I met her and this was unfathomable to me. During one of our many morning coffee talks, I asked her what the first stamp in her new passport should be. "I want to go to Paris in April," she had said.

"Wow, now that is quite a wish and lucky for you," I told her, "I can do that one." So we planned a trip for just the two of us where we would stay at the St. James Club, our company's sister property in Paris. We had been on other trips together, but not out of the country. We travel well together. In the beginning, I was the brains and she was the fun, but she quickly came into her own. She was street smart and bright, but it was her sense of complete fun that was magnetic. She gave me more than I could ever give her. Together, we were an unstoppable, one-in-a-million pair and it showed.

Anyway, we are finally off to Paris, after a one-year delay. No matter, this trip will be awesome. A week or two before we go, I get a call from Renada, the membership director at our club in Tampa.

"Hey, I hear you guys are going to Paris without any husbands," she says.

"That's right," I answer.

"Can I join in and meet you at the Charles de Gaulle Airport?" she asks.

"Sure, we will be in Paris for a few days, then on to Venice and ending up in my beloved Florence," I tell her.

"I just want to be in Paris while you are there. Is that okay?" she asks.

"Sure, the more the merrier," I reply. "We are going to have a ball."

A few days later, I get a call from my other dear girlfriend, Lael.

"Hey sunshine, what's this word on the street that you are going to Italy? Without me? I think not. I have business in Rome, but I want to meet up with you and Debby in Florence. When will you be there?"

I give her the dates. Before I know it, Lael's friend Tracy's husband gets wind of the trip. Knowing his wife is in desperate need of a vacation, he buys her a surprise ticket for her birthday. We will be five by the time we hit Florence. The city will never be the same.

My only regret is that I must leave my new amour, Tom, behind. We only connected a few weeks ago, but I have already rented an apartment for Brittany and me to move into starting mid May, just as soon as the school year is over. I see him whenever I can, but remember that I am a wife and mother. I make dinner every night for my family and attend every sporting event my daughter plays in. I have a sales career with the biggest quota in the company and I work out. There is no free time.

Yet I know for sure that Tom and I will be together. I never planned for it to happen this way. I wanted Brittany to graduate from high school and go off to college. Then it would be my chance to make decisions with only myself in mind, instead of thinking about what is good for everyone else. I guess I didn't plan on being caught totally off guard. It was cosmic. Even now, that sounds too *hocus pocus,* even for me, but I must say, it was more real, for sure, without-a-doubt-right than anything I ever felt. I can't explain it; it was definitely stronger than me, and remember, I am a two-time Ironman tri-athlete. I know gut-it-out-tough, and this was bigger.

April 14th arrives, Debby's birthday, the day we have been planning for. Tom's taking me to the airport. It is a bittersweet goodbye. He insists on parking, going inside, and walking me to the very farthest point he can without having a boarding pass. Sweet, I think, but silly. I know the Orlando Airport like the back of my hand. So does he. He was the top major account manager for BellSouth Telephone Company for twenty years or so. He traveled most of his life, some commercial and lots of private planes. He would fly in the cockpit and co-pilot. He's had his pilot's license since he was sixteen-years-old.

When it's time to go to the gate, we walk together to the security checkpoint. I hand the officer my documents and turn to Tom to say good bye.

"I guess this is it," I say to him.

Out of his coat pocket he pulls some documents and his passport. "Unless this will get me on your flight," he says as he hands me his boarding pass.

In disbelief, I jump up and down and laugh and scream. "You're kidding right? Where are your bags?"

He came to the airport earlier today, checked his bags and got his boarding pass. Several weeks ago he called Debby to get her okay to "steal me away" from our trip for a few days. He arranged for a suite at the St. James in Paris, the same hotel where we are staying. After we pass through security and the tram shuttle, I take Tom's hand as we walk down the long corridor to the gate. About half way there, he squeezes my hand and raises it to his lips. As he kisses it, he turns to me and says, "I have walked these halls many times and would always notice other couples walking holding hands and I never had anyone's hand to hold. From now on it will be different."

Debby is waiting for us at the gate with champagne she smuggled in her carry-on. My feet don't touch the ground as I float onto the plane. This is a trip I will always remember. Once on the plane, Tom pulls out a pint of Crown Royal, his liquor of choice, for the flight and we make drinks for the three of us. It is an overnight flight and not completely full. Debby, well-trained, takes her Tylenol PM and stretches out on the extra seats next to us. The cabin lights are out and the plane is quiet, settling down for the eight hour Trans Atlantic journey. Tom and I are like teenagers and can't sleep a wink, kissing and giggling, making plans for Paris. I get up to go to the bathroom and must pass over Tom to get to the aisle.

On my return, I lean down from behind him and whisper in his ear, "Excuse me, Mr. Ison but I need to pass by." Entering the row facing forward, I straddle both his legs and sit on his lap.

"Oh, excuse me, pardon me," I tell him wiggling. "I seem to have lost my footing." Moving sideways now, I am sitting on his lap like Santa Claus.

"Would you like to make a wish little girl?" he asks.

"I can think of several wishes," I reply, cooing softly in his ear. The cocktails and kissing and new love giddiness go on for who knows how long until the flight attendant comes by to confiscate our bottle, and leans down to inform us in a delicate manner that this is a family flight and that I will need to get into my own seat. We look around the plane and we are the only people awake. This sends us into hysterical hushed laughter. This story would be told again and again. One I will never forget.

The St. James Club, a chateau-turned-five-star hotel and club, exceeds all my expectations, which is not an easy feat. We enter the walled property through huge iron gates, drive up past the sweeping lawn, circle around the fountain, and wait for the uniformed doorman to open the door. Yes, I am a princess; I have just arrived at my palace and Prince Charming is with me. I must be dreaming.

The hotel is old and grand. Tom and I check into am amazing suite that was once the wine cellar. The brick arched ceiling and gilded king-size bed are perfectly surrounded by ornate floor to ceiling drapes. The bathroom is all marble and dark wood with a giant tub. Oh, what fun we are going to have here. I am in the most romantic city in the world with a new love. How lucky am I?

We meet Debby and Renada in the library bar. It too is grand. Books line the shelves three stories high and tall ladders appropriately lean against the walls. Black and white photos of all the celebrities that have stayed here are displayed everywhere. A black baby grand piano sits off in one corner. We toast our good fortune and make plans for the next few days. The girls will go off sightseeing while Tom and I will spend just three days together. He will go on to London when we go to Venice.

The first night I don't think either of us sleep. We are too excited and silly to sleep. For the next few days we stroll the streets of Paris, wrapped in each other's arms, stopping at little sidewalk cafes to drink wine and coffee. We shop and kiss and take pictures of each other. We take the boat ride up and down the River Seine. We tour Notre Dame, and of course, climb to the top of the Eiffel Tower. I didn't know there was a restaurant in the tower. When we ask about reservations, they graciously tell us it takes months to get a table there. It is a very special place.

One day we discover the most delightful little restaurant and go back later that evening. All I can see are stars. Stars are in the sky and little twinkle lights fill the city streets and outline the series of arched bridges that cross the river. There are little lights twinkling on the ceiling of the restaurant and candles glow on our table. Walking home that night, we stop at a little corner shop and buy some champagne and strawberries. I light candles and put them all around the tub while running the bath. Champagne on ice and a bowl of strawberries, everything is perfect. I hop in the tub and call for Tom. He is speechless. His eyes fill with tears as he kneels down to kiss me.

"Join me," I tell him.

"I have never had a bubble bath before," he says. "I never thought I would fall in love again. I thought that part of my life was over years ago. You have changed everything for me. I love you."

We sleep until two o'clock in the afternoon. Tonight is our last night in Paris together. Tom announces he has something special planned for all four of us. We are to dress up and meet in the library at 5:00 p.m. We each try a different champagne cocktail in anticipation of our special evening and then climb into a waiting Town Car.

"To the Eiffel Tower," Tom tells the driver.

"You didn't!" I scream.

"Yes, my darling, we are having dinner in the Jules Verne Restaurant at 7:00 p.m. so we can see the view in the daylight and then watch the sun go down and the city lights come up," he explains. Debby and Renada each kiss one of Tom's cheeks at the same time. He is grinning from ear to ear. "Now who is the lucky one?"

Course after course, bottle of wine after bottle of wine, the view, the food, and the romance of Paris make my heart just want to burst. Look where I am! If I say it once, I said it ten times. "Yes dear, we heard you," Debby says. "One more time and I am going to hurt you."

Eight hundred dollars later, we ride back to the hotel. This is one night I will never forget. Our last night in Paris, and oh, what a night it is.

In the morning, we all check our bags with the bell captain and go off to the Louvre before we go our respective ways. We girls have an overnight train to Venice at 7:00 p.m. and Tom has a 2:00 p.m. train to London, so we all go to the museum together. Standing there, right in front of Van Gogh's *Starry Night*, Tom turns to me and says, "I must say goodbye. I have stayed as long as can. If I don't leave right now, I am not going to have enough time to go back to the hotel, pick up my luggage and make my train. I really want to miss my train, but I have taken you away from your friends for long enough." Hugging and kissing goodbye is the hardest thing. I watch Tom walk away and turn back to one of the most famous paintings in the world. More stars. Paris really is the City of Lights.

After a day at the art museum, we too, return to get our luggage. Attached to my bag is a single red rose and a note. "Until I see you again, Love Tom." Carrying the rose and note, I rush down the grand staircase of the hotel and slide into the backseat of the waiting car. Never did I dream that this little card would be all that is left to remind me of this moment, these last few days. I didn't know that I would never again return to Paris. This trip would be enough to last a lifetime.

# Chapter 6
*Alaska - Week 1*
*June 2006*

## Day 1—801 miles

Five o'clock on Tuesday morning and Dad and I are standing out on the back porch of my childhood home. Lush green rolling hills surround his oasis. A big bright moon is just coming up over the treetops. The camper was thoughtfully loaded over the past several days with everything we might need. After Dad says a prayer of thanksgiving for the gifts we are about to receive, a request of mercy and protection, and an invitation for God to join us, we are off. We head for the Pennsylvania Turnpike. "West, go west!" we laugh. That will be our direction for the next few weeks. Dad is in the driver's seat with me in the back, snoozing until a decent hour.

Home for the next six weeks is a reconfigured Mercedes Touring Van, nicknamed Black Beauty. Dad has taken the seats out and put a bed in the back, added a refrigerator and microwave. There is no running water. The entire vehicle has big picture windows on all sides. Dark tint lets us look out but others can't look in. Perfect for the type of trip we are undertaking. We have already decided that seeing the sites and getting into remote areas is more important than luxury. I may re-think this later.

The Pennsylvania rolling hills turn into mountains. Ohio farms turn into Indiana farms that turn into Illinois countryside. After a solid nine hours of driving, we realize we will be hitting Chicago at rush hour. Taking into consideration the time change, we optimistically think we'll get through without too much delay. Immediately we hit road construction and traffic as we near the city.

"Dad, have you ever been in downtown Chicago?"

"No, I try to stay away from the big cities."

"Why don't we go into the city because everyone else is coming out?"

Pulling out my trusty map book, which spreads way out over my lap,

I flip through the pages, find the state of Illinois and then the city map of Chicago. A turn here and there, and we are soon down by the waterfront headed for Navy Pier. Our van is too tall to fit in the parking garage, so we find a corner pay parking lot.

Walking to where boats are all lined up, we choose the architectural/ lake tour. We must go through the locks to get into Lake Michigan. I know Dad will love this. I have been to Chicago several times before and am happy to play tour guide. The water is blue like Florida, not at all what one would expect. After an-hour-and-a-half, we have learned more about Chicago, the buildings, the amazing engineering feats and the famous residents than we can possibly remember. Now for a bird's eye view of the lake and city, we rise to the top of the Ferris Wheel. What a wonderful way to spend rush hour.

I make dinner for us in the van in the parking lot. Renting the space costs more than our entire jaunt in Chicago. After soup and sandwiches, we are back on the highway. Once out of the city, we choose the first rest area to sleep for the night.

After Dad is asleep and the night is still, I remember today is Tom's birth- day. For his last birthday, I surprised him with a trip to Niagara Falls. Every time I asked him where he would like to go on a trip, he would always say, "Niagara Falls." Not like me, I wanted to go to Morocco, Tibet, India, or Bali. Let's get Niagara Falls crossed off of his list so we can move on to more fun places. So on his birthday, I gave him a big colorful coffee table book of beau- tiful scenic places to go in the USA. In the pages that featured Niagara Falls, I slipped an envelope that contained airline tickets and hotel reservations so when he flipped through the pages, he would find it. The hotels had tacky honeymoon suites with heart-shaped tubs, round beds and mirrored ceilings. When in Rome, do as the Romans, so I went for the red heart-shaped tub with jets. Boy, did he get a big laugh out of that when we checked in.

Lying there in my sleeping bag, in the back of a camper, along the high- way somewhere in the Midwest, I wish Tom a Happy Birthday.

Eight hundred and one miles—not bad for the first day.

# Day 2—752 miles

Dad is up at the butt-crack of dawn. There is a one-hour time change; he normally gets up at 5:00 a.m. Eastern time at home. He has already been to the rest area and refreshed with a bird bath and clean teeth, he pokes around the van.

"What are you doing Dad?"

"I was thinking of moving out."

"Moving out! What time is it?" I say confused.

"Six o'clock. I have been up for an hour."

It is broad daylight. I am sure it doesn't get light in Orlando this early, but I am game.

"Sure, Dad, let's roll."

In Wisconsin the farms get bigger, then Minnesota and then finally South Dakota. Our goal for today is the Badlands. I had no idea how big the states get in the West. Most of our day is spent in overcast skies and light rain at 65 degrees.

When it's time, we stop to buy gas from a lady, probably in her fifties. She is a pig farmer who grew up and has lived in the same county all her life. She and her husband farm 2,000 acres and raise pigs. She has two teenage sons and hopes they will go to college. She works at the gas station to supplement the family income since farming is less profitable now than it was for her parents, also farmers. She is happy for the rain because it has been dry way too long.

We get off the highway in Sioux Falls, South Dakota. To my surprise, we make a few guesses at the streets and wind up right at the falls. We go into the visitor's center to pick up information and walk into the middle of a singing contest. Young boys and girls are singing the national anthem a cappella while a man from the local TV news is video taping them. The boy we listen to is really good. Imagine singing a cappella right there in the visitor's center among the tourists buying postcards. What a sight.

The falls are really cool, much bigger than I thought. Not a big drop-off like Niagara, but wide with a series of drops making the most wonderful soothing sound. The brochure says the falls were discovered in 1856 and 7,400 gallons of water go over per second. Dad is interested in the engineering that powered the old grain mill and later the electric plant.

Back on the highway, the farmland is flat as far as the eye can see. We pass the first of many billboards for the Corn Palace. You can't miss this, my dad says. Dad has been out west before, but not all the way to Alaska. Now I know we are in South Dakota and we have driven for hours passing by miles and miles of fields, but come on, *I* am stopping off to see a building made of corn? Is this what my life has been reduced too? This is me, Barbara. I have dinner in the Eiffel Tower. I do Christmas in Aspen and sip cocktails on Santorini overlooking the Mediterranean. I am stopping to see the Corn Palace?

We exit the interstate at the town of Mitchell, South Dakota, home of the Corn Palace, which is a convention center with the outside façade crafted from thirteen different kinds and colors of corn. The corn is cut in half and attached to the building. Husks are used too. The entire front is removed every year and a new intricate design is created, at the cost of over $100,000. This has been going on since 1901. A photograph of every year lines the interior hallways. The building is used for local basketball games, graduations, and concerts. It is actually really cool. The brochure lists the entertainment line-up for the summer. As I review the list I see an entertainer I know.

"Hey, Eddie Money is coming in August. I'd like to see him," I say.

The girl taking the ticket says, "Who is Eddie Money?"

"Who is Eddie Money?" I reply in shock. "Come on! How old are you?"

"Twenty."

Same age as my daughter and she probably doesn't know who Eddie Money is either. "You know, Eddie Money... the song, *Two Tickets to Paradise*," I coax her.

"Oh, yeah, I know that song."

Poor Eddie Money, reduced to performing at the Corn Palace in South Dakota.

For miles and hours, we drive. The road in front and back looks the same, fields or shrubs on either side. We talk for hours about everything. Dad reflects about growing up. He was the second youngest of sixteen children growing up on a farm in rural Lancaster County Pennsylvania during the depression. They made the best use of everything they could. He remembers using ration stamps to buy shoes, sugar, and gas. They still needed money, but the stamps too.

Rubin Weaver, his dad, bought and sold farm implements in addition to farming. Later the family moved to town, had a small grocery store and farm equipment shop. The girls ran the store and the boys ran the tractor repair and sales. In the summers, my dad along with his siblings, were spread out among different relatives to work and live, always at least two together. They were too poor to keep all the kids at home, and other families were happy for the help. This was usually for a summer, but for some of the children, it lasted for several years. My dad hated this. He was about ten years old and terribly homesick and would cry. He remembers it being very far away, but tells me it was really only about fifteen miles. His temporary family would bring him home on an occasional Sunday whenever they could. He remembers one of his jobs for his grown, married sister was to pull her baby in a wagon until she fell asleep. Every Monday, Dad would walk up and down the sidewalk leading from the house to the barn, pulling the wagon while his sister hung clothing on the wash line to dry. Every Monday was laundry day.

"I think it was a law back then," he remembers, "because everyone always did laundry on a Monday."

Only eleven of the sixteen children made it into adulthood. The oldest daughter died at six-years-old of measles and a few days later, the two-year-old died. Martha, his mom, pregnant, grieving and exhausted from caring for her other sick children, gave birth to a premature baby that only lived a few days. Life was hard, but Dad remembers being loved and wanted. There was always enough to eat. He didn't know they were poor. Everyone was the same. Me, on the other hand, I knew we were poor. We were different. Having eight children in the 1960's was odd.

The only socializing families did in Dad's day was church on Sundays and visiting afterward. Several families would gather at homes of relatives or neighbors. It wasn't every Sunday and not everyone participated. For fun, the boys would play hide and seek in the barn and a game called "Boom Bag." Knots were repeatedly tied on top of each other to create a big ball in the middle of a burlap bag. The boys would throw the knotted bag at each other like tag ball. They also played another game that was called "Volley Over" where kids would stand on either side of a small barn and throw a ball over the roof, then chase each other around the building. It was like a game of tag and volleyball combined.

Dad always wanted to be a farmer. For the first four years after he and my mom got married, they farmed dairy, tobacco, and cattle. He is still sad over my mom leaving him, now some twenty years ago. He never remarried, neither did she. They were married for about thirty years when my mom left. He never saw it coming. My parents have very different memories of their marriage. My dad thinks he had the best marriage. He was completely happy. He had everything he wanted. He would love to get back together with my mom. He is full of regret for not doing things right, but the ironic thing is, he didn't know he wasn't doing it right.

Dad was raised in Mennonite tradition and people didn't talk about feelings—they were deeply religious, God-fearing people. You did what the Bible said, worked hard and took care of your family. If you did that, it was all supposed to be okay. Divorce didn't exist. Dad says if he had known then that he was supposed to do things differently, he would have. He was looking forward to the kids growing up and then he and Mom would travel. Now he has the time and no one to go with him. Don't get me wrong, the man gets around. He has been to Africa and the Holy Land with his church, but he genuinely dreamed of traveling with Mom. Now he knows that won't happen.

Remarriage is a problem for Dad. He is totally hung up on what will happen after he is gone. If he remarries, what will happen to the kids' inheritance? Who should get his money, his kids or his new wife? He also worries about what people will think if he blows it all in the last years of his life. This baffles me. All of us kids are doing fine, none of us needs or is counting on a big inheritance. After all, there are eight kids. Even if he was a millionaire, anything divided eight ways is not going to drastically change our lifestyles.

He and Mom ran away to get married. Dad picked the girl of his dreams. He wanted a Christian girl who was a reformed Mennonite, a farmer's daughter, someone who shared his ideals and outlook on life. They dated for six months, only on the weekends, and usually their dates involved going to hear a traveling evangelist at a tent meeting. They went together to Mom's father, to ask permission to marry. He said. "No, I won't sign."

Shocked and speechless, Dad had asked, "What do you expect us to do?"

Grandpa had replied, "I guess you can run away."

My parents came up with a new plan. Pennsylvania had a law that the girl and the boy had to be eighteen years old with parental signature. In Maryland, the girl could be eighteen without parental permission, but the boy still needed a signature until age twenty-one. Dad's father agreed to go along and sign, which allowed Dad to marry at eighteen. Mom turned eighteen-years-old on July 28th, and he would be eighteen on October 12th, so they drove to Maryland on October 15th with Dad's sister, Elva, and her husband, Henry, to be the witnesses. Dad and Mom got married in the minister's living room with his wife playing the piano. This was not the first three-day waiting period wedding they had performed.

With the marriage done, the happy group drove home only to find Hurricane Hazel of 1954, bearing down on them. It was dark when they got home and the power was out at Grandma Weaver's, so with a borrowed car from Grandpa, the newlyweds went to their apartment three miles away to start their marriage in candle-light romance. Not quite—the neighbors were out with flashlights, checking the trees to make sure they were not going to fall on the houses. Tears are streaming down my dad's cheeks as he is relaying this story to me. All they wanted to do was be in private to celebrate their union of love, but that moment got postponed for hours and hours.

"If this is what it took for our love to become real," he said, "then we knew we could overcome anything."

My dad really does want my mom to come back, but I don't see that happening. Life was hard for my mom, raising eight kids in a rural area on a farm with little help or money. She was totally devoted to the family while the kids were growing up. I don't think that my dad really thought much about what she needed. Mom was the oldest of twelve children and knew how to work hard and live on a shoestring. She also knew how to keep the peace in the family. Her father was an unpredictable man with a temper. I am sure a psychologist today would take one look at their family history and write it off as *train wreck waiting to happen*. At any rate, as a child growing up, I never knew of any conflict. If there were problems between my mom and dad, they were kept in private.

Dad and I stop for the night at a roadside rest area just outside the Badlands. To our shock, it is 90 degrees and incredibly windy, with warm winds blowing over the amber waves of grain. A barn swallow is having a ball playing in the wind, flying high and then dive bombing toward the ground. With the time change, it is ten o'clock at night to us and broad daylight.

## Day 3—311 miles

Again, Dad is up at six o'clock in the morning which is really four o'clock Eastern Time, and wants to get into the canyon for daybreak.

Still asleep in bed, I say, "Let's roll."

We wait at the ranger station for the park to open. I make an executive decision that tonight Dad must wear the blindfolds I have been wearing at night. It is totally light in the van from streetlights, not to mention the natural light from 5:00 a.m. to 10:00 p.m. I know he is so excited to be on the trip, but we have forty days ahead of us. I decide to let him drive to his heart's content. There is no way he can keep this pace.

Badlands, South Dakota was so-named by a French fur trader who was letting others know these were *bad lands* to travel through. All I can think of is, what in the world would I do if I were traveling by wagon train? Coincidentally, the closest town is called Wall. Once the bottom of the lake, this town is really like hitting a wall with its odd formations cut deep into the earth like canyons and others that jut up to the sky, layered with multi-colors of silt showing the years it took to create. I can totally see diving through this place when it was filled with water.

Wall is another South Dakota tourist attraction and the only town for miles, so we stop. Like the Corn Palace, we have seen a billboard every mile for the last twenty miles promoting the town. It's a throwback in time and looks like a cowboy town in a western movie with little shops selling trinkets, Indian jewelry and leather. We pop into the Cactus Café for breakfast. Our hostess is a beautiful bleached blonde girl with an unusual accent. We learn she is from the Ukraine, Russia, working here on a summer visa. I say to myself, "Sorry to be a downer but they hire kids like you in Key West too, you know."

Seated next to us are two young men. One fellow is wearing a Dive Instructor T-shirt. Dive, I am thinking. Where on earth does someone dive around here? So I ask.

"Oh, no, this shirt was a gift," he replies. "We are from Indiana and we are here to go hunting."

"Really, what do you hunt?"

"Prairie Dogs," they answer with a gleam in their eyes.

"Hummm, what do you do with prairie dogs?"

"Shoot'em."

"Do you eat them?"

"Oh, no, we just shoot them. They are actually a rodent and are considered a nuisance. We are just helping to keep the population down."

"Is that sport, entertainment or public service?" I wonder.

Next we meet Veronica, our server. She has lived her whole life here and has never left the state or flown on an airplane. One time she left the county, driving to her sister's wedding. She owns a ranch about eighty miles from town and only gets to go there on the weekends. She needs a job that pays cash money, but her heart is at the ranch.

The café is unbelievably busy. Dad and I are seated at a table and the place fills up. In addition to the Indiana surfer and his friend, in comes a family of four, another couple just getting off a motorcycle, and then a group of ten cowboys. They look at me funny, I think it is because I look like I don't belong here.

I need to go to the restroom before we travel again. Inside the ladies' room, I do not recognize the girl in the mirror; this is not the Barbara Singer I know and love. In the mirror is a girl who is wearing a black and red baseball cap that advertises cowboy boots. She is wearing jeans, sneakers, and a lighter colored jean jacket with two pins. None of her borrowed clothes are figure-flattering, she is wearing no make-up, her skin is blotchy and her lips are pale. She looks like a local, maybe she does belong here. Who is this girl in the mirror?

I head for the checkout counter to pay the bill. Shirley, the cashier moved back home after living in Buffalo, New York. She must be in her fifties. Why would anyone choose to move to Wall after living in Buffalo? She seems happy with her decision. This is home.

Back on the road, I ponder why people live where they live. Just because this is where they were born, does it mean this is where they stay? Is it because of family or familiarity? Is it because this is what they know and what is safe? I guess not everyone has the wanderlust or curiosity to see what else is out there like I do. I guess each of us must decide for ourselves what our dream life looks like.

Traveling down a dirt road off of Route 44 in search of a country route instead of highway, we stumble upon the second-largest Indian Reservation in the US and the home of the Ogallala Indians. What a disgrace to our country's heritage. We have robbed our nation's first people. Among a row of buildings that looks like the abandoned set of an old western movie, the town appears totally deserted, except the bar is open. The neon "Bud" sign in the window doesn't match the totally wooden structure, complete with a front porch and a fence to tie a horse. For decoration, the entire building is covered with sun-bleached cattle skulls. Other buildings are made of rusted tin roofs, wagon wheels, and dust. This is Main Street, Scenic, South Dakota.

We pull into what kind of looks like a gas station, but I can't tell if it is open because there is no sign of life. Once inside this dark, throw-back in time, no-longer-used restaurant, we meet Lee Ann. To my shock, her laptop on the counter is open to eBay.

"Wow, you can get Internet way out here?" I ask.

"Yes, by telephone line. It's slow, but it works."

"What are you buying?" I ask.

"Oh, I am not buying, I am selling."

"What are you selling?"

"Native American Indian Jewelry," she says.

"Really?"

Now Lee Ann isn't any more Indian than I am. She tells me she grew up around here and lives on the reservation now. She has two grown daughters. Looking me straight in the eye, she says, "They are half-breeds." She waits for my response. A clue to whether I am friend or foe. I have no response. I tell her I too have a grown daughter. Motherhood is an International common ground. I come in peace. The floodgate opens. She tells of her life living out here in the remote desolate belly of our nation. She is very smart, well- read and up-to-date on what is going on in the world. She has a book propped next to the cash register.

"What are you reading?" I ask.

"*Under the Banner of Heaven,*" she answers. "It's pretty good. It's about the Mormons and how they searched for a place to practice their religion in peace and how they ended up in Utah. His other book, *Into Thin Air* was better. I am glad I am not Mormon," she says.

"How ironic," I think to myself, "I am glad I am not living in Scenic, South Dakota."

⚜

We make it to our next destination—Mt. Rushmore, in the Black Hills. We get a peek of the famous heads carved in stone as we wind our way through the mountains. There are many funky giant rock faces along the way. As I look at the natural rock mountains, I realize that I would have never come up with the idea to carve faces of the presidents in them. Who thinks of this stuff? We get our first sightings of antelope, buffalo, and deer. The bridges and tunnels are made of natural wood that reminds me of Lincoln Logs. We hit the other attractions in the area, Crazy Horse Memorial, Mt. Rushmore Cave, and Custer's Park.

For the night, we stop at Whispering Pines Campgrounds, a charming roadside place tucked in the Black Hills. Big deep green mountains surround our little piece of heaven down in a small valley. No cell phone service here. Our little campsite has a picnic table, fire ring, and is near the bathroom.

The first order of business is a real shower. I have gotten good at bird baths and brushing my teeth on the run, but am looking forward to a nice hot shower and washing my hair. In the van I pack my shoulder bag with the toiletries I will need. This little bag and my carry-on suitcase have traveled all over the world with me. They remain packed at all times with everything I need to travel except clothes. I have been known to pack for Europe in less than ten minutes and rarely ever travel with more than a carry-on suitcase and this shoulder bag, which I put my purse inside so that it doesn't count as an additional piece of luggage.

Looking inside this pre-packed bag, I have to smile. I guess I should have gone through it in advance. There is a blow up neck cushion, socks, mini toothbrush and paste, book light, Tylenol PM, two catnap eye blinders, a pen from the Park Tower Hotel in Buenos Aries, a notepad from Long Boat Key Club, travel size baby wipes, yellow highlighter, business cards, several packets of my special green tea, a couple of panty liners, and an umbrella. I add two towels—one for my hair and one to dry off with—plus a hairdryer, brush, make-up, toiletries pouch, and clothes that I will probably end up sleeping in. With the little bag over-flowing, I take out the towels and sling them over my shoulder. Well, here goes. Wearing my white terrycloth slippers embroidered with the logo of the Gritti Palace Hotel in Venice, I shuffle along the gravel path to the community shower building. The contrast between the memories of the luxurious hotels I have stayed in to collect these items against the ruggedness of the campsite makes me chuckle.

This reminds me of back-packing through Europe when I finished college. All I needed were a few things, a Euro-rail pass, and a hostel guide book. I rinsed socks and underwear in sinks, slept on a cot in the girl's dorm or on the train and ate pizza for practically every meal. It was inexpensive and filling. Otherwise, it was bread, cheese, and wine. What a great experience. I have already told my daughter if she wants to go, I will be happy to buy the ticket. I know it is different today, but traveling and meeting people from around the world is much too good to miss because of fear.

This old building made of white concrete block has an outdoor double laundry sink for washing dishes, a couple of soda machines, and his and hers bathrooms. The front room has several sinks with a mirror above each and a floor length mirror. Homemade wooden bathroom stalls are down the hall on the left, and a row of white shower curtains down the other side. It is old, but clean. I pick a shower and set my bag down on a little bench that looks like it belongs at the beach. I take off my brightly colored pink Lilly skirt and white cotton T-shirt and put them on the hook. That skirt definitely belongs in Florida, not South Dakota. Yet it was plenty warm enough today for a skirt and sandals. Now that the sun has gone down and I am naked, I realize it is really cold in here. No wonder, looking up I can see the rafters of the roof go right outside leaving about a one foot gap for ventilation.

Oh well. Out of the shower, I dress in clothing I borrowed from my sister. With my hair in a towel turban, I move all my gear to the sink. The plug for my hairdryer is a socket that is part of the bare bulb white porcelain fixture above a mirror that looks like it was made back in the 1940's.

I remember what it was like growing up in our house with one bathroom that we all shared. It had an original pedestal porcelain sink with old-timey twirly hot and cold handles and a floor with tiny black and white mosaic tiles. Only *business* was allowed in the bathroom. All other grooming was done in front of the hallway mirror.

With my hair dry, I brush on a little make-up. Why bother, I wonder to myself as I look into the floor length mirror. My skin is pale now that my spray tan is gone. My fingers look short without fake pink and white acrylic nails. I have my real eye color, still blue, but not what I am used to looking at. No painted toe nails. I can't remember the last time I went without.

On my way back to the campsite, I pass a young maintenance man wearing a lifeguard T-shirt. "Where's the pool?" I asked

"Oh, I wish." he says. "This shirt is from last year. I was working in Hawaii."

"How did you get from Hawaii to South Dakota?"

"Oh, I like to try different places. Just like to keep moving."

"Hum," I say, just like that—Hawaii to South Dakota.

After a shower, fresh clothes and a cold beer from the camp store, I light a fire. I think I will start a tradition of having a beer after a shower. Soon the neighbors come by. It's going to get chilly.

First we meet Charlene and Bob who are working at the campground for the summer. They are from Bethlehem, Pennsylvania, but now live mostly in their fifth wheel RV in Crystal River Florida, near Cedar Key. She is a nurse, and he loves to golf and works at a course in Florida. They find a summer job somewhere in the US each year by logging onto a website called campworker. com. Last year was Tennessee, this year they picked South Dakota.

Then along comes another lady who has been a full-time RV'er for the past eight years. Her husband is disabled. Rather than sit at home and feel sorry for her plight, she loaded him up in the RV and travels the country. They have two children they visit—each for three months out of the year—and the rest of the time they wander. She picks up odd jobs at campgrounds in exchange for a site for their motor home. She must be in her sixties. I never meet her husband. Wow, now there is a lady to admire. We really can choose anything we want.

As I sit around the campsite, I look at the faces of these other folks who have the bug, the travel bug. They too must keep moving. It has become a lifestyle, not a dream or a week's vacation once a year for these people. Life as a vagabond, could I do it? Why not just *do* it. Others are. Did I choose to have my life fall apart or did it just happen? I can look at what happened to me as a curse or a blessing. Then I remember, today is exactly one month since I haven't had a job. This is the first time in my life that I haven't worked. Is this good or bad?

## Day 4—Vore Buffalo 53 miles

Passing by a brown national monument sign that says, "Vore Buffalo Jump," my dad says, "Hey, that's where the Indians stampeded the buffalo over the cliff by the hundreds and then butchered them for meat." Sounds like folklore to me. The road sign says two miles. Why not? If it's true, it could be really cool. We hang a U-turn on this little two-lane country road. Approaching the little roadside *attraction,* I see nothing that resembles a cliff. Hope improves as we see a teepee, port-a-potty, covered wooden sign and two cars. As we pull into the dirt parking lot among the miles of open field, sure enough there is a big hole with a steep drop off. If I didn't see it, then a herd of buffalo running full speed ahead surely didn't either.

To my surprise, this is a manned historical site. Kaleb, a young, freshly-graduated college student greets us, asks us to sign the register and tells us the story. Between 1500 and 1800 AD, 20,000 buffalo were herded by five different Indian tribes and stampeded over the 200 foot wide and 50 foot deep drop-off, plummeting to their death, about 100-150 at a time. Usually done in the fall, the kill would provide food for the winter. The buffalo were drug up the hill and butchered, using every part. Sure beats hunting them one at a time with a bow and arrow.

We are invited to walk the gravel path around to the hole at the bottom where a tented archeological dig is marked off exposing lots of bones. There we meet Tiffany, a music student, working for the summer. She shows us a buffalo bladder used as a water bottle and another one made into a pouch. After I get over the grossness of it, the flexibility and durability of the material is amazing. There is also a piece of leather that is not leather at all, but a buffalo brain that started out as a mushy matter, then was patted and worked into a thin, soft skin. We pose for a photograph holding a buffalo skull. What a surprising little stop!

We make a quick pass through the famous tiny town of Sturgis. It is a modern town, but practically deserted today. During Bike Week, it will fill up to overflowing. Sturgis is the Midwestern equivalent to Daytona Beach, Florida. Dad knows all about it and just wants to drive through so when he watches it on TV, he will know what he is seeing.

Next up is Devil's Tower, our first national monument. We get a sneak peek at this giant tooth-shaped monolith along the winding road. This amazing geological oddity juts straight up from relatively flat, rolling grasslands far off into the horizon. The dormant volcano violently erupted from the ground and now stands 865 feet tall. As we get closer, this natural wonder gets bigger and more magnificent. Framed in deep blues skies above and yellow wild flowers below, it is an awesome site.

At the base of the Devil's Tower, we learn that legend has it that long ago a bear attacked seven Kiowa Indian sisters. The girls climbed onto a rock and prayed for their lives. Suddenly the rock rose into the sky, the enraged bear tried to get to them but his claws kept slipping, creating the great scratches on the side of the rock. The sisters continued to rise toward the heavens and today are the seven stars of the Pleides Cluster. When I give my postcards to the attendant to mail, she tells me there will be a special postal stamp commemorating the 100th anniversary of Devil's Tower. Yet another pleasant surprise.

Heading west, yes, I did say west, we aim for Cody, Wyoming, our goal for the day. As we get onto the interstate, we drive over grates that keep the cattle from crossing the road. Imagine that, special accommodations to allow the cattle to graze along the highway, but still providing a passage for the cars. Just beyond we see a local rodeo corral. Deserted today, but surely on a special day the paddocks would be full of horses, bulls and cowboys while the bleachers exploded with colorfully dressed onlookers cheering loudly. There is also a series of fences along the highways facing north. Dad guesses the fences are to hold back the snow and prevent it from drifting on to the highway creating havoc. We pass a coal mine, which looks just like I think it would—a big, solid, dark, black hole, dotted yellow trucks, plows and backhoes which remind me of playing in the dirt with Tonka trucks when I was a child. From a distance, they look tiny and artificial.

We also pass by several mechanical graveyards, which are clusters of old tin shacks mostly fallen down, and hundreds of rusty old farming tractors and other implements. We drive by pastures with strange cows that look like panda bears with their white heads, black bellies and white rumps. Crazy!

As we roll along the flat yellow fields, it occurs to me that I am more interested in gas mileage and the mechanical gadgets we use in the camper than I am about lipstick and hairspray. Dad is interested in all the engineering contraptions needed to run a town. Driving along, he explains how water towers work. He tells the story of what kind of farm we pass by, whether it is pig or dairy and he counts the number of silos and grain bins. He knows every make and model of tractor machinery. Dad knows what kind of grain is growing in the fields, like alfalfa, hay, wheat, barely or oats and when they need to be harvested.

He also can't hear when his turn signal has been left on—although it has been more than ten minutes—but he can hear the music I am listening to on the headphones I am wearing in the back of the camper. He can't stay awake past 7:00 p.m., but he can wake up at 5:00 a.m. regardless of the time zone we are in.

Rounding over the top of a hill, we get our first glimpse of snow-capped mountains far off in the distance. At first glance, I think they are shadows on the outstretched land or clouds, but sure enough they are snow-capped mountains. My first guess is the Rockies but we are still several hundred miles away from Yellowstone. Nope, it's the Big Horn Mountain Range. The closer we get to it, the more amazing it gets. The vista is spectacular! We are up so high, the ground looks like the view from an airplane. Dad spots a moose in the valley along the stream. He is smiling from ear to ear. He is in his glory. He loves driving. The sign says, *Next 14 miles downhill at a 10% grade. Beware. Hairpin turns. Road open summer only.* The current temperature is 80 degrees.

I refer to the maps that litter the queen-size bed which has become my desk. I am surrounded by travel books, my computer, a trusty note pad and pens, camera, books to read, pillows and a panoramic view as far as my eyes can see. Look where I am! The higher up into the range we go, the more amazing the vistas become. I have never seen anything like this before.

We roll into Cody by late afternoon. There is a big banner across the street promoting the rodeo tonight. I tell Dad we should go. I have never seen a live professional rodeo.

Dad agrees to go, but insists tonight is the night we sleep in the Wal-Mart parking lot. He has been itching to do this ever since we left. Apparently RV'ers can sleep in the outer areas of Wal-Mart parking lots for free. He has only heard about this, but in each town we have passed through, he has been on the look out for a Wal-Mart. I don't get it. Why would you want to spend the night on asphalt with bright streetlights shining in on you all night long when you could be out in nature somewhere? And besides, where do we go to the bathroom during the night? This Wal-Mart is not open twenty-four hours. Oh well, this one is for my dad. I guess we all dream in different sizes. So we scope out the parking lot and pick our spot, but we will have to come back after the rodeo because wherever we go, our house goes too.

The rodeo is the real deal with big bleachers full of seriously intense cheering fans and corrals full of bulls, horses and steers. It begins with little kids roping and riding small animals. I guess this is Little League for cowboys. Then, there is barrel racing for the ladies, roping and wrestling for men, bronco riding, and for the big finale, bull riding. It is major rough and tumble.

From my vantage point, I can see all the cowboys hanging on the fence along the ring of the arena. Dressed in tight jeans, chaps, western shirts and cowboy hats, they are like rock stars at a concert and I am starting to feel like a groupie. They bend over to cheer for their fellow cowboys and then jump off the fence when the bucking horse or bull comes too close. Perhaps I should join them down on the fence and say hello. What am I thinking? I am traveling with my dad, and he would not be amused. Then it occurs to me that for the first time in my life I am not in a relationship or traveling for an extended period of time with a man. No big deal, surely I can go without sex for six weeks. However, those cowboys sure are hot.

## Day 5—Yellowstone 594 miles

This is the big day we have been looking forward to. Dad has been here before but this my first time. The sheer vastness of the park is the first indication that this is a special place. The first animal we spot is a wolf; they were reintroduced to the park a few years ago to naturally help control the population. There are herds of buffalo and deer grazing along the road but off in the distance.

Then we come to a traffic jam. Traffic jam? This can't be. As we creep along, Dad realizes only one or two cars have come from the other direction. "There must be an accident," Dad says. After about ten minutes, we discover not an accident but hundreds of buffalo hanging out in the middle of the road. People are honking at them even though the rangers have warned us not to mess with them since buffalo have been known to attack and do some serious damage to cars. We decide it is best to wait. We are not in a hurry.

As we roll along, we learn the park was started in 1872 by Ulysses S. Grant, our eighteenth president. Along with Old Faithful, Yellowstone has a collection of the world's most extraordinary geysers and hot springs. It also has the Grand Canyon Region and a Lake Region that spreads across three states, Wyoming, Montana, and Idaho. We drive through miles of burnt trees. It doesn't look recent, but still charred and desolate. According to the guide book, in 1988, several different fires destroyed 36 percent of the park.

## Day 6—Father's Day 184 miles

Sunday morning at six o'clock, we wake up to 34 degrees. From my sleeping bag inside the van, I can see my breath. We slept in the parking lot just outside the welcome center and cafeteria. We wait until there are signs of life and make a run for warmth and hot coffee. The room quickly fills with people from a tour bus. Taking the table next to us is a very cold young man. His cheeks and nose are bright red and he is wearing an Indiana Jones hat, a backpack and what appears to be all the clothes he owns.

"Hey, you look as cold as we are," I tell him. "Did you spend the night in a tent?"

"Yes, so as soon as daybreak came, I tore down and came here to warm up."

I invite Joe from Dallas to join us for breakfast. We discover he flew to Idaho Falls yesterday, rented a Harley and drove to Yellowstone, arriving later than he planned at his campsite here at Canyon Falls. He is single and traveling alone, none of his friends were interested in riding a motorcycle through Wyoming for a week.

Later that morning, Joe and I pass on the trail to the lower falls. He is coming down and I am going up. It is too steep for Dad. When I arrive back at the top, Dad says, "Hey, did you see Joe?"

"Yes, we passed on the trail."

"Come over here, look at his bike," Dad says. He is totally impressed with the bike, a shiny, brand new, royal blue 2006 Harley complete with saddle-bags and a big windshield. Dad is planning on driving his motorcycle, along with some other guys, to Florida later this year. He really is a kid at heart.

Back in the RV and riding along, we are hailed to slow down. Off to the side of the road we see all kinds of rescue vehicles, but it doesn't look like a car accident. Dad guesses they are doing some kind of rescue training from the lookout. The following day we learn that a lady tourist stepped outside the fence to get a better view for a photo and slipped, falling to her death.

Less than an hour later, we are pulled over by the flashing lights and siren of a police car. A young officer comes up to Dad's window and asks to see his license and registration, which Dad provides. The young man comes back and returns our papers.

"Do you know how fast you were going, Mr. Weaver?"

"No," Dad says, "I was just enjoying the scenery."

"Well, a little bit to fast, sir, but I can see that you have a commercial driver's license and are probably used to cruising on the highway. Remember, you are here with lots of animals, so you will need to slow it down a little. I am not going to give you a ticket or anything, especially since it is Father's Day."

"Thank you," Dad replies. "Are you a father too?"

"No sir. Not yet. But if I am lucky, I will be someday."

To my surprise, my dad says, "Well. I am a father, but it wasn't luck that gave me eight kids."

The young cop bursts out laughing. We learn that he grew up in Pennsylvania and always dreamed of being a ranger. He wishes us well on our trip to Alaska and we are off again. That was the most risqué thing I think I have ever heard my dad say.

By late afternoon, both Dad and I are sleepy. "Let's pull over, have a little snack and take a nap," I suggest. We are driving along a huge beautiful lake with a snow-capped mountain off in the distance. The view is perfect for a little snooze. This is a treat for both of us, and definitely not a *Weaver* thing to do.

As dusk greets us, we arrive in Jackson Hole, Wyoming. Dad is very excited to show me this town. "Lots of famous rich people live here," he tells me. Tonight, in honor of Father's Day, we get a hotel room and eat dinner in a restaurant. Both are expensive for the quality. We decide that we like camping better. This would be the only hotel room of our entire trip.

## Email, June 18

Hello from Wyoming,

Wow, what a trip so far. All is well. We are having a ball. Cell phone has been spotty and Internet non-existent until today. This is our first week and we have traveled about 2,800 miles; our round trip is estimated at 10,000. So far, we've spent $342 on gas. See attached file for Daily Travel Log. We live in an amazing country. The terrain and sites have changed dramatically.

Dad and I make great traveling partners. He loves to drive and has been behind the wheel most of the time. I navigate, read the travel guides, plan the itineraries, take care of the meals and keep up "the house." He is a big teddy bear and easy-going. We have decided that seeing the sites is far more important than luxury; I may re-think that. I don't recognize the girl in the mirror—make-up is long gone, hair pulled back in a pony tail under a ball cap (however it is Louis Vuitton!!), jeans (toothbrush in back pocket), jean jacket and sneakers— yes, me who NEVER wears sneakers unless I am running or going to the gym.

Dad doesn't know it, but he is on a health kick during the trip. I am in charge of the food. He needs to lose a few pounds and I don't want to gain any, so we are eating well and walking as much as possible.

Although we are in an RV/van, we are really more like camping. We don't have a kitchen or running water/shower, but do have a microwave and refrigerator. We do have a pro-pane cook stove if we want. It works great for two adults.

We are meeting really cool people!

Will send photos next time. Much more to come.

Love

Barbara

## Day 7—401 miles
## Week 1—$342 gas 3207 miles

Idaho is flat but greener than we've seen so far. We pass potato farm after potato farm. I would not know this except Dad can tell because of funky little half-moon buildings built into the side of the hills. They are root cellars and hold the harvest and seed crop for the next year. There are hundreds of them.

After several hours of driving, we get stuck in road construction. We are on a two-lane road in the middle of nowhere, but today it seems as though there is a mile of cars lined up on the steaming hot state road. We are just outside of Craters of the Moon National Park. I take the wheel while Dad gets a little shut-eye.

"Wake me when we get to the park," he instructs. I listen to music on my headset while I creep along.

Moon Crater Park really does look like the surface of the moon. An old volcano created this barren wasteland where tiny black rocks stretch as far as the eye can see. The road looks completely out of place. We stop and check out a few sites and climb to the top of a lookout. Who knew such a place existed in the middle of Idaho.

From there we pass through the town of Stanley, Idaho, population 100 according to the sign. Then we head to Hailey, Idaho, famous now because of its movie star residents, Demi Moore and Bruce Willis. As we drive through this charming little red-bricked town, we see a marquee announcing that Bruce and his band will be playing there on the Fourth of July. Sun Valley, the famous ski resort area, is just down the road. We start our climb into the vast green forest of Lola State Park.

# Chapter 7

*Double Ultimatum*
*2002–2004*

In May of 2002 Brittany and I move out of our big beautiful home in the suburbs for a hot, chic, seventeenth floor apartment in *the* building downtown. I am hoping this will somehow soften the blow of the gossip and reality of what her mother has done. She has her own car and will continue to drive herself to her private high school. At least one thing in her world won't change. I walk through my home and pick out only the things I absolutely love. A fraction of what fills our four-bedroom four-bath home, but I do not care. I am so happy to get rid of the baggage, the stuff and the weight. I call my husband to tell him I am out. He is stunned at what little I took. Gary and I share an attorney and are divorced in twenty-one days. We never talk about anything.

I take the next year to revel in my blind, head-over-heels love for Tom. I do not see the destruction that this union has caused. I do not see the pain and the loss my daughter feels. I do not feel anything except complete love, adoration and an amazing tugging on my heart for Tom.

He is so fun and full of life. Even though he is twenty years older than me, he has more energy and zest for life than people half his age. We are always on the go. If we are just sitting around in the evening, he will jump up from the couch at ten o'clock at night and announce that we are going to Steak and Shake for an icy. One day he shows up with a big bowl of cherries. "Life is like a bowl of cherries," he says gleefully.

Although he is officially retired, Tom still owns and operates Lake Susan Lodge, a restaurant, bar and fourteen little concrete block fishing cabins in the country on a chain of lakes. The marina has some twenty slips and a boat launch for the locals. The camp is a total throw-back in time. He bought it for a song about fifteen years ago. Patrons come by boat, motorcycle and car to eat at the restaurant. He keeps a big pontoon boat and loves being on the water. He also loves being the owner and mingling with the customers. Tom usually has a drink in his hand, is always up for a party, often has a band at the pier bar and sets up a volleyball net in the water. In the winter, he builds huge bonfires down by the water's edge.

Tom is well-known and well-liked in his community. He was the mayor for twelve years and brought a lot of development to the town. Still active in local government, he sits on several boards and feels it is important to stay involved.

I enjoy going to the Lodge on the weekends. It is totally relaxing being on the water and out in the country. Brittany won't come along. She hates me going and staying the night. She thinks the people are hicks and she disapproves of the drinking. I think it is probably the first time she has ever seen me drinking. Most sixteen-year-old kids would have liked the freedom, but she wants things the way they were. She was used to being the center of my world and now I am the center of someone else's world and she is being *dethroned.*

After a year of living in the trendy high-rise building, Brittany and I move into a newly renovated beautiful 1920's cottage in the historic district of downtown Orlando. I bought it several years earlier and desperately wanted to live in it, but Gary and Brittany wouldn't hear anything of the kind, so I rented it to strangers year after year and cried all the way home whenever I signed a lease with the new tenants. "I want to live here! I am allowing someone else to live in my dream house. I can't do this!" I told myself. Now, I have asked the tenants to move out and have made it perfect. It is finally *my* adorable little house with hardwood floors, a fireplace, a swing on the front porch and a big Jacuzzi bathtub in the master bathroom. I believe it will be a place suitable for my daughter to live, somewhere she can be proud of, a place she will be able to bring her friends that live in the world of the 'haves.'

Oh, how wrong I turned out to be. We could have moved into a mansion, but she wants no part of anything as long as Tom is involved. She knows *he* is the one that split up her family. He so desperately wants her to love him. He lost his only daughter; Kelly's dying was the darkest day of Tom's whole life. He tells me again and again how lucky he is to have another chance to be a father to a daughter. Oh how he wants to dance at Brittany's wedding and take flowers to the hospital when she has a baby and push the stroller. How he wants to help her buy a house and change the oil in her car. But it is not meant to be, not on her part or his.

Tom gets very involved in the remodeling of my cottage. He needs to be needed. He stops at the house, talks to the contractors and shops for all kinds of supplies. His corvette becomes a pickup truck. I am always amazed at what he can fit into that car. He is happy to do it. Many a day, I come home from work and change into jeans and a T-shirt and go to Amelia and work side-by-side with Tom, doing demolition or whatever.

Two years pass quickly for us. If there are red flags, I don't see them or if I do see them, I choose to look the other way. He is charming and very charismatic. He takes care of me. He takes care of everything. He decides if we are going to eat in and then stops at the grocery and picks up whatever we need. He drives me to work in the morning and meets me at the athletic club in my building after work. He is constantly with me and I love being taken care of. I went from the one doing all the giving, to the one receiving.

Tom also insists on opening and closing my car door. I have to be trained, though. If I immediately start to open it, he puts his hand on mine and says, "I'll get the door." I am used to being independent and always rushing, he changes this. One day I reach to open the car door myself and he stops me, opens the car door and watches me slide into the seat. Then he leans down, kisses me and says, "Don't ever deny me the pleasure of watching those legs get into my car." I finally get it! He isn't doing it for me, I am doing it for him, or at least it is a win-win. He doesn't have to remind me again to let him get the door!

We begin making plans for when Brittany graduates from high school and goes off to college in the fall. Tommy, Tom's son, is older than Brittany, but still very dependent on his dad. It is time to get him out of the nest too. We talk about traveling and doing the RV thing. Tom is ready to *really* retire.

Lake Susan needs to be sold. The restaurant has seen better days, but the land is incredibly valuable. Tom has been working on plans to tear down the little cabins and build high-end condos. Because it is lakefront property, construction requires special permission from the water management people and both state and local governments. I think Tom really wants to see the project all the way through the construction phase, but I am pushing him to get the approval portion finished, then sell the venture to a builder, and take the money and run. He had already been working on the project for two years when I first met him and now nearly two more years have passed. It seems like an eternity to me. I am itching to get on the road and travel.

As our second anniversary approaches in February, 2004, I am sure an engagement is forthcoming. We plan a romantic ski vacation to Winter Park, Colorado. Ironically, we live near Winter Park, Florida. There is never any doubt in my mind that Tom and I will marry. There is no rush, but I am impatient. We are both single and we spend every waking moment together, although we don't live together. Brittany will have none of that; besides, she is off to college in August and then it will be just Tom and me. He will move in with me so we have a place in town and we will rent his house in Ocoee, but keep a cabin at Lake Susan Lodge until it sells.

Off to Colorado we go. I am shocked when Tom doesn't want to ski since he is athletic and we go jogging together all the time. Come to Colorado and not ski? It is strange to me; I don't understand. Sure there are lots of other things to do, but *hello*! Looking back now, perhaps it was a sign that he was not well. We go for a sleigh ride into the woods for a campfire dinner including a sing-along with a cowboy. One day we rent snowmobiles and go high into the mountains. I insist on skiing. He sits at the bar and drinks while he waits for me.

Our room has a fireplace, so one night we make a fire and there he proposes. It is not a fairytale proposal. After all, it is an ultimatum and it feels like one. After two years of dating and me throwing my whole life as I knew it away to be with this man, yes, I want to be married. In my mind it somehow justifies my decision to walk out on a ten-year marriage and take a total leap of faith. Somehow, getting married is proof that what I did was okay. I thought we would marry as soon as I was divorced. I was shocked when nothing happened on our celebration trip to New York City. I was again disappointed when our first anniversary came and went without a ring. We are two mature adults who know each other well. We are both bringing assets and level heads into the marriage. So as our second anniversary approached, I made it clear that I wanted to get married or I would move on. Never did I think Tom and I would not get married.

Since the engagement on February 22nd things between us are beginning to feel strained. I begin voicing my opinions and trying to get an exit strategy from Lake Susan in place for us and Tom is dragging his feet. His jealousy is starting to show. What at first was *wanting* to spend all our time together, is now starting to feel suffocating for me.

Why does it feel like I am always persuading someone else to buy into my dreams? Doesn't he want this—a life of travel and adventure? He is retired and says he wants to travel. I can't believe that I have found myself once again in the same position. I just want to be free. I want to have time to travel. I want the weight and responsibility of a job and parenting and even Tom to lighten up. "I just want them off of me," I complain to Debby, even demonstrating by sweeping my hands down one arm and then the other. I have no idea of what I am commanding the universe to do for me.

In my journal I write that proximity is power. I must surround myself with people who think and believe like I do. Rather than meeting a man and trying to get him to want the life I have dreamed of, why not find someone who is already traveling? I don't have to reinvent the wheel. I can go to where people are already living the vagabond lifestyle I dream about. Better yet, why not do it on my own? Traveling alone would be different for me, but I love people and meeting them is easy. There are no strangers, only friends I haven't met yet.

Brittany graduates from high school in June and moves into the dormitory at college in August. September is my dear friend Lael's birthday, and we have planned an all-girls trip for a week in a villa just outside of Florence in the Tuscany region. I love Italy and have visited it many times. There will be fourteen girls sharing a seven-bedroom villa with swimming pool and manicured grounds, not to mention a wine cellar and a cook. We are going to party like rock stars. I have been planning this trip for months, going on and on about how much I love Italy and all things Italian—wine, architecture, art, culture, history, leather and fashion.

In fact, I am in the process of starting a tour company that rents villas to American tourists and then plans holidays for them. After so many trips to Italy, friends and associates who learn of my travels want to rent villas too, but don't know how or where to go. If I help others rent villas, then I will have a place to stay and perhaps get to spend whole summers there. For me, it is just another way to be able to spend more time in my beloved Italy. Why not use my knowledge and love of travel to earn a little money? I can't quite pinpoint what the draw of Italy is for me and many others, but of all the places in the world I have traveled, Italy is the place I long for.

I own a sea foam green Vespa and drive it to work, yes, even in a skirt and heels. After one of my trips to Italy, I put a basket on the front of my bicycle so I can carry my groceries home. I ride my bike to the market every day, even to buy only one thing. I walk my little dog to the Italian restaurant in my neighborhood after dinner for a cappuccino. I try to bring the Italian lifestyle home with me to Orlando.

Tom just can't get over the thought of me *on the loose* in Italy. Now it is no secret about Italian men, but I am a grown woman engaged to be married in six months. If I want to fool around, I can do it just as easily in Orlando. Jealousy is eating him up. He can't sleep. He is drinking more than usual. He is miserable. The night before my departure, Tom sits me down on the couch in my living room. He is strangely serious.

"I don't want you to go to Italy," he says.

"What!" I say. "Why?"

"I know what is going to happen there. We are going to be married soon. We should be together. You shouldn't be going away without me. I will take you there, anywhere you want to go, but I don't want you to go without me."

"That's crazy, Tom. You can't mean what you are saying. I love to travel. I have gone a million places. I am not going to stop traveling because you have a wild imagination. If you don't trust me, we have nothing."

"It's not you I don't trust. I know what men are like. I know what they are thinking. You girls all parading into a club or a restaurant and those Italian men will be all over you."

"You aren't thinking right," I plead. "I am a big girl. I can handle myself. I didn't get to be forty-two-years-old with a ton of stamps in my passport by being a little naïve waif. Come on Tom. I am in love with you. I understand that we will travel together after we are married, but my girlfriends and other relationships mean a lot to me."

"I don't want you to go," he says flatly.

"What are you saying? I am going. I leave tomorrow. Everything is already set."

"If you go, I want the engagement ring back," he responds sternly.

Stunned, my mouth drops open and I stare at him in disbelief. I am trying to get my head around the words that have completely changed the meaning of this trip to Italy. A line has been drawn in the sand. The gauntlet has been dropped.

Desperately, I look deeply in his eyes for some kind of understanding of what he is saying. Then I see it. It is a hollow cold steeliness in those crystal clear blue eyes I have looked into a thousand times. Not the blue I have come to find comfort in, but the hollow cold steel I also, unfortunately, have seen before. It is a place where Tom goes to shield himself from things that are happening to him that he cannot or will not accept. It is similar to how a rape victim, in order to tell the story of their ordeal, goes to a place in their mind where it feels as though the horror is being done to someone else, which protects them from the gross violation of their own body. Tom has gone to the place he has created in his mind to stop the hurt of his mother choosing men and booze ahead of him, to stop the hurt of killing in the military and to stop the hurt of punches he endured in the boxing ring. It is a self-inflicted place he retreats to when the pain is more than he can bear.

I too can feel my back bow up in conflict and challenge. No one is going to tell me what I can and can't do. I cannot live in a marriage like this. I can't be with a man who thinks this way. I am mad, sad, outraged, but mostly disappointed.

In complete disbelief, I look down at the sparkling diamond ring on my finger. In slow motion, I slide the ring from my finger and hold it out to him. He takes it from me, stands from the couch and walks out the front door without a word.

That night, I go back and forth. What do I do? I can't live a life without trust or travel.

I love Tom. He is just being insecure. I can help him through this. Should I patch it up with him when I get back?

On the other hand, be strong. Don't call. Move on. This is your chance to strike out on your own. Live the life you have imagined. Why do I keep trying to fit a square man into the round peg of my life? Is he looking for a way, an excuse, to get out of this engagement? Does he really want to live my dream, or is it lip service, like before? I don't need Tom to live my dream life, but I want him. I love him. So, I get on the plane and I don't call him, even once, the entire time I am gone. I'll deal with it when I get back.

# Chapter 8

*Alaska - Week 2*
*June 2006*

## Day 7—385 miles

We've been driving for at least an hour in 100 percent natural forest and haven't passed a single car. Dusk is coming fast and our windshield is being pelted with bugs that proceed to create a mess, making it hard to see. It is a dangerous time to be on the road because animals begin grazing at this time of day. Hoping to spend the night somewhere with a little sign of life along this road, we finally give up and pull into the next state park campground. We drive off the main road onto a dirt road for about a mile or two. I am not comfortable at all being this remote. Should anything happen or if someone came up to our camper, what would I do? So we drive back onto the main road; the next camping area is closer to the road, but totally desolate. No ranger station or check-in area, nothing. It is getting dark very quickly, so Dad steers the headlights at the only sign. I take an envelope, fill it out, put the money in, and drop it in the locked box. Five dollars per site, half for Golden Eagle Pass Holders or senior citizens with a National Park membership, and no more than sixteen consecutive days.

You've got to be kidding me, the honor system for $2.50? I dutifully follow the directions and deposit the money. We drive into the loop and take the camping spot next to the restroom, or more appropriately, the outhouse. There is only still silence among the towering trees. This should be a treat, a blessing, a coup, but it is not. I am feeling very responsible for my dad. We have no cell phone service. After we are snug in our sleeping bags, I lay out a plan.

"Here's the deal, Dad," I tell him. "If someone knocks on the door, do not open it for any reason. Even if they say they are being attacked by a bear. The keys are in the ignition and the flashlight is on the hook. The camper is backed into the space, so we can pull straight out should we need to."

I think I am being paranoid. In reality, there were more wolves and other dangerous creatures in the clubs I went to in my old life than there are out here. So why am I worried about being in this amazing place where we have seen no other humans for at least the last hour? Why wasn't I worried about sleeping in the Wal-Mart parking lot?

I can still see some daylight through the heavy forest from the big picture window by my bed as I look up at the sky. The pine trees creak as they sway gently in the breeze. I say a little prayer for protection and try to enjoy this wonderful seclusion.

## Day 8—646 miles

We wake to 32 degrees in Lola Campground in Sawtooth National Forest, Idaho. In true Weaver tradition, Dad is up at daybreak, has started the engine to warm the cabin, and is behind the wheel. He asks if I need to go to the bathroom before we roll. The thought of getting out of my warm sleeping bag to walk to the outhouse in freezing temperatures isn't appealing. I'll wait, coffee *and* bathroom, now for that, I'll get out of my warm bed. Pulling out of the campground, we see three elk grazing alongside the dirt road. Traveling less than ten miles, we come up to an old Chevy Blazer in a ditch at the side of the road. It is an old beat-up vehicle with Nevada license plates. A young man is on the road, vigorously flagging us down. Immediately, my guard goes up. I hate this about me, but after last night and being so remote I am leery. I sit up in bed in the back of the van.

"Hey there. We broke down last night. Can you give us a lift to the next town?"

"Oh, we thought you got run off the road or hit a deer," Dad says. "How many people do you have?"

"Just me and my girlfriend."

"Sure," Dad says, "go get your things and hop in."

"No, definitely not," I shout in a hushed tone. "We are not picking up hitchhikers in the middle of nowhere. Tell them we will call for help." Okay, the cell phones aren't working, I know from last night. "Tell them we will call for help as soon as we are within phone range. Don't let strangers into our car."

"No," Dad says forcefully, "We are not leaving these people in the middle of the woods without heat. They are cold and stranded."

"Dad, we will get them help, we don't have to take them!"

"Barbara Elaine, we are NOT leaving them here," he says. "What is wrong with you?!?"

Suddenly I am twelve-years-old and I know that is the last word. "Great, just what I need," I say to myself.

As he clears the maps from the passenger seat, I grab my trusty notepad in which I have been journaling and tear out a clean sheet of paper. I quickly scribble: we picked up a couple who broke down just outside of Lola campground at 6:00 a.m. Tuesday—Nevada license tag … and slide it under my pillow. Barely awake, I grab the map. I haven't had any coffee and it's cold. Dear God.

Justin gets in the front seat with Dad and his girlfriend sits on the end of the bed with me. The next town on the map is Lowman. We will drop them there. The ride is quiet. I try to make conversation but feel like I am interrogating them. After all, it is just after six o'clock in the morning, and they were in a car without heat all night. He came up here for a job interview and they are spending a few days camping in the area. They would be happy to move to the mountains and get away from the dry heat of Nevada. We arrive at Lowman to discover the entire town consists of one deserted gas station and Log Lodge which is closed. We can't leave them here. The next town is Idaho City, twelve more miles, so we keep going.

We have been in Idaho almost all day yesterday and I don't have a whole lot of faith in the word *city*, but with no other option, we keep going. Around a bend, a twist and turn after turn, we finally see signs of civilization. We pull into the first gas station we see and our young passengers are graciously thankful. We all head for the bathroom and to get some coffee. They find a pay phone and make a call. After a few minutes we say our farewell. I go to the register to pay and the attendant says, "It's been taken care of for you by the young lady."

"Hmm," I say, feeling embarrassed and then deeply saddened by my warped sense of humanity. Ninety-nine percent of the world is made up of good people. I have watched too many newscasts and movies; I have no trust in the human race. They were just two young folks stranded by the roadside, hoping some *nice people* would come by and save them.

Happy to be on an Interstate, we head for Oregon. We hope to make it through Northwestern Oregon and into Washington State by nightfall. A campsite with a shower is in order. We'll need to fill up with gas but want to wait until the "idiot light" comes on, a little game we have been playing. Without any road changes for at least five hours and flat brown dusty landscape all around, I relax and get into my Sudoku puzzle. Dad is chatting along and I give him a gratuitous grunt every now and then. Neither of us is hungry since we ate so well yesterday. I am going to make all our meals today so we can keep on moving and eat light.

An hour or so passes and Dad announces the gas light just came on. We travel to the next exit and pull into the Red Neck Café and gas station. These two buildings are the only things at the entire exit except dust. As far as I can see in all directions, there is nothing but dust. I am not even sure the gas station really is a gas station or if it is even open. No brand, no sign for prices, just an old, hand lettered sign that says, "Gas Station." Dad pulls up to the pump while I get my shoes on to go inside to pay. There definitely isn't a card swipe machine at the pump here. The handwritten piece of paper taped to the pump says, "$3.26 a gallon." That is twenty-five cents a gallon more than we have been paying.

"Should we fill up or just get $25?" Dad asks.

"Just fill up," I tell him. "We are here now and finding a better deal could be more hassle than it's worth." It will cost an extra $7. In my old life that is half a glass of wine at my favorite trendy spot.

Inside, I look around the store. It's like a mini grocery store from yesteryear. Everything is organized, and they have a surprising selection. I spy some red licorice, my favorite, but am determined not to give in. I haven't let Dad have any junk, so neither can I. I ask the counter girl if they have any microwave popcorn. They do and it's Pop Weaver brand. How appropriate, but it is full of butter, so I leave it on the shelf. At checkout Andrea, the thirty something cashier, says she will sell us just one package of popcorn for fifty-nine cents and she'll even pop it for us. Okay, we'll splurge and buy a single package but will pop it later in the van. Andrea tells me she has lived here for eight years, after living in Key West for fourteen years. Wow, she gave up Key West sand and sun for Oregon dust. Unbelievable.

Dad comes inside and I ask how much the gas was. He doesn't know. There are no dollars on the pump, only gallons. We learn it is $84, it should have been $75, but Andrea tell us that we are in Oregon now and gas will get more expensive the farther west we go. "But you get free coffees with a fill up," she adds proudly. We are surprised to find out we crossed the border. Climbing back into the van, Dad remembers he needs to clean the windshield. After last night we decided that it is a new house rule: must clean the windows at every gas station. I tell Dad Andrea's story and he wants to know why she moved here. Silly me, I forgot to ask. So, I go back and find Andrea outside pumping gas for a burly old man.

"Hey, Andrea, do you pump gas for everyone or just the cute guys?" I tease her.

"Nope, for everybody, it's the state law, everything but diesel. It's to create more jobs. We have high unemployment," she explains. "I only make minimum wage and with Union dues of $35 a month, it's hard to make a living."

"I forgot to ask you why you came to Oregon," I tell her.

"Gold!" she says.

"Gold? Like dig the dirt and shake it in a pan, gold? You're kidding right?"

"No, I'm not. All you have to do is look up the gold claims that have expired and start mining. You get the gold rights as long as you are actively working the claim."

"Really? How did you find out about this? On the Internet?" I inquire.

"No, my husband has been coming to this area all his life."

In an amazed stupor, I climb back into the camper. I relay the story to Dad. We pull out of the Red Neck parking lot in silence trying to digest what we have just heard. I know I have made a lot of changes lately, but I thought I was still in the same century. I have been around gold diggers before, but it usually involved a wallet, not a shovel. What a paradigm shift! I had no idea people are actually still looking for gold. Too stunned to talk, we ride along in silence for awhile.

We are out of the wilderness and cruising now. The big four-lane highway stretches out for miles ahead and behind. Coming over a sweeping hill and a turn in the road, the view is spectacular and so is the drop off. I suggest that Dad slows down a little.

"Why?" he says.

"Cause you are going over eighty-five miles per hour," I reply.

"I know," he says with a boyish grin, "but now that I *can* go fast, sixty miles per hour feels like I'm crawling. Everyone is in the slow lane but me," he says proudly. "Look, all the way up the highway and behind me. Nobody's there."

"There is probably a reason for that, you better get over," I tell him.

"Why? I thought the rule was, slow traffic stays to the right and I'm going fast."

I burst out laughing. That's my dad. I give in. Hey, he's driving. Let him do what he wants.

We pop over the ridge and Dad sees a huge telephone tower. "Hey, I bet you can get service now," he says. I turn on the phone to call Brittany. She tried to call several times yesterday, but we only played phone tag. I would call her when I was in range and she would call me back when I was roaming. The clock on the phone let's us know we have moved into yet another time zone. How does it know?

After driving along the big Columbia River for about two hours, we head toward the Oregon wine country. Just outside Portland, we can see Mt. Hood. It is just over 10,000 feet high touting the only year-round snow skiing in the USA. At the base of the mountain, we drive along the Columbia River and see all the pretty sails of the wind and kite surfers. All this is part of the Cascade Mountain Range, the perfect place to grow grapes, making this prime wine country.

We leave the highway at Exit 62 following a billboard we saw and drive just a few miles, passing a beautiful old hotel, small grape vineyards and then finally pulling into the Cathedral Winery. It is picture postcard adorable with an old rustic building, perfectly manicured green lawn, old wine barrels overflowing with flowers and rows and rows of vines as a backdrop. We go inside for a little wine tasting. I love the names of the wines, Rock Star Red and Exit 62. I wonder who the wine maker is? He must be fun. I use the expression *party like a rock star* all the time. What would I name a wine if I had the chance? Dad tells me he only ever tasted wine once in Germany when he went to visit my brother who was stationed there in the Army some thirty years ago. I am worried that he shouldn't drive when he asks me what it feels like to be drunk. Dad has never been drunk in his entire life. "Do you feel dizzy like this?" he asks, doing his best imitation of a drunken person. I just laugh and shake my head. Two sips of wine, I don't think so.

Back on the highway, we head toward Mt. St. Helens. It is too early to stop for the night, but we are both feeling washed out. Not over it or tired, just feeling like taking a break. According to the map, there is camping on a lake on the small road leading up to Mt. St. Helens. After passing a few privately owned places, we choose Lake Silver Lodge. It is a throwback in time. A series of small cabins dot the landscape leading down to the lake where the camp store and marina are located. Rustic, charming and reminiscent of 1940, the Lodge reminds me so much of Tom's Lake Susan that I could cry. Memories of being at the Lodge with him flood back to me. We are definitely staying here tonight.

We pick out our site, get the gas stove set up on the picnic table and make dinner of turkey burgers, string beans and red beets. Dad has never actually cooked on a gas stove. I remember camping as a kid and all those times, it was my mom who did all the cooking.

We chat easily. After dinner we get the atlas out. It is time to get serious about our route leaving the USA, going through British Columbia, the Yukon, and finally into Alaska. Dad thinks we need three days from the US border to mainland Alaska. Pennsylvania to Vancouver is about twice the distance between Pennsylvania and Florida, and Vancouver to Alaska is once again that distance. That still gives us three weeks in Alaska and one week to get home to Pennsylvania. We both agree that three weeks could be too long, until we get to the Alaska map to discover the mileage per inch isn't twenty or twenty-five miles like it has been so far with all the other states, it is 150 miles per inch! This means that Alaska is about as big as the whole United States of America. I look at my Dad with big blinking eyes and ask, "Are you sure? This can't be right, and if it is, why on God's green earth am I only discovering this now? I think I should have looked a little closer at the map before I agreed to this trip." We both crack up laughing. We are two peas in a pod, ready to take off on an adventure and work out the details later.

Then I discover he hasn't actually looked at a map! He just knows other relatives who have made the journey and they loved it. Juneau is southern Alaska, Fairbanks and Anchorage are a whole different story. Juneau to Fairbanks is another 650 miles north. Oh well, we ARE going to Denali National Park. We clean up camp and head down to the lake for the community bonfire that starts at 9:00 p.m. A big fire ring made from stones is surrounded with log stumps for chairs. Other campers are already there.

There is lively conversation about where the families are from and how long they have been coming here. The kids are roasting marshmallows. We turn in for the night at about ten o'clock. We agree to sleep in and get a slow start, showering in the morning, since we know we are all smoky from the campfire.

## Day 9—214 miles

We sleep until a record 8:00 a.m. It is a little chilly, so when I get up to walk to the bathroom, I swing by the camp store and pick up some wood. Dad hates to pay for firewood. He is sure we can find what we need if we just look around. This is Washington and everything is damp. The sticks and fallen trees will take weeks of sunshine to dry them out. I don't understand why he doesn't know this. I remember going on driving/camping trips all the time when I was young. All eight of us kids piled into a camper on the back of his orange Chevy pickup. I loved it. I am working on the fire when he comes back from the restroom. Making fires or camping was never really his thing, he admits now. He just liked to drive. I guess that is another thing my mom used to do that I never noticed.

Sitting around a campfire makes me happy. Even though Florida is home, I still have a fire ring. I have been known to light a fire in my backyard. Different neighbors would smell the smoke and come out to see what was going on. I would invite them to pull up a lawn chair and before I knew, there were eight or ten people around the fire. I love to poke and stir at the fire. The hotter it gets, the better I like it.

After a breakfast of eggs and green tea, I tell Dad a boat ride is in order. He is not so sure, so I talk him into just one hour. Down at the marina, they rent pontoons, row boats and boats with motors. I want my exercise before

I take a shower. We learn there is a two hour minimum and the cost will be $22 for two hours. He only wants to go one hour, but that's okay.

"Great, we'll take it," I say. Dad looks at me disapprovingly, paying for two hours when we only want one? I decide we are going to splurge.

"Get the one with the motor," he says, "I am not rowing." Now this is my Dad's theory, why walk when you have a perfectly good engine and can ride?

"You are going to have to do the driving. I don't know how," he says.

"You've been on a boat before right?" I ask.

"Only once or twice, I grew up on the land, not around water, you know."

No, I didn't realize he had never been around boats.

With his lifejacket on, Dad unsteadily gets in the boat and sits down in the center. I crawl to the back, with one good pull start the motor and take off from the dock. Armed with a map and a six-horse-power Mercury engine, I take our little green boat out into Lake Silver and head around the right side of the island into the middle of the lake. The girl at the store told us that we should be able to see Mt. St. Helens from this spot. It is the mountain peak with the clouds around it. Sure enough there it is, snow and all. Far off in the distance, the high peak is still magnificent.

"UUUUWWEEEE!" says Dad. He is starting to relax and enjoy the ride. The water is flat, but we take our time anyway. The sound of the water lapping against the side of the boat makes me happy. With the warm sunshine on my face and the wind in my hair, I miss the water. Why don't I live on the water? I've always had a boat and a swimming pool. I love the ocean. Note to self: move to the water.

"Stay out in the middle, don't go in the weeds," Dad instructs.

For a guy who doesn't know about boating, he sure is good at doling out instructions, I think to myself.

"Do you want to drive?" I ask.

"No, no," he answers.

We continue to putter along. After a while, he says, "This is really nice. All I remember of going on a boat is going really fast, and the boat bouncing on waves and slamming down really hard on the water," Dad explains. "It was fun and all, but this, this is really nice."

I open it up a little more and announce, "That's all she's got, Dad."

"Well, that's all you need," he says. Then he adds, "The motor is missing a little. It needs new spark plugs."

We see the world totally different. I am all about the senses: smell the lake, feel the sunshine, taste nature, see the mountains and hear the water. He sees the world mechanically: how does this work, what is this machine doing, how did they get that dam to make electricity, that rock face got like that because the freezing and cooling caused a crack, that valley is perfect for corn because the rain falls this way and the sunshine hits it that way and so on.

Following the edge of the lake, I find the entrance to a canal. Dad checks his watch. To his amazement, we have been on the water over an hour. Interesting lake houses, quirky little docks and boat houses dot the canal and make for easy conversation. At the turn-around point at the end of the canal, I tell Dad it is his turn to drive. He doesn't want to. Now here is a man who has tinkered with every motorized toy under the sun and he doesn't want to drive a little putt-putt boat. With a little coaxing and a lot of wobbling, we switch places. "Just take your time, go slow, get the feel of the throttle," I explain. The canal is a no-wake zone, so we need to go slow anyway. In no time, he is grinning from ear to ear. He likes it. Once back out in the big lake, Dad makes the boat zigzag, getting the hang of steering and opens it all the way. "Hey, this is really fun," he says with child-like zeal in his voice. I am so happy to give my dad a new experience.

We pass a big lake house. Dad comments on how nice it would be to have a summer place. I tell him he could have one, too. There are lots of little lakes in the mountains of Pennsylvania. He doesn't know if he could afford it. "I always had the things I wanted," he reflects. "I never knew I wasn't successful. I thought I did okay in life until I learned about what other people had. Then I didn't think I did so well." The melancholy tone in his voice makes me sad. There is a paradigm shifter. If he didn't know, he wouldn't know. Is it better to leave the Amazon Tribe alone or give them computers and let them see what else is out there? Or is it only better to know what is out there so I can appreciate how good I have it? Or is the key being happy with what you have, regardless of your *position* in the big picture? Some existential food for thought.

Before we know it, we are back at the dock. Dad is elated that we used up our full two hours. We drop the keys off at the camp store and get our second treat for the day, red licorice. They sell it by the piece. We each get five pieces. Wow, does it taste good!!

Now that the temperature has warmed up about twenty degrees, the thought of getting naked to take a shower is manageable. Back at the van, I pack my shoulder bag with fresh clothes, two towels and make sure I have all the toiletries I'll need. I also take two pots and the spatula to wash. Dad asks me if I have enough quarters.

"Quarters?" I question. "What will I need quarters for?"

"To use the shower, every ten minutes is twenty-five cents," he explains.

"Get out!" I retort. I didn't notice that when I checked out the shower. I just noticed there was only one and I hoped no one was using it right now.

Well, here goes then. Fifty cents should do it. I didn't know I would burn up the first quarter trying to adjust the water. I approach the old wooden clapboard building. Inside, there are two toilet stalls to the right, a sink, counter and mirror directly in front and one very large shower stall to the left. The big changing room is great, even if it does house the exposed hot water heater. There is plenty of room on the bench for my things. I insert my first quarter into the ancient machine following the instructions, twist the knob and sure enough, the water turns on. I wait until it is hot, strip down and stand on my sneakers so I am not standing on the cold concrete floor. I make the water a little hotter, a little colder, then again a little hotter and jump in. I get right down to business and shampoo my hair. It is so dirty that the shampoo barely lathers up. So I do it again. The water temperature doesn't stay steady and before I know it, I am freezing. Back out of the shower, I am standing on my sneakers again, shivering, head full of suds, fiddling with the knobs. Hot again, now too hot. Hot is better than cold. The shower stall is very tight. Now, I am small, yet I can back up against the wall and touch the opposite side with my flat hand. My elbows are bumping against the sides when my hands are over my head unless I turn sideways and let one elbow hit the dark green shower curtain. Get the conditioner on quick. I would love to shave my legs, but my goose bumps are too big, which will probably leave a rash, besides who is going to notice my legs anyway? The shower cuts off, announcing the end of the first quarter. Where did I put the second quarter? Of course, I put it on the ledge at the far side of the room. Dripping wet, naked and freezing, I slip my feet partway into my sneakers and shuffle across the room and back to feed the machine to give me some more hot water. Laughing at what a sight I must be, I hope there aren't any peepholes that the regulars know about.

I dry off quickly, putting on layers of pants and tops. With my hair wrapped in a towel, I gather my things and move to the sink with the counter and mirror. I brush my teeth, dust on minimal make-up and comb out my hair. Pulling the hair dryer from my bag, I go in search of a plug. No plug, not one. There is a light overhead, so there is definitely electricity to the building. Guess I'll wash the dishes instead. I must say I have never washed dishes in the same sink I just brushed my teeth in before. Stuffing my towels, toiletries and the pots into my overnight bag, I guess I will dry my hair back at the camper.

Here goes another first. I have never dried my hair standing up in an RV, looking into a rear view mirror, using a hairdryer that is plugged into a converter that is plugged into the cigarette lighter in the middle of Washington. Once finished, after a big sigh, the girl in the mirror looks human again. I think I know her.

The Mt. St. Helens' visitors' center is modern. No wonder, the old one was totally destroyed, and the new structure serves as a representation of the events of the big eruption in 1980. The story that impresses me the most is of a cantankerous eighty-year-old man who was told to evacuate, but refused. He lived his whole life up here and he would rather die here than start new somewhere else. Within days, the man and his house were under twenty feet of ash.

After paying $5 for a cup of coffee, Dad and I decide it is time to buy our own coffee maker. On the drive back down the mountain, we notice a multitude of young trees that were planted twenty-five years ago. The branches are so green and delicate that it makes me feel like I have double vision. I squint, trying to figure out what I am seeing. Dad confirms it is not just me, thank goodness.

We pass through Seattle on our way west, toward the Olympic National Forest. Yes, there is something past Seattle. I can tell I am near the water because of the smell and the calming effect it has on me. This peninsula is the home of the Quinault Rain Forest, famous for some of the world's biggest trees.

We camp for the night under a big pine tree after dutifully paying $16 via the honor system, just like we did at the other unattended state parks. It's 8:30 p.m., so at home it would be 11:30 p.m. Here I sit with a little wine and a little bluegrass playing on the radio. Big pines surround our little piece of paradise. It smells so good. As nightfall comes, the green lawn takes on the color of the rich, deep green forest that surrounds us. I am so happy watching the night unfold, complete with the buzzing of hundreds of katydids. Bliss. My shoulders are down. This is paradise.

Then Dad opens the back door of the camper and shouts, "What is that hollering?"

"What are you talking about?" I call back.

"The music," he answers.

"It's your bluegrass CD," I say shaking my head.

"Well, turn it off. It sounds horrible," he grunts.

"Okay, but it is the same one we have been listening to since we left Pennsylvania," I tell him.

So much for being in the moment, I think to myself. Guess I'll go to bed too. I like lying in bed at night. It gives me time to think. I think about where I have been, where I want to go, what I wish for, but mostly, who do I want to be?

## Day 10—223 miles

In the morning we travel along a shoreline dotted with adorable fishing shacks. The area is well-known for Hamma Hamma Oysters. I want to stop and take a picture at every turn in the road. Soon we realize that the only road system is around the entire National Park which is a four-hour loop going in the other direction. In search of the rain forest and the biggest trees in the USA, we backtrack about an hour. No worry, the scenery just keeps getting better. This peninsula has it all including a bay, logging, ranching, harbors, Pacific Ocean, mountains, fields of wildflowers, a rainforest, Indian reservations, groves of moss covered trees, picturesque Crescent Lake and a Victorian port town with a ferry. I love it here. We have had picture-perfect weather, apparently not the norm. This place gets twelve feet of rain a year! One lady told me it is no wonder I like it so much, I have been here the three days it hasn't rained this year!

We see the world's biggest spruce tree. Signs are posted along the road directing hikers back into the woods to see a specific tree, so with a little coaxing, I get Dad to pull off and have a look. After hiking about half-a-mile into the forest, we come upon the most amazing Cedar Tree, fifty-eight feet around and twenty feet in diameter. It is mostly hollow inside so Dad and I can both get in. The silence is amazing. The smell is wet and rich. We play around and stick our head and hands out the hollow knobs of the tree. I try to climb up, but immediately slide down the decaying bark. We are like kids.

A bit farther down the road we see another sign marking a famous hiking trail. Dad tells me to go on alone. He would rather take a nap amongst the trees and says he can feel the majesty just fine from the bed in the camper. The three-mile loop will take about an hour or so. We agree to make lunch when I return.

The trail is not a disappointment. Not even 200 yards in, I come upon a giant towering tree. What a treat! I can't wait to see what comes next. The earth is damp and lush green plants surround me. I walk along in pure amazement. Who knew a place like this existed and I am not even in Alaska yet. The trees get bigger and closer together the farther down the path I go. First I think about the silence. Actually it is absence of sound, but it is not silent at all. I hear the trees. They are talking. I can't walk and feel them at the same time, so I scan the path for the perfect tree to stop and listen to. I plant myself firmly at the base of a gigantic old tree and ask the universe to open my heart to receive. Resting against the tree, I imagine having a direct link coming straight down from the heavens. I feel small against this huge tree and I feel close to God. I am overwhelmed and start to weep as I sit with my back propped up against a tree. I feel its power. There is an unbelievable presence with me here in the woods. I am definitely finding what I came here for. "Who am I? What am I here for? Show me the way," I ask. Peace washes over me. I am not alone. I sit and soak up this wonderful sense of being alive. I am in the right place. Everything is happening as it should. Trust, believe, receive.

I sit without regard of time, then get up and move along the path with new eyes. Everything is a miracle. Everything is more green, more giant, more delicate and more perfect. With pure joy, I walk through this amazing forest.

Back at the camper, I find Dad puttering around. I tell him to walk down the trail just a little bit to the first huge tree. It's not far, but well worth the short walk. I start lunch by unpacking the cook stove and firing it up. When lunch is ready, I set the little picnic table next to us. I pull out my trusty little pad and jot down a few notes. Then I walk to the restroom at the other end of the parking lot. I am in my own little world until I start to wonder where my dad is. How long has he been gone? What time did he leave?

Maybe he stopped to sit under that first big tree. It's not far, so I will just walk back there to check on him. I stroll back to the tree and don't see him anywhere. That's strange. I call out to him. "Dad, Dad, where are you?" I shout. Nothing. I look all around me, thinking maybe he walked off the trail. I walk a little farther, then remember seeing a little creek down a ravine. Maybe he went down there. From the top of the hill I shout again, "Dad, Dad, are you down there?" Nothing.

Oh, my God. Where is he? How long has he been gone? How far could he have gone? Oh, my God, I have lost my dad! Maybe he got confused and went the wrong way. Maybe he is having a heart attack and is slumped over under a tree somewhere. My mind starts racing. Dear God, where is he? I start calling his name again and again. My heart begins pounding even though I am trying to stay calm. I backtrack to the big tree, this time scanning the woods, not the trail, thinking he is off the path somehow. Nothing.

Maybe he decided to go a little farther up the path. The trail gets steep a little way back. I don't think he could make it up here, but where else could he have gone? So I start to head farther into the forest. Now I am running along the path, calling for him. "Dad, Dad, can you hear me?" I don't know if I should go fast to get to him or slowly to scan the woods. I am totally out of breath by the time I reach the top of the hill and come upon a little group of hikers coming the other way.

"Have you seen my Dad?" I ask trying not to sound completely panicked.

"No, we haven't seen anyone."

Oh, my God, I am in middle of nowhere and I have lost my dad. How did this happen? What do I do? Keep going? Go back? Stay calm. Think. Oh, my God. If he is having a heart attack in the woods, I must find him fast.

The hikers tell me they are going back and will keep an eye out for him and that I should keep going forward. I don't think he could have gotten this far, but maybe. I just don't know how long he has been gone.

I start to run again, along the ridge now, breathing hard. In the same place where just an hour ago I sat in complete peace and harmony, now I am in sheer panic. How did this place go so quickly from love to fear? I go back past the huge trees, past the giant ferns, past the fallen logs, past the mossy vines, past the little footbridge. Nothing. "Dad, Dad, where are you?!" I scream.

I run around the last turn and down the path that leads to the parking lot. There is my dad sitting obliviously at the picnic table with his feet up and a drink in hand.

"Are you alright?" I ask.

"Yes. Why, were you worried?" he asks.

"Yes, I went into woods looking for you," I say still out of breath.

"I thought so, when I came back and you were gone. I went a little past the tree and took the path down to the creek," he explains. "Then I saw the bridge for the road and thought it would be easier to walk back along the road than on the trail. I didn't mean to make you worry."

"I am just glad you are okay. I thought maybe you got hurt or something."

We sit down to have a little lunch. I am not hungry anymore. What just happened? This *in* and *out* of bliss thing. What does it mean? What is the lesson here?

Later, about an hour down the road, we come to the Pacific Ocean where big cliffs hang over the beach. With some simple directions from a stranger, we park and walk down a rugged trail to the ocean. Blue skies and white surf make the perfect backdrop for thousands of huge bleached logs that litter the beach like toothpicks. We climb on one that is ten feet in diameter. Giant rocks just off-shore are a playground for bald eagles. To our shock and amazement, five bald eagles are playing in the surf just down the beach. We sit on some rocks and watch the show. The birds are gigantic with a wingspan of about four to five feet and have white heads and tails. One swoops down and drags its claw in the ocean right in front of us. They are calling to each other as they land in the trees behind us and on the rocks right in front of us. We are completely blown away and we haven't even left the USA!! The Pacific Northwest is my favorite. I decide I would like to spend more time in Oregon and Washington, especially in Puget Sound and the San Juan Islands. Maybe by boat, bicycle or motorcycle! We finish the day with Chinese food and sleep in the parking lot of a Tru-Value Hardware store.

## Day 11—441 miles

In the morning we head to the port town of Victoria, take the ferry back to the mainland of Washington and head for the Canadian border crossing into British Columbia at Vancouver. I drive through the city. We log another 200 miles to Lillooet, driving on Route 99 with its high mountains and hairpin turns. Crossing the border the temperature is 82 degrees—the warmest we have had so far. Dad is still sure it will be 100 degrees in Alaska. He makes me laugh.

The days seem long because it gets light at 4:00 a.m. and stays light until 11:00 p.m. Dad likes to start early and we don't realize how late it is until we are tired, and by then it is 10:00 p.m. We take turns driving and napping. I sit propped up in the *Queen's Throne* typing away while the panoramic view passes me by. I am so happy. When Dad is in bed, it is the *King's Throne*. He is happy, especially when I play Johnny Cash or John Denver for him! We are having a ball and getting along great. We have definitely found our stride.

We stop in the parking lot of a public library and use their wireless Internet. We thought we would spend the night in this location until a local man comes and taps on the window and wants to know what we are doing here. He kindly tells us to move on when we are through. So we find a quiet street and call it a night. I hang a little curtain across the front window, but it is still light inside the camper. I don't sleep very well, worried that someone will wonder what we are doing parked on the street in front of their house, but no one seems to mind.

## Day 12—502 miles

We drive all day through the rural mountains of Canada and sleep along the road in a random parking lot.

## Day 13—593 miles

A repeat of day 12.

## Day 14—603 miles

Another day driving through the rural mountains of Canada. Light rain falls. The sky is overcast as we travel down Route 1. We are in the Yukon! Once again we sleep along the road in a random parking lot.

This week: Gas–$453 Miles–3,222

Running Total: Gas–$795 Miles–6,432

# Chapter 9

## Getting the News
## September 2004

"Would you like something to drink?" The flight attendant asks.

"Yes, I would," I answer.

Debby, who is seated across the aisle from me, just shakes her head and laughs. "Not for me," she says, "I am in detox."

"Oh, come on, we have eight hours left of our vacation," I protest.

The flight attendant says again, "What can I get you?"

"How about something Italian?" I say. I am thinking Super Tuscan, perhaps a Chianti."

Debby laughs.

The flight attendant is not amused. She gives me *the look*. Lady this is an airplane, not a cruise ship. I am a flight attendant, not a sommelier.

"How about red wine? Make it two." I open one and slide the other one into the seat pocket in front of me. I take out my trusty notepad and pen from my carry-on. On a fresh sheet of paper, I write, "Quotes from the Trip" and underline it. #1. Note to self: I don't smoke, referring to the night in the villa when we got the brainy idea to smoke cigars and woke to the world's most awful dragon breath. I could have peeled the wallpaper off with one huff.

I pass the paper across the aisle. Debby reads it and bursts out laughing. She adds a line and passes it back to me, I read it and snicker. #2. The wine cellar is not your friend. We had a wine cellar available for our use and my bill for the wine cellar was more than my share of the villa rental. I add another line. In less than five sentences, she succumbs.

"I'll take that wine now," she says. We play our little game and easily fill page after page. Flooded with memories, we relive every moment of our trip. This one goes down in history as one of our best trips ever. We *did* party like rock stars.

Once we are on the ground in Orlando, we head for baggage pick-up. I wait by the luggage carousel and Debby goes to the nearest pay phone to call her husband, Glenn. They live minutes from the airport and in no time he will be at curbside pickup. I always leave my car parked in the street at their house.

"Hey honey, it's me. We just landed," she informs him.

"Debby, I have something very important to tell you. Do not respond to what I am going to say. Do not say a word. Tom died while you were away. Don't tell Barbara anything. Let's just get her home first," he says sternly.

Too shocked to reply, she hangs up the phone.

As we pull up to Debby's house, I see my car right where I left it, except it has a big dent in the side.

Glenn says, "Oh yeah, I forgot about that. Our neighbor accidentally backed into it a few days ago. She is sick about it. It is so low to the ground that she never saw it in the rear view mirror of her SUV. All her insurance information is inside."

"A pain in the ass," I quip, "but at least it is drivable. Oh well, if that is the worst thing that happened to me while I was away. I can deal with it."

Even that does not ruin my mood. I am still flying high from the trip. We are chatting about our travel adventures, the weather and so on.

"So, anything exciting happen while we were away?" I inquire of Glenn.

Glenn looks at Debby. She goes into the other room taking three-year-old Parker with her.

"Come over here. I have something to tell you," he says, patting on the dark green leather couch. "I have never had to tell anyone this before. I am terribly sorry. Tom died while you were away." The words hang in the air.

"No. No, no, no, no! When? How? Where is he? Am I too late? Oh my God, no."

"He died yesterday, in the morning at 9:30 a.m. We couldn't reach you at the villa. We thought it would be best to tell you when you got home, rather than have you suffering on the long flight. They think it was a heart attack. Tommy found him on the kitchen floor."

My head is spinning. "Oh, my God, Tom is gone."

Just an hour ago I was reveling in bliss and now I am gripped by grief. I have never been so happy and so sad in such a short period of time. How can this be? Tom is gone. I can't believe what I am hearing. I must try to see him.

I feel like I have been stabbed— I am hurt and bleeding, but can only look at my wounds. I don't know what to do about them. Jet-lagged and stunned, I call Tommy.

"We are all at the house," he says. "You should come over."

"I'll be right there."

Debby takes me into the bathroom and starts the shower. She helps me pick out something to change into. I can't think. A hot, hot shower will help. Nothing will help, but I step in anyway. The water stings my face as much as the tears do. The sounds of the shower drown out the animal like groans that are coming from my throat. The moans I hear from deep in my chest are not human. This is not real. This cannot be happening.

On the drive, I try to remember where I was on Thursday at 9:30 a.m. That would be six hours later, Italian time or 3:30 p.m. That day we all went to Florence. We were walking around the city and I remember being all shopped out and telling the girls that I was going to find a place to sit and relax, and that I would meet them by the Ponte Vecchio at four o'clock. I found a place to sit on a bench directly in front of the Duomo and was resting in the sunshine, thinking that I was the luckiest girl in the world. Look where I am. I had an hour to revel in the amazing site. The irony of what was going on at home and how it would change my life forever is immeasurable.

I pull into the driveway of Tom's house. Tommy meets me by my car. We are both crying and clinging to each other. We walk through the front door together.

A lady walks up to me and says, "You must be Barbara."

"Yes, I am."

"I am Pat. I am so sorry."

Pat was Tom's first and only wife. They were married for eighteen years, but divorced about fifteen years ago; she has since remarried twice. They had a friendly relationship. We have never met before although we almost met once when Tom had outpatient surgery and Pat brought him some homemade goodies. His door was never locked, so she stopped in on her way to work at about seven in the morning to make the delivery.

"Tom, it's me Pat," she called from the other room. "I just stopped by to check on you and bring you some food."

"Thanks." Tom called back from the bed. "I am not alone. Barbara is here."

"Oh, sorry to interrupt." She said, "I didn't realize. Hello Barbara."

"Hello Pat," I winced.

"Are you okay then, Tom?"

"Yes, I am fine."

"Okay, I'll just put the food in the fridge and be off then. I hope you feel better quickly. Nice to meet you Barbara."

"Nice to meet you too," I replied.

Today, she greets me with a warm embrace. "I am so sorry. I had to make some decisions. They needed to know what he should wear. I picked a blue shirt, red tie and navy blazer. I hope that is okay."

"That is exactly what I would have picked." I tell her. Tom wore it often. It made his vivid blue eyes stand out even more. Just the thought of it makes the tears flow again.

Pat holds me in her arms and tells me she wants me to be included in everything. I am to ride in the car with the family. She has made funeral arrangements before. For Kelly, for her late husband, for her mother, and now for Tom. She will take care of everything. She is so kind to me and I am grateful.

The living room is crowded with people, most of whom I don't know. Furniture has been rearranged to accommodate everyone. The house already doesn't smell like Tom's house. Now it smells like cleaning products and other people's food. Pat leads me into the bedroom where we can be alone. She is changing the sheets on Tom's bed.

"Please stop," I beg her to myself. "Do you have to do that right this minute?" I scream inside. "Just stop!" Everything is changing so fast. I pick up his pillow from the floor and draw it to my chest. I bury my face in it. It has Tom's scent. I breathe in again and again. I don't want to forget this smell. This is the last place he was, this is as close to him as I will ever be again. I take the pillowcase off and keep it folded in my hand. This pillowcase would become my comfort during the many sleepless nights ahead. It would be carefully tucked under my pillow during the day and pulled out at night for me to hold onto like a small child with her blankie. It would stay there until the very last smell of Tom was gone.

Pat and I sit on the end of the bed.

"Do you think we would ever have gotten married? Did he really love me?" I ask.

"Do you really want to know?" she asks cautiously.

"Yes, I do."

"He really loved you. He talked to me before he proposed. He was struggling about it, but once you were engaged, he was happy. But no, I don't think he would ever have gone through with it. Believe me, it wasn't because of you. He adored you. It was something in him. Is there anything you would like to take? I am sure you have personal things here. Is there anything you want?"

"I would like my engagement ring."

"Do you know where it is?" she asks.

"No, I don't. It may not even be here. He may have thrown it out of the car window for all I know," I answer sadly.

"Well, if we can find it, of course, you may have it."

We go back into the living room. For the first time I meet nieces and nephews, other relatives, neighbors and some people who work for the city.

I am deflated. I sit on the stone ledge in front of the fireplace. I feel very small. Skip, Tommy's uncle, Pat's brother, comes and sits next to me. We had met briefly a few times before at Lake Susan.

"Are you okay kiddo?" Skip asks kindly.

I don't want to look at him. My eyes are red and puffy. I am exhausted. My head is spinning. "No, I'm sorry, but I am not."

"Is there anything I can do for you?"

"Yes, there is, actually," I say.

"Name it." Skip answers, eager for something to do.

"Someone hit my car and the wheel well is scraping when I go around the corner. It is cutting into the tire and I think I might get a flat," I explain.

He gets up to check out the situation. He comes back and asks me for the keys.

Tommy hands me a beer. Pat brings me a plate of food. I am too shocked to know if I am thirsty, hungry or sleepy. It hurts to breathe. I don't want to be here. I don't want to go home. I don't want any part of this. The beer tastes good, but I am already numb and don't feel its effect.

Skip is back. "Your car is fixed," he reports. "The tire will be okay for now, but you should replace it."

"You fixed it already?" I reply, surprised.

"Sure, I just ran it down the street to the body shop and they bent the metal back far enough so it won't scrape."

"Wow, now that's service. Thank you."

"Happy to help," he says

Skip doesn't leave my side. He knows his family and is concerned for reasons I don't understand.

I need to sleep. Pat asks if I want to stay here. The thought of sleeping in Tom's bed is unbearable. Skip volunteers to drive me home, but I want to be alone. I have been gone for ten days.

✳

In the morning, we all go together in one car, Pat, Skip and me. The funeral director greets Pat in the reception room. They are chatting like old friends. My knees are weak. They chatter on. "Let's just go inside. Please stop talking, I scream to myself." I just want to see Tom. I think I am going to be sick. Finally, we move on.

Walking down the aisle of a small room that looks like a chapel, I see Tom in an open casket. The three of us are walking slowly, arm in arm. I well up with tears as we get closer. This isn't happening. This isn't real. My Tom isn't dead.

Standing close to him now, I say, "He looks so old."

Pat laughs and looks at me. "He was old," she says.

Tom was sixty-four-years-old but had more vigor and playfulness in him than anyone I knew. "He was never old to me," I say. Other than that, he looked good.

The wheels are in motion. There will be two viewings—one in Ocoee, for all the city employees and residents (after all he had been the mayor), and one in Clermont for the Lake Susan people. After the funeral service at the church, Tom will be buried at Woodlawn Cemetery next to his daughter, Kelly.

I know exactly where the cemetery plot is. I have been there many times with Tom. Little did I know that when I was there, holding Tom as he cried at the foot of his daughter's grave, that later I would be the one standing there weeping.

At some point in the middle of all the funeral arrangements, there was the reading of his will. Again, we all drive in the same car to the attorney's office together. This time it is Pat, Tommy, Skip and me. We are all sitting at an oval table in a dated conference room. The attorney tells us that the will was written about twenty years ago and, to his knowledge, it was never updated. He asks if we know of any other wills. None of us does. According to the attorney, it is no longer valid because it lists Pat as his wife, it lists Kelly who is now deceased and, of course, Tommy. Pat will be disqualified because they are divorced, leaving only Tommy.

"Even though it is invalid, does anyone have a problem with Tommy as the only heir?" the attorney asks.

All eyes turn on me. If it was Tom and Brittany sitting at this table and I was the one who died, Tom would have done the right thing. Besides, we were not married and apparently never would have been. I am a grown-up girl who can take care of herself. Tommy is just twenty-six-years-old.

"Of course, Tommy should have everything. I am sure that is what Tom would have wanted," I say.

There is relief in the room. It isn't a surprise to Tommy, Skip looks impressed, and Pat is pleasantly shocked. The attorney breaks the silence. "Very well, then. I will draw up a document for you to sign Miss Singer and we will be through." I am not a threat and this act confirms it.

Without realizing it at the time, that one single response totally changed my reputation for a whole lot of people. I guess this issue had been discussed when I wasn't around, and this is what greatly concerned Skip. Tommy always knew that I was in it because I loved his dad, but apparently, lots of people thought otherwise. I am not a gold digger. I know full well that today I am walking away from millions. Tommy has Pat to help him with the estate and the mountain of papers that are to follow. Finalizing all the details will take years, if ever, and I want no part of that.

Besides, I have my own daughter to look after. It hurts me that she didn't come home from college for the funeral. I called to tell her the news several days ago. She had tests and papers and studying to do. Besides, she has no pity for me. Remembering her own pain, she had lashed out at me, "How does it feel to be left behind? He died of a broken heart, you know." Perhaps it is better if she stays away. I couldn't take her steely glare on top of all this heartache.

My whole body aches as the day of the funeral finally arrives. It has been days of non-stop events. What little sleep I got was fitful. I used up all my tears. No make-up is going to help hide the pain and sorrow on my face. I dress carefully, choosing exactly the same black Armani suit, light blue blouse and vintage jewelry that I wore the night I stayed out all night with Tom. I drive to the church early to display several posters with lots of photographs of Tom when he was very much alive. He would have wanted to be remembered on his boat, at the lodge, winning sales awards, playing with his kids, flying his plane, cutting the ribbon at ground-breakings and so on.

Tom's casket is already loaded in the hearse and the line of black cars is in place. Pat and Gary, her husband, ride in the front with the driver, and I'm in the back seat with Tommy and Skip.

"Oh, I have something for you," Tommy says. He reaches into his pocket and produces my engagement ring. I slide it onto to my left hand, back to where Tom had originally placed it just six months ago. I am engaged to a man who no longer draws breath.

"I know the timing is terrible," Tommy says, "but I thought you would want it as soon I found it."

Tommy made a compilation CD for us to listen to during the ride. The music is his last gift to his father. The plan is to go from the funeral home to Tom's beloved Lake Susan Lodge, and then on to the church. I do fine until we get to Lake Susan. The cars pull in and make a big sweeping U-turn down by the water. The driver gets out and opens the back of the hearse. I can see the casket inside, draped with the American Flag. With hands folded in front, the driver bows his head for a moment of silence. This scene, with the music Tommy so carefully picked out, is more than I can take. It is all just so sad. This shouldn't be happening. The tears roll down my cheeks.

After a drive that seems like an eternity, we pull into the packed parking lot of the church. It is filled with fire engines and police cars complete with men and women in uniform. As we near the front door, I do an about-face. "I am not going in there. I am going to be sick."

Skip grabs my shoulders and stops me from running away. He looks me straight in the eyes and says, "You can do this. I will be right by your side the whole time."

"I need to use the restroom." Once inside the stall—a moment of quiet where no one can see—I have a melt down. I am wailing now. My Mom is knocking on the door. She and my sister-in-law, Patti, had arrived earlier today from Pennsylvania.

"Barbie, it's Mom. Come out." I open the door and fall into her arms.

"I can't do this Mom," I sob. "I can't go in there. It is so final. I don't want it to end."

She holds me and rocks me, gently swaying me back and forth. "You are going to be okay. If I could take your pain away, I would. I love you."

We come out of the restroom and I am handed off to Skip. The family is waiting for me and we walk down the aisle. I feel dizzy and reach out gripping Skip's arm. We take a seat in the first pew. I am between Tommy and Skip. I am visibly shaking. I feel like I am in a freezer without a coat. The shudders won't stop. Skip reaches over and takes my hand. I hold on so tightly that his fingers turn purple instantly. I don't let go.

The sermon goes on forever, words, words, words. More words. I am listening, but I hear nothing. Please let this end. More words. The procession starts and the first people to come by Tom's casket are from the club, my co-workers. I am deeply touched. Others come through the line, mostly strangers to me. The line finally ends.

One final thing to do. Place a lock of Kelly's hair in Tom's coat pocket. He showed it to me on the first night I was at his home. It was cut from her head the day she was buried, safely kept in an envelope that read, *bury it with me next to my heart.* Pat didn't know it existed. Never did I dream that I would be the one carrying out this request. The four of us are standing at his side for the last time as I tuck the lock of hair into his breast pocket. Tommy pulls out a miniature liquor bottle of Crown Royal, his drink, and tucks it into the other side. We chuckle. It was perfect. We all needed to lighten up.

At the gravesite a light breeze comes over our sad party. It is a beautiful sunny day. The blue sky is dotted with white puffy clouds. A great day for flying I think; I am sure Tom would agree. Just as I am reminiscing, I see a bird with a wide wing-span catching some air just above us. Gently soaring, circling, and clearly having fun in the wind. That's him. That is Tom, having a ball. The loud crack of the military gun salute brings me back to reality. I jump with every fire. At last, it is done.

I never go back to Lake Susan or Tom's house. That part of my life is over. There is nothing for me there. Driving home that day, my diamond engagement ring glistens in the sunlight. I didn't want the ring, I wanted the man.

# Chapter 10

## Day 14—603 miles

Now that we are traveling in Canada, we must adjust to buying gas in liters and judging mileage in kilometers. At the grocery store I *rent* a shopping cart for twenty-five cents and pay 14 percent tax on a six-pack of beer that costs $13.

At roadside rests in Canada, it is common to have toilets in the middle of nowhere. I guess it is because we are in such a rural area. Where else would you go? At one rest area we meet a man from Holland who is in his early thirties and traveling alone. He bought a camper here when he arrived and will travel around for a month and then sell it before he goes home. What a concept.

The last three days have been long. We take turns driving, although Dad is at the wheel most of the time. I am cranky. I want a manicure, pedicure and a facial. I don't feel pretty. My skin is blotchy. I want all my stuff. My hair is brown and dirty. My legs are flaky from dryness. Who packed my clothing anyway? I don't have anything I need. After a shower at the Nugget City campground, I feel better. The people's faces are changing. We are seeing more brown, flat faces, Eskimo Indians I suppose.

There are more animals along the road now. We see two black bears and a moose. Dad has a great eye for spotting them. We see our first sign for the Alaska Highway, 752 km away or five hours. Today we get another chip in the windshield. That makes three so far. The stones fly up from the gravel parts of the road. In Canada they seem to do construction in ten-mile stretches. On this stretch there is actually a cop giving out speeding tickets for people going too fast and passing in a construction zone. Doesn't he have anything better to do?

The temperature is 42 degrees with clear blue skies. After 200 miles, we fill up with gas at White Horse and head for Dawson Creek. I see a sign that says, "restaurant open 21 hours a day". Silly, I think. Why not just go three more hours and make it twenty-four? What is the guy going to do for three hours? Count the money?

At the gas station I buy a country and western CD. Dad likes this better than my music. I play John Mayer for him and try to get him to appreciate the lyrics, but he doesn't listen to the words. It reminds me of Brittany and me. She tries to get me to appreciate rap, but I can't understand most of what they are saying.

Dad fusses at me when I drive. When he is not driving, he wants to tell me how to do it. I don't say much until he reaches over and tries to adjust stuff. That's where I draw the line and tell him to stay in the passenger seat or go take a nap. Within an hour, he is ready to drive again.

By lunch we roll into Dawson Creek, home of the Yukon Gold Rush of 1896, and from the looks of the town, nothing has changed since. The old wooden clapboard buildings are literally propped up with poles. We walk up and down the muddy streets and read the historical plaques on the dilapidated buildings. I am fascinated by the graveyard. Small headstones—some white stone and some old wooden planks—dot a green field surrounded by a white picket fence. It looks forgotten and sad. Apparently almost no one lives here anymore except in the summertime when the population swells and two-thousand workers come in to support the *tourist trade*.

The short story of the gold rush is that the strike was in Yukon, Canada not in Alaska, and it was a party of just three people who actually found the gold—a woman, an Indian and a white man. George Carmack was officially credited for the gold discovery because the actual claim was staked in his name. The group agreed to this because they felt that other miners would be reluctant to recognize a claim made by an Indian, given the strong racist attitudes of the time. I suppose a woman couldn't stake a claim either, an Indian woman at that! They were with another group when they were told to move out because one of the men in the group was prejudiced and didn't want the Indians around, so they moved on up river and found the gold.

News reached the USA in July 1897, when the first successful prospectors arrived in San Francisco setting off the Klondike stampede. One year later, the population in Klondike may have reached 40,000. To get to Dawson Creek, the stampeders landed in Skagway, Alaska, then hiked some twenty-five to thirty-five grueling miles then built rafts that would take them the final 500 plus miles down the Yukon to Dawson City, near the gold fields. The stampeders had to carry a year's supply of goods, about a ton, more than half of it food, over the passes to be allowed to enter Canada. The irony of the whole thing is that only a small percentage of the stampeders ever found gold. Most stampeders ended up working to support the town and live off of the riches of the lucky few who found gold.

In celebration of the incredible spirit of the Sour Dough Boys, as the first ragtag miners from San Francisco were nicknamed, we decide to go to the local saloon for a little dinner and can-can show. Dad even plays his first slot machine. After the lively show and with tummies full, we figure we should gas up tonight since the "idiot light" came on and we want to get an early start in the morning. Tomorrow is the *Top-of-the-World*, a famous drive known for its 100 miles of scenic dirt road. Here we will cross the border and finally be in Alaska.

Could I have been a stampeder or a treasure hunter? Could I have braved the cold and harsh conditions for a "maybe?" Was it for the money, the thrill of the hunt, the going into the unknown or the camaraderie of it all? Somehow, going treasure hunting in the Caribbean for a sunken ship sounds much more inviting to me. Could I?

We soon discover that the only gas station is closed for the night and will open at 8:00 a.m. "Perfect," I tell Dad. "We will just camp out right here at the station and be ready when they open in the morning." Lucky for me, I can get Internet from the campground next door, at least until my battery wears out. After that, I read until well into the night. It is broad daylight inside the camper all night long. I can read as much as I want and this time Dad can't complain about my flashlight bothering him. I still don't understand how my light can bother him when he is definitely sleeping, as evidenced by his snoring!

## Day 15—369 miles

It's six o'clock in the morning and Dad is awake and headed to the bathroom in broad daylight. I could literally have read a newspaper from my bed all night. I was wearing my blindfolds, but Dad was not. Each time he stirred, I uncovered my eyes to see what was the matter, 1:00 a.m., then 3:00 a.m., now 6:00 a.m. We are parked at the gas station, waiting for them to open at 8:00 a.m. We agreed last night that we would stay put until they opened, so we can fill up and head for the border. I cover my eyes and go back to sleep. The next thing I know I am rolling back and forth in my bed, bouncing along the road. From the bed, I call out, "Dad, what are you doing?"

"Looking for gas."

"I thought we were waiting until eight o'clock."

"I think I can find gas at the other end of town. Someone in this town should be open."

"Whatever," I snap and pull the covers over my head.

In less than five minutes he shouts, "Holy cow, the road ends! There is no more road! They are motioning me to get onto the ferry. Should I go? I'm going."

What is he talking about? I sit up and take off my blindfold to figure out what is going on. Without my contacts in, I don't see far away very well, but there is definitely a river next to the road, only trees in front of us and, sure enough, some cones marking off lanes to board the ferry. Dear God, tell me this is a dream. Ferry? I didn't see anything about a ferry. Did he buy a ticket? We have no gas. The light came on last night. We are empty. Where does the ferry go? If I thought my bed was bouncing before, that was a warm up. The dirt road leading to the ferry literally looks like it was scraped in the dirt by a snow plow, and there is no dock. The ferry comes right up to the gravel shore wherever it can. The river is moving fast and looks about half a mile across.

"Don't get on!" I shout. "Ask the guy if there is gas on the other side. Back up!"

A man guides us right between the cones and onto the ferry and in less than ten seconds after boarding, the chain snaps across the back, the *all clear* whistle blows and we are chugging across the river. I spring from the bed, jump into the passenger seat, get the map book out and try to figure out what went wrong. There are two other cars and a motor home on the ferry. That is about all that fits. No bridge across this big river? I guess it's not worth building one. Not that many cars must pass by. Not a good sign. We are washed down shore quickly. When we are mostly across, the ferry turns straight into the current and works it way back up to the makeshift dirt dock on the other side. It rams right into the riverbank, balances the engines to steady itself, and drops the loading ramp. We drive off into gravel and up the hill onto a dirt road.

Eyes wide open, there is nothing to see. There is nothing on the other side. Not one building, just road and trees. We are going uphill. There is a sign—struggling to read it, I think it says "Top of the World Golf Course." Can't be, I tell myself. Lord, help me, where are my contacts? I reach into my pocket while I pull down the visor and vanity mirror. I look like a hamster, squinting my eyes, exposing my two front teeth. The sight is more than I can take. I burst out laughing. I look like hell: big eyes blinking wide open with yesterday's mascara smudged underneath, pale lips holding in morning breath, with greasy bed hair sticking straight up, tangled in a yellow blindfold that says *Cat Nap* strapped to my forehead. And here I am, the gas light is on empty and I am in the middle of the Yukon.

In complete calm, my dad says, "Let's just drive on a little and see what is ahead." Scouring the map, I figure it is seventy miles to the border of Alaska via a beautiful remote road that is only open May through September. Dad thinks he can make it if he uses the two gallons of gas we keep in the back for an emergency.

"I guess this is an emergency," he says.

"You can go ten miles," I tell him, "and that's it. If there is no gas station, we are going back. Let's be safe rather than sorry." I check the odometer.

We travel down the road for a while, eventually making a u-turn and going back. Still not ready to give up, Dad turns down the only road, following the signs to the golf course. This very windy road leads up to a lookout with a stunning view of Dawson City. From here the town looks much bigger and so does the river. We wind along the road until it finally leads to a "clubhouse" with a row of about six golf carts. The clubhouse is actually a mobile home. How many days a year can they actually golf? A man comes out looking more like a lumberjack than a golfer.

I am not getting out. Please, let's not drag out this nightmare any longer than we must. Dad goes over and chats with the man. Driving in the camper back to the ferry, Dad tells me the man is from Nova Scotia. He came to Dawson to visit his son who was working at the golf course. He liked it so much that when he retired, he moved here. He does go back home for the winters because they are milder there. Let me get this straight, he moved from north of Maine to the Yukon, but goes back east for the *mild* winters? Someone, please get me out of the twilight zone!

Back across the ferry and into the parking lot of the same gas station where we spent the night, we fill up with the most expensive tank of gas yet, $126 for twenty-six gallons or $5 a gallon. Now for the third time, we ride the ferry. This time, the captain comes over to talk to us. We tell him our story. He sensed that's what happened. We gave him his chuckle for the morning. He says not to worry, that he goes back and forth all day no matter who is on board.

Off to The-Top-of-The-World. Twisting and turning, climbing and climbing on a dirt road, we truly are on top of the world. With steep drop-offs on both sides of the road, we can see green mountain ranges far off on the horizon either way. Climbing more, it seems like we are driving right into a cloud. "We are going to run into the ceiling," Dad says.

As we drive along, we can see the horizon way off in the distance. Around the next bend it's a white-out. We are in a cloud. A headlight from an on-coming car is all we can see. This goes on for miles. To our surprise, we see a sign for the border patrol. We know it is along this road somewhere, but here in the clouds? How do these people get here everyday? Five or six RV's are in line ahead of us. While we wait, I look at our passports and learn that Dad's middle initial H stands for Hoover, his mother's maiden name.

After the usual questions by a very nice young border patrolman and a look at our passports, we pull ahead to see the "Welcome to Alaska" sign. We hoot and holler. I know we took the long route, but finally we are in Alaska. Can't see a darn thing more than ten feet in front of us, but we are here. We drove sixty-seven miles since the ferry, and it took three hours to get this far.

Back on the road, I don't want to miss anything. Sometimes we are in total whiteness and I can actually see the clouds blowing. It looks like snow. We are listening to the lovely piano music of Jim Brickman. It seems appropriate for this ethereal landscape. The view keeps changing; even here in this harsh climate, summer brings fields of beautiful purple flowers. The washboard road makes it impossible to read or write.

We enter Forty Mile Park, which will take us to Chicken, Alaska. After miles of bumpy, muddy, dirt road with forest on both sides—deserted except for passing other RV's—we come to Chicken, Alaska. There is an old rusty dredging machine down by the creek, several small buildings, and a main gift shop lined with cars covered with yellow dirt except for the windshields. Some crazy people made the trip on motorcycles. Free coffee and free panning for gold make this stop a must. After traveling 108 hard miles since this morning, we are ready for a break. As we pull in, we see our Canadian tablemates from last night.

I read the legend of how Chicken got its name. I thought this was the place people stopped who chickened out of going any farther, but the truth is this area was abundant with Ptarmigan, a little bird that resembled a chicken. The miners came here in search of food during the harsh winters. The correct spelling of the word couldn't be agreed upon by the town's people, and they didn't want to be the source of ridicule so they decided on Chicken. I like the folklore better.

We putter around and chat for a while, then take our pans down to the creek. Dad finds one little gold fleck. Heck, I think to myself, I get more gold in a shot of *Goldschlager* than I found out here all afternoon.

We make it back to the Alaska Highway or Route 1 and follow the signs to Fairbanks, 216 miles away, our goal for tonight. Dad tells me about Clatty Martin. Clatty is an old friend and farmer from Pennsylvania. He came to Alaska by bus last year on vacation and ran out of money before he could buy his bus ticket back, so he is working here, somewhere, saving up money to get home. Apparently he had a heart attack and decided to make the trip to Alaska before it was too late. He left his wife and grown sons at home to run the farm. It seems that things go better when he is not there. Dad wonders where Clatty is living. Alaska is a big place. I suggest that we call his wife and ask her where he is. I can't tell if Dad thinks what Clatty is doing is good or bad.

Highway 1 runs out and we are now on Highway 2, at the town of Tok headed to Fairbanks. With 100 or so miles to go, we stop at Delta Junction for the night. We could push it, but it is already 6:00 p.m. Dad drops me at the grocery store and finds a place to rotate the tires. Today the odometer turned 50,000 miles, so he thought it was a good time to do it. We find a lovely spot along the mostly dried riverbank to pull over. The sun is shining brightly and the van is hot inside, so we open the windows.

We putter around the campsite. Dad wonders what his co-workers and friends are doing back home. I don't understand why he is even thinking about home. I have traveled with other people who talk about this. I don't get it. Dad is asleep by 8:00 p.m. About ten o'clock the sun goes behind the clouds and it gets chilly, about 65 degrees and still broad daylight.

Today we are as far north as we will be on this trip. We also will only back track a small section of the Alaska Highway. Our goal is to get off the big roads and see the natural beauty. This is the second time I am second-guessing myself about our route. After three long days of driving, maybe we should have taken the direct route. Dad reassures me that we did the right thing. He will be really upset if someone asks him if we saw this or that when we get home, and we had missed it. He wants to see everything. He doesn't know if he will get to come back in the next ten years or maybe never. So let's hit it all. Yes, sir. No stone in Alaska will go unturned by us.

Today starts our second week and we have planned on three weeks until we need to be at the Alaska border heading home. We have the time. There is no rush. I am wondering what to do with the second half of my life and here is my Dad, hoping to fulfill his dreams before he is out of time completely.

## Day 16—151 miles

Dad starts driving at o-dark-hundred while I am still in bed. Soon he pulls off the road and putters around until I stir. "You won't want to miss this," he says. "It's the North Pole, the home of Santa Claus." It really is cute. I sit up in bed and look around. There is a big gingerbread house with a giant Christmas tree in front. Red and white striped telephone poles line the streets. A reindeer and sleigh complete the perfect little town. In a shop we read a postcard that says, "What is the difference between a caribou and a reindeer? Reindeer can fly!" Really they are the same thing. Reindeer are domesticated and caribou are wild. Just a little Alaskan humor.

A few hours later, we roll into Fairbanks. "I wonder if this is where Clatty Martin is living," Dad says.

"Alaska is a big place Dad," I reply. "If you want to find Clatty, we really need to call his family."

The town is a bit of a disappointment. It is just a regular town with regular stores. We find a Wal-Mart and decide to get supplies and make photographs so I can clear my memory chip. I buy four photo albums, two for Dad and two for me. Dad thinks I am being extravagant. We break down and buy a coffee maker and thermos. We are spending too much on coffee and decide that making our own is better. Chris at the photo counter is super helpful and explains that we are very close to the pipeline and Chena Hot Springs, both very popular tourist spots, and we should check them out before leaving town.

On the way out of the store, Dad gets on the scale. He has lost eleven pounds. I've stayed the same. According to my phone, we lost another hour in the time change. I don't know how that happened either. How does it know?

About five miles out of town, we see the sign for the pipeline. We pull into the parking lot and there it is, running along for as far as we can see in each direction. It is about ten feet in diameter and a few feet off the ground in all its shiny metal glory. This is what all the fuss is about. We snap a photo or two, read the plaque, and jump back in the camper. Pipeline. Check. Another thing marked off my list.

An hour later, on a sunny 70 degree afternoon, we roll into Chena Hot Springs, known for its healing natural springs. As we cross over the bridge leading into the campground, we see some men clearing the brush using machetes and chain saws.

"There's Clatty Martin!" my dad shouts as we roll past.

"Sure Dad," I say, completely unamused.

"No, no, really, I think it's him!"

"You must be imagining things," I say. "It can't be him, Alaska is a big place. He could be anywhere." Then, I look in the rear view mirror and sure enough, there is a man running after the camper waving his arms. Oh my God, what are the chances of this happening?

Dad stops the camper and jumps out. He is like a little kid and Clatty Martin is so happy to see a face from home. They are like boyhood friends, high-fiving and slapping each other on the back. Introductions are made and Clatty instructs us to go to the office and check in, then he will come to our campsite after work and we will catch up. He is the horse wrangler and usually is out giving trail rides, but he didn't have any tourists today, so he was helping clear brush. If we want, we can take a ride tonight. How lucky are we?

As we set up camp, we see a helicopter land and take off several times. Later Clatty tells us that they are geologists studying the wilderness looking for gold. The pilot drops them off and they take soil samples and bring them back for testing. There's that gold thing again.

I am eager to get into the springs and soak. The water in the man-made pond is clear and steaming with a little smell of sulfur, but not too bad. The bottom is gravel with big boulders around the outside, giving it a very natural feeling. It's nature's hot tub. I am glad it is not a swimming pool, like the indoor one. As I move around the pond, the water temperature gets uncomfortably hot, so does the gravel under my feet. There is a big rock in the middle to crawl onto. I feel a bit like a seal, lounging on the rock.

Here I meet Brad and Yolanda, a young couple from Canada. They are very athletic and have raccoon suntans.

"Where have you been on holiday to get those silly tan lines?" I ask.

"We have been on a quest to climb Mt. McKinley," she says.

"Wow, I am impressed," I tell them. Mt. McKinley is in the heart of Denali and is the highest mountain in North America, coming in at 20,320 feet. The latitude makes it particularly dangerous to climbers. In addition to the cold, the oxygen is thinner.

"Unfortunately, we didn't make it to the summit. We came about 200 meters, but the weather was so bad, we had to turn back," she says. "We sat at base camp for five days, hoping for a weather window, but it never came. We ran out of time, so now we are spending the last day of our holiday here."

Her words cut through my heart like a knife. I am enough of an athlete to know the preparation, anticipation and perseverance that went into that effort, to come so close and have to turn back. It's like the Ironman being cancelled due to weather. It just makes my whole body ache for them.

After dinner and a lovely visit with Clatty, we go to the horse stables with him and pick out our rides. It is 10:00 p.m. and broad daylight. Dad hasn't been on a horse in fifty years and isn't sure he wants to ride now. With a little coaxing, we are off. This is a once in a lifetime opportunity. Take it!

## Day 17—0 miles

We wake to a teenage moose strolling through our campsite. We can see him clearly through the big picture windows, but he can't see us.

We are so relaxed here that we decide to stay another night. It is our first day with zero miles. Dad's friend is here. We will have a chance to do laundry and I have all the Internet access I want.

After lunch, Clatty brings his boss, Bernie Karl the owner, to meet us. Bernie is quite the entrepreneur and inventor. He also manages the campground, a self-sustaining organic hydroponics garden, and of course, the Ice Palace.

The Ice Palace, written up in Forbes as one of the most ridiculous business ideas in the world, is a year-round indoor ice sculpture complete with chess set, bedrooms and a bar with about eight seats and yes, martini glasses made of ice. Why would anyone make an ice palace in a place that is frozen most of the year? Temperatures here have been recorded at 100 degrees below zero.

Apparently Japanese are the most popular tourists to Chena. They come in winter to see one of the best views in the world of the Aurora Borealis, an atmospheric light show that is considered to be a spiritual experience. It is also legend that if a woman sees the Borealis on the night she conceives a baby, the baby will have a wonderful life, hence, the palace with bedrooms. I like Bernie's spirit. What do those city boys know about making money in Alaska?

## Day 18—270 miles

In the morning we wake to 51 degrees, cold, rainy and overcast skies. I pull down the sun visor to put in my contacts and my skin looks great. I look rested; hair is blonde, eyes are blue, no puffiness and no blotches. I wonder if it is the magic of the hot springs or the fact that we haven't moved for one night.

Today I discover that my dad was twenty-five years old when I was born, and that is the same age I was when I had my daughter. He is fussing over being old and tired and I tell him it is all in his head. There are plenty of people much older than him out there living life to the fullest. After all, he is only going to be seventy.

"Yes, well, you wait another forty years and see what happens to you," Dad says.

"I am forty-four. That would make you eighty-four. Hey, you are only twenty-five years older than me," I say. That's a scary thought. My dad is only twenty-five years older than me. The world he grew up in was totally different than it is now. Will the world I am living in now be totally different in another twenty-five years? Will I seem like an out-dated, out-of-sync person to my daughter the way my dad seems to me? Twenty-five years, it's not that long. I am not even two times twenty-five years yet.

We are off to Denali and arrive by noon. Dad is greeted by disappointment. He thought he could drive wherever he wanted. I am surprised too. Here we are at the entrance to one of the greatest National Parks and out of the six million acres, we are only allowed to drive the first eleven miles, which of course we do. We have a great view of Mt. McKinley, but not the summit—too many clouds. The rest of the sixty-eight miles of road are only for the tour buses, so we buy a pass for the next day. Dad wants to be on the first bus of the day. He thinks we will see the most animals early in the morning. We catch a dog sled demonstration.

Parked in the lot right in front of the visitor's center, we settle in for the night. I finish putting photographs in our books. The first book is filled with 500 pictures. Dad has been very patient about stopping and letting me get all the photos I want. In exchange, I want to make sure he has a book of all the pictures I have taken.

## Day 19—120 miles

It's five-thirty in the morning and we are standing outside the visitor's center waiting to go on our eight hour tour of the park. It is 50 degrees and cold. For eleven hours, we bump along a winding dirt road in a school bus. Without the driver pointing out the wild life, I don't think we would have seen much more than the majestic ram horn sheep. We do see two Grizzly bears and several cubs, some caribou, a moose, more sheep and more bears. The guide says a Grizzly adult weighs about 800 pounds and the cubs weigh around 400 pounds. Unfortunately, they are far off in the fields and can only be seen with binoculars. Dad is disappointed with the number of animals; he thought they would be everywhere. The park is more about the landscape than the animals. The vistas are beautiful and vast, the wide-open spaces amazing. Mt. McKinley does pop into view for about ten minutes. It has been under a cloud for the last nine days. All white. I guess if we had come directly here we would be impressed, but we have been seeing breathtaking views for days now. We decide that we are scenery-numb and must make a point to remember how lucky we are to be here and have the chance to see all this amazing natural beauty. We are fully aware of our good fortune and start each day with a prayer of gratitude.

We leave Denali and roll into a charming little village nearby called Talkeetna. If there is a town of Denali, this is it. It's going to be a big weekend with a fishing tournament and street party. We are lucky to get a campsite close to the water. There is lots of activity in the town and at the boat ramp. Around happy hour, I hear a band strike up, so we walk toward The Fairview Inn, an old wooden saloon. The guy at the door looks like a left-over hippie from the sixties. He cards us. I have my wallet with me, but Dad doesn't.

"Sorry," he says, "no one gets in without ID."

"Excuse me," I reply. "I think you can tell by looking at him that he is over twenty-one."

"Sorry lady, it's the law. No ID, no entrance."

I volunteer to run back to the camper and get Dad's ID, but he has already decided the music inside is too loud anyway. He thinks everything is too loud—everything I listen to anyway. I wonder if his hearing is good or bad. He complained the radio was too loud, so I bought a headset and he said that was too loud too. He can't possibly hear it. I think he just wants to control everything. Of course, the radio preacher isn't too loud.

## Day 20—135 miles

Finally we get a warm day, it's 66 degrees and sunny. Our little campsite is damp, but I try to start a fire anyway. Dad wants to help get the campfire going with car oil. I just look at him. I think not.

It's time for a shower before we head out of town. I pack my toiletries in a bag and walk to the public building. Inside is a gift shop/laundry/shower. I buy a token and wait my turn in line. No "boy" or "girl" showers, just the next available one. There are three people ahead of me. After puttering around, I take a seat next to a young military man who has a crew cut and muscular build. I ask him if he is stationed near here, then realize I don't know where I am exactly and that means I don't know where *nearby* is anyway. He is cute. I wonder how old he is—too young for me. I wonder how old he thinks I am. Would it matter?

We chat easily. He is here with some buddies for the big fishing tournament. They did well yesterday and are excited about being here. For the first time in my life, I am learning about me without the package. As I sit and talk to a total stranger about anything and nothing, what do I choose to say about myself? Other than the obvious, I am traveling in a camper with my dad, blah, blah, blah. Who am I? I know the things I have done in the past. Now, I have nothing around me to tell others of my status. I am important, I am successful, I am smart. No, today, I am just a girl sitting on a chair waiting to take a shower. Did I really live in such a small world that I didn't have to think? Where all the trappings that surrounded people made me decide who they were without their even saying one word? Did I overlook people who were really cool and interesting because they were the ticket-taker or the cashier?

Back on the road, we head for Homer, passing through Anchorage. We see a sign for the Alaska Native Heritage Center and decide to stop. The visitor's center looks like a new log cabin and is filled with native artifacts, giving us a glimpse of what life was like for these people. We walk around the outdoor park filled with displays and examples of homes, hunting, and even the bones of a huge whale.

The demonstration of singing and athletic games is the most interesting to me. Local families, including children, dress in traditional garb, sing songs in their native tongue and perform dances with lots of hand motions. Before each song, the director explains what they are singing about. It reminds me a lot of Hawaiian dancing. Even their faces and dark shiny hair look Hawaiian or Tibetan. It is beautiful and I am so glad it has not been lost or forgotten. The songs are passed down from generation to generation and are about nature, protection, survival and the hunt. Then the teenage boys take the stage and demonstrate native games of strength, balance, concentration and wrestling. These high school boys are proud to show off their heritage and physical prowess.

Teaching our children about other cultures opens their minds to alternative ways of thinking. Get them off the treadmill. It is not the American Dream to strive for, but the world dream. Humanity is the precious commodity, not money.

We roll through Anchorage, a town similar to Fairbanks, but it is on the water and a bit more interesting. Main Street has all the kinds of shops I like: a dress shop, tanning place, nail salon, and a book store. We are back in civilization. We stop for dinner and splurge on a restaurant meal at a cute rooftop place. I order an Alaskan summer ale beer and it comes in a bottle with a jumping Orca on it.

## Day 21—347 miles

Bright and early, Dad is behind the wheel. Today our goal is Homer, famous for halibut fishing. We pass through the beautiful high mountains and snow-covered nubs of Girdwood. When we hit Chugach State Park it is 40 degrees. We decide to pull off at a rest area and make coffee. Two bald eagles fly by.

Our vehicle is a magnet. Other travelers are curious as to how the inside is configured. It is definitely not a regular camper. This model of van is used all over the world as a utility vehicle, including an ambulance. It is narrow and tall so it can drive through the narrow streets of Europe, and tall enough for people to stand up inside. Additionally, it is diesel and automatic, making it economical and easy to drive. As for the inside, the best part is the huge tinted windows, perfect for touring. At this stop-off, our fellow campers come over to have a look inside. It's not glamorous, but it does the job.

One couple is curious as to who we are and what our travel plans are. They are envious, as many others have been, about my getting to do this trip with my dad and tell me how lucky I am to get to spend the time with him, adding that most people don't get this chance. The truth is I haven't spent much time with him other than a Christmas or Thanksgiving here and there. My memory of Dad when I was growing up is that he was the fun parent. We had all kinds of motorized toys, like mini-bikes, go-carts and snowmobiles. He wanted to play.

He seems like a teddy bear, but he is not. He is passive-aggressive. When I am reading while he is driving, I try to read out loud to him but he is not interested, even when it is Joel Olsten's book, a very popular Christian TV minister. I bought it specifically to read to him, yet Dad complains that it is too motivational and not God-based enough, even though each chapter quotes a Bible scripture.

Dad and I are of a different religious belief. I was raised on hell, fire and brimstone, taught that God was a mean, vengeful God and you better walk the caulk line because if you don't, the devil is hiding behind every corner waiting to get you. Oh, and by the way, you were born a sinner and you don't even have a chance. I wanted no part of that. My God is kind and tender and loves me no matter what. Dad doesn't approve of my beliefs and reminds me of this often. The only hell I believe in is the one I create by not remembering who I truly am ... a child of God, the universe.

When I do read, he talks to me constantly. When I put the book down, he doesn't have a word to say. He just wants me to sit there and ride along. I understand now the things that must have made my mom crazy. She was the manager and the disciplinarian; he was along for the ride. Lucky for me, I am not married to him and I am not trying to raise eight kids on a shoestring. I just love him.

The closer we get to Homer, the more beautiful the views become: sky, sea, and snow-capped mountains in every shade of blue, gray and white. We get our third chip on the windshield. As we drive along, we encounter all kinds of vehicles supporting a race. I think it is a marathon. What a great stretch to have a road race! Then I discover it is not a marathon, but a wheel chair race. Wow, I have got to give those guys credit. What a challenge! I just came up with a new thing to write in my gratitude journal. I am thankful that I can run, jump, and walk.

# Chapter 11
## *Recovering*
## *September 2004*

The Monday after Tom's funeral, I am back at work. No time to cry over something that is over and done with. No time for pitying myself. I am not that kind of girl. I am on my own now. Because I work on sales commission, I don't get paid to show up, I get paid to sell. No one wants to buy something from someone who is depressing, so I put on a happy face and play the game. By day, I am okay. It's the nights that get to me.

I can't go home. It is too sad there. It is too painful passing the white swing on the front porch where we had morning coffee in our bathrobes or a Crown Royal night cap on a warm summer evening. In the kitchen, I remember Tom and me literally ripping the old kitchen cabinets down and scraping up the cracked tile floor that seemed melted directly onto the linoleum. It hurts to walk past Brittany's old bedroom—full of stuff, but void of the personality that made it come alive. My big super-comfy bed with the best linens money can buy is no longer a love nest, but a place of dread. My little dream house has now become a house of pain.

So I do what Barbara Singer does best. I get busy—busy with everything and anything I can think of. I work out at the end of my business day and then go out after that. Every night is booked. By the time I walk into my house, I am exhausted. I change my clothes, brush my teeth, take out my contacts and go to sleep. This works until about 3:00 a.m. Sometimes I get lucky and can sleep in blissful oblivion a little longer, but not often. Then the quiet comes, that awful silence. The stillness when no one sees the pain deep in my heart. Lying in the darkness, hours pass. I beg for sleep but my mind won't let me go. Other times a noise will wake me. I used to be a great sleeper, but now I hear everything. Before I could drink coffee or be out dancing, yet the minute my head hit the pillow, I was out. Now sleep eludes me.

One night I am startled awake with my eyes wide open, frozen, too terrified to move, straining my ears to hear, trying to figure out what on earth the scratching and scrambling sound is, and where it is coming from. My heart is pounding loudly as I try to decipher what in the world is going on in my living room.

"Definitely two robbers," I tell myself, but what are they doing? Fighting over what to steal? For God's sake, take everything, please don't harm me! I lie as still as I can, trying not to breathe, so they won't know I am in the other room.

My house has a raised floor, which means, the house is built about three feet off the ground. This was to allow for better ventilation back in the early 1920's, before air conditioning. To my chagrin, I finally realize that there are two nocturnal raccoons under my house. These little critters may look like bandits, but they were not in the living room stealing my candlesticks. I can't live like this.

The next day I ask George to move out of the apartment he rents from me. It is detached and over the two-car garage located just behind the little cottage. "In fact, let's just trade," I tell him. "You can have the front house and get a roommate and I will move into the back." He ends up finding a place across town and will be out by the end of November. Perfect. I can stick it out for a few more weeks. New Year, new place, new start. Once again, time to simplify some more, this time into a one-bedroom.

Now that I am on my own, I am free to do whatever I want. I have no one to answer to but myself. I have my job, but my heart isn't in it any longer. I am not happy. I had a great run, but it is time to do something else. Time to make a plan and work the plan. This I know how to do, so I get to work. It is time to change my life. I get out my journal and start visualizing. What do I really want to do? Where do I want to live? I write in my journal, "Jobs I Want" and list: travel guide, hotel inspector, travel writer, Italian villa rental company, run a bed and breakfast, adult hostelling, be a personal assistant, caretaker, life coach, secret shopper or work for a destination club.

"To Do List:" send resume, learn Italian, get to an island, give up regular job, meet the right people (boaters, travelers, Italians), go to marina, car shows, polo, mediate, home exchange. All I have to do is make it happen. After writing all that, I realize what I really want is time and freedom to travel.

My next step is to get on the Internet and start researching. It doesn't take long until I find an on-line ad for a caretaker for a small hotel on a remote island off of Puerto Rico. They are looking for someone to run the place in their absence for six months. The small salary includes living quarters. I have a hotel background and Puerto Rico is still in the US, which means I don't need any special visa to work there. I email the owners and we exchange information. I take a friend and fly into San Juan, take a taxi to the port and get on a ferry to the little island of Culebra, home of the famous Flamenco Beach.

When I arrive, the wife shows me to my room, a complete disappointment and informs me that the position is filled.

"What?" I say, shocked.

"Yes, we have found someone more suitable for the job," she says.

"And you couldn't have told me this yesterday?" I ask her.

On top of that, she is charging me full price for the room. The place is a dump. Everything is old and falling down. I try to make the best of my trip so we rent scooters and go all over the tiny island. The beach is beautiful and a handful of unique restaurants make it doable. After two nights, I can't take it anymore and tell her I am leaving. She says she will have to charge me for the three nights, since I reserved it. "Do what you have to," I tell her. I think it was a scam to get people to come to their hotel. I don't think there ever was a job. I never talked to the husband. The whole thing was a huge disappointment.

⚜

Brittany wants to visit Seth at school in Atlanta, so I volunteer to drive her up for a long weekend in October. I am so happy to have somewhere to go. I am hoping the drive will give us some time to reconnect, but she sleeps most of the way. We head straight for the campus. She stays in the dorm with Seth and I find a no-name motel by the highway. It will do, it's just me anyway. In my usual *modus operandi*, I bring more than I can read in a week, but it doesn't work this time. There is too much pain too close to the surface. Time by myself is not for me.

With the afternoon free, I find a trendy area and shop. I walk into a home-furnishings/antique shop in a beautiful old 1920's house and the woman who owns it greets me with a friendly smile. In the display case are pieces of handmade jewelry made of crystals along with other spiritual trinkets. Cleverly, each price tag has a small crystal stone and a blue-black butterfly glued to it. I don't ask what that means, but I think about how different and special it makes the thought of money. Blue-black butterflies are all over the store. Equally fascinated with the house as with the items for sale, I stroll around. Old houses with character and yester-year charm have a lot of appeal for me and the original dark wood-paneled walls of this house give each room a warm feeling. The fireplace, in the once-living-room, has unusual green tile around the hearth. I notice an original triangular porcelain sink in the corner of one of the downstairs rooms. It has the old-timey twirly black and white fixtures.

"How odd for a sink to be downstairs," I comment to the shop lady.

"Yes it is," she replies. "This home was once owned by a doctor and this was his office. He practiced in this house for over twenty years and raised four daughters here." Little tidbits like this warm my heart. There is so much history here. I love imagining what must have happened in this place over the past eighty years. I wonder about all the people who came through this room, some for happy reasons like pregnancies and births, and some for troubling reasons like illness and death.

Out back on the porch, wind chimes and other whimsical lawn art fill the outside space. I am in no hurry at all and this is such a soothing place. As I stand admiring the artistic display, a light wind blows over the porch and all the chimes starting ringing and tinkling around me. The cool breeze blows softly over my cheeks and the chimes sound like they are talking to me. A powerful feeling erupts from my heart and spills out into tears running down my face. I am overcome with such emotion right here in this lovely little house, I weep. I am completely overwhelmed. Totally embarrassed, I try to stop, but I can't. How do I get out of this place without making a scene? I am clearly upset and the shop lady, bringing me a tissue, comes over to comfort me.

"Are you okay?" she asks. "What's wrong?"

"I just lost my fiancé a few weeks ago. I am sorry to make a scene."

"Don't be silly," she says gently. "Let the tears come. Stay out here as long as you need."

When I am pulled together enough to make an exit, I bid this sweet lady goodbye and head down the street. Popping in and out of eclectic shops takes my mind off of my misery. A bookstore is the very best place to get lost in. After an hour or so of scanning thousands of titles and fanning through dozens of books, I am hungry. Taking a table for one at a charming outside Irish Pub, I decide a beer and a snack are in order. Sipping on my pint of Guinness and inhaling the smell of a newly opened book, again the tears come.

What is it about this day, this place, this uncontrollable crying? I try to hide behind my book, using my beverage napkin as a tissue, and I weep. It won't stop. I am making a spectacle of myself. Dear God, will this sadness ever leave me?

The waitress comes over and says, "Are you okay?"

"Yes, I am fine. I just lost someone I loved. I am sorry to make a scene. "

"Oh, honey, don't you worry. I wish I could help."

"Thank you, I am going to walk around the block to clear my head. Just bring my salad whenever it is ready. I'll be right back."

I walk not even three storefronts down to discover, of all things, an oriental meditation garden complete with coy pond and waterfall. It is totally out of place. A black wrought-iron fence surrounds it on one side, a lush green hedge on the back side, and buildings on the two ends box it in. It has benches and rocks thoughtfully placed along the well-groomed walkways. It is peaceful yet happy as the birds chirp and warm sun fills the air. I sit on a rock near the waterfall and feel my sadness wash away. I am calm now. My shoulders come down about four inches, and the intensity in my body goes down a few octaves. I am relaxed.

Before my very eyes, a blue-black butterfly lights on a small rock just beyond my feet, rhythmically flapping its wings back and forth. I look again. It is exactly the same as the blue-black butterflies from the little shop. This feeling of calm, of peace, it is Tom coming to me, comforting me. His presence is so real I can taste it. Oh Tom, I miss you so. Another strong eruption comes from deep in my heart, but this time it is not tears, it is peace, a knowing, an understanding. Tom is with me and I should not be sad. It's going to be okay. The butterfly stays at my feet for a long time, then flies up to a leaf on the tree, and then finally flies away, leaving me peaceful and exhausted.

I take my salad to go and head back to the motel. All I can think of is a hot bath. I always travel with a candle or two, so I can turn any nondescript bathroom into a spa treatment. I slide into a tub of bubbles up to my neck. Oh, this is the life. What a day it has been.

With Christmas just a few weeks around the corner, I start to worry. This will be my first Christmas since Tom. Brittany has plans and I will be alone. One night, I am having dinner with my girlfriend, Anne, and she mentions she is going to Aspen for Christmas. She has a boyfriend there and is going out to see him and ski. He will be working a lot since it is *the season,* and she will be skiing alone during the day. She is flying out on December 19th and coming home on Christmas Day. My birthday is December 20th and I can't think of anything I'd rather do than ski in Aspen, my favorite village. After a bottle of wine or two, she says, "Come with me. You can stay at his house with me and we'll all hang out together. You can't be alone for Christmas."

In the morning, I go online and to my surprise, I find a flight. At a reasonable hour, I call Anne. "Good morning Sunshine. Hey were you serious about me coming to Aspen with you?"

"Yes, of course I am serious. I will be alone a lot and would love your company." She doesn't have to ask me twice. I hang up and buy the ticket.

⚜

We celebrate my birthday at the Little Nell hotel bar at the foot of the mountain after a fantastic day on the slopes. For four days, we ski and shop and eat and drink and walk all over town. I especially love walking along the frozen-over stream behind the house. The trees are dripping with snow as ice tries to cover up the slow moving stream. It is a postcard.

Christmas Eve rolls around, and at about four o'clock in the afternoon, we come off the mountain for *Après Ski* or happy hour. We have just one drink at each bar we visit. At one place Anne chooses the wine, and at the next place, I choose. Around 8:00 p.m., we stumble out of the St. Regis Hotel where we sat by the huge fireplace and had a fantastic wine called Ménage a Trois or blend of three grapes. Now we are walking arm-in-arm, holding each other up, not sure if it is the wine or the icy sidewalks, but it doesn't matter. It is snowing in one of the most perfect places in the world to spend Christmas, and I am happy.

"I have to eat something Anne," I tell her, "or I *am* going to fall down."

"Okay, the next restaurant we see, we will go inside and eat."

We find the Wild Fig, a charming little restaurant with just ten tables and a lovely little bar. Still arm-in-arm, Anne and I stagger to the bar where we are greeted by a young man, barely old enough to drink. "Well ladies, here it is Christmas Eve. What can I get for you?"

Anne, with just a little slur in her words, says, "We just came from the St. Regis Hotel and had a fabulous Ménage a Trois, and we'd like to have another."

The young bartender's face lights up and he rubs his hands together. "Ladies, Ladies, you have come to the right place. I knew this night wouldn't be a bust. Santa is my man. Allow me!"

Of course, we have to explain. We ring in Christmas morning at the bar, drinking shots along with the rest of the staff and the manager. For this night, we are family. This is Christmas and I am not with strangers, I am with friends I just made. We close down the bar and walk home. It's cold outside, but my heart is warm.

⁂

The New Year proves to be a whirlwind of travel. Out of pity or opportunity, I go. Whenever someone asks me to go somewhere, I accept. I ride on the back of a Harley to Bike Week in Daytona, take a trip to Chicago for the weekend, go to the Coeur de Elegance car show in Amelia Island, cheer on the horses at the Kentucky Derby, travel to Market in Atlanta, tour villas in Italy as an American representative, spend a long weekend in New York City at the Plaza, cruise the Greek Isles ending up in Venice and finally, a wine and culture tour of Chile and Argentina. It is a fantastic way not to think.

I am thinner than I have been in years. I think I look great, but my friends are worried.

One day I look back in the pages of my journal. These are some of my thoughts.

*Change the situation or change your response to it.*

*Dream Big. Send it into the universe. Listen to your inner voice. She is the guide and the universe is your helper.*

*If you are unhappy with your choices, simply choose again.*

*Love your work and you'll never work
another day in your life.*

*Be Happy. Focus on Good. Daily. Now.*

*I am confident, capable and courageous.*

*Trust; everything is happening exactly as it should.*

*Change the internal before the external.
Get out of your comfort zone.*

*Dare to live the life you have dreamed for yourself. Go forward and make your dreams come true. -Emerson*

*Happiness is the best revenge.*

# Chapter 12

*Alaska - Week 4*
*July 2006*

## Day 22—0 miles

We are camping at the most unbelievable place. Our site is on the beach, directly facing the surf with snow-capped mountains behind it. We are on the Homer Spit, a narrow piece of land that juts out into the water about two miles and is 300 yards wide with one road running down the middle between the beach and a marina. Lots of colorful shacks, shops and fishing charters dot the road. We are camped between the Eagle Lady—a woman who feeds hundreds of bald eagles in winter—and the Maritime Memorial. Tomorrow is the 4th of July and we plan to go on a fishing charter. I look forward to fireworks, until I learn there aren't any here. It doesn't get dark!

We have had amazing divine intervention on this trip. With no reservations and no real plan, we have hit everything just right. We are camping on this big holiday weekend at the most popular spot in Alaska, and just happen to walk into the office as a cancellation for a prime spot was being called in. Talking with locals and other travelers has been our real travel guide. We know the general direction we want to travel, which is easy considering the roads are very limited, but we have truly been guided on what to actually see and do.

Our pace has slowed considerably since Chena Hot Springs where we were both so relaxed. The *always daylight* has gotten us out of sync for sleeping so we easily stay up until midnight and still get up at a normal time, but have started napping in the afternoons. We joke about how brutal the summers are in Alaska. We can't get any sleep around here because it is daytime all the time!

We both seem to realize we are here now, so the rush to get to Alaska is no longer hanging over our heads. The sights to see are much closer together, a few hours drive rather than a few days drive. The scenery still changes dramatically with each turn and so does the temperature. We go from 40 degrees at daybreak to 77 degrees in the afternoon sun. Right now the lady next to us is sunbathing in a swim suit; I am wearing a hooded coat. Out of the wind, it is warm. A bald eagle just flew overhead!

Today is Day 22. We have logged 7,707 miles, taken one hotel room, spent $1,051 on gas and taken 631 photographs! Most are already developed and in albums. I can't help it, I am still a Type A person—okay, maybe an A- now. Give me another three weeks on the road and I could become a B.

We are getting along just fine. Dad complains about my driving, that things are too expensive and about my music, but lets the turn signal stay on for miles. Car manufacturing companies really should change the pitch of the turn signal blinker. It apparently isn't audible to anyone over sixty-five-years-old. They should make it the sound of rock and roll because Dad can hear that at any volume, headset or not. I fuss at him about walking and eating. He has been a real trooper about letting me cook. He has lost over fifteen pounds so far, getting him under 200 pounds, something he hasn't seen in over two years. I stress over making sure we see everything. I don't want either of us to miss out.

This morning I am propped up in bed having my morning coffee and the view out my window is a gift. I am 100 feet from the sea. The beach is filled with smooth, light, black, fist-sized rocks, one bleached log with a picnic table next to it, and beyond the lapping surf, children laughing and calling to each other, with snow-capped mountains of different shades of gray off in the distance. The sky, without one cloud, is yet a lighter shade of gray. I can hear the chugging of a boat coming into the harbor. I smell a fire on the beach, but I can't see it. I love a fire. What a luxury. Fire and water. Living and loving. Impatient and spontaneous.

Life is so simple. Today I do not have a care in the world. It is amazing to me how we complicate our lives. It appears to me that life now is a lot like the American legal system. In the beginning, we needed a few rules of justice, then for over 200 years, we kept adding more until we have this unbelievable big pile of rules. That's how life got so complicated. It started out simple—fall in love, have a family, buy a house—then it turned into investments, tax advantages, businesses on the side, college tuition and trust funds. It has gotten too complicated.

The people we meet who are living on the road have exchanged security for adventure. The ironic part is there is no such thing as security anyway. Yet we trade our joy, freedom and adventure for a *secure* plan that we really have no control over. How can this be? Is it a cruel joke? Even if you do everything right, you can get dumped, fired, downsized, sick, or have a car accident. The stock market can crash, someone can die or your kids can make bad decisions. Nonetheless, we still choose to invest our precious days and all our energy in things that we have no control over, rather than what we do have control over like choosing joy or carefully selecting what we allow into our world. We continue ahead mindlessly, not stopping to screen each choice to decide if it fits who we really are or if it is how we want to spend our time and thoughts.

Why is stepping off the treadmill so scary when it is the real path to happiness? What do we really need? Are we brave enough to peel away the "protection" of following the *social handbook* instead of our *personal heart book*? Can this be taught to our kids or does life have to play out for them? Something I read yesterday said, "Trust because you are willing to accept the risk, not because it is safe or certain." This I ponder today.

The event for the day is halibut fishing. Yesterday I bought tickets for us to go out on a boat with guides. Dad doesn't want to go because it is too expensive. There is nothing to decide. We are here. We are going. We board a trawler just after eight o'clock in the morning and head out to sea with a total of fifteen people and two guides. The charter company has everything we need and after a little instruction, we are fishing. Halibut are fighters and fun to catch, but we keep them only if they are over twelve pounds. Our fishing permit allows each person two fish. Dad hasn't done much fishing but manages to catch the biggest fish of the day, a whopping seventeen pounds.

The ride back from a successful day of fishing is my favorite part. We each caught our bounty and watched the crew slice and dice fish after fish. The sun sparkles on the water like diamonds. I am sitting on the bow of the boat with my back resting against the captain's cockpit. I love riding the waves in unison with the boat as it hits the water. I let the boat rock me, pushing me back and forth. Light spray splashes my face. The water tastes salty. I rest my head back and close my eyes, breathing in the sea air that smells so good to me. I am warm and cold at the same time. I like the power of the boat beneath me.

At the dock I feel a little dizzy as I get off the boat, trying to get my land legs back. The scene at the harbor is like a bee hive with lots of comings and goings. There are many fishing charters coming in all at once. Our boat is greeted by the shipping company that will transport our catch to our respective homes.

A crowd is gathering next to a boat across the way. A very muscular fishmonger is spearing huge, weird looking fish by the mouth and hanging them onto a transport cart; he is wearing nothing but muck boots and bright orange rubber pants held up by suspenders. Everyone is taking pictures of the fish and discussing the incredible catch. I am snapping pictures too, but not of the fish. After a while, the crowd dissipates but I am still there. One of the men on the boat calls down to me and asks if I want him to hold up a fish. "No thanks," I shout back, "but you could ask that beautiful specimen to turn around and hang ten from that bar for me so I can get one more shot of his rear deltoids, lats and biceps." Just then, a band of older ladies standing on the next dock over start laughing. I turn to them and they give me the thumbs up. Now I know what it is like to be a sailor just coming into harbor after being at sea.

We are at the half-way point of our trip. The three things I vowed to give up on the trip were coffee, wine and sex. So far, sex is the only thing left. After twenty-two days, I am showing signs of weakening in that department too. Thank goodness for great showers and I am sneaking licorice. Dad is doing so well on his diet. I don't want him to eat junk.

It costs $100 to send the flash frozen fish home. Dad thinks we should just keep it, but there is no way we will be able to eat this much fish without it spoiling. I make the decision to go ahead with the shipment.

I buy my only souvenir of the trip so far. It is a small mask wall-hanging made of caribou fur and hoofs wearing a pair of white polar bear earrings. The mask represents prosperity.

Back at the campsite, I invent camper aerobics. I figure out how I can use the camper to do leg lunges and triceps dips. Gallon jugs of water make great weights. I could make a video and become famous. I miss being cute. My fingernails have actually grown out and aren't completely flimsy anymore. Unfortunately, my hair is growing out too. I can see gray! This will never do.

I get great Internet for $8.95 per twenty-four hours. My phone works too. It has for the entire trip so far, I just don't know how much the roaming fees are costing me.

The ladies in the campsite next to us are having happy hour and invite us over for a drink. Dad isn't so happy to go. They are gay and now we are drinking alcohol. They ask him why he wears the white cap. He always wears the same chauffeur's style white cap and he explains that he has many of them. He is a driver of white rabbits, so he thought wearing the white driver's cap was appropriate. When the ladies ask about the rabbits, he tells them they aren't going to be happy, but he drives the rabbits to laboratories and hospitals for testing. I am surprised that he is concerned they will not like what he does for a living. He grew up around the farm. He, like me, understands "perform or be eaten." Dad goes for a walk while I visit with the ladies.

I learn they work in the school system in Anchorage as crisis counselors. Evidently suicide is very high in Alaska, especially among the natives because it is hard for them to fit in with modern culture. There is pressure to maintain their heritage and yet be successful in the outside world. There is also a lot of prejudice and the weather plays a big part too, with daylight for six months followed by darkness for six months.

This couple is not the first gay women we have met, there seem to be a lot. I wonder if Alaska holds an attraction for alternative lifestyles, or if people who are at peace with who they really are have made the decision to live in such a beautiful, authentic place.

## Day 23—83 miles

After a short hop we arrive in Seward. It's a cute town. We go down to the harbor to check out all the boats in Resurrection Bay and buy a ticket for tomorrow to see the fjords. This is what we came to see; this is the real Alaska.

We stop to pick up supplies at a grocery store that has a good selection. Dad shops for price and I shop for nutrition. I don't know how much a gallon of milk or a dozen eggs cost. If I want something, I buy it. He complains that bananas are thirty-five cents a pound, but doesn't mention that beef is $10 a pound.

We find a great spot by the water to park and make lunch. We grill some halibut and I open a bottle of Shiraz, my favorite wine. It starts to drizzle so

I find a nice spot to read and Dad takes a nap. Later he asks if I want to walk around, but I tell him I am happy to stay here. He wonders how I can read so much.

"It's interesting," I tell him.

"Not to me," he replies.

My dad can't read, or a least not very well. Raised in a rural farm family, he only attended school through the sixth grade, and in a one-room schoolhouse. He also had a hard time in school. He probably had a learning disorder, but back then he was just labeled dumb and was teased mercilessly. He had a very high fever when he was a kid and someone told him that it did permanent damage to his brain and that is why he can't read, and he believes this. My dad is smart and can fix or build anything. I ask Dad if he would like to learn to read, but he doesn't want to. Why learn now when he has gotten along fine this far? I truly believe that he thinks he can't learn. What a tragedy. It is amazing the power of the mind, and how what we believe can change our whole life.

I continue to read and drink wine while Dad goes off on his own. Soon I am playing dance music and having my own little party. I play Tony Braxton over and over again. I miss going out, dancing, using my body and feeling alive.

## Day 24—61 miles

The Kenai Fjords Cruise boat pulls out of the bay in heavily overcast skies. We bring our warm coats and binoculars. The cruise to the glacier is three hours, but we have a good chance of seeing wildlife along the way. Our captain has the underwater radar on and is in constant contact with other boats for optimal animal spotting. We are not disappointed. An orca whale pod, adults and kids, surfaces to breathe just off the side of the boat. They are beautiful and huge. We see walruses sunning on a rock and lots of different types of birds. I am surprised at how blue the water is.

As we near the glacier, we start to see all different sized chunks of ice floating in the water. The glacier itself is a big chunk of ice with vertical cracks in it. Other boats get closer than us, but they are much smaller. I am glad we are on a big boat. Once in a good spot, the captain quiets the engines so we can hear the glacier *calving,* which is when ice chunks break off. It sounds like thunder off in the distance. I can actually hear hundreds of little cracks and then a roar as it splashes into the water. This has been happening for thousands of years. I am watching one of the most majestic shows nature offers. How lucky am I?

Once back on land, we follow the signs to Exit Glacier, a different glacier that we can actually walk to and get a closer look. It's a longer hike than we anticipated, but Dad is a trooper. We take our time and follow the path to the end. Finding a seat on a rock, we take in this purely awesome site.

Like the kid I am, I want to get closer and climb on the ice or at least just touch it. The glacier is clearly roped off and marked "dangerous." I duck under the rope and stroll down the gravel path. Soon I am hopping rocks and I get close enough to touch the bluish ice. I am surprised how dirty it is until I learn later that it has been here for hundreds of years and that the dirt has been accumulating all this time. The cracks are much bigger up close and it's not very cold.

On the way back to the parking lot, a mother black bear crosses the trail with her little cub. They are so cute. Now that we have gotten our wish to see the animals up close and personal, we realize that this is a little too close.

## Day 25—495 miles

Today is the turn-around point. We drive back to Anchorage to catch the highway going east toward Skagway and take a side trip to visit some relatives Dad knows. Joe and Sandy are Mennonites from Pennsylvania who live here now. Because of their religious beliefs, they are home-schooling their two children. I admire them. To me, home-schooling is a huge responsibility. I can't imagine tackling such a task. She is a stay-at-home mom and he works the night shift. In the summer, Joe goes to Nome to mine for gold. There is that gold thing again!

We get out the map and start to plan our route back to Pennsylvania. The excitement is dwindling for Dad. "No more Alaska," he says. "What will I talk about now?" He seems to complain more, but the next day he doesn't remember it. He wants to eat junk food and is tired of eggs, fish and cereal. He thinks if he makes the trip again, he would fly to Anchorage and start there. I try to encourage him by telling him that we have all the islands to see yet and that most people who come to Alaska only see this part. He is convinced he has seen Alaska and it's finished.

On a rainy afternoon, we drive along sloppy dirt roads and cross the border back into Canada. We are given the gift of a beautiful double rainbow.

## Day 26—435 miles

We drive 400 miles or so in the rain. It forces us to slow down and is actually quite calming. We stop at a roadside place to use the bathroom and get gas. I call home from a pay phone on the porch and try to stay out of the rain dripping off the roof. Inside, the TV is showing CNN. It is the first time in weeks that we see the news, and it seems unbelievably silly. Who cares about this stuff? The owners of the roadside store are a young couple from Oklahoma. They live on the property and have two small children.

I am envious of people coming toward us, most are in RV's. They haven't been there yet. I am not ready to go home. We cross the border again for the second time today. Yes that's right, a double border-crossing and a double rainbow. Now we are back on the famous Al-Can or Alaska-Canada highway. The road was built by the American Military to make it possible to protect our 49th state.

# Chapter 13

## Meeting Warren
## February 2005

"Membership, this is Barbara," I answer the phone at the Citrus Club.

"Hello, I am responding to an invitation I received in the mail about coming to the club for lunch and a tour," the voice says.

"Wonderful, who am I speaking with?"

"Warren."

"Great Warren, when would you like to come in?" I ask.

"I was thinking of next week," he answers.

"Let me check my calendar; any day but Tuesday looks good. We serve lunch from 11:30 a.m. until 2:00 p.m. What works for you?" I ask.

"How about Thursday at noon?" he suggests.

"Super, would you like to bring a guest? You can bring a friend or if you are married, you may want to bring your wife because she will automatically be a member too."

"I am widowed," he says flatly.

"I am so sorry to hear that," I reply, trying not to let the sting of the words show in my voice.

There is a silence on the phone. I am caught completely off guard. My voice inside says, no one wants to buy anything from a sad salesperson. Don't cry at work. Leave it at home for the nights when no one can see.

"I just lost my fiancé five months ago," I say. "It was very sudden." I can't say I was widowed. I can't say he was my everything, so instead, I politely ask, "How long ago did your wife die?"

"A year and a half ago," he answers softly.

"I am so sorry. Does it ever get any better?" I say, realizing that I have no right to ask, but needing so desperately to know.

In a sad reflective way, he says, "I am sorry to tell you this, but no. It doesn't get any better, it gets worse."

"Worse! Dear God, I can't do worse," I say, being so honest that it surprises even me.

"The thing is, you don't really know what you have lost until you try to live and everything reminds you of what is missing. Nothing is the same. We were married for eight years and she truly was my partner. We were a team, and now I am lopsided without her beside me. She died very suddenly and it was all just so shocking. I am lost without her."

I feel the sorrow in his voice coming across the telephone wire. My pain is buried, his is raw and completely on the surface.

"I wish there was something I could say or do, but I know there is not," I tell him sadly.

"Just letting me talk about it is good," he says. "Anyway, I am sure this is not what you expected to talk about today, huh? I will bring a guest and see you next Thursday."

"Okay, I look forward to meeting you, Mr. Foley. Goodbye." I hang up the phone not knowing what to make of our conversation.

On Thursday, Warren Foley and a guest come to the club and have lunch. Just as they are finishing dessert, I join them for the usual fifteen-minute pitch. Warren is a perfect gentleman, rising when I introduce myself, and pulling out my chair. He is wearing a dark suit and yellow tie. He is fair with perfectly trimmed short blonde hair and vivid blue eyes. He is my second of three lunch appointments and I am rushing. I go over the membership information with them. He is very clever, making little jokes. We banter back and forth. After the nickel tour of the club, I walk him and his guest, Andy, to the lobby. The conversation flows easily. I like his sense of humor, he is much younger than I thought and cute too. With a goodbye handshake, I go back upstairs to my next appointment.

I would learn later that Andy asked exactly what he and Warren were doing at the club that day. "Looking into a membership," Warren answered.

"No," Andy said, "that is not at all what was going on there."

"What do you mean?" Warren inquired.

"If I have to explain it to you, you must be blind," Andy quipped.

Later in the afternoon, Warren calls to thank me for lunch. He is not sure if the club is a right fit for him or not, but he thought we had a lot to offer. "Do you remember talking to me last week?"

"Yes, I do," I answer.

"I didn't want to bring it up at lunch because I know bringing up the death thing can really be difficult if it catches you at the wrong moment. That's how it is for me anyway."

I understand what he means. There are still times when I run into someone who doesn't know Tom died, and I have to go through the whole story again. Then there are times when it feels like everyone has already forgotten that he was ever alive. And there is the proverbial, *How are you holding up?* I know people mean well, but what am I supposed to say? I feel like shit and want to stay in bed all day, or I'm doing great, I just haven't slept in five months.

"Have you been to any grief counseling?" Warren asks.

"No." The thought of it makes a wall go up. There is nothing to talk about, Tom's gone, get over it.

"Do you have a church or anyone you can talk to?" he asks.

"No," I answer flatly.

"Well, I found it really helped. Anyway, I just wanted to say thanks for a great lunch."

"You're welcome," I reply. "Let me know what you decide. If I don't hear from you, I'll call you next week."

About an hour later, Warren calls again. His voice in gripped with pain. He is weeping.

"What's wrong?" I ask.

He is in his car at his wife's grave. The cemetery is a few blocks from the club. He just needs someone to talk to. I don't know what to say to comfort this man, so I just listen and absorb the sadness of loss. I know it well. He talks, I listen. Long silences run between the sobs. I listen. I cry with him. He has two more years of experience at this death thing, and yet he feels it as though it is new. He is apologetic for the call. He doesn't have anyone else who understands. It's okay. There is a kinship among those left behind. I would soon learn that either I am a magnet for widowers, or I have always met people who have lost their spouses and never noticed before. Now, I notice it is everywhere. We say goodbye. I sit back in my chair at my desk, rest my head on its high back and ponder what just happened. This grief thing, this man—oh, how it hurts to be left behind.

A few days later, Warren calls again. He says he has a book for me and wants to drop it off. I think it is very thoughtful.

"I'm downtown and can be there in a few minutes," he says. I look at my watch. It is just before 5:00 p.m. and I am eager to go home and walk my dog and enjoy some warm fresh air.

"I am just leaving work, but if you would like to join me for a walk around Lake Eola that would be great. Warren agrees to meet me at the Pagoda in ten minutes. I zip home and get my little three-pound teacup Chihuahua, Pooka, and go. I live only a few blocks from the club and walk to the lake.

Right on time, Warren is waiting for me. We walk around the lake and talk. It is pleasant and easy. Back at the Pagoda, I turn to say goodbye, but Warren asks if I have plans for this evening, and I don't. He is starving and invites me to dinner. I agree, but I need to take Pooka home. "Let's drop her off and then we can walk to a little Italian place in my neighborhood," I suggest. This is one of my favorite things about living downtown.

We walk to my little apartment above the garage that I have named the tree house because it feels like I live in the trees. The blinds on the windows are somewhat see-through, so from inside looking out, all I see are tree tops. The apartment gets light with the sunrise, which I love. My little hideout serves me well. I don't think I will be here very long, but I did decorate it with only things I love. It came together nicely, Pottery Barn with a little whimsy. It's old and I love all the details of the crown molding and funky door handles.

Stepping into the living room Warren says, "Wow, it's really small."

At this point, I don't know he lives in a mansion on prestigious Park Avenue.

"It's cute though, it fits you," he adds. Chatting from the bedroom, I take off my hose and heels and put on more comfortable sandals. I come out and announce I am ready.

"Don't you want to change?" he asks.

"No, I'm fine." I like to dress up and rarely wear jeans. I have been wearing a suit every day for eight years now. I am comfortable.

Once outside we discover it looks like rain. Warren's umbrella is in his car, which we left parked by the lake, so I get a big one from my car. I don't think we'll need it, but Warren insists. We walk and talk. He tells me the story of how Lisa died. It was tragic. She died suddenly in her sleep, leaving two small children, Michael, age two and Rachel, just eight months. Warren found her in the morning in their bed and tried to revive her, but she had died in the night. He didn't go to work for months and took care of the children. She was the same age as he, forty-two at the time. He married again only eleven months after Lisa's death. They barely knew each other after dating for only two months, but he was desperate to move forward. They married for all the wrong reasons. After just five months of marriage, she walked out just days after finding out she was pregnant. This would be Warren's fifth child. He has a grown daughter, twenty-four and a son, fourteen, who lives with his mother.

Over dinner, I tell him my story. I went away to Italy on vacation. Tom didn't want me to go, so before I left he asked for his engagement ring back. I never called him while I was away and while I was gone, he died. Not knowing that we would become lovers, I tell Warren the *whole story*. About how I threw away my marriage and life in the suburbs, destroyed my relationship with my daughter, and turned my whole world upside-down for a man who was never going to marry me. How I stayed out all night and scared the life out of my family and had an affair that the whole world knew about. I don't know whose story is more tragic. We are some pair. The talk is easy. Warren is sweet and charming. He needs a friend as much as I do.

As we leave the restaurant, sure enough, it is lightly raining. Holding the umbrella, we huddle together to stay dry. I love walking the streets of my neighborhood and in the rain, well that makes it even better. Warren suggests we swing by the lake since it is closer to his car than it is to my house, and then drive home. As we cross the street, we get out of sync and I reach for Warren's hand. We walk this way for a block or two, then shifting the umbrella, Warren puts his arm around me and I do the same with him. Now, we are walking arm-in-arm in the rain on a warm summer evening in perfect step. This feels really good. I am close enough now to smell his cologne, a fragrance I won't soon forget. At his car, he opens the door for me and we drive the few blocks to my place. He walks me to the door. I thank him for dinner, he thanks me for the company and we say goodnight. Warren turns to walk away and then turns back, slides his arm around the back of my waist and pulls me tightly toward him. We kiss. With his face just a few inches from mine, he gives me a crooked smile and squints his eyes just a little. It is as though he is asking me where that kiss came from. I felt it and so did he. Looking into my eyes like he is looking straight into my soul, he hesitates and then turns and walks away. I close the door and climb the stairs of my little tree house, take off my clothes and slide into bed. That was quite a kiss.

We talk every day after that. We have so much to share. To my surprise, Warren shows up at my office unexpectedly one afternoon.

"Can you get away early today?" He asks.

"Sure, but why, what's wrong?" I ask.

"Nothing is wrong. I know today was Tom's birthday and you haven't been to his grave since the day of his funeral," Warren explains. "I want to take you there."

"Oh, no. I appreciate it, really, but I can't. I don't want to go."

"Don't worry," he says, "I will be right there with you."

"I don't want to go," I say firmly.

"You need to go, Barbara. It's all part of the healing. Come on, get your purse," he coaxes, "I'll drive."

We pull out of the parking garage into a steady rain. The windshield wipers are the only sound in the car. Neither of us speak. I don't want to do this. There is no point in standing there and talking to the ground. My Tom is not there. He is soaring in the clouds, just like I saw him doing the day of the funeral.

We arrive at the cemetery and I instruct Warren to turn here and then there and we pull over to where Tom is buried next to Kelly. Their graves are under a big tree. Tom picked this site for Kelly, not thinking that he would be buried on this protected spot. Warren takes out an umbrella and we huddle together underneath as he holds it over us. I am shaking as tears well up in my eyes. We stand there in silence until Warren offers to say a prayer. A prayer. Wow, that is the last thing I think to do. I am talking to Tom, not to God. I look to Warren to see just what he is going to pray about. Tom's soul is long gone. Warren asks God to lift the burdens on my heart and to care for Tom's soul. For the first time, someone prays for me.

We stand there on the soggy ground at the foot of Tom's grave. His headstone is a small bronze plaque level with the ground, just like Kelly's. It seems like it was so very long ago, not just a few months. The smell of rain is all around us and I shiver from the dampness. Through all this, I have peace.

After a few minutes, Warren puts his arm around my shoulder and guides me to the car, opens my door and I slide into the seat. We drive along silently, until we make a wrong turn in the road.

"Where are we going?" I ask.

"You'll see," he says. We turn here and there and then onto the lane leading to the city cemetery. "This is where Lisa is buried," Warren says.

We pull up to an open iron gate. Warren points to two flickering gas lanterns on each side of the gate. "I donated those in honor of Lisa. They are perpetual. It is the same flame that was lit when they were installed. They burn all the time. She hated the dark," he says.

We wind around the road past hundreds of graves. It is an old cemetery with lots of big trees. Lisa's headstone is huge, long actually. There is a place for four people to be buried on this continual family plot. Two planters and a photo of her are carefully placed. Warren tells me he designed the whole thing and had it made. He spoke at her funeral. He mourned on a whole different level than me. I, the doer, did nothing. He, the thinker, did all kinds of things.

But here, on this rainy day, we are simply two people who lost our loves. I wish I could say a prayer for Warren like he did for me, but I haven't prayed to God—his God—in a very long time. I haven't been to church in twenty years. He prays. He prays for Lisa's soul, he prays for his children, he prays for his in-laws and I end our prayer with a single sentence for him, "And may Warren find peace."

# Chapter 14

*Alaska – Trolling on Saturday Night in Skagway*
*July 2006*

## Day 27—3 miles

We drive into Skagway on a winding road with one breathtaking vista after another. We pass Destruction Bay and Emerald Lake, appropriately named for the brilliant green color of the water. I make Dad pull over so I can take a postcard-perfect photograph of a red canoe on a mirror-flat lake surrounded with mountains.

I am psyched to get into Skagway, the gateway to the inside passage. I expect a bustling harbor with ferries and seaplanes to whisk us off to the plethora of islands surrounding this popular destination. This is the northernmost town that 90 percent of the visitors to Alaska see. Driving through town I get a little concerned. A small section of local housing leads to a main street called Broadway, which is about ten blocks long and two blocks wide. It is 7:00 p.m. and most everything is closed. It is 55 degrees and windy. This is a major port for cruise ships. Where are all the people? Broadway Street is adorable with cute shops and a train station at the end. Dad is dying to go on the old steam-powered train until he learns it costs $95 per person. "Dad, when you are sitting on your chair this winter, I think you would rather have seen this passage than have $95 in your bank account," I tell him. "I am going, so you can go too or wait for me right here until I get back." He guesses he will go. We make the arrangements for tomorrow.

We need to do laundry. There is a Laundromat next to an Internet place, just down the street from the liquor store across from the train station. Sounds like a street that has everything I want. Within a few minutes, I find out the Laundromat closes in ten minutes and the Internet site is down waiting for the technician. Please let the liquor store be open! Dad doesn't think we need showers and he can wear his dirty coat from fishing, no one will notice. I think not! I know fish stink.

The girl at the liquor store is listening to a political radio show with Bill Moyer. I am thinking; you live in Alaska, who cares! Anyway, she is sweet and lets me know the town is dead tonight. Only about 1500 people live here, mostly seasonal workers. The Red Onion will be hopping later. That's where the locals go. They are all off tonight. Saturday night is the slowest day of the week here. Wednesdays, when the big ships come into port, the town swells to 11,000. Great, my big Saturday night and it is dead.

We passed another Laundromat at an RV park just outside of town, so after my beer purchase of Moose Drool, in honor of my upcoming shower, we head to the RV Park. It's perfect. We can do laundry for $4, buy soap for $1, take a shower for $1 for six minutes and surf the Internet for $5 per hour. This is my kind of place. My kind of place used to be tawny Park Avenue with posh boutiques, trendy restaurants, and a day spa with spray tans, nails, massages, and facials. In the laundry room, I see two cute girls, tan with very pretty white teeth. Not locals. After a few pleasantries, I learn they are from Florida and are seasonal employees who go back and forth, working high season in both places. I inquire as to where a girl can go out on Saturday night and they both confirm, The Red Onion Saloon. Lucky for me, I know right where it is. Great, they invite me to The Onion or just a few doors down, another local favorite spot called Moe's. Somewhere in the translation, I get confused. I was looking for an ordinary Joe, but here they are called Moes. Moes are locals like Joes, but mountain men are called Moes. So, is this after-hours place for locals called Moe's or are guys I am looking for called Moes? At least this is worth a big laugh to these twenty-something girls. They have pity for me when they learn I have been traveling with my dad for twenty-six days of a forty-two day trip. The clarification of the Moe situation would cost me a round of drinks at the Red Onion. Happy to supply the libations for my new friends, I agree to meet up with them later.

I head for the shower. Picking out my clothes is quite an ordeal. Who packed this stuff anyway? My cute low-rise jeans can only be worn with heels and the only heels I have are sandals. My feet are always cold. I hate cold feet.

This time comfort wins over fashion. So I will wear borrowed jeans from my sister and my black fur-lined boots. I am 5 '1" without heels. Dancing in boots is not easy, but I really want to cut loose. Oh well, I have heard time and again, the ratio of men to women in Alaska is ten-to-one in my favor. I was also clued in that if a girl wears make-up and shaves her legs, she is immediately put on the "A list." Sounds easy enough. Look on the bright side, I will have just showered, washed my hair and I think I still own make-up.

I'm hurrying as usual because it's cold and I only get six minutes per dollar. The money is not the problem, having US quarters is the problem, I strip, shower and try to condition my super-dry hair. The weather has completely changed my skin and hair. None of my old beauty routines are working anymore. Once again, the goose bump situation prohibits shaving my legs. Oh well, I have just dropped to the Alaskan "B list."

Besides, I wax. In order to wax, one must build up a pretty good growth for the wax to grab. Six weeks of growth should give Kim, my salon girl, a thrill. This growing leg hair long enough has always been a problem. Too short, most hair doesn't come out and still hurts like a mother, only to discover you must come back in another two or three weeks. Long leg hair takes forever to grow, and God forbid, someone should notice the forest growing on your legs. Like poor Brandon, my new friend, who sees this horror growing on my legs. "So are you European or what?" he asks.

"No, I have a waxing appointment in three days and wasn't expecting to be close enough for anyone to notice," I explain. Clearly, he could tell I was a girl telling the truth. No one could come up with a story like that on the fly!

Anyway, out of the shower with my hair up in a towel, I notice a big pimple right on my nose. Probably from wearing sunglasses along with all the moisturizer I have been applying. I have not had a pimple for at least ten years, but tonight I have one. Great. It will go well with my long underwear top, which I will be wearing under my jean jacket with my ill-fitting jeans that are even baggier now without my long underwear underneath. This is the first time I am not wearing two pairs of pants since I left Pennsylvania. Now for the last big decision for the night, polar bear earrings or the puffin bird ones I bought at Seward. What should a girl do?

By the time I am ready, the laundry is done, and one hour of wireless is over; it is 11:30 p.m. and Dad is long asleep. I told him I would park the van in front of the train station, which opens at 7:30 a.m. We will get up in the morning and ride the train. The *Red Onion* is just down the street. After a quick survey of this tiny town's streets, I am certain I can find my way back "home." Off I go in search of Joe or Moe or at least a good laugh with my fellow Floridians!

By midnight the place is packed and the band is rocking. It's good to be out. I head to the bar and immediately run into my new girlfriends. They know everyone and introduce me around. It is very loud in the bar and I can't hear exactly what Beth and Nan are telling them, but I am greeted with high-fives and lots of toasts. I overhear that I have just hit the road, love the vagabond lifestyle, am never going back to the traditional treadmill, and am looking for a place to land. I am welcomed into the world of adventure. I learn that the girls are trail ride guides and live in a barn with no electricity. They come to the RV park to shower and do laundry. I meet the girls who clean the train, carpenters from Seattle, a guy on crutches with a broken leg from a motorcycle accident, and an adventure guide with a broken hand. He recommends that I don't choose his company. I am impressed by the girl wearing a sundress with sandals—after all, it is summer. However, she is talking to a guy wearing a flannel shirt. Most live in a tent at a campsite for $300 for the season, and shower for twenty-five cents a minute. Keep it simple, travel light and keep moving. There is a whole culture of people doing this. They are all ages.

This is not a usual night at the Red Onion, the band is playing a special engagement. They played last night and word quickly spread that this is the place to be. We are dancing, laughing and drinking. The owner of the bar is completely drunk and attempts to group hug on the dance floor, loses her balance and takes about five people down with her. Andy, one of the guys in our group, hands me a Corona.

"How did you know I drink Corona?"

"Because you are a Florida girl," he answers. "I worked the Key West thing for a few seasons." It is the first Corona I have had since I left Orlando and it tastes like home. Funny thing is, Orlando isn't home anymore. I really don't know where home is or will be.

The band plays until 2:00 a.m. and is persuaded to play another hour. After that, we are pushed out the door into broad daylight. It is so bizarre. "Hey, let's walk down to the lookout," someone suggests.

"Where's the lookout?" I ask.

"Down by the docks and over the footbridge where a trail leads to a clearing by the water with a killer view of the Skagway harbor," Andy answers. The six of us head out. It is cold, but I don't want to be a wimp, so I go into Ironman mode and suck it up. The trail is like a mobile party. There are other people out here walking around. Apparently it leads to a camp area where people live and they walk this trail to get to town. My new friends know everyone. The view from our rocky perch is worth the cold mist blowing on my face. I am visibly shaking. Andy tries to give me his coat, which I refuse because then he will freeze. "Just take the windbreaker," he says. "I have two other layers underneath. It is the dampness that is making you cold."

No, I think to myself, not wearing my long johns and fleece turtleneck is why I am cold. I take his jacket, stop shaking, and listen to the stories of these vagabonds.

We all walk back like a posse of bandits strolling around this wild western, lawless Alaskan town looking for trouble. I feel like Soapy Smith, a local swindler and con artist who was killed on this very street after a shoot-out in 1898. I say goodnight to my posse as I will probably never see them again. Andy walks me home, which is two cars down. I give him his jacket and a hug of gratitude, and turn to go inside—that is, unlock the door and climb into the passenger seat! To my surprise, my dad is sitting on the end of the bed, wide awake and has just watched our band of strays walk into town and my gentleman caller bid me goodnight.

"What do you think you are doing? Do you know what time it is? Where have you been? I saw you with that man!" my dad says disgustedly.

Now I know I am living way outside my comfort zone, but come on. I am forty-four years old and being scolded by my dad for coming in late.

"What are you doing up?" I ask. "I thought you would be fast asleep. We are at the train station, all ready for tomorrow morning. Just go back to sleep."

Six o'clock in the morning, we're up and at 'em for breakfast. The ticket office opens at seven-thirty and the train leaves at eight. Sitting up in bed, the thought of bending over to the microwave on the floor to make eggs after two hours of sleep is painful. Trying to make amends for my behavior last night, I suggest breakfast at the Sweet Tooth Cafe. Coffee, lots of hot coffee, will make my head feel better. This is the third time in twenty-four hours that I am reminded of my age. I really need to act my age. A big greasy breakfast should set the world straight. Dressed in my ever so fashionable Louis Vuitton hat and red parka, we walk a few blocks to the restaurant. The cold wind on my face is a welcome wake-up call. In the bathroom I put my contacts in, take an aspirin, brush my teeth, wash my face and prepare for the day.

After a full day of sight-seeing, a steam engine train ride and historical tour, we head to the ferry to figure out how to travel the inside passage. This will not be an easy feat. Take the camper or not, how many islands, etc.? The schedule is different every day and there are fast ferries and slow ferries. After lots of help from the ticket agent, we have a plan.

We agree that tonight's 11:45 ferry arriving at 6:45 a.m. in Juneau with an immediate transfer to Sitka arriving at noon would be our best option. Best Option?!? There are other routes, but the auto cargos are sold out. Only one catch, we can't stay in the camper on the ferry. No passengers are allowed on the auto deck. There are lounge chairs, similar to airplane chairs, or you can bring your sleeping bag and sleep on the floor. A flashback to when I was twenty-years-old and backpacking through Europe comes to mind. Let me get this straight—after two hours of sleep and nursing a hangover, I am going to get on a ferry at midnight and travel for twelve hours, making a boat transfer with the camper!?! This cruel twist comes on the heels of my sitting up in bed night after night from about seven o'clock on, watching my dad sleep, getting more shut eye than I have in years. And now on the one day I decide to burn the midnight oil, I get to pull a double all-nighter? Double rainbow, double border crossing, double all-nighter? Is this the universe trying to tell me something?

With my game face on, I sit like a seasoned traveler in my chair. The only real problem is the chairs don't recline because I don't have enough body weight to make mine stay lying back. Daylight doesn't allow for much napping, so I watch the world go by. Twilight cruising. This is a first for me. At Juneau, we are delayed for our transfer due to a docking situation, and I am concerned about making the forty-five minute connection. We make a plan. We will get in the RV and I will make a pot of coffee. While it is brewing, Dad will drive off ferry A and pull up to the terminal. I will go inside, get the proper boarding documents and lane assignment for the camper, pour the coffee into the travel thermos, drive onto ferry B, pack a snack and my personal items so I can freshen up on the next four-and-a-half hour leg and be out of the camper by last call for the auto deck. Dear God, could I have picked a crazier schedule? Remembering my new motto: I am open and eager to see what comes next. I am in the right place at the right time. Life is meant to be fun and I am willing to enjoy it, I say, "Let's roll or perhaps, even more appropriately, let's float!"

Dad loves cruising. He has never been on a big boat like this. He is up and around checking out everything. Talking with the boat workers, he learns all about our vessel. He loves to be on the move. He is up at the window, has been on every deck and surveyed the entire boat. It's all about you Dad, you go boy!

To date, we have driven 8,939 miles and traveled eleven hours on a ferry.

# Chapter 15

## The Mourners Path
## September 2005

Everyone says not to make any major changes after someone you love dies, so I don't. I go to work, put on a happy face and stuff my sadness deep into my heart where no one can see. I try to move on, take my licks, and shake it off, but my heart just isn't in it.

It is Warren's constant insisting that I go to grieving class that really opens my eyes to just how much I am suffering. He had been through the class after his wife died and found it to be really helpful. I guess he can see how much I need help, even though I can't. He is not the only one who sees that I need help. My co-worker, Molly, gives me the name of her therapist, a very wise, spiritual counselor whom I start to see.

In the fall I start a ten-week class called the Mourner's Path. The meetings are conducted through a local church. I walk up the stairs, looking for room 202. Tonight is the first class. I am not worried or sad. I am doing this because I am supposed to, something I am used to doing. The big room has a little circle of chairs placed in the center. There are nine participants, all of whom have lost someone they love. The ladies who run the program are very sweet and kind.

Our first exercise is to go around the room and say our name and the name of the person we lost. Most people are older, except Roberta and another Barbara. Then we pair up in two's and are instructed to tell our story to the other person and the other person is going to relay the story to the group. Roberta, in her late thirties, lost her very controlling mother whom she nursed for the last years of her life until she died a few months ago, then she found her live-in girlfriend dead on the kitchen floor just a few weeks ago. She is the saddest person I have ever seen. She feels totally let down by her church and has no one to turn to. Then there is another forty-something Barbara, who lost her best friend of the same age to breast cancer. She is mad at God for taking such a beautiful person so early in life and leaving two young children without a mother. We go around the room and listen to the stories of loss. Then it is my partner's turn to tell my story.

This is Barbara. She lost her fiancé, Tom, to a sudden heart attack. She changed her whole life to be with him and they dated only two years and were planning to get married on February 22nd. Just six months before the wedding, Barbara was planning an all-girls trip to Italy to celebrate a girl-friend's fortieth birthday. Tom was very jealous and didn't want her to go. The night before she was to fly out, he told her that if she went, he wanted the ring back and the engagement was off. Shocked and hurt, Barbara gave the ring back and went to Italy. While she was there, he died. She never called him during the trip and only found out about his death when she landed in Orlando. He was alone when he died.

Hearing the story out loud, told by a stranger—a very compassionate stranger—and looking into the faces of others who were also suffering, it oc-curs to me that my story really is tragic. It is totally devastating. I was totally blind-sided. My story has it all, lost hope, love, guilt and pain, all wrapped into one small, gigantic package.

Over the next ten weeks, I don't miss a class. I need to go, but it becomes increasingly difficult. All the sadness that was hidden gradually comes to the surface. I cry the day I have class. I cry the day after class. I cry at my desk at work. I cry on the treadmill. I cry in the shower. I can't stop. The sadness is as real as when Tom first died. My reality check comes the night we do a little quiz and answer questions on a scale of one to ten about how we feel. The categories are physical stress and emotional stress. Being an Ironman and se-rious athlete, I have no physical signs of stress. I completely mastered physi-cal self-discipline. I exercise to the point of exhaustion in order to sleep, fill my days to the brim with stuff, and don't allow self-pity.

It is the emotional test I flat-out fail. I can't see the future. All the hopes and dreams I had are gone, buried with Tom. I am just going through the motions. My first glance at the results is a bit of a surprise. I rank in the serious to dangerously depressed category, but hell, I know I am struggling. Yet seeing the words *Dangerously Depressed* gets my attention. I have always been known for my happy, optimistic outlook on life. I was told repeatedly,

"If I was on a sinking ship, I would want you on it." Now, to see the label Dangerously Depressed is shocking, not to mention the serious reaction the directors of the program have to my results.

"What about a leave of absence?" someone suggests. "Maybe you can take some time off work and take a break?"

"Take a break!" I think, "Are you nuts? I am alone. If I don't work, I will starve and worse yet, I don't get paid to show up, I have to sell. I have a mortgage and a daughter in college. Yes, I have investments and stuff, but that's not meant to live on. I have to work! I need to support myself. I am independent. I can do this."

"Yes, yes you can," the director soothes me, "but you don't have to. Have you looked into other alternatives?"

"Other alternatives, like what?" I question.

"Go and see your health care administrator and find out what benefits you have," she says.

"But we weren't married? He wasn't a family member?" I throw out.

"It may not be for grieving, you may get help for depression," she says softly.

"Depression?" I repeat in horror.

"Yes, and maybe the counselor you are seeing can give you something to take."

"Take? Absolutely not! I have never and will never take anti-depression drugs! Those are for wimps!" I retort firmly.

"But if it will help you?" she urges.

"Help me! That will just send me down a road I am not taking," I protest. But the idea of taking a break, slowing down, and dropping the facade that *everything is fine* does sound appealing. Just letting me entertain the idea of escaping this place I have put myself in is enough. The window cracks open. I am tired. No, I am all used up. My well is dry and I have nothing to give.

Still there is something I can give that is so small, so silly, yet it could mean the world to someone who is hurting. Roberta, the saddest girl in my class, feels truly abandoned. She feels that no one cares about her and that she is all alone. As crazy as it seems, one of the concerns she talks about repeatedly in class is that her yard needs to be mowed. Her lawnmower broke and she tried to borrow one from the church she attends, but they needed it back. It isn't about the lawnmower, it is the fact that she asked for help from the one place she thought would come through for her, and they let her down. A lawnmower!! We are not talking about a house getting foreclosed. This lawn thing is a daily reminder to Roberta that no one cares about her.

I can buy her a lawn mower. For that matter, I need a new one too. A lawnmower, for crying out loud, we are not talking about brain surgery, here. So I ask the director for Roberta's name and phone number. Warren has a mini-van and volunteers to take me and the lawnmower to Roberta's house. We go to Home Depot, buy two lawn mowers, and follow our Map Quest directions to Roberta's modest little house. I know we are at the right place when we pull up because the grass is very high. She knows I am coming over to bring her something, but she has no idea what it is. The look on Roberta's face is pure surprise and then the realization of what is really happening hits her. She gives me the biggest bear hug I have ever received. She holds me tight and just lets the tears come. Someone heard her cry for help. Someone cares about Roberta. Someone knows that she is alive. There we are, two crying women watching Warren put the handle on the lawn mower and adjust the wheels. What a sight. It is a lawnmower, not a million dollars, but it means the same to Roberta. There was one tiny drop of water in my well and I gave it to the person who needed it the most. It gives me hope that I still have something left to give.

At the urging of my grief counselors, I contact my HMO at work to see if there is any help for someone in my situation, and there is. Maybe I can get a leave of absence and get paid, but it won't be for grief, it will be for depression. I don't feel good about that because I really don't believe I am depressed. But I am really tired and the thought of stepping off the treadmill and dropping this façade sounds right. My hopes rise as I jump through bureaucratic hoops, filling out form after form as I am passed along from administrator to administrator. Mine is not an easy case to pinpoint. It isn't like I broke my leg. My injury is less obvious. My hope evaporates when I am told that the counselor I am seeing is a licensed practitioner and not a Ph.D. In other words, she isn't a real doctor and I am not taking medication. That's crazy. I'm not depressed enough and the only way to prove it is to take drugs. My counselor tries to help, but I will need to see the Ph.D. in her office for at least three visits so she can make a decision about my diagnosis. Then I can fill a prescription for Prozac, even if I choose not to take it. This doesn't sound right, not to mention that the visits are $150 each out of my pocket and visits to the PhD still won't guarantee that I will be approved for medical leave. I don't want Prozac and I don't want to be labeled as being treated for depression. I am grieving. I am grieving a terrible shocking loss. I lost my future. I lost my love. I lost my soft place to fall. I lost my everything. More than that, the timing of it all is insane—Brittany went away to school in August, Tom died in September and Debby quit work in December. My entire world changed in a matter of a few months. The party is over and I am the only one still on the dance floor.

In the end, my claim is rejected. Now that the door is open for me to have an escape route, I can't get it closed again. When I finally admit to myself that I am miserable, I know I have to make changes.

Roberta isn't the only person who needs help, so does Warren. His nanny isn't working out and Christmas is coming. He can use the help with the kids and I sure want to be needed. We need each other too, and by now I am crazy about him. We talk for hours about everything. No two people understand death and all its complications better than us. We cling to each other. We cling together for love, strength, guidance and reassurance.

When I tell my boss I need some time off, he understands and gives me an unpaid leave of absence until the end of the year. My sales plan is ahead and will carry the club through the end of the year.

"It's too bad," he says, "you have really improved this past year."

"Improved? What do you mean?" I ask.

"Well, you seem to be getting along much better with the other department heads. You seem more relaxed and let things roll off your back more," my boss says.

"Funny thing," I reply, "I have never cared less about the club and its members than in this last year. When I was passionate about delivering what I was selling and made sure the club held to the highest standards, I was labeled a trouble-maker, and now that I don't care about the product I am selling, I am complimented for *getting along*." I really don't belong here anymore. This is clear.

Warren's two children are a delight and I adore them, but they are work. Rachel is a love. She reminds me a lot of my own daughter when she was little, but Rachel is as Irish as my fair-haired Warren. She has red hair, clear blue eyes and the whitest skin I have ever seen. Mike is smart as a whip and tests every move. He has mastered the art of manipulating the string of caretakers he has had since his mother's death. He is a piece of work, but underneath all that is a little boy who misses the showering of attention that was his life, until death changed all that. He holds a special place in my heart.

I am determined to make some memories for Rachel and Mike. We go to the pumpkin patch and bake cookies. When Christmas comes, we buy a big tree from the tree farm and decorate it, stringing popcorn while sitting cross-legged in front of the fireplace. I even get them little chef's hats with gingerbread aprons. They stand on chairs to reach the kitchen counters and we cook. We have fun. At night when we are all together, we make a picnic and eat dinner on the living room floor, or snuggle together on the couch and eat popcorn while watching a movie. I spend most of my time at Warren's home with him and the kids, although I keep the tree house intact. I promised Brittany I will always keep a place for her to call home, even though no place feels like home to me anymore.

It's all good, but it is a real job, this being a mom, and I am almost twice as old as when I did it the first time. I just graduated from the job of motherhood and as time passes by, I know that I don't want to do it again. They are just babies, not to mention the new baby, Warren's son from his six-month marriage. He is an infant and that means starting at ground zero. Custody is still being arranged, unfortunately, amidst faxes and angry letters, accusations and hurt. This isn't the only battle in Warren's life, which is a constant caldron of conflict. He has been married five times, twice to the same woman and the one that died, but that still leaves three ex-wives and a lot of hate. The pot just keeps stirring and I get thrown in too. Someone anonymously called the Department of Family Services and a report is filed that I hurt Michael. Of course it is complete bunk, but the children are interviewed and their little bodies checked for bruises. The social worker comes to the house and interviews me, Warren, and the children's grandparents on both sides. It is all horribly painful and happens just days before Christmas, on my birthday. I get a first-hand taste of hate and don't like it. This kind of conflict is foreign to me; I am not used to all this turmoil. Sure, I have had ups and downs in the past, but nothing like this. As time goes by, I come to realize that Warren is the common denominator in every issue. I keep telling myself when this is over things will settle down, but I soon realize it is never going to settle down.

Warren runs his corporation from a home office and has a personal assistant who comes in daily. The phone rings, faxes come in, deliveries are made, and someone is always in the house. Even though it is a huge house, there are few moments of peace and very little down time. After a month or two, I know I can't sustain this lifestyle, so after Christmas, I start to look for a job. I know I can't go back to the club, so I give my permanent notice. I move back into the tree house. I remember what my counselor said. My new mantra is "I am open and eager to see what comes next. I am in the right place at the right time." Be brave. I added that part myself.

I don't feel brave and I don't feel like I am in the right place, but I am exhausted from trying so hard to make *something* work. I want so desperately to fit in somewhere, to belong again, but this isn't the place.

# Chapter 16

*Alaska - Week 5*
*July 2006*

## Day 28—49 miles

Sitka. Ah, beautiful Sitka. This is our first island of the inside passage and the ferry ride over is spectacular. The channels to get here are quite narrow for our big barge. Heavily forested islands line both sides of the waterway; at the dock, there is no town. To our surprise Sitka itself is seven miles away, and the whole island is only fourteen miles from end to end. Happy we decided to bring the camper, we're off to downtown to see what we can find and to our delight, the fishing/seaport town is a postcard picture. Nine thousand people live here year round. This island has it all including fishing, rocky shorelines, whales, bald eagles, rainforests with super big trees, native history and most surprising, Russian history. I find this fascinating.

The highest peak in town was once the lookout of the native Indian tribe, then later became the home of the Governor of the Russian-American Land Company, and then in 1867, became the actual site where the papers were signed selling Alaska to the USA for $7.2 million, or nineteen cents an acre. After the fur trade was depleted and without much use for this vast expanse of land, Russia thought they had better sell Alaska before they lost it since it was too difficult to defend from so far away.

During the time of the Russians and the Americans, the natives were forced to convert to Christianity, and were forbidden to speak their native language and to practice their dances and rituals. Today there is a huge resurgence to teach the children the old ways. We meet a woman in her 70's who cannot speak her native language, but her three children all do and they know the customs better than she does. They are not Eskimos. There are only two clans of Eskimos who are actually descendents of Siberia, and they live much further north. Natives of Sitka are from Australia and speak a totally different language. Today, different clans still get together for a pot-luck or a big party, dress in beautiful costumes, and perform old dances.

The natives belong to one of two tribes, either the Ravens or the Eagles. Eagles always marry a Raven and a Raven always marries an Eagle; they are called "the love birds." Art displaying the tribal symbols may only be created by someone of that tribe.

Totem poles have one of four purposes: They tell the ancestry, tell a story, honor a person, or serve as a mortuary holding cremated remains. They are painted using three colors: black, red, and turquoise. These colors are made from ingredients found naturally on the island.

In the afternoon, we hike up a dense, deep green wooded trail to an old Russian cemetery with an incredible lookout to the sea, and as we sit quietly we hear the birds calling and rustling in the trees. To our amazement, a raven and a bald eagle fly right into the cemetery.

I love it here. I'm told the winters are mild, staying around 30 or 40 degrees and with the sea level elevation and the salt air, there is very little snow. The summers are busy with tourism when the big cruise ships dock, but the winters are quiet with natural beauty everywhere. One thirty-something girl I meet says it is a very deep-thinking, spiritual community. Sounds like my kind of place. Sitka reminds me a lot of Olympic National Forest in Washington State, still my favorite, although there seems to be a lot more job opportunities here. With seventeen days still ahead, I will keep looking! Or perhaps, as my new adventurer friends tell me, *travel light and keep moving. Stay for a while and when the urge comes, pull up stakes and go.*

We find an isolated campsite on an estuary at the end of the road. Dad is amazed that the road actually ends. He knows he is on an island, but in his mind the road always keeps going. We check in at a cute little log cabin that is actually the home of the campsite manager. The husband and wife team arrive in summer and go back home to Oregon in the winter. Their job includes housing. This is their eighth year coming here.

## Day 29—36 miles

We wake to a picture-perfect morning in our little campsite in the forest, except it is chilly. Dad and I bicker over who is going to get out of bed and go to the driver's seat to turn on the heat. I want to start the engine and get real heat, and he wants to use this little secondary heater that barely throws any warmth. He is convinced the heat is the same; I am convinced the secondary heater is worthless. I end up getting up, so I start the engine and really fire up the heat.

Wet green forest is all around us. I love the smell. The ground is too damp to find wood for a fire, so I make chicken apple sausage and eggs on the cook stove.

After breakfast, we tour the island and find a small college with about 300 students. We visit the on-campus fish hatchery and sea aquarium. Marine biology and forestry are popular majors.

Later we find the Raptor Center with its many native birds. Dad falls asleep during the presentation and misses seeing the giant eagle up close. These amazing birds have a seven foot wing span but weigh only fourteen pounds and can see eight times better than humans, which means they can read a one inch newspaper headline from across a football field. They have the ability to turn their head 210 degrees. These Eagles live for about twenty years in the wild and have been removed from the endangered list. Flying all over the island, they create an unbelievable sight.

On this quiet and serene island we are surrounded with lush forests and mountains. Back at the campsite we walk all through the estuary soaking up the natural beauty while looking for spawning salmon. Our day ends with the gift of an awesome sunset.

## Day 30—74 miles

Dad is up early and ready to go. He is cranky and wants to leave now, even though the ferry doesn't leave until 1:30 p.m. He hates not being able to go when he wants. We go back into town and Dad is convinced I am meeting a man here and that is why we stayed for two days. He seems to have forgotten about how we struggled to make the ferry schedule work for us. He gets loud and starts talking trash when a stranger passing by tells him to cool it and stop yelling. "We don't act like that here," the man tells him. I've never heard my dad talk like that.

We are parked by the library next to the harbor, which is currently filled with three giant cruise ships. I can't get phone or Internet service and when I ask a local, they tell me it is because the cruisers jam the system. On the other days, it works great.

We get tickets to see a Russian dance performance. The show is charming with beautiful costumes, and the narrator makes the dances come alive for us. We are surprised to learn all the dancers are women, even though some are dressed as men. Apparently the men are not interested in dancing.

After the show, we drive through McDonalds for Dad (the first fast food of our trip), and head for the ferry parking lot even though we are about two hours early. Dad would rather sit there and sleep than drive around. He wants to go and that is that. I think he feels trapped on an island. We argue. He tells me I am pushy. I think he is homesick. He talks all the time, but we don't really have a conversation. He isn't interested in what I have to say and thinks my views are *way out there*. It is clear he doesn't approve. His Pennsylvania Dutch accent is heavier than I remember.

On the ferry to Juneau, I meet Quinn, a woodsy kayaker guide from Vail who comes to Alaska during the summer. I am in my groove and talking up a storm. Dad makes it clear he has had enough of me and my *meeting people*. He is being ridiculous. Quinn has made this ferry trip many times and makes arrangements for Dad to go to the Bridge. I am happy for the break. When he returns, Dad says he thinks the captain thought he was a spy. He is like a kid.

It is late when we arrive in Juneau, so we drive to the top of the mountain to a great overlook of the city. Evidently the overlook is a ski resort/campground, so we call it a night right there in the rest area. It is 10:00 p.m. and the sun is setting after eighteen hours of daylight.

# Day 31—131 miles

We wake to a chilly rain. Large cruise ships are in the harbor here, too, but the phone works. Juneau is a big town and the capital of Alaska. We learn there is conflict about the capital being on an island since it is not easy for the residents to arrive here, and it's not centrally located in the state. However, if it wasn't the capital of Alaska, Juneau would lose its tourism. We take a trolley ride of the town and tour the capital building.

A heavy mist is hanging in the sky like a lid. I want to fly over the glacier in one of the little planes that fly there, land and take off on the water. Unfortunately, they are not flying today because of the weather, so we will try again tomorrow. Dad isn't thrilled to go because of the cost, but again I insist. What he really wants to see are the salmon jumping. We are here at the right time of the year and thought the streams would be filled with them. We put this on our list for tomorrow.

Late in the afternoon we drive to the far end of the island to Echo Bay and camp for the night. Dad wants to park right down by the water rather than take a real campsite. He lies down in the back and I go find a perch on a rock by the water. More picture-perfect stillness with water, mountains, sky, and quiet.

After a while I notice a little activity over at the boat ramp. The mail boat has arrived and bundles and packages are being loaded from a van onto the boat. I walk over and learn that the boat comes once a week to pick up mail and take it back to a remote camp store that services some fishing lodges and summer camps for churches.

From here, I see two fly fishermen wading out into the water about knee deep. They look like they came directly out of an Eddie Bauer catalog. I am impressed when they catch one huge salmon after another and release them back into the water. I wonder why they don't keep them, so after a while I stroll over and ask. They explain that they are old friends from college and come to Alaska every year at this time for salmon fishing. They only have a few days left of their holiday and have already caught all the fish they can eat and ship, so now they are just doing it for sport.

"Sport?" I question. "What about dinner? I will make you a deal," I tell them. "You catch them and I'll cook them. I have the stove right over there in that camper." In a minute, we have a plan. They will catch and clean the fish and I will whip up some potatoes and whatever else we have.

I have a front row seat on a beautiful evening somewhere in Alaska to watch my dinner being caught. I start a little fire on the beach in preparation of another chilly evening. Dimness is setting over our little camp and the sky turns beautiful shades of pink and orange. To my surprise it is almost 9:00 p.m. The fishermen are experts at cleaning their catch on a makeshift rock table and toss the carcasses on the beach toward the water. To my pure delight, a bald eagle swoops down and picks up the fish remains in its claws and flies away. Does it get any better than this?

It does get better when one of the fishermen returns from their car with a cooler full of ice cold beer. Now this is the life. That is until Dad wakes up and strolls down to the beach and sees our little party. He is happy about the fish and mad about the beer and my new friends. As the night goes on, the fire gets bigger and we are laughing and having a great time. Dad went to bed long ago. I finally call it a night too and to my shock, I am not in my bed for more than ten minutes and the camper is bouncing down the road.

"Dad, what are you doing?" I shout to him in the driver's seat.

"We are leaving. I did not bring you here to act this way," he says angrily. "You are not going to carry on with those men."

"What are you talking about?" I retort. "You are crazy for driving around in the middle of the night. Where are you going to go?"

"I don't know but we are not staying here."

"Do what you want," I snap back, pulling the covers over my head.

## Day 32—331 miles

In the morning I wake up in the parking lot of McDonalds. Great, this is the one place Dad knows. He is inside having breakfast. When he comes out, he acts like nothing happened, but something has happened.

Dad has had it. I think he would like to skip a scenic trip home and just get back. We have a discussion about it. We agreed to six weeks. I tell him that we are not having another night like last night, and that driving away in the middle of night was dangerous and stupid. I think he is tired of the trip and thinks if he acts like a jerk, I will throw in the towel and agree to drive non-stop back to Pennsylvania. But I don't want to cut the trip short, we have ten days left and I am not ready to go home. I tell him we have three choices, but we are not going on this way. He can fly home and I will drive the camper back; I fly home and he drives back; or we sell the camper and both fly home. I think he is truly surprised. The idea of me driving his camper home is not appealing, he can't navigate his way home alone and he definitely doesn't want to sell. He says he will think about it. I don't understand what the hurry is to get back.

It is still cold and cloudy when we drive out to Mendenhall Glacier in silence. It is beautiful both close-up and far away. With our last chance to fly looming over us, I call the bush pilot and learn that he is flying and we can be on the ten o'clock flight. He won't land on top of the glacier, but the visibility is quite good.

The floating plane takes off right on the river downtown next to the cruise ships. The flight over the glacier is absolutely spectacular as we see breathtaking views of landscapes that appear otherworldly. I love taking off and landing on the water, but the glacier itself is the most amazing part—miles and miles of blue-green ice surrounded by forest and lake. We are in a little ten-passenger propeller plane and our pilot narrates as we fly. I snap photos and remember that at this moment I am the luckiest girl in the world.

One last thing we must see before leaving Alaska is salmon jumping. We have made every attempt to go to the streams where they should be, but no fish. As divine intervention would have it, as we are using the restroom just after the flight, we bump into the same couple we met yesterday. They ask if we have seen the salmon jumping and to our surprise, they tell us the hatchery is just a few blocks away.

There they are, thousands of them in the water and in every compartment of the concrete ladder. It is nothing like what I imagined. According to our guide, the salmon return to their birthplace to mate. After they mate, they die, so the *fishermen* built *ladders* to *help* the fish *climb* up from the water into the tank where they will be *caught* and harvested. We can see them jumping, from little pool to the next pool higher and higher, until they make it to the big tank at the top. There are literally thousands of salmon in this tank. They are separated boys from girls then split open and the eggs are dumped into a bucket. Then, like nature's perfect recipe, sperm are added to the same bucket, stirred around with a paddle and poof! Baby salmon are made. When they are big enough, these salmon will be released returning in a few years to be harvested. This should be illegal. They literally swim right into the tanks to be caught and butchered. In the gift shop, we can purchase smoked or canned salmon, yet for some reason, it is not so appetizing.

By 4:00 p.m. we are off to the ferry and back on land leaving Skagway. Hitting the road with a full tank of gas, we head straight for the border. Under heavy clouds, we can't see half of what we did when we arrived. Goodbye Alaska, hello Canada. It is 47 degrees when we cross the Canadian border again. The guard checks our passports and asks if we have any guns or liquor on board. These are the same questions we have been asked all along, but this time I am lying. I have wine hidden in the back, but it is hidden from Dad not from the Canadian Border Patrol. There is tension in the air now between my dad and me. This well-trained guard knows we are lying about something, wants to search our camper and asks us to get out. We stand in the freezing cold wind while he hops in and looks around. In a minute we are back on the road driving in silence until it is time to sleep.

# Day 33—704 miles

Dad is on a mission to get back into the lower forty-eight states and we make great time. I drive 400 miles today, most of the time with my headphones on listening to my music. Now I am acting like Brittany, a kid who doesn't want to talk to their *out-of-touch* parent. I have completely changed roles. When I am not driving, I lie in the back.

We stop at Liard Springs, another famous hot springs. The hot steaming bath is a welcomed tension-reliever. Light rain feels good against my hot skin as we take the wooden walkway back to the parking lot. Here we meet two more lesbian school teachers from Colorado traveling together in a new VW van. Dad is interested in the van and all its unique camping features.

At the bathhouse, I take my best shower of the entire trip in a portable trailer that looks like a walk-in freezer. The super hot water gushes from the showerhead like a waterfall. I please myself. I really need to have sex with someone else. I know how to make myself feel good, but it is not the same. All that pleasure is a bargain at $5 for unlimited time.

Dad doesn't think he needs to take a shower, and I don't argue. I am tired of telling him to brush his teeth and wear deodorant. "Yes, Dad, you must do it everyday," I tell him repeatedly. By this time, I have developed significant sympathy for what my mother endured all those years.

Today, Dad is struggling with his dream being over. This is his last chance, he will not come back to Alaska. I am struggling too. I feel lost. I want to feel good and be cute. I want to go out and socialize. I miss being with a man.

As we leave the hot springs, Dad gets confused as to which direction we came from. I say to go left and he insists we should go right. I let him drive the wrong way for about five miles until he figures it out and turns around. I think this really bothers him although we never talk about it.

After a full day of driving, I have a headache and an ear ache from the dampness. We get our fifth chip in the windshield and at 5:00 p.m. we hit the 10,000 mile mark of our trip. We hoot and holler. It reminds me of the first time I hit the 100 mile mark on a bicycle ride training for the Ironman. It happened somewhere on a country road in Lake County, Florida on a hot summer day when I was with my buds, Mike, Scott, and Todd. Riding along now—passing lots of motorcycles and bicycles on the road of ever-changing landscapes—makes my heart ache a little as I remember my training days. Seeing the bicycles makes me want to take up cycling again. I want adventure and a physical lifestyle.

We drive for hours past beautiful Alberta farmlands. I am surprised to see such huge farms so far north until I figure out that even though the season is short, twenty-hour days of sunlight make the growth intense.

We sleep at Grand Prairie. It gets dark enough to see the bright white half moon. We are both confused about the time change since we passed two time zones in one day. Apparently all of Alaska keeps the same time zone, but Canada, which is in the middle, in some areas doesn't.

## Day 34—707 miles

Before I know it, it's morning. We are awakened by a big beautiful sunrise— the first one we have seen since leaving Pennsylvania. We have been in some shade of daylight for thirty-three days. I look at my watch. It's 3:30 a.m. Can't be, I think. Squinting, I look again. Why not, everything else in my world has changed, why not when the sun rises? Dad decides to roll at 4:00 a.m. on this Sunday morning. When I wake about six, he is convinced it is Monday morning. We have lost a day somehow.

"What makes you think that, Dad?" I ask.

"Because the roads are packed." Look at all the work trucks. There are tankers, foreman's pickups and men surveying," he says. "It can't be Sunday." I look at my log book and check the calendar. I don't think so, but I guess it is possible. Just as I am trying to figure this out, a ladybug lands right on my arm! It's a sign. Ladybugs mean I am trying too hard. I don't have to hunt down life, I can let life come to me. Anything is possible. We stop at a gas station and I go inside.

"Excuse me, what time is it?" I ask the lady.

"Eight-thirty," she answers.

"What day is it?" I ask.

"July 16th," she answers.

"No, I mean what day of the week is it?" I hesitantly inquire.

"Sunday," she says slowly, looking at me like I am a total freak.

When I return to the RV, I announce that it is still Sunday but it is 8:30 a.m., not 6:30. All we can do is shrug our shoulders and chuckle. Funny thing, without being told, do we really know what time or day it is anyway?

We spend another full day driving. I lie in the back and read the entire book of *Angels and Demons*. We don't speak much even when we drive through the Canadian Rockies and breathtaking Banff and Jasper where amazing high, snow-capped mountains jut down into emerald green pools below. Jaw-dropping views appear at every bend. I skip Lake Louise and the gondola when I refuse to get out of the car. "Go see it yourself if you want," I tell Dad. "I am staying here."

"Two people can play this game," I think to myself.

About two hours later, at 8:30 p.m., we cross the border back into the USA and into Montana. "Welcome Home," the border patrolman says. It feels good to be back in the lower forty-eight. We are in Big Sky Country now and the terrain changes into miles and miles of honey brown grass.

Just outside the gates of Glacier National Park, we stop for the night. So far we have logged 11,427 miles and bought $1,513 of diesel. That comes out to about thirteen cents a mile and we are averaging twenty-three miles to the gallon. At the start of this trip, I would never have imagined that I would care about these details, but today they are important statistics. Signing off in my journal for tonight, as a good news reporter does, I say, "Until next time, this is Nanook of the North and Dad, reporting live from the unmarked UPS van."

# Chapter 17

*Getting Fired*
*May 2006*

Being in the tree house is like living in a dollhouse. It truly is filled with all the things I love. During each move of the last year or so, I have trimmed down until I am now left with only a fraction of what I started with, but it is the best. I am surrounded now only with the things I really love like my favorite paintings, sparkling crystal and china, special pieces of furniture, and lots of *happys*, as I call them. Little reminders of my travels, little sayings, and lots of pretty note cards. These are the things that make me happy.

I still lie awake at night, but for the first few weeks, I am so tired that sleeping is not a problem. Waking up in the morning is the best part. Out of my windows, all I see are trees, lots of trees. The blinds are bamboo and quite see-through so I wake with the light and birds chirping. It doesn't take long for me to love to come home to my little hideaway. I look forward to walking to my front door which is lined with terra cotta pots of all kinds of blooming flowers. I completely fix the front door with new paint, a screen, and add a stained glass window. I brick the walkway and carpet the stairs leading up to the second front door. There I create a little oasis on the landing with more little treasures that make me happy. Sunflowers, ladybugs, and a little toy Vespa on the ledge under the mirror.

Preparing my bed is a major production. I sell the bed Tom and I shared and buy a full-size bed that will fit in my tiny bedroom. To my dismay, fabulous sheets are not made for such a small bed. No market for it I suspect. Anyway, my mattress is extra thick and topping it with the fattest feather bed I can find makes queen sheets fit just fine. I cover it all with a 600 thread count duvet that is to die for. I make the bed higher by using blocks, so I practically have to hop up to get into it and pile it high with feather pillows. It's a dream. I feel like the Princess and the Pea. I am hugged all night by plush bedding above and below me. On the nightstand, I place an Eiffel Tower lamp and a tiny vase of tea roses. Next I add a bed tray filled with more things that make me happy and of course, my journal, a pen, and a yellow highlighter. From here, I have coffee in bed each morning, feeling totally decadent.

My little home is filled with music, candles, and books. I used to have quite a collection of books, but now it is whittled down to only the very best—those that are still powerful to me. I think I have read every self-help, metaphysical, motivational book ever written. Now I keep only the best ones. The rest I read, highlight, and journal the most important parts for quick memory. I dig those books and journals out and start to re-read every one of them.

My favorite place to read is on the little porch. I buy a swing and downstairs in the garage paint it white. As the warm weather comes, I start to take my coffee out there and the mornings on the porch become my special time. I slide out of my warm, feathered nest, play Vivaldi's coffee song on the stereo and brew coffee in a tiny two-cup coffee maker. Nestled in a white robe and white slippers, I use my best china cup and saucer and settle in for an hour of reading. Awakening really, not "wake-up" like I am sleeping, but wake up my soul, like it was asleep. These mornings on the porch are re-awakening the girl inside that was lost. I was sleepwalking. I understand intellectually how the universe works, but never really got it emotionally. Now, with an empty slate for a life, I finally start to understand that I never really trusted the universe. I always thought that making a plan and working the plan was how things got done. But here, for the first time I see it differently, I get it. *Knowing what I want is the only thing I have to do and then let the universe handle the rest.* Just get out of the way and trust that what is happening is exactly as it should be. This would never happen to Barbara, the go-getter. *I should be doing something. Nothing happens unless I make it happen.* Wow, that was my ego talking. But today, sitting on my little porch reading and praying, I get it so clearly now, I really wake up. Every day I trust more, open my heart more and as time passes, peace comes to me, glorious peace.

I make up little three-by-five index cards and read them every morning and every night. At first they are simple little sayings and then I keep adding to them:

*I am always Joyful, Loving, Grateful, Accepting and Blessing.*

*Ask, the universe always answers, not
always in the package we expect.*

*Thankfulness is a powerful statement to the universe.*

*Listen to your inner voice. She is your
guide, the universe are your helpers.*

*I receive your grace and abundant gifts.*

*Live joyfully now. Operate life from a position of joy.*

*Nothing is permanent. Everything is
constantly changing. No guarantees.*

*Be quiet, still and open to see what comes next.*

*I am flexible and adventurous.*

*I am curious and interested to see what will happen next.*

*I am in the right place right now.*

*Everything is happening at exactly the right time as it should.*

*My timing is excellent.*

*Whatever you resist—persists.*

*Judgment keeps us from joy.*

*Expectation makes us unhappy.*

*Life is always a result of our thoughts.*

*All "problems" that arise have a solution with them.*

*Focus on the gift of exchange. Giving and receiving. Win-Win.*

*Let go of the attachment to the outcome.*

*Proximity is power.*

*Get a vision and draw it to me like a magnet.*

I still am not sure what I am doing or where my life is headed, but it is different. I have not been looking very long when my dream job falls right into my lap. I am referred by my girlfriend, and start on February 1st. I am now the membership director for a new kind of club, a luxury destination club where members pay $200,000 to join, annual dues of $15,000 and have privileges to use multi-million dollar homes all over the world in the hottest vacation destinations. It is a new concept and has all the elements that appeal to me: travel, luxury, and a private club. My job is to develop a referral program where current members invite their friends to join the club at parties the club will host in their city. I will travel around the country and host these parties. It is perfect for me.

The drive to the office is farther than I prefer, but it will only be temporary. Soon enough, I will be on the road more than in the office anyway. I use the drive as my little learning library. I re-listen to the tapes of *Conversations with God* by Neale Donald Walsh and *The 7 Spiritual Laws* by Deepak Chopra and some of my other old favorites. Time in the car becomes an extension of my spiritual lessons and a chance to soak up the Florida sunshine.

The days pass quickly, but it is my time on the porch that becomes sacred to me. I begin to set the alarm earlier and earlier. Now I get up at five o'clock to read, pray, meditate, and journal until I have to get ready for work. I read *Many Lives, Many Masters* by Brian Weiss again and his latest book, *Messages from the Masters*, a book literally dropped off on a whim by my dear friend, Chocky. She just happened to stop by one day and casually left it on the table. "I picked this up today and thought you might enjoy reading it, if you like," she said.

I was given this book and others at exactly the time I needed to read them. It becomes life-changing for me. I open a book to just the right page for what I need to hear that day. I read my old favorites again, but see them with new eyes. The clarity of how the universe works is totally different this time around. I re-read *Creative Visualization* and really think about what my true purpose is. What are my natural talents? What do I really love? What makes my spirit soar? Slowly over time, my true love and purpose come to me—freedom, unburdened with *life stuff*, travel, time, and helping others understand how the universe works. Becoming comfortable in my own skin, I slowly start to hear my inner voice telling me to get out of the way and trust in the universe. Great things are at my fingertips if I just *stop doing and be.*

At my new job, the learning curve is huge in the beginning, but it is just what I need, a new start and a new industry. For the first month, I study how the industry works and research the competition so I can sell against them.

That isn't the only learning I need to do. I need to get mobile. After the training period, my job will be primarily traveling. I know how to use a computer, but at my old job, the software programs were industry-specific. I didn't have a laptop or a need to look up things on the Internet. I don't have a Blackberry, a digital camera, or an I-pod. Now I need everything. I have a lot to learn. I add a new statement to my morning meditation: *Technology comes easily and effortlessly for me.* I am going mobile all right, but not for the reason I think.

The owners of the club are learning too. They have only been in business one year and have just seven homes. It's a very small company compared to the handful of similar clubs in the marketplace and our fee to join is much less. I haven't yet gotten the referral program off the ground when one of the sales people leaves and my boss asks me to focus on sales for a while as this is what the company really needs at the moment. Since all of our leads are coming from the Internet website, this means telephone sales and I love the phone. It isn't cold-calling, but selling a $200,000 membership over the phone is a bit daunting because we're a new club and most of our members joined just a few months ago, haven't gone on a trip yet, and aren't ready to give us a reference. They are not ready to promote the club to their friends and associates and if leads do come in from referrals, the owner gets them because he was the original sales person.

It doesn't take long for the wheels to fall off the bus. I have my first referral party from neighbors of my boss. They don't know him or anything about the company and if they do, they have already *been sold.* For whatever reason, it is a terrible flop.

After two months or so, I am miserable, but I force myself to put on a happy face. The phone calls are awful. I can feel the stress chemicals pouring through my veins. One Wednesday, on my way back to the office after lunch,

I call my best friend Debby.

"I can't go back in there," I croak. "I hate it. I am so miserable. This is not what I signed up for." I start to cry making my face turn red and my eyes puffy.

"Take a deep breath," she soothes. "It's going to okay."

"I'm going to quit," I sob.

"Don't do anything rash. Don't quit until you have another job," Debby counsels.

"I can't go back in there. It's awful. The pressure is ridiculous. It's so wrong."

"Look, just get through the afternoon. Go home tonight and sleep on it, and if you feel the same way in the morning, then do something. Aren't you taking Brittany to Atlanta this weekend?" she asks.

"Yes." I answer. "Maybe I'll ask for a few extra days off. Okay, you're right, just get through today and tomorrow. I will think about it, and if I feel the same way later, I will quit."

I go back inside and make up some excuse about getting upsetting news. I also ask for Friday and Monday off to take Brittany back to school and get her new apartment set up. I struggle through the afternoon, and when six o'clock finally comes, I get in my car, throw down the top and drive home. Get through Thursday and I have a four-day weekend to look forward too. "I can do this," I counsel myself.

In the morning I arrive at work as usual. My boss asks to see me in his office and the controller joins us. "It is never easy to do this," he says, "but things aren't working out here for you. We love you and your enthusiasm and know that you have lots of talent, but we aren't ready for you to do the referral program and telephone sales aren't for you."

I am stunned. I am getting fired.

All I can say is, "I am so relieved. I am miserable." The energy in the air is odd. I tell them that I love the club, the concept and maybe at another time or place things could work out between us. He gives me a document to sign and we wish each other well. I go back to my desk to pack what few personal things I have here and tell my two co-workers that I am leaving. Then I remember the bottle of champagne I have in the refrigerator to celebrate my first sale, so I open it and we all toast to friendship. My boss carries the box to my car, we hug and I drive away the happiest girl in the world. It doesn't matter to me whether I quit or got fired. I am free. With the convertible top down and music blaring, I fly down the highway. Free to be outside in the sunshine and free to breathe. I am so happy. I should be scared, but I am not. I am relieved.

The next day Brittany, Seth, and I drive to Atlanta and get the keys to her first apartment. It's a big deal, at least to me. I am so excited for her. This weekend is all about her. We are going to paint her room and get new bedroom furniture.

At 2:00 p.m., we have an appointment with the financial aid advisor at her college. I want to meet her in person and make sure we have done everything to receive all the aid we possibly can, especially now that things have changed. We meet with Prudence Goss, a lovely young woman who is a graduate of Emory. I give her copies of my tax return and other documents she needs. I tell her how much it means to us for Brittany to come to such a fine school, and that I know it will make a difference in her life to have a diploma from Emory. I also explain that it is a huge stretch financially for us, but it is important enough to do whatever it takes to make it happen.

"Have I filled out everything I can?" I ask. "Is there anything else I can do?"

"No, it looks like everything is in order. Unless anything has changed since you filled out these papers," she adds.

I look over at Brittany sitting next to me; she knows what has changed. I am embarrassed to say it out loud. I look at the floor, tears well up in my eyes and I turn back to Prudence.

"Something has changed," I say. "I got fired yesterday." It hurts to say the words out loud.

"That's wonderful," she exclaims, clapping her hands.

"It is?" I ask, totally confused.

"Do you have a letter?"

"Yes, not with me, but I do have a termination letter at home," I tell her.

"With that letter, I will be able to get you more money. A lot more money," she says with a glint in her eye. "A lot of families come to this school as though it is just the next step in their children's education. It is not every day that a family comes to my office that is really grateful for the opportunity. You both really know what an Emory education means, and I love knowing I can help."

I can only imagine the look on my face. I can't conceive what has just happened. Prudence and I talk many times on the phone after that. I never have to introduce myself, she always recognizes my voice. "I know who you are," she always says. "You are one of my favorite families." That letter ended up giving us $16,000 off of Brittany's tuition.

That night I read and re-read my three-by-five index cards:

*Events become blessings, one and all.*

*All "problems" that arise have a solution with them.*

I never thought the miracles would happen so fast.

# Chapter 18

*Alaska - Week 6*
*July 2006*

## Day 35—505 miles

At five-thirty in the morning I wake up with a headache and bloody nose. I think it is from the transition of damp to very dry air. Dad is a new man and very excited about being in Glacier National Park. I think he is happy to be somewhere he has been before as he seems excited to show me around. We never really talk about how to handle the rest of the trip, but we map out our return route to Pennsylvania putting us back home on day forty-two, just as planned. I don't know what the rush is to get back because Dad is retired and takes work when he wants too. I think he does it for something to do rather than just sitting around the house. He thinks his work needs him, but he refuses to call and check in. I am not ready to stop, and would extend the trip even longer. We decide to go back on a route that is farther north, going up over the top of Lake Michigan, crossing into Canada again, then heading for Niagara Falls and crossing back into the US at New York. We add a stop-off for Dad at a Christian Retreat he and Mom went to some forty years ago. It is clear that I am lucky to get the full six weeks, so I am grateful for that.

Glacier National Park is smaller than I thought, but very dramatic with lots of sweeping views, winding roads and no guard rails. It is chilly in the high altitudes, about 50 degrees. We stop at a lookout and are greeted by long-haired mountain goats. They walk past us without a care in the world. I feel like Heidi; this could be Austria and I should have my hair braided.

A ranger is directing traffic for some road work and while we wait to pass, he tells us that he is a retired airline pilot. He is a lot younger than sixty-five, but says this is the best decision he has ever made. "It is impossible to be stressed living here," he says.

Traveling south, we head to Helena, passing miles of flat yellow fields and plains. For hours, we can see the Rockies faintly off in the distance. Helena is a charming town with lots of beautiful brickwork on the old houses of Main Street and the gorge, which is filled with shops and outside eateries. The flags on the streetlight poles say, "Voted Best Small Arts Town." At the grocery store I ask two teenage girls what it is like to live here. They tell me it gets really cold in the winter and the weather can change dramatically in just a few hours. It can swing 50 degrees in no time. They go outside for gym and lunch unless it is below zero degrees. Guess I won't move here.

By the time we reach the Choteau Mountains, the temperature is 100 degrees and hot wind is blowing across the plains. It feels like being in a giant hairdryer. This area is home to the Blackfoot Indians. From what I can tell, this reservation is not as desolate as the others we have seen. Eastern Montana turns into the rolling plains where Indian history is narrated by roadside historical landmark signs. We pull over often to read the history, which makes for a pleasant drive. Next, we stumble upon Egg Mountain and I vaguely remember hearing that in 1978, a huge nest of fossilized dinosaur eggs was uncovered here. It's just a big hole in the ground now, but the nearby town has a big display.

We pass a series of strange handmade billboards and a sign for a campaign against the use of the drug, methamphetamine. One is a cartoon drawing of the grim reaper and another one is a little kid saying, "My mommy loves me, but she loves meth more." These seem out of place in this rural heartland of America with its rolling hills and yellow rocks. What else is there for the kids to do out here?

We sleep in the parking lot of a public park. Stars, stars, stars. It is hot, so we open the windows and side door of the camper. A deer walks by our open door. From then on, I don't sleep well, thinking that the deer or anyone else can just walk into my home. After midnight, several cars of drunken teenagers arrive. They are playing music and tag football. I don't think they know we are in the camper.

## Day 36—702 miles

At 6:30 a.m., we are awakened by sirens. We aren't sure what they are for, but my guess is that it is some kind of a warning, like for tornados. We decide to roll right away and find out. The guy at the Coneco station says they do it every morning and not to worry.

Yellow fields turn greenish about halfway through North Dakota. Another hundred miles goes by. We pass the town of Home on the Range, North Dakota. Yes, it really is a town. As we drive, we see five wild horses standing high up on a ridge letting the wind blow into their faces, waving their manes. I expect a band of Indians to come flying over the hilltop like a scene from a western movie.

After another hundred miles we see sign after sign for the World's Biggest Buffalo in Jamestown, North Dakota. Okay, I'll bite. I've seen the world's biggest spruce tree and it was pretty amazing, so yes, I want to see the world's biggest buffalo. Going out of our way much farther than it originally appears, we arrive and discover we have been taken. The world's biggest buffalo is a concrete statue, although huge. Our saving grace is that there actually is a live buffalo on display in the same tourist trap. Oh well, here is to making lemonade. I coin the phrase, "invent-a-tourism," kind of like the Corn Palace. I can't blame them, and obviously, we aren't the only travelers looking for a little entertainment during the long hours of driving.

Flat yellow land and miles of open fields stretch out before us for hours. We stop for gas in the little classic western town of Richardson, North Dakota. The welcome sign is an old covered wagon filled with flowers. Driving down the only dusty little street, we pass the red brick building of the Elkhorn Bar, the Prairie Rose Café with its white lace curtains and turn around just past the American Legion, complete with a deer statue in front that has been knocked over by the wind. This little town is plopped down in the middle of miles and miles of fields.

What kind of life must a young girl born here dream of? Does she dream the same things that a girl born in the city dreams about? Does she live small but happy? Does not knowing about all the material things make her not want them and feel less pressure to *get ahead,* or does TV change all that? I am loving the isolation from the outside world. Not knowing is good for me. As I am pondering these thoughts, a ladybug lands on my arm. It's a sign. Is it possible, a ladybug in the middle of nowhere? Yes, anything is possible.

Another hundred miles or so later the landscape turns to green farmlands, corn, and wheat. Brittany calls. She is happy and we chat for a while. We cross the border into Minnesota, with its ten-thousand lakes, according to the license plates.

Dad adds two notches on his belt buckle. He thinks he has lost between twenty and twenty-five pounds. The best part is now he can sleep on his stomach for the first time in years.

We camp at Strawberry Lake Christian Retreat in the Woods. Dad remembers being here forty years ago. The man he came to hear no longer preaches, but his son has taken over. We have dinner in the fellowship hall and meet everyone. Dad is surprised when I agree to go to the evening church service.

The people in the congregation are of all ages and some have shaved heads and tattoos. I actually like the service. It is informal and relaxed. Dad falls asleep halfway through it. The sermon is leaning on the motivational side. The preacher sounds a lot like Joel Osteen. As we walk back to the camper, I tell Dad I enjoyed the service and got a lot out of it. Dad says he never heard him preach this way before and liked his elder preacher's services better. I guess I can't win. I go to sleep thinking about life.

## Day 37—206 miles

After breakfast, we go back to church for the Sunday Morning Service. It is a little more organized than last night, but still has the same easiness. This time I take notes because it helps me remember things better. The big take-aways for me are: First, get tunnel-vision. Repeat again and again, "I have to hear your voice." Continue to ask to understand. Decide to have daily conversations with God. The way will be shown if you truly ask to know. And the most important is that the mind is a battlefield, so *get out of your mind* as often as possible. Stop thinking and accept things as they are. Hummm.

After lunch we pack up and head out following parts of the Lewis and Clark Trail. We stop off at Wal-mart and develop more photographs. We pass through Akeley, Minnesota, the home of Paul Bunyan, and I must stop to take a photo of Dad sitting in the palm of this giant plastic figurine with a blue ox next to him. I love these funky pieces of Americana. We drive on to Leech Lake and Stoney Pointe Campsite. It looks a little out of the way on the map, but I insist we go. I have a good feeling.

Leech Lake is not a disappointment. It is *On Golden Pond*. The loons are calling as the sun slides into the water and a sliver moon pops out to put the icing on the cake. I don't leave my spot by the water all night. I have found paradise. I am the luckiest girl in the whole wide world.

Another ladybug lights on me. Is this a sign that I am trying too hard? Sit back and let the universe handle the details. As the great philosopher Deepak Chopra said, "Flowers don't try to bloom, they just do." Tonight as I lie in bed journaling and thinking about the last few days, I sign off with "Nanook of the North, reporting from the Spy Van."

In the morning I stay in bed as long as possible, listening to the loons and the lapping of the water against the rocks. It is the most peaceful sound. Dad sleeps late too. I make coffee and serve him in bed. He doesn't know this world and calls it *The Life of Riley.* I don't know any other world. In my old life I drank coffee in bed almost every morning. He never has.

Dad is not open to new things. His is a solitary life. He stopped learning and growing at fifteen-years-old. I understand that he believed with all his heart that if he was a God-fearing man and worked hard and followed the rules of the Bible, his life would be great. But it didn't work that way. He didn't change with the times and has now backed himself into a corner with no choice but to live by the old rules, the only rules he knows. I admire him for that.

I am grateful that Dad wants to drive so much, but I would have gone slower, stopped more, rested more, and read more. Instead Dad complains until I give in and he gets to control his world. Do I do this too?

I want to keep my world small. Is that good or bad for the global environment?

I miss my skin against fabulous sheets and being wrapped in the arms of a lover.

I miss Brittany so much. I want to stay around young people. Maybe I should move to a college town like Boulder.

No more reading. I don't want to bring in any new influences. I have enough to think about.

## Day 38—563 miles

Sunrise comes to Golden Pond, or actually Stoney Point, with the loons and the lake. The rocky side is loud with the lapping of the water and the beach side is quiet and gentle. Dad follows me everywhere. Is he worried I won't come back? Is he scared of being alone and that he won't be able to find his way home?

As we leave town we stop for fuel and meet Wanda at the gas station. She is married, retired and would love to travel in an RV. I see the glimmer in her eye, but know in my heart of hearts, she will never do it. She is waiting for the timing to be right: the right camper to come along, the right financial situation, the right blah, blah, blah. The reality is that the universe will provide everything for you once you take a leap of faith, not the other way around! It will never be perfect. "Just do it! Just go!" I want to scream at her over the counter, but she is a lovely country lady with dreams. I understand her.

We pass through Duluth, Minnesota, the coldest city in America. I know this because in Florida I worked with a man from Duluth and every day on the morning news they would announce the coldest place in the United States and everyday it was Duluth. I am intrigued by this big industrial town that is apparently frozen most of the time.

We drive on through the wooded area of upper Wisconsin that soon turns to America's Dairy Land. Dad is surprised when I suggest we stop for ice cream. It has been a very long day of driving and we are in the land of milk and honey. We discover we are back in the east coast time zone for the first time in almost forty days. We drive all the way around the top of Lake Michigan and camp just outside of Mackinaw City. The sunset on the beach of yet another picturesque lake is absolutely beautiful. Our campsite offers unlimited showers, Internet, and a million stars.

Dad won't call his work to see if they need him; he is determined to go to work on the day he told them he would be back, even if there is no work. He won't stay on the road longer and I am not ready to go back. Perhaps he is ready for something familiar. Perhaps he wants to be back with his work buddies and sleep in his own bed again. Perhaps he is sick of me. Perhaps he just wants to go home. For me, I don't know where home is.

## Day 39—410 miles

We sleep until 8:30 a.m., a luxury, then drive to the dock to take the ferry to Mackinac Island. No cars are allowed on the island and the only means of transportation are bikes and horses. We take a carriage ride tour all around this cool island that is only open during the summers.

I am in awe of a huge white hotel called The Grand and try to go inside to look around. I learn there is a fee of $15. I am happy to pay it and for the first time, let Dad off the hook. He will not appreciate it the way I will. It is truly grand inside. I love the sweeping staircases and long ornate corridors. Passing through the restaurant, I notice all the wait staff are black with very dark skin, and they are dressed in white jackets with black bow ties, a total throw-back in time. Then I hear a wonderful Jamaican accent. Of course, it makes perfect sense. They come north for work in the summer because tourists don't go to Jamaica then because it is too hot. Since room and board are probably included, it's a perfect deal. I really feel like I am in a different era somewhere in the Deep South.

I stroll into an art gallery and meet Barbara, the seventy-seven-year-old shopkeeper. She is reading the book, *A Million Tiny Pieces*. I ask her how she likes it and what she thinks about all the controversy over the book. She tells me she is a little lacking on news these days because she just returned to the states after getting out of the Peace Corp. The Peace Corp? I do a double-take. She explains that after her husband died, she didn't want to sit around and get old, so she joined up. She took this job because it included housing. She lives in the girl's dormitory house, but has her own room. It includes meals and use of the golf course, so on her day off she plays golf. It's temporary, but gives her something to do during the summer. I walk out of the shop in a daze. She is seventy-seven-years-old and still has the wanderlust bug. She is my hero. I love her. I tuck the card with her email address in my pocket. Wow. Clearly, I am a baby at this vagabond game.

By 4:00 p.m. we are back in the RV and drive toward the 1,000 Islands. Dad has been here before and is sure I will love it. On the way we pass a lighthouse. It reminds me of Tom and sadness washes over me. He collected lighthouses and had a huge painting of one in his bedroom. We decide to skip Niagara Falls on the way back and take a different route. We have both seen the Falls before and I think it will be too painful. We pass through the town of Flint, which reminds me of Michael Moore's movie *Roger and Me*. At 9:00 p.m., we cross the Canadian border for the sixth time. The border patrol asks if we are going to gamble. I think not.

We sleep by the roadside in a heavy equipment sales parking lot. It is already late and we will be taking off early in the morning. It is hot, so we sleep with the windows open. It makes me nervous, but we have no choice. We must have tripped a silent alarm, because some time in the night a police officer shines a spotlight right onto our faces as we sleep in the back of the camper, making me sit up wide awake and blinded by the light. No harm done, but I don't sleep well after that. It could have been someone looking for trouble and not a cop. In two seconds they could have been inside the camper. Not good.

Morning finally comes and neither of us has gotten much sleep. Disoriented, we stop for coffee. My cousin is getting married in Cody, Wyoming sometime in October and a big group of family is planning to take a bus and go. Dad thinks he will pass on the trip. He has had his fill of driving for a while.

Brittany calls to tell me she wants to take a year off from school. I don't think it is wise. "Just finish the four years and then take a break before graduate school," I suggest.

## Day 40—July 352 miles

We drive through London and Bellville, Toronto, a charming little town with beautiful old brick buildings. Queen Anne's lace and periwinkle grow along the roadside. Stopping at Lake-on-the-Mountain, we learn of a wonderful old Indian legend that is the love story of two Mohawk Indian teenagers. She lived in the lake on top of the mountain and he lived in the bay below. Her sisters showed him a crack in the limestone where he crawled through to be with her. In spring, the lake overflows and creates a giant waterfall into the bay. In the legend, the three sisters were bean, corn, and squash.

The little towns of Bloomfield and Picton look like Pennsylvania where I grew up. We pass a winery and a fun little town called Birdhouse City. We are in farmlands and driving on winding country roads. I spot a license plate for Ontario, with the slogan, *Yours to remember.*

A little side trip to Sandbanks Provincial Park is in order. Someone told us not to miss it. It is Canada's version of the Sahara Desert where mountains of tan sand are a playground for kids and adults. We make the climb up the dunes and slide down on our rear ends. The world is a big playground, so why do we keeping playing in our same old sandbox, even after it gets dirty and the cat peed in it? What are we so afraid of?

Brittany calls and we talk about school and what she should do. She wants to transfer to Rollins College near Orlando. I tell her no. She transferred once already and I want no part of that mountain of forms again, not to mention that some credits won't transfer and that will only add time to completing her degree.

Sadness creeps in on me. It is day forty and soon our trip will be over. The thought of re-entry causes a lump to grow in my throat.

Dad says next time he will take an airplane or a boat.

# Day 41—243 miles

We wake up in the parking lot of a marina along the St. Lawrence River in 1000 Islands. After a quick breakfast, we buy our tickets for the boat tour of the islands with a stop at the famous Boldt Castle. We are told to bring our passports because the castle is on an island that is really part of the USA.

The boat captain tells us not to count the islands because there are actually many more than 1000. Some are so small that they don't even count. The rule is it must be above sea level 365 days a year, be at least one-foot-by-one-foot, and have one living tree to be registered. Currently, there are 1,793 registered islands. I hope the one tree on an island doesn't die. One rock is even marked with a line drawn down the middle and has a Canadian flag painted on one side and an American flag on the other.

After clearing customs, we get the tour of the castle that was built by George Boldt, the millionaire-owner of the Waldorf-Astoria Hotel in New York City, for his wife. It is a huge gray stone mansion with six stories and 120 rooms, lots of turrets and other little buildings. It was meant to be a surprise for her and took four years to build. Unfortunately, she died before it was finished and never saw it. In his grief and sadness, Boldt stopped work on it and never returned to the property, letting it fall into disrepair. Seventy-three years later, the government got it and has been slowly restoring the mansion back to its original splendor.

We learn the story of how 1000 Islands salad dressing was invented. Supposedly the chef of the Waldorf grew all the fresh vegetables for the hotel on the property. One year there was a banner crop of pickles. Trying to come up with a thousand ways to use the pickles, he tried adding chopped pickles to mayonnaise and ketchup and poof, the salad dressing was created and was a big hit.

On the boat, we meet a lady whose daughter is a cop. She works for three years then takes one year off. This next year she will be spending it on a boat in the Bahamas. Wow, I am impressed. There is that vagabond thing again. Everyone is doing it.

By 5:00 p.m. we cross back into the US driving toward Syracuse, New York and end the day sleeping under the stars in a field off a dirt road, somewhere in the green mountains of Pennsylvania.

## Day 42—187 miles

It is day forty-two and our last day on the road. Exactly six weeks, just like we planned. We are driving through central Pennsylvania when Dad mentions that my brother Stan, a tractor-trailer truck driver, often makes a run to Scranton, which is nearby.

"Let's call him on the CB radio," I suggest. We haven't used it at all, but I get it ready and Dad talks. To my shock, my brother's voice comes across the radio. He is about ten miles from us and we agree to meet for breakfast. We pull off at a greasy spoon, and sure enough, there in the parking lot filled with big rigs is my brother and a fellow trucker. Divine intervention is the only answer. We have a lively meal and make plans for later.

Looking on the map, I see a little town called Jim Thorpe. I remember how cool it was when I went there as a kid. I wanted to go to college at Lehigh University, but it was a private school and the tuition was way out of my reach. I remember visiting the campus, which is nearby. We agree to make this our last stop of the trip before home. The town is nicknamed *America's little Switzerland* and *The Gateway to the Poconos* because of the picturesque scenery, mountainous location, and charming architecture. I think the chimes of the church bells make it feel like Europe, but whatever it is, it warms my heart. Imagine! I knew this at age sixteen when I first came here!

The town is named after arguably the greatest athlete in the 21st century, Jim Thorpe (1887-1953). He won two gold medals in the 1912 Olympics for track and field and excelled in football and baseball. When he died, his wife wanted him to be buried in his birth state of Oklahoma and for a monument to be erected there in his honor. When the state refused, she found a little town in Pennsylvania that was looking for a new name to promote tourism. She struck a deal with them and the little town of Mauch Chunk was renamed Jim Thorpe. We visit the park where his monument still stands today. He was a Native-American Indian and the father of seven kids.

Our next stop is a tour of one of the most magnificent Victorian mansions in America, the home of Asa Packer. Asa came to Pennsylvania from Mystic, Connecticut and made his fortune in railroads, hauling coal from the mines. It was the first railroad in Pennsylvania, Lehigh Valley Railroad, commonly called the *Switchback Railroad,* and boasts being the first roller coaster.

The three-story mansion has eighteen rooms, with 11,000 square feet, and took two years to build at a cost of $14,000 in 1861, which is about $2.3 million today. In 1878, Asa planned a huge 50th Anniversary party and some 1,500 guests were invited. Many modern updates were made to the house such as a cooling system that used huge blocks of ice.

Asa and his wife, Sarah had seven children, but all died at an early age except Mary. A bit of a bohemian, as history so politely records it, Mary was fond of art, music, literature, and travel. In 1885, she was single, forty-six-years-old, and the only member left in the immediate family. Women were viewed as second-class citizens back then, so in order to gain control of her father's fortune, Mary needed to wed. Charles Cummings was a close family friend who worked for the railroad. Mary, who was very intelligent and way ahead of her time, had Charles sign a pre-nuptial agreement, the first of its kind to be filed in the area. It said that if the marriage ended, Mary would receive the home, the property, and most importantly, the family business and Charles would receive $100,000 in railroad stock. They were married April 7, 1885. Mary retained the title Mrs. while inheriting $54.5 million which made her the wealthiest woman in America, second in the world just behind Her Majesty, Queen Victoria of England. Mary and Charles divorced in 1893. He eventually remarried to a woman named Sarah. Mary and Sarah became great friends and traveled extensively together. Both Sarah and Charles remained close to Mary and were even named in her will. Mary saw twenty-two states come into the Union during her lifetime.

When she died, Mary left the mansion and all its contents to the town.

Not sure what to do with it, the town let the house sit empty for forty-two years, unchanged without anything being removed or vandalized. Today the government operates tours. What a precious slice of American history!

An hour or two later, we pull into the driveway of my dad's home. He pulls the camper around the back into the yard next to the kitchen to make it easy to unpack. We drag the queen size mattress from the back of the camper up the stairs and back onto his bed. I put on clean sheets. In less than an hour, we are finished.

Six weeks, five chips on the windshield, $1.829 in gas, 14,056 miles, 790 photos and millions of memories. My childhood memories of my dad are better than the way he is today. Back then he was the happy-go-lucky, fun one and I was too little to know his struggles. He played with us kids and I don't really ever remember him being mad. Now I feel sorry for him. He didn't keep up with technology and learning, and he is lost. He lived his life the way he thought he should and it didn't work out the way he thought it would. Or maybe he did it just right. He believed in something and held to his morals and convictions. In the end, no one knows. Mostly, I just love my dad.

# Chapter 19

## Homecoming from Alaska – CPR
## August 2006

It's my first day back in Orlando since I left on the road trip with my Dad. I am so eager to see my daughter, but here I stand in the middle of the tree house, disgusted. Brittany knew I was coming home today and look at this place! It's a wreck. How could she leave it a mess when she knew I was coming home today? Is this the way she treats our home? I know she is on summer break, but she must still clean up. Thank goodness she is at work until noon. I walk around the apartment and look at the empty cans and dirty dishes, clothing piled everywhere, and trash bags that need to go to the curb.

I go outside onto the balcony, sit on the swing and try to get a grip on the situation. Part of me wants to call her up, rant and rave and tell her that I will be back tomorrow and this place better be cleaned up and put back together. Another part of me—the calm, rational part—tells me to step back and look at the big picture. I haven't seen my daughter in almost two months. What is the most important thing about coming home and seeing her?

The clear and most pressing thing about my homecoming is to talk to her about college and make sure she goes back to school in the fall. She is thinking about taking a semester off, taking a break from school because she really doesn't know what she wants to do and feels like taking the wrong classes is just a waste of time and money. She is thinking about coming back to Orlando. None of this sounds like a good idea to me. Everyone knows when a student takes a semester off, there's an overwhelming likelihood they won't go back.

I also want us to just have some downtime together, to get back in sync. I miss the old days when she was silly and I giggled, when things between us were easy. When she was adorable and I was loving and accepting. Now our relationship is strained and difficult. The dialog doesn't come easily; I am guarded and she is critical.

Do I make a scene about the mess of the apartment or do I focus on what she is feeling and try to understand her issues that make her want to take time off? Yes, she is being disrespectful to my things and our home. Yes, she is hurting and struggling as a twenty-year-old who is supposed to decide today what she wants to do with the rest of her life, when here I sit not knowing what I want to do with the rest of my life either. What do I really want to achieve in these few days we have together? What is really important?

I sit on the swing and gently glide back and forth. The rhythm is comforting to me and soon my breath is in sync with the swinging. I remember all the mornings I spent on this porch and all the wisdom and "ah ha moments" I had out here. That's what I need, a moment of clarity. All I have to do is what I did so many times before, out here, on this very swing—ask the universe for divine intervention, sit quietly and let my inner voice speak. My inner guidance knows what to do because I am a child of the universe. My soul is tapped into the big picture, so back up, slow down, and listen to what is in my heart. If I could raise myself up and see the situation from a different vantage point, what would I see? Just like when Tom and I used to go flying, how different my neighborhood looked from a hundred feet in the air instead of the way it looked driving home every day. From my vantage point, I see things one way, but from Brittany's vantage point, she sees something totally different. I need to see things from her perspective. And just like that, it becomes clear to me what my objective is. A dirty apartment is not the issue here but seeing things from her vantage point and hearing her out is what's important. On the swing this warm August day, I pray to be in the right frame of mind when I see Brittany. I seek understanding of what is really important and what is really going on with her and ask for help to do what is right for her not letting my dreams for her overshadow her own.

It is about nine in the morning and I know what to do. Clean up the apartment, unpack my suitcases, go for a run, and be ready for a girlie-girl lunch at her favorite trendy restaurant at noon. Cleaning up the place will make me feel better, and going for a run will change my chemistry and flush out these stress toxins I've got going on. There are several ways to change chemistry such as drinking, drugs, food, meditation, or exercise. Exercise is my drug of choice. I get to work, blast some dance music, and whip the place into shape, running up and down the steps with suitcases, trash and laundry. The phone rings several times and I chat to different girlfriends, making plans. It keeps getting later and later and I keep telling myself I better get going. It's getting hot. Finally, at 11:15 a.m., I leave the tree house and head for Lake Eola. It is almost 100 degrees and 100 percent humidity. I'll just do three laps around, that makes three miles.

As I round the lake for my second lap, I come upon a man lying on the sidewalk and two young men in white shirts and ties standing over him. They are calling 911. "What happened?" I ask, out of breath.

"We don't know," they reply. "He was walking along and just fell down, maybe from the heat." The man lying on the sidewalk is unconscious. He is old and bleeding from a small cut on his forehead just below his brown receding hairline.

I run to a nearby restaurant for a cold cloth and some ice, thinking that he is suffering from a heat stroke. The restaurant is closed, so I run around the back, find the ice machine, grab an old cloth and plate and scoop up as much ice as I can, then quickly run back to the man. I wasn't gone even a minute. To my shock, when I get back and dump the ice down his shirt and hold some on his forehead, the man has turned a horrible ash color.

"You guys, this man is not breathing. Did you check for a breath?"

"We don't know CPR? Do you?"

Stunned, I am thinking, you don't know CPR? I thought everyone knew CPR?

"Yes, yes I do," I reply.

Kneeling over him, my knees crush into the concrete sidewalk. I slap his face and shake him, begging him to wake up and start breathing. "Come on buddy, you've got to breathe," I tell him. The reality of what is happening clamps down on me. I am shaking and start to cry with fear. I lower my face over his mouth and pray for a breath. I put my hand on his neck and press my fingers into his vein. Nothing.

"Oh God, man, come on here. Breathe," I beg.

His vivid blue eyes are partially rolled up into his head.

"This guy is dying here," I cry out in panic. I am scared out of my mind. I've got to do it. I pinch his nose and pull his head back and breathe the biggest breath I can muster after my running and crying and with my own heart pounding wildly inside my chest.

I am not prepared for that sound, the sound of breath leaving a dead body. It is hollow and guttural. It comes from emptiness. I give another breath and when I raise my mouth up from his, I see his false teeth have fallen out and are lodged in his mouth.

"Oh, dear God," I cry, wringing my hands, "I can't do this," I say through the tears and the sweating. "Please don't die, please don't die."

Yes, I can do this, I tell myself. I must. I couldn't help Tom, but I can help this man. This man looks just like Tom did. Tall and slim, receding hairline, vivid blue eyes. Tom died this exact same way. He had a massive heart attack, fell down, hit his forehead and laid there until he died because no one was there to save him. But this is now and I am here and I must try to save this man.

I turn his head to the side and pull out his dentures and drop them on the sidewalk. With another breath, the lower dentures fall into his mouth. Again, I retrieve the plate and throw it down. He is not moving at all and getting blue. Oh my God, he is dying. He is dying right before my eyes, I scream to myself in shear panic. I go into full-on CPR, ten chest compressions to one breath. "Please, someone help me!" I shout. I am pumping and breathing, trying to concentrate and not let the terror totally overcome me. I can hear the sirens. Please don't die, I beg. Dear God, someone hurry.

A bicycle cop who heard the call on the radio crosses the street and is heading across the park toward us. "Hurry," I scream, "This guy is dying here!" The cop arrives and opens a small kit and puts on gloves and little device that covers the man's mouth. He instructs me, "You do the compressions, I'll breathe. Let's do two to thirty and do the compressions faster, not as deep." I follow his instructions. We follow this rhythm until the paramedics come and take over. Suddenly there are lots of people attending to the man. They have all kinds of equipment and boxes of gear all over the ground around him. They cut his shirt open and stick the electrodes on his bare chest.

I back away. My eyes are bulging out of my head as I watch the scene. With my hands over my mouth I beg for him to be all right. I am too stunned to cry, although tears are streaming down my face. Along with the two whiteshirts, I stand in total disbelief as we watch them get out the electric shock paddles, trying to jolt some life back into the man. His body lurches about a foot off the ground and then he projectile vomits high into the air. I immediately turn my back and start throwing up myself. A lady cop in uniform comes over to me and puts her arms around my shoulders to comfort me and hands me a tissue.

"Are you going to be okay? Do you want some smelling salts?" she asks.

"No, no, I'm okay, thank you."

The electric shock must have done the trick. In no time, they load him onto the gurney and a whole entourage rolls him to the waiting ambulance and they drive off with full lights and siren. The bicycle cop who was the first one on the scene comes over to me and looks into my eyes and sees the shock.

"You did well," he says. "What just happened is going to stay with you for a long time. This can be very traumatic. You are going to be exhausted."

Tears start to well up in my eyes, so I look down at the ground and squirm. "Can I go now?" I ask, wanting to escape.

"I just need a little information from you," he says, pulling out a little spiral notepad.

"Is he going to be all right?" I ask.

"They got him stable enough to transport him to the hospital. He is a very lucky man that you came along at just the right time."

"Where are they taking him?" I ask.

"Orlando Regional Medical Center," he says. "I can give you his name and you can call the hospital later if you like. He was homeless and lived at the Salvation Army."

I hear his words, but they mean nothing to me. He was a man who wasn't breathing, nothing else. I give him my name and address and he gives me his business card and writes the man's name on the back. I stuff the card into my sports bra and head for home. It is 12:15 p.m. and I'm late. I run the mile or so back to the tree house and find Brittany there waiting for me. I haven't seen her in two months and I fly through the door, give her a quick hello, and run to the bathroom. All I can think about is brushing my teeth.

"What is going on?" she asks.

"I just gave CPR to a man in the park," I answer, eyes still wide open and tears hot on my face.

"What?"

I briefly explain what happened as I get out of the shower and rush to get ready. Twenty minutes later I have a glass of wine in my hand as we sit in a chic restaurant, listening to the pulsating sound of techno music. I look around the room of the hip urban environment and it is as though nothing happened this morning. The world really does go on. It just happened so fast. This is surreal.

My absolutely stunningly beautiful daughter is sitting across the table from me chatting away. She tells me about her classes, her boyfriend and who's back in town for the summer. We catch up on celebrity news as I listen and shake my head a lot. Literally in shock, I can't say anything. I just listen. She talks about school and the future. I listen. She talks about how worried she was about me when I was gone and how relieved she is that I am home. I listen.

After lunch, Brittany is off to be with her friends and I am back, sitting on the porch swing, desperately trying to get my head around what happened. I prayed for clarity about what is really important and I gave CPR. Then it hits me. I asked to know what is really important and the answer is *life and death*. Appreciate life because it can be taken away in just a few minutes. I asked to be in the right frame of mind with Brittany and was still in shock and barely able to say a word. All I could do was listen. Dirty dishes, what school, or what major are not important. I needed to listen and hear her out. I roll the thoughts around in mind and then a little grin sneaks onto my face.

"Wow, okay, okay," I say as I look up to the heavens, "I get it already. Could you take it a little easier on me next time? I get it, I get it. You don't need to beat me over the head," I laugh to myself. Is this really how it works?

The next day, I call the hospital, but can't find the man, so I call the cop. He tells me he went to see the man at the hospital this morning and he was sitting up talking. He did have a full-fledged cardiac arrest and if he hadn't gotten help immediately, he would have died. *I was in the right place at the right time*, for him and me. There is that win-win again. I don't go to the hospital to see him. I can't. I am still too freaked out.

A few months later I get a call from the Orlando Police Department. They are honoring civilians who helped others and I am invited to come to the ceremony and be presented with a plaque. I don't go to that either.

# Chapter 20

## Moving to Matlacha
## August—December 2006

After being back in Orlando for a few days and running the roads, hitting my old spots, I am certain I can't live an authentic lifestyle and stay in my town. I will fall back into my old patterns. If I stay here, I will not find what I am looking for. I don't know what is out there or exactly what it is I am looking for, but I feel deeply compelled to find out. I want to live on an island and experience a slow isolated life. Moving to a place where I don't know anyone seems so right. Other people don't understand and I am not sure I do either. Up until now, I have packed as much into each day as I possibly could. More than once I was told, "You do more in one day than I do in a week", or "I am exhausted just listening to your schedule." The more I accomplished, the better I felt. Then one day, I didn't want that anymore. Death is a wake up call for the living. It is like a sheer veil was lifted from my face and I can see clearly that all *that* was not *it* at all. Somehow, I am way off-track. Although I am not sure what the right track looks like, I do know that the one I am on has come to a dead end.

I decide to move to a tiny little artsy fishing village called Matlacha (Mat la shay), near Ft. Meyers, about three hours from Orlando on the Gulf of Mexico. I had driven through it just once before with my friend Brandon. We went there to visit his friend Buddy. It is the cutest little town I have ever been to that I didn't fly to visit. It is a real island with brightly colored buildings filled with art galleries, coffee shops, a pizza place and a bait shop or two, and only one road running through it. The sea can be seen on both sides of the road. I had no idea that a little piece of paradise actually existed on the mainland. I can live on an island and still be able to drive away if I want to. It is perfect.

I call a girl that Brandon knows who was in real estate there. She has a place for rent, is out of town, but will have someone leave the key and I can come, see the place, stay the night, and let her know by email if I want to rent it from her. I find the cottage just fine, but no key. No one answers the phone numbers I have. So I drive around and check out a few things then call Brandon to get Buddy's phone number.

Buddy remembers me from my prior visit. He says to come to his house and he will help me out. We never do get the key, but Buddy has an extra room and invites me to stay there. He is happy to drive me around and show me the lay of the land. We go for a late lunch and early Happy Hour. He is fun and seems to know everyone in the little town.

The next day, we talk about my situation. I don't really want a whole apartment because that means bringing all my stuff with me, and I don't want to do that. All I really want is a room and use of the kitchen and bath. He offers to let me come and stay with him. He had a major operation just a few months ago and needs some help with the house and yard. He was in Vietnam and suffered the effects of Agent Orange and he never got his strength back. It isn't as easy for him as it used to be. He is spending a lot more time at home since he isn't working anymore, and would enjoy having some company around the house. I think I can help him with nutrition. I see it as a win-win situation. We set my move-in date for September 1st.

I make the decision to give up the tree house. There is no reason to keep an apartment that no one lives in and I don't need the expense either, so rather than having an expense, I can have income. I hire movers to take what little possessions I have left, after whittling down three times, and put them into a five-feet-by-ten feet storage unit for $125 a month. The $825 of rent money will go towards Brittany's expenses in Atlanta. I quickly rent my adorable little hideaway to a girl who is relocating from Palm Beach and I give Pooka, my dog, to my friend Sharon who is crazy about her and happy to give her a new home.

Moving is no easy feat. I live upstairs, so all the stuff has to go down the stairs and into the truck, driven to the storage unit, loaded onto trolleys and into the elevator up to the fourth floor, then arranged and stacked like some kind of sophisticated Rubik's Cube closed behind a big grey metal roll-down garage door. In anticipation of using this storage as a giant closet, I keep all the things I think I may need close to the door. When I roll up the door, there across ten feet are racks of clothing, an armoire packed full of boxes of shoes and purses for weather and lifestyle different than the sunny little island I am headed for.

There, now. I am officially homeless. As much as I love the tree house, I am happy to have my freedom. It feels good to me. Go, go and live the life of your dreams. I just want to try something else. I am completely mobile now. I pay what few bills I have, health and car insurance, cell phone and storage unit on auto-pay each month and check my banking on-line.

What will I do for a job when I get there? All I know for sure is that I want a no-brainer job. I don't want to take my worries home with me. I want to go in, do my thing, make money and go home. I want to work somewhere on the water, with a great view, be around happy people, and be outside. I want to bartend at a Tiki Bar on the beach.

Brittany is my worst critic. She doesn't understand at all. Why would I throw away everything I have worked so hard for to be a waitress? "You have a terrible short-term memory," she reminds me. She doesn't like the idea of her executive mom who went to work in suits and heels slinging drinks. She doesn't want to tell her friends what her mom is doing. I have always pushed for the best education money can buy for her. Knowledge is power. I want her to have more choices in life than I had. I don't want her to struggle and have to scratch and claw for every scrap she gets. So why am I giving up the very life I have paved the way for her to have? In some ways, I think I am putting her on a bigger treadmill than the one I just jumped off of. She would like things the way they were, normal parents who live in the same house she grew up in, with normal, steady jobs. She is worried that I am unstable.

I think it shouldn't matter to her. She's tucked away neatly at school. She has a great apartment and money in the bank for her expenses. All she needs to do is focus on her classes and making good grades. Not like when I went to college, working a full-time job, maintaining an apartment, paying for tuition, and going to classes. I did have something she doesn't, and that is a place to call home. Even though I hardly talked to my parents the years I went to school, I always knew where they were. They never came to visit me, never saw my apartment or knew my roommates, but I could always go home.

Two suitcases and my computer are about all I can fit into my little sports car. Buddy is expecting me around 5:00 p.m. Map in hand, water bottle, sunglasses, CD player loaded, I am off. Three hours is plenty of time to get there. Unfortunately, I miss the short-cut exit costing me an extra half-hour or so. I arrive unscathed, and to my surprise, to a little dinner party with Julie and Bobby and another couple, Frankie and Betty who have come over to meet the new girl. Buddy pops the champagne and we toast to my arrival in Matlacha. What a lovely welcome.

Buddy likes being the life of the party. He is happy when he is around people. He has led an interesting life and just a few years ago, was at the top of his game. He purchased a new three-bedroom house, had a new truck, boat, a Harley, and a girlfriend or two. The air conditioning business in Florida provided him with a good living. With no children or alimony to pay, life was all about Buddy and having fun. He has a good circle of friends he has made over the sixteen years he has lived on Matlacha. He knows everyone in the local bars where he spends his time.

I like hanging out with Buddy and his friends, but I need to work, so during the day, I go off job hunting. I had no idea how seasonal this area of South Florida is, but none of the restaurants are ready to hire and I don't want to drive into town to work. I came here to live and work by the water, not in town. I also thought I could work in a very popular island vacation spot, Sanibel Island, the next island over. But I quickly realize it isn't easy to drive there and when season comes, the traffic will make the commute much longer, which is not something I am interested in. I apply at golf courses to drive the beer cart and at restaurants as a bartender or server, but it is too early in the season.

So for a week or so, Buddy and I go boating, take turns cooking and running the roads. I love it here and I love being on the water. Each night, around seven, I look out the window and see the glow that will soon be sunset. I persuade Buddy to jump into my convertible and ride to the bridge to watch it. This becomes my routine, morning and night. I rise early, take my coffee with me and go to the bridge. It is perfect on chilly mornings. The view is fantastic, the dolphins glide by and the boaters make their way to their favorite fishing spots. Buddy says he has watched more sunsets with me in just a few weeks than he has the whole time he's lived here. After just a few days, I know I have to have my little sea foam green Vespa to ride around the island. So I bring it to Matlacha. I loved riding my little scooter in Orlando and now, having it here is even better.

Each morning, *The Apache* shrimp boat comes back from sea and docks in her slip. I watch the young muscular sailors work the ropes and unload today's catch. After a week or two, they start to wave to me on the bridge and shout, "Hello scooter girl!" I feel at home here. I feel like I belong.

My little yellow bedroom is perfect for me. I have a white wicker headboard and dresser. I add a few personal touches and bring way too much clothing. I don't know what my job will be or the type of clothing it will require. I have the space, so no harm done.

One day I find an old Tony Robbins motivational CD and pop it in as I drive to the airport to pick up Buddy and Julie. "You are not in a relationship because you don't want to be," Tony says. "Even if you say you want to be. Because you have associated more pain with being in a relationship than the pleasure you will get from it. You may want love and companionship but..." Boy, did that ring a bell with me. Buddy and his friends don't understand why I am doing what I am doing or why I am not in a relationship. They don't know my pain.

I start to work in a charming little art gallery filled with light and color. Everyone who works at the shop is female. We have fun together and I will get more hours when the tourist season starts. I think I will need to work two jobs.

In September, I apply for a job at Portobello's, a nice marina bar, not on the island but not in town either. The moment I walk in, I know it is the place for me. The manager, Jon, hires me on the spot. I have no experience, but tell him I do. I have never waited on a table in my life. Perhaps he knows, perhaps it doesn't matter. I feel an instant unspoken attraction between us. The way he walks, the way he speaks, the way his eyes look like dark chocolate pools with long eyelashes. He is always a gentleman, a proper young man with appropriate upbringing. He is wise beyond his years. He is like a cat who silently positions himself around the restaurant. From his strategic perches, he can see everything, but go unnoticed by everyone. Sometimes he is stretched out and relaxed, and at other times he is alert, ready to pounce. He goes unnoticed by everyone but me. I am acutely aware of his presence. I completely lose my concentration whenever he comes close. All he has to do is come within a few feet of me and my whole body becomes aware of him, his rhythm, his breath and his scent.

When he comes up behind me when I am at the computer putting in an order, I can barely breathe, let alone think. Jon is easily a foot taller than me, especially when I wear my Croc's (boat shoes that make excellent server shoes because they don't slide) making me five feet tall. He towers over me as I stand between him and the computer screen. All I want him to do is gently kiss the back of my neck. He is attractive and handsome to me, but it is inappropriate. I can never let him know how I feel or what I want. He becomes my protector. He later tells me that if he said it once, he said it night after night to inquiring restaurant patrons, he didn't know about my personal life. Suitors would inquire and he would ward them off. I just worked there. With his great silent wisdom and my unwillingness to let anyone see into my past wounds, we understand each other.

Although he is a man of few words, he does give me some great pieces of advice, this being the most important: twenty years my junior, he asks me, "Did you come here to make friends or money?" So simple, but more times than I can remember, I heard his words. I don't make any girlfriends working here. It is an odd relationship. We are co-workers, us against them (the customers), yet we are competitors. Who gets the best tables or makes the most money?

So I work my tables. Without a friend in the world, my tables become my friends. I laugh and joke with them. I play with them. When a big roar of laughter rises up from a table, there I am, right in the middle of it. Teasing Jon, I say, "See there, you get a comedian and a server for the price of one."

"Yeah, I see the comedian, but where is the server," he shoots right back.

I may not be the best server in town, but my people have fun. I really enjoy my customers. I am asked out practically every day, and every day I give the same response, "I am not dating. I have gone through a tragedy. I am recovering."

One day as I am going into the kitchen, I pass the reception area of the restaurant and notice a blue-black butterfly painted on the wall as part of a beautiful mural. Just like the ones in the little shop in Atlanta.

"Was that butterfly always on the wall right there?" I ask the hostess.

"I don't know, I never noticed it before but the mural has been there since we opened."

Hmm! It's a sign that I am in the right place.

I share little pieces of my life with my tables. Once I told some people from Georgia that my daughter was a third-year college student at Emory. They taunt me about what a party school it is and they are sure she is living it up instead of studying. When I bring them the check, I slide it carefully across the table and say, "Now remember, I said Emory and the tuition is forty-four-thousand a year, so help me out a little." I am not too proud to go for the pity tip. They burst into laughter and request me to wait on them whenever they come in the restaurant.

Each night as I leave, I take a to-go cup filled with club soda, go to my car, exchange my work apron full of tip money for a towel from the trunk, and head for the deserted pool and hot tub across the parking lot. I would have enjoyed the company of my co-workers, but know that it would quickly get out of hand, and late-night laughter would turn into drunken parties that would alert security. So, I keep to myself. My nightly visits to the hot tub are solo. I strip naked and go back and forth between the steaming hot tub and the heated swimming pool. The lights in the pool go out at ten so by the time I arrive it is totally dark, except for the moonlight shining down over the palm trees and casting a lovely glow. On nights when I am lucky, the stars are so bright, it is like looking into the soul of the universe. The combination of the heat, the cool refreshment of the pool, then back into the swirling heat of the hot tub is dizzying to my aching body. My legs and feet throb. Some nights I am so exhausted from work all I can do is soak, becoming more and more relaxed with each shot of hot and cold. Other nights my body reacts in that familiar way to the intense stimulation. Goosebumps awaken my senses. I become instantly aroused as the hot water swirls around my legs that are spread open wide. Oh how I wish for the company of a lover, but it isn't meant to be. My luck with men is less than encouraging.

Days turn into weeks and before I know it, Thanksgiving is coming. I think it would be fun to have Brittany come to visit, but she wants no part of my new world. I try to explain that Buddy and I are just housemates, that she can stay with me on my side of the house and there is plenty of room for her. She hates the idea of my waiting tables and caring for some "random Agent Orange guy in some random house in some random town." She would rather stay at school than come visit. Besides, I have to work on Thanksgiving and she doesn't want to sit at a table of strangers. I am disappointed, but know I can't force myself onto her. She will just have to come around in her own time.

Two days before Thanksgiving, I get the call. Brittany is crying. The campus is deserted and everyone else has gone home to their families and she is the only one left. She has nowhere to go, no place to call home. Sobbing over the phone, she tells me she didn't think it would be this way. She thought she would be fine, that other students would be staying too, but now she is alone. There is nothing I can do. It is too late to get a flight for her to come to me. It is too far for her to drive, and I am working and can't go to her. My heart breaks as I try my best to comfort her, but there is nothing to say or do to lessen the pain of *not having a home to go to.* Again, the guilt of not being the "Best Mom" and shielding her from suffering, stabs through my heart. My selfishness is causing my child to suffer. I tried to get her to come a month ago, but she refused. Why is that my fault? After a horrible twenty minutes on the phone, we hang up without a solution. The long weekend finally passes.

One day, I am waiting on one of my regular customers, Pete, a nice man who comes into the restaurant almost daily. He has just moved to the marina and is living on his sailboat. We chat easily about lots of things.

"When is your next day off?" He asks me.

"I have Tuesdays and Wednesdays off." Not that it matters to me what day of the week I have off. I have nothing do anyway, so Saturday off or Monday off makes no difference to me.

"Would you like to go sailing with me?" He asks.

"Sure, but I don't know how to sail," I tell him.

"Not to worry, I do. Where do you want to go?"

"I don't know, that's up to you. How about somewhere close, but where we can see the sunset. I don't get to see it actually touch the water because it is blocked by other islands," I explain.

"Okay," he says, "Let's get started early. Come to my slip, P18, around 9:00 a.m."

I think it will be fun. I am looking forward to a lazy day on a boat. So, at nine o'clock Tuesday morning, I find the dock and walk past all different kinds of boats. They are big, small, sailboats, trawlers, and power boats.

I don't really know what to expect other than a sail boat. I am pleasantly surprised when I find Pete adjusting the lines of a beautiful forty-two foot Hunter Passage. She is a beauty, new and modern, white with navy blue trimmings. He gives me a tour. She is very luxurious. I love all the wood.

"All we have to do is disconnect a few things and we are off," Pete says.

"Great, tell me what I need to do," I say.

We motor down the canal, headed out to sea. As we round the bend, there is a sudden hard rub and the boat comes to a quick stop.

"What's going on?" I ask.

"We must have come aground. The boat has a five foot draft," Pete says.

"Okay," I agree, not really knowing what that means.

"It is low tide, but according to the charts, we should be able to pass through this canal," he says, "If not, we just have to wait a couple of hours until the tide comes in."

"I don't care. It is my day off and I am out on the water. So, do you have any beer on this boat?" I ask.

"Yes, I have Corona. Would you like one?"

"Sure, it's five o'clock somewhere, isn't it?" I reply. I am not going anywhere, so why not relax and enjoy the ride.

We sit, stuck for about two hours. Conversation comes easily. The sun is warm, I am happy. My feet are propped up over the side of boat. Finally we break loose and head out to sea. Once in open water with the warm sun glistening like diamonds, we start cruising. I can breathe. I draw in the sea air. I am relaxed. I can't believe what a lucky girl I am. I can feel the drug of being on the open water wash over my body. I am home. I love being on the water. After several hours, we anchor, Pete fires up the grill and prepares a feast for us. I doze off for a little afternoon nap. I have found paradise. We spend the whole afternoon floating, then the sun sets and it is a million-dollar show. At nine o'clock when it is totally dark, the stars come out. It is amazing.

"We can go back tonight or wait until the morning," Pete says.

"Morning is fine, I just want to call Buddy and let him know I am not coming home tonight," I tell him. After what happened when Tom died, I want to make sure I tell someone where I am and how I can be reached. I fall asleep on deck and Pete covers me with a big blanket. I sleep like a baby. I am home.

The next morning we return to the marina at about ten. It is low tide again, and again we get stuck. I am not as patient as I was the first time around, but I am not really going anywhere so why get excited. This behavior will reward me handsomely. I have no idea what it means to Pete. My non-reaction is far more important than my reaction, a trait that is very important in a first mate.

Pete and I take the boat out just a handful of times when one day in December, I walk down the docks and see a *For Sale* sign on the Ooh La La.

"Pete, what is this?" I ask, pointing to the sign.

"Well, you know, I have to sell her if I want to live in a house."

"Live in a house," I question. "why would you want to do that? My God, you have a million-dollar view every day and if you get tired of that one, all you have to do is move. Have you ever thought about taking her island-hopping before you sell her?"

"Yes, of course, it's my dream," Pete says, "I would love that, but I don't want to go alone. It wouldn't be any fun and besides, I can't handle the boat by myself. Who am I going to get to go on a trip like that for three or four months?"

"I'll go," I reply. The words fly out of mouth before I have a chance to even consider what I am saying. It is on my *list of things I want to do.* I have always wanted to live on a sailboat in the islands.

"Are you serious?" Pete asks.

There are a few things to consider. The *season* is just starting and it is a chance for me to make a lot of money at the restaurant. There are other questions. How much would it cost? How far will we go? Will it be safe?

In short order, we have a plan. I will be paid crew. It will be enough to cover my commitments at home and Pete will pay for the expenses during the trip. I will stay onboard until April, around Brittany's birthday, and fly home from whatever island we reach. Pete will hire someone else to get the boat back to Florida if he decides to return at all. We will leave on New Year's Eve. Sharon, my friend, who has been keeping Pooka would love to make her a permanent part of their family. She is happy there. I give my notice to quit at work, which gives me enough time to pack up my room and take a quick ski trip to Aspen for Christmas.

# Chapter 21

*Aspen*
*December 2006*

"Where do you live?" asks the distinguished older man seated next to me at the bar.

"Well," I squirm, "could you start with an easier question?"

Puzzled and intrigued, he bites, "How about, what do you do for a living?"

"Well, that's a tough one too," I tease. "Actually, I am homeless and jobless." Just saying the words brings up two emotions. One complete bliss and optimism, almost childlike giddiness and the other is, what in Dear God's name are you doing?

"Really?" he replies with surprise and skepticism, looking me over trying to decide just how crazy I am. "Well, it suits you," he says with a chuckle.

I tell him my story and he listens with a twinkle in his eye.

"Well let me introduce myself," he says, extending his hand. "I'm Hal."

"I know who you are," I reply.

"You do?" He says with raised eyebrows.

"Yes. We've met before. I have been in your bedroom," I state matter-of-factly.

"Excuse me, but I think I would remember you, especially if you have been in my bedroom," he says.

I lean over and whisper in his ear, "You let me wear your mink slippers."

Now his mind is racing to figure out what I am saying. He does have mink slippers, but he doesn't remember me. Letting him off the hook, I tell him I attended his big annual holiday party last year and the doorman made me take off my Uggs, and since I wasn't wearing any socks, I was walking around the party with bare feet and made such a fuss about giving up my shoes, that the host was alerted. So, Hal had come up behind me and whispered in my ear, "I hear you are the with girl cold feet."

"Yes, I am."

"Follow me."

"Where are we going?"

"To my bedroom," he stated.

"Thanks for the invitation, but I hardly know you," I teased.

"Do you want some slippers or not?" he said, unamused.

I followed him as he opened the door to a huge master suite complete with a king-size platform bed dressed in a dark brown mink bedspread. He glided over to the dresser next to the bed and retrieved a matching pair of mink slippers.

"Put them back in the drawer before you leave," he instructed, as he handed me the slippers and walked out of the room.

He remembers the story, but apparently I didn't make too big of an impression on him.

Today could be different, but as timing would have it, I am ready to get on a boat and sail away.

I love Aspen. Of all the little ski towns I have been to, Aspen is the real thing. It is complete with old buildings and a real downtown, not something that the developers have modeled after Disney World. High in the Rockies, it is hard to get to, so only the serious come to Aspen. It boasts 300 days of blue skies along with lots of snow and sunshine. It started out as a mining town, then in the early '70's became the first Mecca for health fanatics.

I have been coming to Aspen every ski season for years now. I am traveling with Anne again this year. At the last minute, I came along to keep her company. Brittany made her plans for Christmas long ago, she wasn't going to spend another holiday on campus like Thanksgiving. Anne and I just barely make it to Aspen. It is the snowstorm of the decade. I got the last flight out of Denver and the snow is coming down. It is a winter wonderland. We end our day in the outdoor hot tub. It is fun to run across the snow in our swimsuits and jump into the hot bubbling water.

Just a few days later, finally aboard the Ooh La La, I can breathe. Pete drove me to Orlando with the last bit of worldly possessions I own, and we stuffed them into my small storage unit. It seems odd now because possessions mean the least to me. My ski trip to Aspen with friends is what life is about, not some furniture, papers, and clothes. Oh, but I do need the Vespa. How can I be "scooter girl" without it?

I am ready to live on the Ooh La La for three months, ready to slow down and relax. I am ready to sleep all day and all night, ready for hours and hours to pass by without need or want. Oh, how I am ready for everything and nothing. Is this how it is meant to be? Drawn to the water like a magnet, I crave the sunlight sparkling on it, content that it's sunlight and not diamonds. I want miles of blue water. I know I don't fit into the mold. I have had invitations of fortune and fake ones. It doesn't matter to me, because in the end, it is the adventure I seek. Now, at forty-five-years-old, I know this about myself: I am not about the accumulation of material things, I am about adventure. I collect experiences.

# Chapter 22

*Bonvoyage*
*December 31, 2006*

Our two-hour jaunt to Cabbage Key is a delightful warm-up run. I take my place in the cockpit on this great adjustable recliner cushion. It is high enough in back to rest my head. My feet are propped up on the side of the boat and the view is pure open water. The sun dances on the ever-changing surface. Pete, happiest when he is at the helm, takes the captain's spot. Bambi, Pete's dog, sits between us. I bask in the sun and let the gentle rocking of the boat cradle me in and out of a lazy sleep. This is my spot. It's pure heaven. There is something about the water that just relaxes every muscle in my body. My shoulders are down, my breath is full and steady. My brain stops that gawd-awful racing. There is no place to go and nothing to do. I crave this, this nothingness. This will be my life for the next three months.

We arrive at Cabbage Key and ease into a little cove that is perfect for anchoring. We are not the only ones to discover this spot since other boats have already settled in. I thought our boat was big and quite nicely appointed until I look around. Our boat is white with navy blue canvas. The living quarters below are beautiful polished brown teakwood, rounded doorways, dark blue couches, and a flat screen TV complete the salon. The galley has everything—fridge, freezer, microwave, coffee grinder, coffee maker, toaster, oven, and three-burner stove. There is even a grill on-deck. Two cabins, two heads, and lots of storage—way more room than I had in the camper. I brought about the same amount of clothing and stuff, two suitcases and a computer.

When we dingy over to the restaurant, the boats get even larger and more lavish. A cigarette boat is revving its twin 500 horsepower Corvette engines. I can't tell if he is coming in, going out or just showing off. Power boaters and sailors are about as different as night and day. I have always known there is a difference between them, but I thought it had more to do with nature than personality. This will require more thought and observation.

We are dressed in our pirate costumes ready to go to a New Year's Eve party. Actually, we didn't know the party had a theme until yesterday. Lucky for Pete, he was a pirate for Halloween, so he had a costume. As for me, I scrounged around the boat and found a pirate flag and pinned it into a wrap-around skirt. I took a white shirt and tied it as a midriff, threw on some beads and a scull cap and, *viola*, a costume is made. Pete looks great in his triangle hat and outfit complete with boots and cuffs. Everyone at the party is into the theme. There is lots of growling, toasting, and pinching the wenches. We eat a fantastic meal and dance the night away to a great DJ. The restaurant is an old Victorian house with lots of funky little rooms and a huge screened-in front porch. Decorated tables fill every room. The bar is in the library complete with books, wood paneling, and a fireplace. All the other rooms have one-dollar bills taped to the walls and ceiling, I mean covering every inch of space. Some tattered, some written on, but all are the real thing. Even on this remote island offshore, we still have a TV to watch the ball drop in Times Square. Would we have been able to ring in the New Year without it? Would have we been able to know what time it is without it? Some things are just so ingrained in our culture. I guess it is just the way it is.

Alas, we find blue water and clear skies. The dolphins come to play in our wake and the crabbers are out tending their traps, thousands of them. We must be careful not to cruise over the traps and get the lines wrapped around the propeller. The following afternoon, we cross from the Gulf of Mexico into the Atlantic Ocean. The water immediately turns even bluer. We have logged about 135 miles since leaving the marina. Tonight we will anchor at Marathon Key and wait for good weather to make our first big open water hop to the Bahamas.

We fire up the grill and have dinner on deck. The sunset is a bit blocked by clouds, but we do have my first ever moonset. About 7:30 a.m., we watch the full moon go down over the horizon and minutes later, the sun rises on the opposite side of the sea. Has this been going on for centuries and I am only now seeing it? What else happens in nature that I haven't noticed or haven't taken the time to see? Show me more please, Mother Nature.

In the harbor, we make friends with fellow sailors, Jerry and Trish, and decide to make the pass to the Bahamas with them. Jerry is a salty dog, and has spent a long time on the water. Trish is a rookie like me. They appear to be an odd couple. Pete and I make a bet to see who will last longer, us or them. At any rate, we are grateful for his knowledge. We may try it tomorrow, but so far the weather looks better for Friday. No rush, we would rather wait for the best sailing conditions.

Three days go by and we are still in the marina in Marathon but there is a weather break today. Our plan is to motor sail the 100 miles to Chub Cay in the Bahamas leaving at 3:00 p.m. arriving at 8:00 a.m. I am not thrilled about the overnight sail, but that appears to be our best option. We will be in deep water on a straight course.

I like living on the boat. There is lots of time to read. Being outside all the time is the best part. I love watching the sunshine dancing on the water. The moon has been full the past few nights and makes for lovely evenings on deck. We've been in the harbor and have been entertained by all of the activity from the other boats. It is fun to see all the variety in gear and style. When we were in Cabbage Key I thought we were slumming it, now in Marathon I realize we are going first class.

Bambi is proving difficult to live with. She is a seven-year-old Shih Tzu. Pete got her from a shelter and she hates me. She bit me when I tried to move her out of the way. She hasn't learned where to go to the bathroom now that she is staying on the boat all the time. Apparently this was not considered before we left. It doesn't amuse me. Yesterday she peed on my bed, so I spent the day in the Laundromat at the marina. The killer part is she wants to sit by me all the time and sleep right next to me. She does have an adorable face. We'll see who lasts longer, me or the dog.

Finally we are officially cruising for one week. After five days in the harbor, we head out on a sunny, fabulous day with water and gas tanks full. We carry seventy-gallons of diesel, and food and beverages are stocked to capacity. We set motor-sail at two o'clock to cross the Atlantic Gulf Stream, heading to the Bahamas for our destination, Chub Cay, just north of Andros Islands. Traveling at six or seven knots, we should arrive in shallow water eighteen hours later or around 8:00 a.m. The weather is calling for winds from the south-southwest, which means winds on our backs increasing our speed and pushing us in the right direction. We have wind speed of ten to fifteen knots with seas one to three feet.

After several hours of watching the GPS which Pete has programmed, I start to do the math. Now let's think about this. We are only going one hundred and ten miles, so why is it taking eighteen hours? I know people who made the crossing in four hours, although that was in a powerboat, not a sailboat. Here and now, I learn about sailing. Why are we under motor power if we are sailing? We have the main sail up, but it is directly in line with the boat, therefore not catching any wind. We are under motor because the winds are not reliable enough and we are under a time restraint. I learn for the first time that even though we are in a sail boat, true *sailing* without a motor is rare and only lasts for short periods of time, all depending on the wind. Why sail at all? I ponder. Why not just have a powerboat and get there? As the hours and days unfold, I think I will learn.

Is this not what I have longed for? Having hours and hours of unhurried time, with nothing to do, nowhere to go? On the RV trip with my Dad, I wished we had more time to putter, nap in the sun, and smell the deep green earth of the forest. So here, now, is my chance to really take it slow. My wish has come true.

Okay, let's go back to the eighteen-hours thing. Six knots of nautical speed means six miles an hour. I am a runner and that means a ten-minute mile. Yes, that means I can run faster than we are going on this boat. Pete tells me eight knots is about the fastest this boat can or should go, so even if we added *sail speed*, we are going about as fast as we are going to go.

Now, let's talk about eighteen hours of sailing. Pete said he will take the helm until 2:00 a.m., and then I will take over for four hours so he can sleep. That should bring us into daybreak at about six. I have never sailed on a boat before these last few days and I trust Pete because he has years of experience, but Pete trusting me enough to sleep in the dead of night while we are out in 2800 feet of open water? That is a different story. Do I trust myself?

After a few hours, we are blessed with an amazing sunset. The sky turns an array of soft hues from pink to yellow and back. It takes a good hour for complete darkness to set in. We have lost sight of land now and can see faint residual light from what we are guessing is Nassau. Moonrise arrives about 10:00 p.m. It is a big, bright moon, not full but full enough to light up the night. We are able to distinguish between sea and sky all night. It is a lovely night to be on the water.

With the GPS guiding our path and the auto-pilot making minor adjustments to the course, we motor along. We have all our lights on, running lights, anchor light, and steaming lights. Lights from other boats can be seen miles away. Easy enough, I think. Easy enough until the weather forecast is just a little off. A little off on the water makes a big difference. One or two knots of boat speed is a lot. Five or ten knots of wind speed is significant. Seas of one to two feet are steady, three to four feet are rolling, five to six feet raises the stern high into the air slapping it down hard.

I stay on deck in the cockpit with Pete until about 10:00 p.m. The winds are fifteen to twenty knots, the seas are four to five feet—not exactly the smooth sailing we anticipated. We are prepared though. We both have our foul weather gear on and are harnessed to the boat. *Jack lines* or safety lines we can clip on are out should we need to go out on to the deck. We have done the drill, so I know where all the emergency gear is stored. We have the *run bag* out and packed with provisions we will need if we have to get off the boat in a hurry. We ride along, neither of us discussing the conditions or our options. They are what they are. The waves seem big to me, but I have no reference. I don't feel like we are going to tip over, it's like a carnival ride. I am not scared, but wonder how much bigger they will get. At this point, there are only two options, keep going or turn back. We are at about the halfway point. To me going or returning is the same. So we go on.

I go below to sleep. It is loud with the engine running full out, water gurgling on all sides of the boat and the constant heaving and slapping of the boat riding out the waves. I am not strapped into the bed and awake often to the rolling and banging of the boat hitting hard on the waves. Somewhere in my sleep, I do hear a rush of water, like a bucket being emptied, but it doesn't concern me enough to get up. I wasn't able to distinguish if it was outside or inside. So I sleep on.

At 3:00 a.m., Pete comes below to wake me. He has had enough and is ready to sleep. It is an hour later than we had arranged. He decided to stay at the helm a little longer as the seas have changed while I slept. Winds, at their worst, had gotten to thirty-five knots producing six foot swells, but have calmed a little. Now as I take my place in the cockpit and check the gauges, the stats are about the same as when I went below to sleep. It is dark but I can see the horizon, all 360 degrees of it. The moon is bright with some stars, some clouds. The engine and the sea are loud. My earlier concern of falling asleep and failing at my duty goes away instantly. The rocking and rolling of the boat keep me awake just to stay in my spot.

I am alone for the next three hours, just me, the blackness, the sound of the engine, the wind and waves and the glow from the panel of gauges. They become my only companions. I am not scared. I look around, searching for a light. There is none. It is just me, the darkness and the boat on this vast ocean. I like it. I like this contentment of being totally alone. It is new to me. I am okay with it.

I think of Pete sleeping below. We are virtually strangers. Two people whose paths crossed at just the right moment. We are two people who saw an opportunity and took it, along with a big leap of faith, and trusted another person. I don't know if I would trust me as much as Pete does. This boat is his pride and joy and his home or, much more importantly, his everything. We met at the marina, spent only a few odd days here and there at sea or even in each other's company. Now here we are, setting off for three months together.

He is newly divorced. His wife of ten years gave him his walking papers. He has only been married once; Pete was her fourth husband. She is a trust fund baby. She got the houses and he got the boat and a check. He definitely wanted more from life than the way their marriage worked out. Boy, does that sound familiar. He was ready for an adventure, ready to get on with the business of living. Who knows where life will take either of us, but what is the harm of taking a few months to play? We are both in relationship recovery and know that neither of us is in a place to start something new. So we take it for an adventure. By daybreak, Pete comes up to join me. The seas have calmed down now that we are in much shallower water. We are treated to another moonset and sunrise. I remind myself not to get immune to the majesty of these events. Mother Nature puts on a different, spectacular show for us everyday and we are too busy to even look out the window to see it. With hours of solitude on the water ahead of me on this trip, I imagine I will eagerly wait for the shows.

We sail on through the entire day, setting anchor in twelve feet of water and still twenty-five miles from our destination of Chub Cay. During the night, our speed had dropped to three knots or so because of having to fight the waves, so we didn't travel as far as we had projected.

And a beautiful sunny day it is indeed, to be on the ocean with big puffy white clouds against a blue sky. The water is clear and constantly changing from green to blue and back, depending on whether the bottom is sandy or grassy. The sea is calm, one to two foot waves and winds of ten to fifteen knots.

By late afternoon, the engine is shut off and the boat is still, other than the gentle, constant rocking. We go up on deck, toast a safe passage with rum drinks in hand, and lie back on the deck to watch the sunset. Pete is exhausted. I've napped off and on all day and feel quite rested.

Now that we are safe and secure, Pete asks me if I heard the great crash of water last night. I vaguely remember it. He said a huge wave came over the side of boat, swamping the cockpit and rushing down the stairs into the salon below. The weather was not at all what he thought it would be. Immediately, he secured the hatch, earnestly hoping that would be the only wave like that for the night. To our good fortune, it was. He worried that I would get spooked and not want to continue. That was the worst of it for him. I am glad I didn't get up, ignorance is bliss, at least this time.

I suggest Pete get a shower while I make dinner. We are both starving. Everything inside the boat is sticky from salt water and sea air. I light the gas stove and clean while the meat is browning. After dinner, we switch roles. Pete cleans up the kitchen while I shower. To my surprise, I learn that neither the gas stove nor the shower was ever used on this boat. He has owned it for three years. We go up on deck where Pete enjoys a little port sherry and a cigar. It is completely black out with no distinction from sky and sea. The darkest part of the night is between sundown and moonrise. Tonight, that is between eight and ten. I go out on the foredeck in my pajamas and sit, resting my back on the dingy strapped there. All black except a million, billion stars of all sizes and brilliance that fill the sky. Some twinkle so brightly that I don't think they are even stars. Some are so tiny and clustered together they look like a Paeve diamond bracelet. This sight brings tears to my eyes, it is the most amazing thing I have ever seen. I am in complete and utter awe.

About noon the next day, we reach Chub Cay, go through customs and dock in a slip for the next two nights. A cold front is moving in and we want the protection of the marina for the changing winds and rain. I didn't expect to be docking, I thought we would anchor out and dinghy in. We need to come to shore to fill water and gas tanks, but we make our own electricity, so there is no real reason to dock and incur the cost. Oh well, it is Pete's call. I would rather be safe than sorry.

Clearing customs is uneventful other than my surprise when a customs agent drives from the airport to the fuel dock where we are tied up to review our documents. He comes to us? This seems odd until I learn that the three-month entry fee for the boat is $300. That is more than they collect from an entire small aircraft in tourist tax. We have all the right documentation including vaccination certificates for Bambi.

A housing development is under construction right next to the marina. With the constant noise of trucks and hammers, it's hard to believe we are on an island. Who would buy a house here? Other than the marina, there is nothing on the island.

Off to explore, we find Harry's Bar and have a Kalik, the Bahamian beer, then head to the beach for sunset. Later we return to the clubhouse at Chub Cay dressed in elegant island casual and enjoy a feast of lobster, grouper and a lovely bottle of wine. This is another unexpected treat. For some reason, I thought we would be eating on the boat and wasn't expecting the luxury of fine dining. Harry and the staff serve us with that ever so gracious easy island flair. My shoulders are down and relaxed. We have arrived!

We are the only customers other than one couple sitting a few tables away. He is handsome with white hair, but I guess only in his early fifties. She looks to be about in her forties and pretty with long dark hair and beautiful green eyes. Both are tan, fit and trim. We strike up a conversation with them. They live primarily in Switzerland, but keep a place in Vero Beach, Florida and are building a home here on the island. They are currently living in the maid's house until the real house is built. The big house is up on top of the hill with a sweeping view of the sea, and was completely blown away in Hurricane Andrew, leaving only the concrete foundation. They have new plans drawn and are ready to start construction. They will need to move out of the maid's house so the construction crew can move-in and have a place to live. Five Bahamians will build the house and live onsite. Food and housing are part of the building cost on an island. All materials will be shipped in containers and provided by the owners. The key is to have everything on site and ready to go because delays while waiting for supplies are costly. There is no Home Depot around the corner to run to.

The conversation is easy and they are eager to share their story and interesting little things about the island. They are among just a handful of homeowners, but they don't seem to mind the development of the marina and all the new houses under construction. Evidently this is not the first company to come along with big plans. This couple seems to have a *lets wait and see what happens* attitude. Remote island living and hurricanes change things, sometimes quickly, sometimes over time.

We wake to overcast and chilly weather. It rained overnight and to our dismay, we learn that we must have taken water into the V-berth storage area because everything up front is wet. Our only option is to drag the stuff out and put it on deck to dry. Pete also discovers a problem with the head holding tank. We can't dump it. He has an extra macerator pump and hopes that replacing it will do the trick. It is a smelly job, so he sends me to the clubhouse while he works. He instructs me to come back in an hour. I ask the bartender to turn the TV to Oprah.

Two hours later, hungry, I return to the boat. Our beautiful boat looks like the Beverly Hillbillie's truck. Up top is piled with all kinds of stuff including a mattress, blankets and bags. Down below, the floor boards are all pulled up with tubes and tools everywhere. Dear God, did a bomb go off in here or what—and the smell! Pete is dripping with sweat. I hope this situation can be fixed or we are nix-nil on the trip. Not to worry, I am told. We have a good belly laugh in spite of ourselves.

The tank is empty, but the pump is not the problem. Pete rigged the back head to by-pass the tank, but needs more hose to make the forward head work. So we are down to one head and will have to share until we can buy the hose we need. By noon we have the boat put back together and Pete goes to the marina shower to bathe.

Our neighbor at the dock is a thirty-two foot sailboat from Vero Beach owned by Ingrid and Erik, a husband and wife team both German, who have lived in the US since they were young. Later Big Rosie pulls in with Captain

Bob, a stout businessman from New Jersey who listens to classical music. He is traveling from Ft. Lauderdale to Puerto Rico where he will leave his boat for six months, and then return and travel again for a few months. He has hired Jim from an Internet website for ten days of his jaunt. Jim paid for his flight to meet the boat and crews in exchange for room, board, and adventure. They have never met before. Bob has three other crew like this lined up to join him at different stops.

I take my first three-mile run in months. It feels good to be back out on the road.

Our last day in Chub Cay, we take Bambi for a little walk down the beach where scattered on the sand are the most amazing butterfly shells. They are mostly white with pale bands—of yellow pink and coral, but the yellow ones are the prettiest. I tell myself I can't bring home every shell I find, but I can't help it. I have never seen anything like them.

## What I learned after being on the Boat for Two Weeks

Boats are not feet-friendly. Crocs are to be worn at all times.

Weather forecasters lie. Everyone has an opinion of the weather. Do your own thing.

Nothing stays dry.

Living onboard is fun.

Marinas are pure entertainment.

Boats are tree houses for grown ups—the more gadgets and toys, the better.

VH radios are like walkie-talkies. Everything has code names like in a spy movie.

We don't sail, we motor.

We don't go fast. I can run faster than the boat.

You must really love a dog to have it on a boat.

Sailing is a small community. We keep seeing the same people at different ports.

Our dinghy is a pain to take on and off the boat.

After staying in Chub Cay for four nights waiting for smooth sailing weather, we decide it is time to move on. We go only seven miles. The winds are about twenty knots and waves are six to eight feet. Not exactly our best choice, but who knows how long we could have been stuck at Chub Cay. The upside to this crossing is that we are not going directly into the wind. We are on a thirty-degree angle of the waves, so we roll along rather than hitting directly into them making the bow crash up and down.

We slip into a little cove protected by two deserted islands, Bird Cay and Whale Cay. The water is pristine and the sand on the beach is pure white. We anchor in as shallow water as we can, thinking that will be calmer because the winds are making the boat rock. We draw five feet for the keel, so we think we are good in six-and-a-half feet of water. The water is so clear that we can easily see the bottom of the boat. It is too rough to take the dinghy out, so we settle into a lazy day on the boat. I make rum drinks, sun, and listen to happy music. The boat has an awesome stereo system and we are stocked with lots of music. We also have a whole library of DVD movies to watch during quiet evenings. The sun is too bright for me to see the computer screen on deck, so I am typing away downstairs in the salon.

By dark, the rocking of the boat increases and I am not feeling good, not throwing up, not dizzy, just a pit in my stomach. I haven't had this feeling at all since I have been onboard and am surprised that after two weeks, I get it now. I decide to skip dinner and spend the night on deck. The waves become higher and the wind stronger, making the boat rock harder and harder from side to side. Rolling three-foot swells raise the boat up and down in rocking horse style. All of a sudden, there is a substantial crash as though we have hit something. There are no rocks around us. What can it be? We check the water depth. It is five-and-a-half feet. Not good. The tide is going out, something we hadn't planned on this far out in the ocean. The tide can change the water level up to three feet. That means that we could *keel over,* meaning lean the boat onto its side. At worst, we would take on water. Now I know where that expression, *keel over* came from. My mom used to say that all the time. The crash comes every couple of minutes and as the boat rises up with a wave, I squint my eyes and hope.

What we need to do is re-anchor in deeper water, but that means maneuvering the boat in high winds, in the dark, in a small body of water between two islands that have mostly rocky shorelines in two to twenty feet of water. Not good. So first we try letting out more anchor chain, which should float us into deeper water. This works for a little while, but after an hour, we are once again in too shallow water and the horrible crashing on the bottom of the ocean rattles the entire boat. We must pull up anchor and move. Now, to our dismay, we discover this is no longer an option. In order to pull up the anchor, the boat must be directly over the anchor so the claw will release from the sand. We cannot move the boat toward the anchor because the water is too shallow. We must wait for high tide at 2:00 a.m. or cut the anchor. Pete lets out the last 400 feet of anchor chain. It does the trick for the moment. Tide should be on the rise, so our plan is to move the boat in high tide. We can't wait until daylight because the next low tide is morning. The boat is really rocking and winds are twenty knots or so, even here in our little protected cove. About midnight, I go below to sleep; Pete will wake me at two. He will stay on deck, catching intermittent sleep.

At two o'clock, we are sitting on the deck discussing our plan of attack while the boat is rocking and the wind blowing strong. We are both wearing long pants and jackets. Pete will be harnessed to the boat at all times, so should he slip or lose his balance, he won't fall off. To add to our dilemma, the windless, which is the machine that automatically pulls up the anchor and chain, is not working. This means that Pete will be on his knees, bending down over the bow of the boat, hauling in 400 feet of heavy anchor chain. He is a big man, six feet tall, over 200 pounds and not exactly physically fit. I am not worried about him slipping or losing his balance, but I am worried about him passing out and falling overboard. Then he would be dangling, but still harnessed to the boat, and I will have to get him back in. The only way to do this is to lower him in the water and drag him to the swim platform at the back of the boat. No easy feat, but if he is unconscious and face down in the water, I will only have a minute or two to get him out. He doesn't want to wear a life jacket because it is too bulky to work in. I insist he wear a personal flare which will light should he hit the water. I put several dock lines out so I have something to work with. The horseshoe shaped man-over-board floatation device is clipped to the side of the boat ready to go, but it won't do any good if he is unconscious.

With only the glow of the instrument panel in front of me, I take the helm and Pete works his way out to the front of the boat, moving in rhythm with the waves and rocking of the boat in the wind. I can see him struggling. The deck light illuminates him enough so that I can see his red jacket and make out his hand signals, telling me when to power forward. The plan is to keep the nose into the wind until we break free, then turn the boat 180 degrees east toward open sea. We'll then circle around when we are in fifteen feet of water, head back into the wind, and drop anchor again. We can't hear each other at all over the howling wind. It is very dark. I can't make out land, but I can see the glow in the horizon at Club Key in the west and another fainter glow that is Nassau. There is also a red flashing light. These are my only markers.

We are both pleasantly surprised when the windless decides to work. That takes most of my concern away. We do exactly as planned and with luck on our side, we don't drift really fast and the re-anchor takes the first time. Safely back in the cockpit, we are both relieved. It is four o'clock, completely dark, wind whipping, boat rocking, but we are securely anchored for what is left of the night. Sleep is restless and I am awakened often by being rolled over in bed. The pit in my stomach is still there, not better or worse, but definitely not the way I want to spend the rest of the trip.

We wake the next morning to blue skies, aqua water, a light breeze, and warm air. I climb up on the deck and look around. It is truly paradise. What a difference from the last time I climbed up the ladder. A deserted cove and small private islands surround us. There is an old white lighthouse on a cliff at the end, calling for us to come and explore. It's time to lower the dinghy and head for land.

We launch on a little sandy beach about fifty feet from our anchored boat. The water is a little cooler than we hoped. I, for one, am not ready to take the plunge. We stroll the beach and check out a pavilion that is in fairly good shape. A small plane comes in real low. Our little deserted island isn't so deserted. That was the third small plane to land this morning. It is Saturday. Maybe people pop in for the weekend. We follow a little stone path that leads up to the road and then turns into a wider dirt road, which we hope will take us to the lighthouse. It does. We poke around. Going inside, we see no signs of life and it doesn't look like it ever held a light at all. We take pictures and soak up the panoramic view. The water is an incredible blue. That's what I asked for, blue water. Before we left, that's all I could talk about. I just want blue water. But now that I have blue water, I want warm, calm, blue water. I know, want, want, want.

The second night at Whale Cay, the winds come from the east and make two to four foot swells. We roll, but thank goodness no pounding. We decide to move to Nassau, weather or not. It is only thirty-one miles. Once we are under way, my tummy is back to normal, thank goodness. Even Pete admits his tummy felt it too.

# Chapter 23

*Nassau, Bahamas*
*January 2007*

Although the weather isn't what we are hoping for, we make the short, open water pass to New Province Island. We are hoping to make the thirty-mile trip in about five hours. Donning our foul weather gear and harnesses, we are ready for a rough ride. A few big waves hit us, but other than that we just rock and roll along. The seas are seven to ten feet, but look at the bright side, it is daylight. Arriving into Nassau Harbor at two-thirty on a sunny afternoon, we radio Harbor Patrol for permission to enter.

"Nassau Harbor Patrol, Nassau Harbor Patrol, this is the sailing vessel Ooh La La."

No response.

"Nassau Harbor Patrol, Nassau Harbor Patrol, this is the sailing vessel Ooh La La."

Again, no response.

Pete goes below to get the handheld VHS radio and calls from that, still no response. Pete is worried. Not having a working radio in a busy port is not good. We slow the engine and let a huge freighter enter before us. There is a little lighthouse at the mouth of the harbor. We see two cruise ships docked, lots of other boats going up and down and others anchored along near the banks. That is our plan too, to anchor. According to the chart, there are several places to choose from.

After calling about ten times and waiting a few minutes in between, we get a response. A voice with a heavy Bahamian accent says he is looking for the boat calling for Nassau Harbor Patrol. They are just busy; our radio is working fine.

"What is the name of your vessel and your registration number?"

Now we know how they keep track of who made customs and who hasn't. They can also keep track of where you are going and when your visa runs out. Ours is good for three months, then renewable for three more months for no additional cost. We recite our information and are given permission to enter. The water inside the harbor is still that beautiful aqua blue. I expected it to be brown and dirty, but it is not. We decide to cruise up and down the harbor, get an overview and check out the anchorage spots marked on the chart.

There is every imaginable size and shape vessel in this busy place. They range from huge oil tankers down to a jet ski. Beautiful sleek yachts sit next to old Bahamian crab boats. Then there are the ferries taking cars and passengers to the other islands, and don't forget the mail boat. It is a floating town. Hotels and buildings line the mainland side and the towers of the Atlantis Hotel are on the Paradise Island side.

Following the chart, we pull into our first choice anchorage spot and to our surprise, right next to Ingrid and Erik, the brown sailboat with the Hawaiian name we can't pronounce from Chub Cay. How bizarre. There are about twenty-five other boats in this area, so the space is tight. We need enough room to swing around when the current and winds change. We are forty-two feet and will have about fifty feet of anchor chain out.

I take the helm and Pete, standing on the bow, directs me into a spot he has chosen. He drops the anchor, but we continue to drift. The anchor doesn't take hold. It just keeps slipping along the bottom. We are getting too close to the other boats, so we decide to pull up, reposition ourselves, and try again. When the anchor is in sight, we realize that our anchor is hooked in someone else's anchor line. Pete is pulling with all his might, but we are drifting around backwards. Now we are twisted around and can see someone else's line wrapped around our keel back at the prop. This means we can't power the boat for fear that the line will get wrapped around our propeller. We are using every tool we have to unhook the anchors, but the tangle is too far down out over the bow. Pete yells for me to radio to the Texaco gas station, hoping someone will come out in a boat and unhook us. It would be much easier to do at water level than leaning down. I have put fenders out, big rubber bumpers to prevent us from scratching each other's boat as we are now rubbing against each other.

I have never talked on the radio before, I've only listened but we are in trouble, so here goes. I check to make sure we are on Channel 16, pick up the microphone and squeeze the button.

"Nassau Texaco, Nassau Texaco, this is the sailing vessel Ooh La La."

I wait. Nothing

"Nassau Texaco, Nassau Texaco, this is the sailing vessel Ooh La La, do you copy?"

I wait, again. Nothing,

"Nassau Texaco, Nassau Texaco, this is the sailing vessel Ooh La La, do you copy?

I wait, again. Nothing.

Finally a couple comes by in a dinghy, sees our dilemma, and comes to our rescue. They sound Australian and are happy to help. Both men are pulling with all their might and finally release enough tension to get us free. As soon as we are released, the boat swings around, the keel moves away and we are okay to motor out of our situation. Pete is back at the helm, sweating and out of breath. Not hooking and drifting is one thing, but tangling someone else's lines and pulling up their anchor and bumping into another boat is way worse. Even though no harm was done, we are happy to get out of there and move on. Pete is clearly shaken.

The second anchorage spot is on the other side of the harbor, has fewer boats around and more space, so if we drift again, we'll be okay. We slowly work our way into the spot, checking the depth and seeing where the current will push us. I am at the helm and Pete is on the bow, ready to drop the anchor. He gives it another try and it doesn't hold. We are drifting again. A man, sunning on the deck of another boat, yells to us that we are too close. We aren't even settled in yet. After our last experience, we decide to move out. Using the windless to quickly get the anchor up, we can see a four-foot board stuck in the claw. No wonder it wouldn't hold. Pete is again hanging out over the bow, trying to get the board out. We don't have space to drift any further, but I don't want to power up the motor with him out there like that. I shout at him to get back in the boat, put it in reverse, turn hard over, and give her full throttle. This doesn't mean much at all because we are a slow-moving creature. I just need enough space to make the turn. We are headed directly for the side of a boat and with the anchor precariously positioned off the bow, it now looks more like a medieval ramming tool than an anchor. With a sigh of relief, we make the turn and are once again motoring in the open channel. Pete gets the board dislodged and puts the anchor back into its storage position.

We have had enough of trying to anchor in the harbor, so we pull out the chart book, spot a marina, and hope they have a slip available without a reservation. We radio for the office of Yacht Haven. A deep voice with a heavy accent says he will walk the docks and see if he can accommodate a boat with our size and draft. With luck on our side, we radio back to him in fifteen minutes and he tells us to come on in. He instructs us to call when we can see the navy tugboat, Northstar, docked at the end pier and he will guide us in. We follow his instructions, turning here and there, and then we see him waving his arms, ready to grab a dock line. We learn the slip costs $1.75 a foot or about $75 a night, plus water and electric by consumption. The price is much more reasonable than Chub at $3.50 a foot, plus water and electric. I hadn't really thought about staying in marinas. We could just use the dinghy to come to shore. It's Pete's call. We decide to stay for two nights. I feel like we have spent a lot of Pete's money already. I have to get over this. This is not like traveling with my dad. We are not trying to do this on a shoestring. Pete doesn't care. This is just as much his trip as it is mine, and if this is the style he wants to travel in, let him. I am along for the ride. I'll just do my part, be a gracious guest and make him look good. Get along, be happy, and let him be the man. Let him live his dream too.

Once we are safe and secure, Pete is ready for a beer. This anchoring thing is far more harrowing than expected. Pete confides in me that we have done more anchoring on this trip than he has done collectively in all the years he has owned a boat. He is learning too. I find this odd and wonder what else he hasn't done before. Oh well, worry is wasted energy. I am on a trip of a lifetime and having a blast. I am not going back now, especially over something my imagination came up with.

He also tells me I passed the test. The overnight sail was much rougher than he thought it would be, but I didn't panic or ask to get off. He is happy to see that I stayed calm during our late night anchor resetting, and again just now when anchoring got a little hairy. He said he picked me because he knew from seeing me everyday at the restaurant that I was a hard worker, independent, had a good attitude, and physical stamina. Anyone who did the Ironman Triathlon isn't a wimp. He is happy to learn that I am level-headed and thinking all the time. Oh, and he is really glad I can cook.

I put my faith in Pete because he has owned and operated a boat for over ten years. He raced to Mexico several times. In races, the boats are not allowed to use their engines. It's all free sailing and you don't wait for perfect weather conditions, so you just take it as it comes. I know he has lots of experience. He is an engineer by education, but has worked at West Marine for the last several years just because he loves boating so much. Engineers are usually very analytical and not risk takers. Pete is also a small aircraft pilot and as he puts it, he gave up wings for sails. He wanted to try something different. If he took chances, he wouldn't have lasted long as a pilot. This trip is a life-long dream for both of us, so keeping focused on the trip and not the inconveniences is the key.

We toast to our arrival in Nassau and look around. We are surprised to be right next to Big Rosie. Don and Jim were our neighbors in Chub Cay. Other boats look familiar, too. It's funny how we keep running into the same people.

I love reading the names of peoples' boats and seeing where they came from. People are from Texas, Michigan, Canada, even landlocked places like Colorado. Lots are from Delaware, at least registered there, because there is no tax. Some of my favorite boat names are Tenacious, Perseverance, Piece of Eight, Spice of Life, Moody Blue, No Worries, Aquasition, Prozac, Ciao Bella, Reel Pushy, Passport, Reel Easy, At Last, Second Fling, Copasetic, and Heart Throb (maybe he is a cardiologist). If I named a boat, I would choose Be Brave.

The couple across the dock is also on a forty-five foot Hunter, a boat similar to ours. We stop by to compare digs. Pete informs me that having the biggest stick ( tallest mast pole) in the marina is a very important guy thing. Their boat looks very new as they go about the business of cleaning and polishing. We learn they are from Alabama and just last year sold everything, bought the boat brand new, and have been cruising ever since. They are probably in their late fifties and called their three children one day to tell them to come get what they wanted from the house, because everything was being sold, even the cars. Some friends thought they were crazy, but most said go and have the time of your lives. Since then, one child got married and had a baby, so being away has been a little more difficult now. They are heading back to Ft. Lauderdale to have some warranty work done on the generator.

Back at the marina, we climb the stairs to the restaurant called the Poop Deck for a drink. The bar is hopping. The super bowl semi-final is on. Locals and visitors alike are huddled around the TV in the corner. We take a seat at the bar and meet a young couple from Nashville. They are staying at the Atlantis, but like coming here for the local flair.

They ask where we are staying and we tell them on our boat. They ooh and ah and share with us that they would love to do it too some day. I love the response we get from people as it strikes a cord of adventure. So far we have mostly been around other boaters, so it's been a pretty common tale. Although lots of live-a-boards dream of doing a trip like this, they never do. Pete's neighbors at the marina at Burnt Store lived onboard for three years and only went to the Gulf of Mexico and the Keys, but no farther. They said they would like to make it to the Islands. What are they waiting for? That is the difference between a goal and dream. A goal has a deadline and action plan, a dream is just a "someday."

To my surprise, a few seats down from us is Jim from the boat, Big Rosie. We go over and say hello. He is with Arnett, a cruiser from Tanzania who has been on his boat for seven years and is sailing alone. Jim tells us he is boat-less. Do tell. Apparently Don, the skipper, got his days confused and he only booked Jim to be on his boat for one week, not two. Jim's replacement is due to come in tomorrow and Jim's flight isn't for another week. He isn't worried because the boating community is very small and friendly. He will work it out. We offer to let him stay with us if need be. He doesn't seem too worried and orders another beer.

"Can't think of anyplace I would rather be stranded than here," he says.

We follow the maze of docks back to the boat, only to meet an Irish couple who is on the boat next to us. They have had enough to drink, but we invite them for another one anyway. Their boat is a bit worn and tattered and we learn that they too were island hopping until they had repairs to make and had to stay here to work and raise some money. That was three years ago. She gets a little too playful with Bambi and our dog gives her a nasty nip on the hand. In a shocked blatantly Irish accent, she shouts, "The dog took a chunk out of me hand! Can you believe that?"

We apologize. We tried to warn her about Bambi, but she thought she was such a cutie.

"Me hand is bleedin'. The dog took a bloody bite of me hand. I don't believe it!"

Her husband goes next door to get a bandage. When he comes back, he staggers a bit, knocks his drink into the water and falls in when he tries to get it. He is hanging from our fender trying to climb out of the water as his wife is shouting at him. Now it is after midnight and we have been drinking, but this is a little ridiculous. Even with Bambi down below, the party is clearly over.

As I lie in bed that night and review the day, it occurs to me I am in another country. I never thought of Nassau as international, but why not? We have met people from all over the world today. I thought cruising was for the rich, but we have seen and met all kinds of people traveling or not traveling in all kinds of boats. I guess there are Yachties of all classes. I wonder what they think of us. How do we fit into the Yachties hierarchy? What criteria does one use to judge now? All boundaries are gone. Even more strange is the fact that I am just a girl traveling with two suitcases and a computer. The boat and everything in it isn't even mine. None of us really knows anything about anyone other than what we see at this moment. Who are these people? Or better yet, who am I? Who do I want to be? What is really important to me?

No one asks us what we do for a living. Everyone has quit their jobs. No one even asks what we used to do or how we are funding the trip. Somehow everyone is making it happen and besides, each one of us has left that behind. The conversation is all about where have you been, where are you going, and what cool stuff have you seen or how's the boat holding up. The common thread is adventure. It doesn't matter your mode of transportation. Everyone sees the same thing from their eyes. We are all here.

I decide I am going to make a conscious effort not to judge and to accept all. Everyone has a gift to offer. In all my *new age* reading and studying, I have tried to incorporate non-judging into my life anyway, now I have a major jump start. Each person I meet has a story to tell or may have some useful information we need for plotting our next course. I want to learn from them how they have created a life for themselves afloat. After all, I am one of them.

The next morning, we go to breakfast at a local dive and then walk to the grocery store. It's a Winn Dixie with some IGA labels. The store looks just like the ones at home, except this one has a bird flying around in it. We decide to skip produce when we see that a package of celery is $4.99. New York Strip steak is $10.99 a pound. We get what we need and head to the check-out counter. To my dismay, they have the same trashy celebrity magazines for sale as we have in Florida. Even sadder is the fact that I want to buy one. Why do I care? I know they are all lies anyway. I resist. I want to make a conscious effort to choose what I let in to my world. We have gotten little snippets of news and it amazes me how it stays with me. I think about the war in Iraq, what the president is doing and what the consequences will be. It hurts my heart. I am surprised how often it comes into my mind. I suppose it is unrealistic to shelter myself from the things in the world, but what good does it do for me to know and not do something about it?

A long time ago I learned about circles of influence. There is a small circle in the middle—these are things I can influence, then a larger circle around that. These are things that are my circle of concern, meaning things that are important to me, or things I care about and can change if I get out there and get involved. Then a third big circle represents things are that are completely outside of my world. However, once I know about something and it is of concern to me, then it is my responsibility to move it into the middle circle, the one where I can choose to do something about it. Some problems are just too big. How do I make a difference in human suffering in Africa? How many issues can I really influence? Where do I begin? What do I choose? Knowing that there is suffering, yet doing nothing is worse than not knowing. Not knowing only relieves me of guilt, it surely doesn't take the pain away from the one suffering. This "live simply, keep my world uncomplicated" crusade, is this the answer?

By one o'clock we are starving and decide to go to the Poop Deck for lunch, then off for some sightseeing. The restaurant has a second story balcony overlooking the marina. We take a table with a view of our boat and enjoy a relaxing lunch of Bombay Smash drinks, a local rum favorite, and seafood. Feeling the need to walk off a little lunch, we decide to hoof it the mile or so to the straw market and shopping area. We pass by an old church and cemetery where most burials are above ground. Many of the tombstones date back to the 1800's. The church is locked, so we look through the stained glass windows to see the ornate alter and huge pipe organ.

Walking farther long, we seem to have gotten off the main road, so we stop to ask directions from a native couple loading things into their parked car.

"Are you sure you want to walk that far?" he says.

"Well, we didn't think it was much farther down the road," we say.

"Too far to walk," he says. "We are going that way, hop in."

He starts clearing some books and papers in the back seat. His wife is in the front. Both are heavy with very dark skin. The steering wheel is on the right and the traffic drives on the other side.

Introductions are made. They are newlyweds of about six months. They had a small wedding in a church they point out to us as we go by. "Small" in the Bahamas is 500 people. They had a boxed brunch reception at the hall in the church, and made most of the food and flowers themselves with the help of their families. From her purse, she pulls out two photos of the wedding party. White wedding dress for her and white suit for him, complete with matching dresses for the bridesmaids. I think it is lovely that she carries the photos with her. They are saving for a house and hoping to start a family after they get settled in. He is the maintenance man at the Atlantis and she teaches at a private school.

I ask them what is the best and worst thing about living on the island? Weather is the answer to both. The weather is always nice, so we can plan things and don't have to worry. Hurricanes are the worst. There is no place to go. You can't out-drive it. Loss of property and damage is always a threat.

We talk about living in Nassau. It is congested, but that is part of any city life. They vote, they get global news and all the modern conveniences. They are content here. It's a nice life and both their families are nearby. They don't plan to leave.

Pulling up right in front of the straw market, he gets out of the car to open my door. Pete gives him $20, about what a cab ride would have cost, and tells him to put it toward the house. He is too shocked to even respond. We are off before he can refuse, as I know he will.

Now would we have gotten in a car with a stranger back home? Not likely. Would I have given a ride to a tourist back in Orlando? Probably not. How sad.

The straw market is a buzz of activity with row after row of straw purses, hats, jewelry, T-shirts, and trinkets stacked high to the ceiling. They all look the same to me. This could be Canal Street in New York City. Now if I had a booth, I would make something different to stand out in the crowd. Then it occurs to me that as soon as something is different, the others copy it anyway. No patent pending here I suppose. We pass by old lady after old lady sitting on chairs and calling out to the tourists passing by, "Hey lady, buy something for the little ones back home," or "three T-shirts for ten dollars." They sit on that chair, watching over their booth all day in this crowded dark building. Some are sewing, carefully stitching by hand the pretty colorful patterns on the straw bags. How many bags must she have sewn in her lifetime? I look into the eyes of the grannies and wonder what kind of life did they have? Their faces and hands are wrinkled and leathery from the sun, the wind, and of course, age. Most are very overweight. Then there are the young girls, sitting next to perhaps their mom or aunt, learning the trade. Is this a good living for a woman? Are these old ladies giving these young girls a gift or a curse? I wonder.

I also wonder what is considered pretty for a Bahamian girl—skinny, fat, big boobs, big butt, straight white teeth, long hair or tall? Culturally, what is prized? When I was growing up in the USA, everyone wanted the "then" all American blonde look like Christie Brinkley or Farrah Fawcett. That has changed, thank goodness, to include much more variety and dimension. Do the young girls here study *The Star* and fashion magazines like American girls do? And if they do, who are they trying to emulate, I wonder?

And another thing, why is it that we come to the islands to enjoy the slow, relaxed, easy-to-talk-to, quick-with-a-smile, take-your-time attitude of the locals? We love the slow island shuffle, viewed as island time, where back home we think a person who behaves this way is dumb and lazy and looked down upon. Why is that?

We pop into a jewelry store to look around and enjoy the air-conditioning and free rum punch. Pete asks if I see anything I want. He has been so generous already. He has made it possible for me to come on this trip, all I had to do was get onboard. We haven't discussed a budget and I really know nothing of his financial situation. What I do know is that he wouldn't or couldn't make the trip. Sure he could hire crew just like Don on Big Rosie is doing. The truth is, going on an adventure with someone who wants it just as badly as he does makes all the difference in the world. Traveling with someone who wants to have fun, and is outgoing is a totally new experience for him.

Pete is a self-described geek. He grew up as the middle child in a family of three kids living in Kankakee, Illinois. His dad died at age fifty-three when Pete was just nine-years-old. His older brother was eleven and his little sister was only two. Pete's older brother had a terrible stuttering problem and was teased mercilessly at school. Pete was an introvert who tried to stay out of the way of the other kids and the taunting. He was a loner. He had terrible eyesight and never played sports, but he was smart. In college he couldn't get enough of math and science. When he graduated with an engineering degree, he went to work at a battery plant in his hometown just outside of Chicago. He always wanted to be a pilot, so as a hobby he took up flying. He hated living in the cold weather, add boredom to that, and he started gaining weight. Eventually, he moved to Florida and lost nearly 100 pounds. He got married at age forty-three but never had children. Just a few years ago he had Lasik surgery correcting his 20/400 vision. What a life changing moment to never wear those awful coke bottle glasses again. He tried contacts over the years, but could never wear them.

His former wife would never make a trip like this. They talked about it, but she always had a reason not to go. She also had lots of issues that prevented them from taking a trip like this. She wasn't hardy or level-headed. She was afraid and had back problems. It wouldn't have been fun, to say the least.

I know getting his walking papers from his wife was a shock and terrible blow, but I think she held him back. I think his freedom was a gift. The old adage, "within every problem there is an opportunity" rings true for Pete. We can look at all the things that happen to us as either good or bad. Even for me, Tom's dying was a gift. Oh it sure didn't feel like it at the time, but it was a wake-up call. It was an *in my face* message that life is short and I can't control the world. I don't even know if we would have made it together, but I do know that it was life changing for me. It thrust me mercilessly out of my comfort zone. Way out.

Anyway, Pete wants to do things and is so happy to have someone to share them with. His older brother died a few years ago at a young age, so with that family history, he doesn't know how long he has. Helping him live out this dream is a good thing.

The sales lady asks us where we are staying. We tell her on our own boat and that we are island hopping and heading to the Exumas next. She says that is where she grew up. She tries to explain which island, but without a map we are at a loss. I tell her I can't wait to snorkel and see the beautiful water.

"Do you have any recommendations as to the best snorkeling?" I ask.

"I don't know," she says, "I never snorkeled."

"What?" I reply in shock.

"No, lady, I don't know how to swim," she says.

"Unbelievable!" I ask myself. "How can this be?"

We find out that she moved here as a young girl for high school and never went back. She has been living in Nassau for about twenty years. I tell her that can't be right. She only looks to be in her early twenties now. With a grin from ear to ear, she tells me she is thirty-seven years old. "Impossible," I say. Bahamians do not look their age at all. She says it is because of their laid-back attitude and lifestyle. Yesterday, the dockhand back at the marina said something about his grandson. I told him he was too young to have a grandson. I thought he was about thirty-years-old, and he was actually fifty-seven. Unbelievable!

We say our goodbyes and are back out in the street. The shops are all closing up because it's five o'clock. The jitneys are all lined up on the corner and we decide to take one back instead of a taxi. Locals and tourists alike use them. We hop on the one that will take us to the Poop Deck.

As we bump along on our way back into town, I see a billboard that says *Protect Ya Ting! Wear a rubber every time. Prevent pregnancy, STD and Aids.* We would never see a sign like that in the USA. We crack up laughing.

After dinner on the boat, we decide to try our luck at the casino. Now if there is one thing I have learned, it is dress the part. If I want good service and to be treated nicely, dress the part. I know how to do this. I didn't think I would need anything dressy for this trip, but at the last minute, my girlfriend talked me into bringing a few things and thank goodness she did. I have already worn several outfits. Dressed in heels, hair up, in a little red bright print silk cocktail slip dress, we have the cab driver drop us off in front of the Atlantis Hotel. I have been here before, so I play tour guide to Pete. I don't pay much attention to people looking at us, but he notices. I am used to things coming easily. He is not.

We walk around admiring the architecture and décor of this amazing hotel. It is grand with gigantic murals of Gods and Goddesses of the sea and other creatures from a watery world. The sound of rushing water fills the towering lobby. Low lighting illuminates the elegance of the grand corridors. A gigantic aquarium surrounds the entire dining room and is the home to amazing fish, sharks, and a huge man-o-war. We breeze in and out of the designer boutiques. The sales associates are courteous and helpful. We look like we are potential buyers. Strolling outside, we see the beautifully landscaped pools and gardens lit just enough for us to find our way. It's a lovely evening for a stroll. We walk down by the marina where the mega yachts are docked and learn that they charge $8 a foot for a slip. One of the yachts is rumored to be owned by the Smithfield Ham Family. We must come back in the daylight and snap a few pictures.

We play a little slots and a little roulette. We are not lucky and the place isn't very busy. With no entertainment tonight in the lounge, we decide to call it a night.

By lunchtime, we are back at the boat. We decide to have lunch at Hurricane Hole marina on the Paradise Island side of the Harbor and then we can walk to Atlantis and get our photos. We didn't take our dinghy off the boat, so we ask our neighbor, Don, on Big Rosie, if he would give us a lift. On the way over, he tells us his wife is back in the states. I ask why she isn't here with him. She is still working, maybe she will come next year, but he is not in a rush for that. He came down a few years ago with a girlfriend and it didn't work out very well. He finds hiring crew works better, even if he doesn't know them, they know boating and enjoy it.

Hurricane Hole is a small but upscale marina with several big boats. The Green Parrot Restaurant is the perfect little beach bar. Several cruisers have said that it is not to be missed and now we know why. It is nothing more than an open air thatched roof building. The bar takes up most of the place, and almost every seat is filled with men that look like they are from the states on a fishing vacation. There are a few tables on the deck by the swimming pool. The rafters are decorated with T-shirts and boat pennants with hand written messages scribbled on them. There are even a pair or two of panties. Good old rock and roll is playing on the stereo and what bar would be complete without the TV tuned to ESPN? Sad, but true.

After a leisurely lunch and a few Kaliks, the local beer, we walk over to the Atlantis. What a different experience. This time we are dressed in casual boating clothes, hats and crocs. The Atlantis and Paradise Island are the Disney versions of the Bahamas. Everything is new and perfect and also fake. I love grand and I love perfectly manicured gardens and such, but I also love old and original with all its flaws, charm, and character. Give it to me real. Maybe that is why I am drawn to Italy. It just feels so real there.

We walk past the shops to get to the pool area. I point out a purse in the window of the Versace store I hadn't noticed last night. It's white fur. I remembered seeing it in Aspen just a few weeks ago. Pete wants to go inside and see how much it is. The sales girl answers our questions politely, but isn't as chatty or attentive as last night. I know I am the same girl I was last night, but she doesn't. I feel like I am that poor little farm girl from Pennsylvania all over again and people are looking at me like I don't belong here. This is not what I thought I would be feeling on an island hopping trip through the Caribbean. I want to go back to days afloat, reading and writing, back to that world where everyone is about adventure and travel and not about judgment. I want to be the only one judging me. Hey, I don't even want to do that anymore.

"Let's go," I tell Pete. As we walk away, he comments to me about the service. He even felt the difference. "Let's get our pictures and go," I say.

This time we are stopped when we try to walk out to the pool. Two very polite hotel employees dressed in casual uniforms of shorts and polo shirts inform us we will need a pass to go to the pool. It will cost $29 to use the pool and $89 to go into the water park where the famous slide that looks like a Mayan ruin can be found. Even though we just want to take photos, we understand.

Our last night in Nassau, we are off to the Crystal Palace Hotel and Casino to see a show. We heard about a Broadway style show that just opened and is supposed to be awesome. We bought the tickets several days ago and tonight is the only night available. Once again, we dress in our *acceptable* attire, this time I choose a simple black halter dress, a la Marilyn Monroe. Coincidently, just a few nights ago we watched her classic movie, *Some like It Hot*. Just the thought of that movie added a little fantasy to the evening. There is a captain's hat onboard Pete could wear or not. It's odd, in my old life I loved to dress up and go to formal events. I guess I just didn't have this kind of thing in mind for this trip. Oh well, keep it light and keep it fun. Take life as it comes. Expectations of how things should be are the reason for disappointment. And what, dear God, do I have to be disappointed about?

I feel a bit silly walking the docks in such formal attire. Even the security guard at the marina office has to come outside to check us out. He hails a taxi, we slide into the back seat and tell the driver to take us to the Crystal Palace. To our surprise, he says he can't go there. He gets a bad spirit there. He gets out of the cab and walks over to the other drivers waiting in line. Another cab driver comes over and asks us to switch cars, which we do.

"What bad spirit does the Crystal Palace have?" I ask.

Oh, it's not the hotel, it's the other drivers there." He explains that after a driver drops off his fare, he goes to the back of the line of taxis and waits his turn to get to the front and get another fare. In line, they get to drinking and then he can't drive and loses money for the night, so he wants to stay away from that area. Here I thought there was superstition about the hotel being built on ancient burial grounds. I like my version better.

Anyway our new cab driver is young and friendly. He tells us he was born and raised here. His grandfather came to the Bahamas from Africa as a slave. He lived to be one-hundred-eighteen-years-old. Imagine what a man like that must have seen during his lifetime. What was it like to be a slave? Come over on a boat? What were his living conditions? Unfortunately, our driver doesn't know. He said his grandfather never wanted to talk about those days, he wanted them to be forgotten.

Just then there is an awful crash and a scraping sound coming from the back of our car. He tells us not to worry, pulls the car over and hops out. While he is working, I look around the cab and notice he has ties hanging from the rear view mirror. What's that about? My guess is he has to wear a tie as part of his license agreement but doesn't want to, so should he get stopped he can just slide one on.

When the repair job is complete and he is back behind the wheel, I ask about the ties. "Oh," he says, "they are for customers. Some of the fancier restaurants require ties and most tourists don't have one. So, we cabbies keep some, loan them out when needed and get them back. We give them to each other, so most drivers have one or two on hand." What a great system. It is like the bicycles in Holland. No one has their own, yet there are plenty for everyone. Just use them, leave them outside and take one when you need one.

The show at the hotel is first class, chock full of energy, dancing, singing, acrobatics, drumming, great costumes, and fire. It has it all. *Jambalaya* is a mixture of many ingredients just like the heritage of the Bahamians. The dances are a collection of all the rhythms of the Island People. The talent must have come from New York City or Las Vegas. The dancers are great athletes. I know what effort, pain and hours and hours it takes to reach that level. Their physiques are truly works of art and I love watching them move. They are working and playing at the same time. I know what it feels like to be performing at a peak level, to be in the zone. I lived there for several years not that long ago, and loved it.

In the cab on the way home, I think about being in top condition. Now I say I am fat and happy. I am not fat, but I am certainly not ripped either. What is the price I have to pay to be ripped? Am I willing to pay it? I look down at my body and think, yes, I want to be lean and mean again.

"It doesn't take much. I know what to do," says the little Barbara on my left shoulder.

"Oh, come on, you have the rest of your life to be lean and mean," says the little Barbara on my right shoulder. "Don't do it on the trip. Who cares how you look?"

"You'll feel so much better about yourself if you are ripped and fit," Barbara on the left says.

"Yeah, and you'll be stressing about eating real butter on your lobster and drinking the local rum and beer," touts Barbara on the right.

Okay, okay. I am getting whiplash from this internal dialog. Barbara on the right wins. Relax and enjoy the trip, although it wouldn't hurt to reel in the eating and exercise more.

# Chapter 24
*Exumas Bahamas*
*January 2007*

Allen Cay is our first stop in the Exumas and it lives up to our expectations. We read about the Iguanas living on only this island, and that we should leave Bambi onboard. Sure enough, before we even set anchor, we can see them crawling out of the brush and onto the white sandy beach. As we are loading our stuff in the dinghy, to our shock and horror, a big tour boat with about twenty people onboard motors by and launches right there on the beach. I guess we are not on a remote deserted island like we think. Where did they come from? Georgetown is only about 100 miles away; a speed boat like that could make the trip in about an hour or two. We won't get to Georgetown for another week or two, but we will be over-nighting along the way. There is no rush, remember?

We pop off to another island and when the coast is clear, we head to what we named Iguana Beach. These creepy pre-historic reptiles come right up to greet us. The book said not to feed them, but it is clear they are looking for food. Teenager Iguanas, about the size of a dachshund, run fast right at me and stop only a short distance from my feet. I don't like this. There are hundreds of them, the biggest ones are about two feet long and have red skin hanging under their chin like a rooster. They are not attractive animals. I will be doing no sunbathing on this island!

Back on the Ooh La La, it's time to shower. The plan was to shower off the back of the boat on the swim platform, but it has been too cool, so we have been showering in the closet. Well, not really. The shower in the rear head was converted to a closet by installing a removable bar and hanging our clothing on it. Up until now, when we wanted to shower, we just laid all the clothes on the bed, took out the bar, showered, dried it, and put the stuff back. The bar doesn't fit in the forward head and we are using that one for storage and the ice-maker It's been cumbersome but not totally unreasonable. This time I am going to *brave it* and shower outside.

Before I get wet, I have all my stuff ready—shampoo, conditioner and so on. On the swim platform, there is a little door into a cubby that houses the hot and cold faucet and a three-foot shower hose. It is a little chilly and breezy for this but I give it a try anyway. Hot water is precious, so once I get a good temperature, I turn the dial on the nozzles to stop the water flow. Letting it run while I shampoo is not a luxury we can afford. I wonder if someone from another boat is watching me but then I decide *who cares?* This is camping. We are all in the same boat anyway. I chuckle at this old saying that now has a new meaning. At this point, I am freezing so my entire shower takes less than two minutes. Remember, I was the fastest girl in the transition tent in the Ironman. The key is to bathe before the sun goes down. I certainly hope things warm up or I will have to go back in the closet.

Now it feels like we are island hopping in the Caribbean. I like anchoring much better than docking. Natural beauty is all around us with unobstructed views of sunrise and sunset. It is quiet, private and pristine.

We move five miles to Highborne Cay with winds of ten to fifteen knots and seas of one to three feet. As we motor sail along the coastline, we pass by one deserted island after another, some so small, I don't even know if they count. They all have rocky shorelines and sandy beaches.

At Highborne Cay, there is a small marina and store and the snorkeling should be good. The water temperature is warmer than we have had so far. This is a good thing since we are both eager to snorkel. We load the dinghy up with all our gear and head for the marina.

The dock master comes out to greet us looking just like I imagine, a jolly round man with white hair and a white stubbly day-old shave. All body parts that stick out of his uniform—a worn out T-shirt, shorts, and sneakers—are deeply tanned and wrinkled. He gives us permission to walk around and invites us to go up to the store and the office.

The building is new with yellow siding, lots of windows and a wrap-around porch. As we approach the front door, there is a bucket of water with a sign that says, "Foot Wash". We dip our feet, shoes and all, into the bucket and head toward the door. I chuckle and say to myself, a woman must run the place because a man would sweep the floor every night and just think sand is part of the deal. It's like those old commercials for ring-around-the-collar. Hey, rocket scientist, how about scrubbing your neck?

The inside is pristine and tidy with neatly lined shelves full of boat merchandise, souvenirs, and groceries. It is very pricey. We don't need anything, thank goodness. A package of Oreo cookies is $9.90 and a bag of Corn Chips Scoops is $6.95. I am certain that if I had been at sea for several months and had a craving for an Oreo, I would spring for the ten bucks! It's all about supply and demand.

We meet Barbara, who has been running the place for fourteen years—I knew it was a woman—and another lady who just flew in from Nassau for the day. Both are fair-haired Bohemians. Built after Hurricane Andrew, the building is only three years old. There is a flat-screen monitor and keyboard for the Internet, ($5 an hour), a phone, and several other radios. The whole place is self-sustaining, they make their own electricity, collect and purify water, and all communication is by satellite.

After sending a postcard to Brittany, we walk to the top of the hill. The stop sign looks normal until we get close enough to see that even it has island flair. Painted on it is a palm tree, yellow sun and waves on the bottom. Like good tourists, we snap a few pictures, check out the view, and head back to the dinghy to find a good snorkeling spot.

Snorkeling does not disappointed us. The coral heads are just feet from the shore, so we swim right to them. Tired and satisfied, we lay on the sand to dry and warm up a bit. As the sun is getting low in the sky, we head back to the boat. We are relaxed, and tanned, reveling in our good fortune. Pete lights a cigar. I am actually getting used to the smell, it's becoming a trigger to relax, a signal that all is well and we have at least a half-hour to chill. With a rum cocktail in hand, we watch the sunset off the back of the boat, gently rocking, listening to great acoustic Spanish guitar. We are the luckiest people in the world with three more months in paradise ahead of us.

About fifteen boats are anchored around us and we can see a couple rowing their dingy back to a catamaran. Using the binoculars, we discover the boat is named Lioness and Pete remembers helping push them off the dock in Nassau. Once they are onboard, Pete radios to them on Channel 16 to see if they need help.

"Lioness, Lioness, this is the sailing vessel Ooh La La."

They radio back and we learn they are having trouble with the dinghy.

They ask if we have any starter fluid, but unfortunately we don't. We are talking back and forth until another voice pops on the radio, "Channel 16 is for hailing and emergency," the voice says sternly. "Switch to a working channel." Duly noted, neither of us talks again. We have been scolded. She is correct. Everyone listens to channel sixteen all the time. Then when you have reached your party, the caller who initiated the call chooses the new channel. Switch to fifteen, one five, or any channel you choose up to eighty-eight.

In about fifteen minutes, Lioness calls to us. We switch channels and he asks if we will tow him to the dock in the morning. We agree on eight o'clock.

Rain clouds are moving in, but it is hard to tell how close they are until that all-too-familiar smell of rain drifts across the water. We run to batten down the hatches—another tree house term for close the windows. Each little one-foot-by-two-foot window has four dogs, or latches, to hold it down. Overkill, I thought, until we rocked and rolled across the Gulf Stream and had the windows underwater. The funny thing is stuff still gets wet. How does water still manage to soak our clothing and all my toiletries in the head?

A little sprinkle comes, our first rain since Chub Cay. The clouds look threatening with heavy gray bottoms, but no real rain comes; then to our pure delight, a rainbow appears. Not the faint mamby-pamby kind that you can hardly see at the horizon, I mean a big, full, end-to-end brilliant rainbow. The whole color spectrum is clear and each band of color—red, orange, yellow, green, blue, indigo, and violet—seems to be at least a foot wide. And then, as I learned in Alaska, there are always two rainbows if you look hard enough, and to my amazement, there is a second partial arc. I guess it is true. Here I am, forty-five-years old, and never knew to look for the second one. What a waste. What a shame. At least I did know about, ROY G BIV, the way to remember the order of the colors. Red, orange, yellow....

Dusk is falling and the dark water makes the rainbow even brighter. All around us are dark clouds, but behind the rainbow it is bright. The way the light plays off all the aspects of the 180 degree panorama is full of variety and surprise: dark, light, gray, deep blue, yellow, white, near and far. How can all this be happening in one sky? Propped up on my recliner cushion, I watch the show until I am in total darkness.

Too lazy to cook, we decide we aren't that hungry and opt for a movie and popcorn instead. We watch *Something's Got to Give* with Diane Keaton and Jack Nicholson. A great ending to a great day.

We wake to completely different water than we have seen before, flat calm, only a ripple here and there. The sky is barely distinguishable from the sea and a low band of short puffy white clouds hangs at the horizon. Everything is silver, white and pale blue-gray. A soft haze makes the seascape fuzzy. It looks like we are flying in an airplane just above the cloud line, more than like we are on the water. So far we have had similar weather, but last night and today have given us completely different scenery. In my old life, I would not have noticed the subtle changes in the clouds.

Pete takes the dinghy over to the Lioness while I stay onboard. He is gone about an hour or two and when he returns, he reports they are a really nice young couple who are on their first adventure. Neither has ever sailed before. Wow, they are brave.

We motor to Norman's Cay, a whopping twelve miles. The total mileage for the trip is 465 miles. I must stop comparing this to Alaska where we were clocking up to 800 miles a day. This is totally different and besides, one thing I would have changed about Alaska is that I would have stayed in places a little longer, had time to meet our neighbors and just plain putter. We do have a litany of islands we want to stop at, but are becoming a little more discrete about which ones to take in and what they have to offer. I guess the new criterion is: *is it anchor worthy?*

Norman's Cay is probably the most famous of all the islands in the Exuma, thanks to a cocaine smuggler, Carlos Lehder, who used the island in the 1970's and 1980's. His career ended in a shoot-out and sentence of life in prison with no chance of parole, plus another 175 years. I guess they wanted to make sure he was off the street for the rest of his life. Bullet holes can still be seen in some old buildings on the end of the island. We take the dinghy into the cove to check out the rusted, decayed carcass of an old DC3 airplane that crashed into the water many years ago. With the remains partially sticking up out of the clear water, we can see part of the prop and one wing still attached; the other wing is nowhere in sight. I guess that's what caused its demise—the pilot banked too low or just plain old crashed into the water, breaking off a wing. No need to snorkel here, we can see everything from the boat.

So off to check out MacDuff's Restaurant, reported to have the best burgers on the island. That shouldn't be too difficult as they are the only eatery on the island. We are planning to have dinner there. Riding in the dinghy, we round the rocky tip of the island and head toward the white sand beach. "I see two brightly colored island style buildings, relatively new," I report, looking through the binoculars. Almost in unison, we say, "Must have been Andrew." Hurricane Andrew was devastating to this part of the world and is used as a reference when discussing time and history.

To our dismay, there is no sign of life, both buildings and a little village of about five other buildings look deserted. The walkway between the buildings has a colorful fence and other cute island-y touches. A new car is parked next to one of the houses and two huge above-ground tanks are next to a noisy generator running full blast. I ask Pete how long our boat could run by making electricity using one of those fuel tanks. He guesses three years. Someone must be here. We knock on a few doors and find Chareen, a tall thin local with corn rows braided in her hair. She tells us the restaurant has been closed since last year. New people took it over and they hope to be opening next month. We joke later, that means next year in *island time*. She and five others live on the island. Chareen gives us the "Okay" to putter around, so we walk out to the airstrip and down to see the bullet holes in the buildings by the fallen-down dock.

Six people live here—it blows my mind! What do they do all day? Fish, drink, have crab races on Friday night? I don't know. The whole island isn't but a couple miles across. It is intriguing and fun to ponder as I have done many times back home, but standing here now, looking around, I don't know if I could do it. Working in the restaurant and meeting cruisers could be enjoyable. Lucky for me this not a decision I have to make today.

Back in the dinghy, we motor to the boat and this time I am driving. I want to learn how to prime the gas, use the choke, start the engine and work the throttle. Just like on the sail boat, I want to *do* things, not just watch. How sad would it be to come away from a trip like this and not know how to run the boat?

With the Ooh La La in sight, I spot a postcard-perfect island just off her starboard side. That's off to the right in "boat language." Port is to the left. Why they can't just say left and right? It's the *guy tree house thing again*, I presume. Anyway, I had a hard time remembering this until I heard the story of how they got the names. Boats always used to dock with the left side at the port and the right side open to see the sky and star side on the right. Left land (or Port), right star (or Starboard), makes perfect sense to me.

We must stop at what I nickname Gilligan's Island, which is a sandy little island about fifty feet long and twenty feet wide with one palm tree in the middle. If I ever thought of being stranded on an island, this is exactly how I pictured it. I beach the dinghy and we hop out. The tide is out, so the whole island is surrounded with ankle deep water. Wading in the warm water with super soft sand, we spot baby conchs partially sticking up out of the water. Hundreds of them. Alive. What is this place, the conch nursery? I wonder why they come here. The shells are so small. Do conchs upgrade their shells when they outgrow them like Hermit crabs, or does the shell grow too? Something to Google or perhaps, the old fashioned way, look up in a guidebook.

Tonight we are having our first cocktail party, so we invite two of our neighboring boats. The Passport is home to a couple from Michigan. This is their fifth trip through the islands. They keep the boat near Jacksonville, Florida in summer and have a smaller sailboat up north that they use there. The boat is an old school sailboat with a dark blue hull and lots of decorative teak trim. It reminds me a lot of the Fantome—the Wind Jammer sailing vessel I traveled on in Belize that later sunk in Hurricane Mitch—just a smaller version.

Our other neighbors are on a tattered boat named Dyad. To our surprise, there are four people living onboard, Mom and Dad, a twelve-year-old boy, and a fifteen-year-old girl. They are French-Canadians; the parents are fluent in English and the kids are learning. The parents would prefer to live onboard all the time, but they will go back when school starts. We learn they speared seven lobsters today. Supposedly we can do it too because our fee for immigration gives us the okay to fish and lobster for our personal use. I dove for lobsters before, but I don't really know where to look for the holes. This will require some further investigating.

Our guests bring snacks and drinks. We are a lively bunch, eager to hear each other's cruising stories. When the sun goes down, I have everyone guess how long it takes from the time the sun touches the ocean until it is totally gone. Most everyone agrees, ten to fifteen minutes. We time it. Three minutes. I have been timing it for weeks, so I know the answer.

When the first star comes out, we toast and I recite the poem, *Starlight, Starbright* for the kids. I say it every night when I see the first star. I know it is a silly little childish thing, but it is one of the things I use as a daily reminder not to forget how precious the simple things in life are. Having never heard it before, the parents translate the poem for the kids, but of course, it doesn't rhyme anymore.

> *Starlight, Starbright*
> *The first star I see tonight*
> *I wish I may*
> *I wish I might*
> *Have the wish I wish tonight*

Darkness comes and our guests hop into their dinghies and motor home to make dinner. I can get used to this.

I awaken to light coming in the open overhead hatch and starboard side windows. Another beautiful sunrise in the making. I hear the water lapping on the side of the boat. That is, until the loud rumble of the generator startles me awake and the smell of diesel fuel wafts over my nose. I know we have no power left because I was up writing in the night until the light went out, and I used the last of my computer's battery. In complete darkness, I climbed up the ladder and watched the stars for a while. What a gift. I have to remember to bring my blanket up there with me. The night air is chilly.

This power thing is a real issue. I don't understand why the refrigerator keeps working when the lights won't. Pete has tried to explain this to me before, but I don't get it. Funny, the power thing was an issue in the RV too. Self-sustaining takes some real technology.

This morning Pete gives me an electricity lesson, complete with a diagram. When we are in a marina, we hook up to water and electric, just like a house. We can use all the power we want and the batteries get fully charged. We haven't been in a marina since Nassau, some seven days ago. When the motor is running, the batteries get recharged just like a car. Same thing when the generator is running. There are two house batteries, A and B. Some things run off of DC power which comes directly off the batteries, like refrigerator and radio, and other things need AC power or regular electricity, like the microwave and my computer. In order to make electricity from a battery, it needs to go through an inverter. The bummer is the inverter uses about 20 percent of the energy in the conversion process. So DC power gets more bang for the buck. Now, how many volts does it take to stock up the battery, how many hours do we need to run the generator and what are we using that depletes our supply? To my surprise, we would have to run the generator several hours a day just to give us enough juice to run the refrigerator and freezer for twenty-four hours.

So at this point, we need to run the generator for our immediate needs and run it even longer to re-charge our batteries. It is not a good idea to leave the generator running when we are not home. In this marina, there is a burned sunken boat due to that very thing. Thank goodness our stove is gas. I guess I will switch to green tea using water I can boil on the stove, rather than grind the coffee beans and plug in the coffee maker. I have been intending to break the coffee habit anyway. There is a third battery, the starter battery, that starts the engine and the generator. For good reason, it is separate from powering *the house.*

Now I understand why some boats have little windmills and solar panels. They are making electricity all the time without fuel, or at least when the wind is blowing or the sun is shining. I also understand why other boaters marvel at our toaster, icemaker, and coffee grinder. Not for the luxury of toast, but for the cost of power. And a hair dryer! That is the biggest power hog of all. Ooh La La!

We have settled into a routine. We wake, make coffee, listen to the weather report on the single side band radio at seven, go up on deck to watch the sunrise, clean up the galley, listen to music, tidy up the boat, read or write, plot our next passage, anchor up, move the boat, go exploring, snorkel, get back to the Ooh La La by four, shower off on the swim platform and dry off before it gets dark and cool, make a rum drink, play some international music, and watch the sunset. Then we wait for the moonrise and look for the first star, make dinner, eat on deck and watch a movie or read. Not a bad day's work.

The weather report is our life-line to the outside world. Caroline's crackling voice comes on the radio at 7:00 a.m. from Nassau. She reads the weather for the entire region and then boats call in from all over the Bahamas with reports from their respective locations, giving a whole laundry list of information like wind speed and direction, wave height, tide, water temperature and such. All times are given in military terms and numbers are repeated like winds twenty one knots, two-one knots. Letters are also repeated according to the International Telegraph Union's phonetic alphabet. Like CAT is repeated Charlie, alpha, tango. I never knew they were standardized. I thought you got to make them up as you go.

Once again, the *guy tree house* thing. Anyway, the reporting boats give their boat name, and to our surprise, we've seen many of them, some are even our neighbors in our anchorage. Weather reporting seems to be a volunteer thing and the reports may not come from the same locations each day. Other messages are passed on as well, such as people trying to contact a friend. This huddling around the radio is a throw-back to the olden days. I remember my mom listening to a radio drama in the kitchen when she was cooking.

We move five miles to Shroud Cay and today I set the anchor. The water is calm and clear with no other boats close by, making it a good spot for my first attempt, which goes exceptionally well. It is easier than I think. I want to be useful, Pete doesn't need to do all the work.

Shroud Cay is unique because it has a river running through the mangroves. We pack a lunch and make a run up the river. I expect the water to be dark and murky from the mangroves, but it is crystal clear, even way back into the wooded areas. The roots of the plants grow every which way, some even four feet long out into the stream. We go all the way through to the other end that leads us back out into the ocean and to the most beautiful beach we have seen yet. We are greeted by miles of soft white sand, crystal clear shallow water sparkling in the sun and every shade of blue and green I can imagine, for as far as the eye can see. Paradise. We climb to a lookout on top of the hill, snap a few pictures and revel in our good fortune.

Once back down on the beach, we are surprised to have company. Kayakers. We haven't seen a soul and here sit two earthy looking paddlers, both dressed in rugged outdoor gear and the man has a big canvas hat and day-old—make that, several days old—shave. They look to be in their thirties. We learn that this is their last day of a week of camping and island hopping. "You've got to be kidding. Everything you need is right here in these two little boats? Do tell," I demand. John and Anne are from Los Angeles. He used to work for Club Med and has always wanted to make this trip. He has been planning it for thirteen years. They flew in with all their gear, including the blow up kayaks, cook stove, food, bug spray, sunscreen, tent and clothing. Anne didn't go with him on his last trip to the Baja and has regretted it ever since. She was determined not to miss this one. How cool! I am amazed at what people do. They make us look like lightweights.

We each unpack our lunch. We have ham and cheese sandwiches, carrots, apples, and of course, rum drinks. They have freeze dried fruit, Oreo cookies, and cold ravioli from a can. They are going home tomorrow, so it is clean-out-the-backpack day. Eat everything. We share. Anne is happy to have a carrot, and I think her dried mangos are really good. Their cook stove didn't work out well, hence the eating from the can. We invite them to come onboard, cook up a hot meal and spend the night. We can tow them to the airstrip in the morning. They will fly out of Norman's Cay and since we just came from there. I can't believe they can actually book a flight on that runway. It looked abandoned to me, or like only a private plane doing a joy ride would stop there. They will deflate the boats and put them in a suitcase-size bag. Who knew?

John and Anne appreciate the offer, but decline. That would be totally killing the spirit of adventure and the goal of roughing it and gutting it out until the end. I totally get that. It would be like cutting the corner in a marathon to save a few feet. You are only cheating yourself.

A highlight of their trip was being greeted by Immigration. As they were paddling along, John thought they might pick up a little speed by making a sail from a tarp. Since they are a little crusty looking and a bit rag-tag, Immigration thought they were Cuban refuges. I can only imagine how they must have felt.

They are equally amazed at our story. They passed the Ooh La La anchored offshore on their way here. She remembered the name and thought it was great, and so do I. Pete named her. Actually this is his third boat with the same name. We tell our story. How I quit my life, my successful job of eight years, liquidated my stuff, rented out my house and traveled last summer in the camper with Dad to Alaska. How I moved to Matlacha, this adorable artsy island community I had driven through once, and got a job waiting tables in the restaurant at the marina.

Pete got the boat in a divorce and has been living onboard since September. He wanted to be at least 100 miles away from his old life. He started looking for a marina slip in Key West and every town north, but could not find anything until Burnt Store Marina, exactly 102 miles away. We both had just moved there and neither of us knew anyone. Pete had the boat for sale and was interviewing for a job to stress-test concrete on a construction site, and instead we ended up here when I suggested an island hopping trip to the Caribbean. It has been a life-long dream for each of us. They both burst out laughing. Sailing the Caribbean or testing concrete? It's still a crazy story, no matter how many times I hear it.

We decide that moving every day is a bit much. Having a day to putter around would be nice. Tomorrow we are hoping to get a mooring ball—a floating ball on a chain that boats tie up to rather than having to anchor—in the Land and Sea Park. Depending on the facilities and Internet, we may stay longer than a day.

# Chapter 25
## Swimming Pigs - Bahamas
## January 2007

Yesterday we radioed to the Exuma Cays Land and Sea Park headquarters to reserve a mooring ball for tonight. A mooring ball is a big ball floating on the surface of the water with a rope tided to it and anchored on the ocean floor below. Another rope, called a pennant, is attached to it and is used to hook onto the cleat of your boat. The pennant should be picked up with a hook rather than your hand since some pennants have been in the water so long that barnacles have grown on them and can give you a nasty cut on bare hands. This is my first mooring ball experience, Pete's too, and we are assigned to E21. I suppose the E is for Emerald Rock, appropriately named for the Emerald water around it. It looks like a great place to snorkel, but the water is chilly. I am going in anyway. I didn't come all this way to sit on the boat. I wish I had a wet suit, but oh well. We hook the ball and tie up the boat with ease. The mooring balls are much easier than anchoring, plus I am sure the park uses them to keep boaters from damaging the coral heads.

After every anchorage, it has become our custom to toast with a rum drink. At one anchor a few days ago, Pete was puttering up and down the cove so long that I came out of the galley with two rums drinks while he was still at the helm.

"Jumping the gun a little aren't you," he said.

"No, I was just hoping that the sight of the rum drink would help you select a spot a little faster," I quipped back.

Now I go below and bring up two rum drinks and am greeted by a growling Bambi. She is guarding her food bowl. Somehow, in our preparation for anchoring, her food bowl got put right in front of the ladder to go below. We know this doesn't work. She will protect her food till the bitter end. So Pete takes a pole and tries to push it out of the way. She reacts with the viciousness of a Rottweiler. She is biting the pole for all she is worth, growling loudly, spilling the food all over the floor. I throw a towel over her so she can't see anything and snatch the food bowl away. Once the bowl is out of sight, she bounces up on deck like nothing happened. We have created quite a stir and now our neighbors in the boat next door shout over, "Is everything okay over there?"

"Oh, sure it's fine," Pete says. "It's just Bambi, our Piranha-Pit Bull mix."

And there is cute little Bambi's furry face looking over at them, innocent as the day is long. I turn to Pete and say, "That's one way to make an impression in the neighborhood. Guess they won't be coming over for cocktails."

We dinghy to the Ranger Station, a rustic building high on a hill with a wrap-around porch that has an awesome view. Other boaters are sitting on the porch using their laptop and WiFi phones.

According to the guide book, the warden has a tough job, but at first glance, no one would know this. He lives here with his wife and ten-year-old son in this great house with a killer view, rides around on a boat all day and teaches people about the cool marina life. Not so fast. The park is off-limits to fishing and lobstering, making it rich with marine life. His biggest problem is poachers, cruisers and locals who are either unaware or don't care. The warden risks his life daily in high-speed chases in shallow water and has even received death threats to the point that he goes out with manpower from the military.

Our days have slowed down considerably with nothing to do and nowhere to go. My favorite spot is in the cockpit, reclining on a lounger with one foot hanging out over the ledge and sunlight sparkling on the water like diamonds. Spanish, Mexican or Italian music plays on the stereo and I could literally be anywhere in the world. If I didn't know, I wouldn't know. I like that. I never get tired of looking at the blue water. The photos look like a swimming pool. The ocean is just not this blue in Florida. I am getting really good at reading the water, understanding that different shades mean different depths. Green means grassy bottom, reef or rocks. Super aqua blue indicates a sandy bottom and anywhere from three to twenty-something feet deep. Waves breaking show that rocks are near the surface or there's a sand bar. Choppy dark blue water means there is a current and the tide is going in or out.

Being outside is the best part. I have learned that most girls on boats get tired of the *primitive* conditions, but not me, not so far anyway. When I get a twinge of restlessness, I remember how lucky I am to have two-thirds of the day to do nothing except read, write, and practice my Italian on the computer.

I have also discovered I like heavy reading where I can learn something. I brought a few pop novels and read two the first week we were onboard, but I was quickly bored. Now I have moved on to *The Road Less Traveled* and a life-management book based on *A Course In Miracles*.

I haven't gotten completely on island time and still feel the pinch of needing to be productive and journal, keeping up with the pace of the trip. Again, the two little Barbaras come to visit, one sitting on each shoulder. Barbara on the right says, "Relax, enjoy, don't ruin the trip of a lifetime by working and feeling the pressure to keep up."

The Barbara on the left says, "You will be sorry if you don't write now. You will never remember everything later. Besides, how much lounging and reading can a girl do?"

Barbara on the right says, "Come on, have another drink, go on deck and sun bathe. Look around, Paradise."

Barbara on the left says, "Write when you are in the moment, it is so much better." They are both right and no one wins this time.

Sunrise and sunset are my favorite times of the day. Not just the actual sun, but the warm glow before and after—the way the sky changes colors. At first glance, I didn't realize that the sky has so many layers. Each band of clouds takes its turn to light up and strut its colors. After sunset, it takes about an hour for complete darkness to come and that is when the colors are the most vivid. How is it that I never noticed all these subtleties before?

Tonight we have a special treat, a crescent moon, just a sliver, with a slight glow of the full moon behind it, and as though that isn't enough, one lone star pops out right next to the moon. When Brittany was little and she saw a crescent moon, she would say, "Look Mom, a fingernail moon." I think back to how quickly her childhood passed through my life. I remember an excerpt about parenting from a Kalhlil Gibran book, *The Prophet*, written in 1698.

*Your children are not your children*
*They are the sons and daughters of life's longing for itself*
*They come through you, but are not from you*

*And though they are with you, they are not yours.*
*You may give them your love, but not your thoughts*
*For they have their own thoughts*
*You may house their bodies but not their souls.*

Funny, I was given that book many years ago and I used the script about marriage for my wedding vows. Just yesterday I read that quote in the book, *The Road Less Traveled,* which I also read some twenty years ago. What does it all mean? What is the universe trying to tell me? Be silent, be still, hear the messages. I am trying to be still. That is the purpose of this crazy downsize, check-out-of-my-life thing. It has to be more than this.

We spend the day exploring all the different islands. When we get back to the boat, we see the harbor has filled up. Lioness is here. We radio to them.

"Ooh La La to Lioness. Ooh La La to Lioness, do you copy?"

"Lioness here," Keith answers.

"Switch to channel fourteen, channel one-four," Pete instructs.

Now we can talk freely, but anyone who wants to listen can also switch to channel fourteen. We invite them for cocktails at five.

Karla and Keith sold everything and bought the catamaran just four months ago. They are in their forties and are just as excited and giddy over this whole *let's throw our lives out the window and play* thing as we are. They are fun and sweet. Formerly from the Traverse City Michigan area, he is an engineer and she is a hair dresser.

That night we watch the movie, *Thunderball,* in preparation for our visit to the famous Thunderball Cave. It was the first James Bond movie ever made and was filmed in the Bahamas near Staniel Cay, our destination for tomorrow.

I have made a peace agreement with Bambi since she was here first and will be here after I am gone. It was my idea for Pete to get her anyway. He really missed his dogs that he had to leave behind. He has the patience of a saint when it comes to her and even though she has an edgy side, he forgives her. Bambi has had a hard life. I have to give it to Pete, that's mighty noble. Then again, maybe that's why we get along so well. He gives me a *hall pass* rather than throwing me overboard. I hope I am much more even-keeled than Bambi.

I still don't like her, but for some reason she likes me. No matter how many times I scoot her away, she keeps coming back. I actually feel sorry for her. I think she is bored and depressed. We don't take her off the boat very much because of the sand spurs and most businesses don't want dogs inside, so we have to tie her to a tree and then she cries.

Anchor up and we are off to Staniel Cay with hopes of civilization and seeing the home of the famous Thunderball Cave. We make one quick stop at Rocky Dundas to see a cave and supposedly a short dinghy ride to the *sea aquarium*, the best snorkeling in the park. After an easy anchoring, we hop in the dinghy and circle the small island where the cave is supposed to be. We can see light from inside, but no clear hole for the entrance. That means we'll need to dive down under and pop up inside the cave. Pete is not thrilled about this. He tells me to go ahead without him, but I know going into a cave alone is suicide. The snorkeling is amazing. We take some underwater photos. To our good fortune, another dinghy comes along, but they have already been inside. I ask if one of them would mind coming inside again with me. Happy to help, the woman jumps in and leads me inside the cave. My heart is pounding as I take a deep breath, dive down and kick hard to come up inside, being careful not to bump my head. When I pop up inside and look around, it is another world. Stalactites hang down from the ceiling in this small but well lit cavern. As Dr. Suess said, *Oh, the places you'll go!* I am so lucky to have the opportunity to see this.

When we leave, she asks me if I want to exit first or last. Neither option sounds appealing. "Go first, I'll follow you out," I say. Once outside, I shout a "thank-you," but she is already swimming away.

Back in the dinghy, we head for the *sea aquarium*, which is several small islands down, so Pete drew a map. Around this island, past this V-looking cliff, through a small channel, we come to what we think is it. Gear on and in the water, we are disappointed. The current is so strong that, even using all our effort, we can't stay still. With noon coming, we decide to head back to the boat and make the rest of the trip to Staniel Cay.

Once onboard, we look at the chart and discover we were not at the right place but really close. I am disappointed. It will take too much time to go back. I decide I am not reading the guidebooks anymore. There is that expectation thing again. If I see what I see, I will be happy. Earlier I was reading about an island that we had already passed and learned about all kinds of things we missed. This is why I started reading a book. I want to just let things unfold the way they do. When I was traveling with my Dad, I didn't read anything until we rolled into a town. The people we met were our guides, we asked them what we should see and were told about cool places and met interesting people. Ask and the teacher will come. Out with the books, in with the locals.

A few hours later, we dock at Staniel Cay Yacht Club, the yacht club part to be taken lightly. Dripping with local color, it is my kind of place. We are not as good at docking as we have become at anchoring. It's windy, making the boat hard to maneuver. I have lines out on all four corners, two at the bow and two at the stern. We don't know if we will be docking on the starboard or port. A dockhand is waving to us, it looks like we will dock portside. Pete expertly steers the boat close. I toss the bow line, the dockhand cleats it off, and I run to the back and toss a stern line and he cleats that off. Then I put a fender between our rub rail and the dock so we don't scrape. It will need to be adjusted later. Pete adds a spring line to keep the boat from moving forward and back from the dock. Now we hook up the water and electric lines. That should do it.

The dockhand is very helpful, giving us the lay of the land. He tells us dinner is one seating at seven-thirty, by reservation only and we choose our meal when we make our reservation. Just be sure to do it by five. I like that, nice and organized. We tip the dockhand and he is off. We can be electricity hogs now that we are hooked up. I am going to use my hairdryer and run the microwave and watch a movie on the big TV tonight, just because I can.

We check out the place. A cute little pool area is surrounded by fuchsia bougainvillea bushes. Little cottages of all different colors are for rent, which includes all meals at the restaurant and for a little extra, a Boston Whaler, a little boat for puttering around. The town is just around the corner and down the road. We learn it has a clinic, a pink grocery, a blue grocery, a ladies boutique, a hardware store and a church. There will be plenty of time to explore later.

The bar is colorful, ratty, sailorish and charming all at the same time. Flags from boats, T-shirts and nautical findings hang from the ceiling. The chairs are made from barrels. White sailor's rope outlines the seats that have been cut into the barrels. Some people are on the Internet using laptops and some are glued to CNN. The VHS radio is mounted on the wall just under the TV. No wonder we couldn't make a reservation for a boat slip when we radioed a few days ago. We called several times around five and got no response. Another boater heard us calling and suggested we wait until after happy hour, because they probably couldn't hear the radio. Now we understand why. At the moment, the VHS radio is being used as a telephone and people are calling in their food orders.

We order two beers from Carl, our young, friendly Bahamian bartender whose dark skin is accentuated by chunky gold jewelry hanging from his neck. He says, "I'll run a tab for you. What is your boat's name?"

"Ooh La La," we answer.

After he understands how to spell it, he gets it. "Oh, I see. Ooh La La," he says with a wink and a sly grin. I love that. The bar tab is by the boat name.

I want to get my shower before the sun goes down and it gets cold. Off the back of the boat, I shower with my swimsuit on, of course. This does not deter a small group of local men from gathering on the end of the dock next to us. I know the only fuel tank in town is at the other end of the pier, but it seems to have gotten much busier. I try to hurry and get covered up. I thought I was getting used to the lack of privacy, but I was wrong.

About nine o'clock, we head inside. There is another young man behind the bar. "He is the new guy," Carl tells us pointing to the young guy behind the bar fiddling with the TV and is now shooting pool. "He must be the manager," I tell Pete.

"How do you know that?" he asks.

"He hasn't done anything since we got here," I answer.

Later we find out that his dad, an American, owned the place. He was called here to run the restaurant when his dad came up missing after a solo flight in his private plane. The son had been in the US going to college. What a paradigm shift! Is that for the good or the bad? Did his father's death save him from the corporate hamster wheel or did it rob him of the American Dream? He reminds me of Tom and Tommy.

And what of the American dream anyway? Doesn't everyone want the same thing, a safe place to raise a family and enough money to support them? How did that turn into a house in the suburbs, 2.5 kids, an SUV, consumerism, greed and climbing the corporate ladder? Being out here and meeting people who are living all kinds of different lifestyles is really cool. It makes me wonder if we were exposed to more cultures and options, would we choose the rat race? I read somewhere that less than 10 percent of Americans have a passport. Most don't know what it is like to live somewhere else in the world.

Back on the boat, we settle in for the night. Thank goodness for being docked without that rocking and rolling we were experiencing before, but now we have a new problem. No breeze and bugs. It's stifling hot, humid and buggy. We are at the dock and hooked up to electricity, so air conditioning is an option. I say, "YES" with capital letters.

In the morning, it is the same dog and pony show on the dock. We are drinking coffee and trying to get the Internet to hold long enough to send some photos. Not only am I hot and frustrated over the Internet, now some local men have gathered in small groups on the dock, ogling me. This isn't working.

Since we are on land, I decide to go to for a run. Fifteen minutes out and fifteen back should be about three miles. Once on the road, I realize I waited too late in the morning because it is very hot and I didn't bring a water bottle. The scenery helps take my mind off the heat. Most of the islands have been deserted until now and I am surprised that with all this peace and beauty, no one lives here. Occasionally there is a house with an airstrip. If it is only me on an island, then I have to be everything, the water and the power company and the grocery store. No neighbors. Wow, I really am out of shape. Three miles was chump change in the old days of training. Note to self: start earlier, run more often.

At last it is time to explore the famous Thunderball Cave. We go by dinghy and hook up to the mooring ball. There is another boat on the ball with us. We are confused about the entrance; it is slack tide, but the current still seems strong. If we use this entrance, we will have to let the current drift us between two very jagged rocks into a narrow channel, and then into a small opening only about as big as our head. The good news is we don't need to dive under the water. Pete is very leery about the situation, but doesn't want to miss seeing the cave. "Swim hard and don't crash into the rocks," I tell him. "I'll go first, stay close to me. I won't be able to help you if you are out of my reach." What am I talking about, helping him? I have no idea what to expect. My heart is beating faster now. "Control you're breathing," I tell myself. "Save it for the current." With a hope and a prayer, I jump into the water and head for the hole.

The water is swift, but luckily going the right direction. I navigate my way between the rocks and into the hole and an entirely different world. Pete is right behind me. It is dark compared to the bright sunshine we just came from. Light shines down from the one hole at the top. Hundreds of tropical fish swirl around us, looking for a treat. So this is the famous Thunderball cave of 007 fame. We take our time and soak it all up.

Getting back into the boat isn't easy. I maneuver my way through the rocky channel and swim as hard as I can into the current and back to the dinghy. With fins on, I definitely have an advantage, but we both successfully make it back into the dinghy.

After lunch, we get the collapsible bikes out and explore the island. Mine seems to peddle hard or maybe my legs are just tired from my run. We come to a little shop and the sign says "open," but the door is locked. Just as we start to peddle away, the door opens and a lady calls for us to come in. She tells us she was picking up supplies from the mail boat and just got back.

Inside, her shop is full to the brim with clothing, T-shirts, straw bags, and other trinkets. With her are a young woman and a little girl about five-years-old. I ask if she is in school. "Not yet, she is too little," the woman replies. "There is only one school on the island for grades one to eight and ten children currently attend. For high school, the children must go to Nassau or Georgetown. Unfortunately, most do not return to this tiny island."

We ride our bikes along the bayside road and soak in the fabulous view of blue water dotted with anchored boats. At the end of the road, we come to an industrial dock that is bustling with activity. A few beat-up old cars, but mostly golf carts loaded with boxes are coming and going. We learn that the mail boat only comes once a week and all supplies come to the island this way, not just mail. The boat belonging to the ranger from Walderick Wells is tied up at the dock too. We learn the boat only comes to the bigger islands and everyone else comes here each week to pick up what they have ordered.

However, for a fee of $500, the boat will stop at other islands. I guess if you had lots of building supplies it might be worth it.

I get a wicked sports headache by afternoon. My run this morning was too hot. I should have known better. This hasn't happened to me in a long time, but neither has a run in the hot sun.

We lie by the pool at the Yacht Club and rest. Next to us is a friendly Canadian couple who have been coming to Staniel Cay by boat for eight years, but have given that up. They think they are getting too old to manage the boat, so now they simply fly in for a week or two at a time.

Dressed and ready for dinner, we walk up the docks to the restaurant. Earlier in the day, we made our reservation and pre-selected our entrees, and the rest is pre-fixed. I like this, very civilized. No reason to rush around. Everything is made to order and they know how much of what to prepare. No waste. No chaos, no *getting slammed* with unexpected business.

Before dinner we have cocktails at the bar. It is very busy. We sit next to the two cute young girls we saw checking in yesterday, suitcases in tow. We say hello and learn they are from Boston. "How on earth did you find this place?" I ask. One girl explains her sister came here a few years ago on a sail-boat and couldn't stop talking about the swimming pigs. So, of course, she goes on the Internet and types in swimming pigs of the Bahamas and *viola*, finds Staniel Cay Yacht Club. We have heard about the pigs, but haven't seen them yet. The girls rented one of the colorful bungalows next to the pool. They are planning on snorkeling and exploring the islands for a week. Getting out of Boston in January is a must.

A very beautiful couple in their twenties hear us talking about the swimming pigs and tells us we can't miss it. "They swim right out to your dinghy," she says. "Don't get too close or they will try to hop in." This I have to see. Tall and thin with brown hair, dark eyelashes and eyebrows, she looks like a model. I can't tell if she is wearing any make-up or is just naturally this beautiful. Her boyfriend is equally handsome—tall and muscular with a day-old shave giving him that Calvin Klein underwear model look. Both are deeply tanned. We learn they are on the sailing vessel Out of the Blue. It's a small thirty-two footer with kayaks strapped to the bow. They are from Canada and plan to spend the winter on the boat. They are so lucky to be making this kind of trip at such a young age. We speculate if Daddy is funding the trip, or if they are in film or television and have the means and lifestyle that they can take some time off. No matter, they are *doing* it.

A new day brings another pretty sunrise. Today I will run again, but much earlier than yesterday. My legs are fine, yet I can tell I got some exercise. As soon as I get back from my jog, we decide to make a run out to Big Major Island where the pigs are supposed to be. We went by yesterday, but didn't see any. Today is not a disappointment. There are pigs alright, but not little potbellies like we expect. They are big pink farm pigs like Farmer Brown keeps. We can see only two and they don't seem interested in us in the least. According to the guide book, the pigs are put there by the local who owns the island. They run free and get fed by the tourists. They are friendly, but can get aggressive. Don't bring your dog and don't get too close to them. We dinghy closer with food in hand ready to feed them when out of the bushes on the other side of the beach runs a little brown pig. He goes right into the surf and starts swimming straight for us. The others follow him. We are a little leery and have our oar ready to beat him off if he tries to climb in. Laughing and giggling at the swimming pigs, we take all the pictures we want then motor away to find some lunch.

Back at the Yacht Club restaurant we find the place hopping. We see the young Canadian couple from last night and say hello. After ordering lunch, we try to use the Internet. A throwback hippie couple walks into the bar dressed in African print outfits; he is wearing a matching hat and she has her gray hair in cornrows. Wow, I guess the islands attract everyone.

We go back to the Yacht Club for lunch and Carl tells us he is glad we came in because the owner wants everyone off the docks by 2:00 p.m. A *blow* is expected later today and we will be pulling hard on the dock, so he wants all of us to move and anchor out somewhere else. This doesn't make Pete happy. Staying on the dock will keep the boat much steadier and if the winds are strong, we have a good chance of slipping anchor in the night. After lunch we settle up our tab, which has been running for three days now, and prepare to move the boat and find a sheltered harbor from the impending northerly winds.

After a sleepless night of rocking and rolling, we listen to Chris Parker, the single side-band meteorologist to the Caribbean boaters, to hear what is coming next. A cold front is moving into the area, and the winds are changing again. We move the boat to the other side of the island where the land will block the winds. Now we are anchored just off Big Major Island, which I have nicknamed Pig Island. It is chilly and windy, too cold to get in the water. We have the perfect vantage point to watch people come up to see the pigs. I hope we get to see the pigs in someone's boat.

In short order, two Jet Ski's and a small boat with a dog in it come motoring along. All three beach right onto the shore and hop off where they are greeted by the pigs. They pet them and the pigs eat right out of their hands. That does it. I am definitely not reading the guidebooks anymore.

I spend the day reading and writing and Pete goes off to explore in the dinghy. Just as I am done journaling notes from the book I just finished reading, *Letting Go of Fear*, Pete returns to announce we have reservations for dinner at Fowl Cay. (fowlcay.com). It is a small first class island compound with a few fabulous houses for rent, a gift shop, and a lovely clubhouse where dinner is served. There is one seating at 7:00 p.m. Dinner is $75 per person and includes wine and cocktails. Tonight they are serving steak and lobster.

This sounds like fun and a chance to dress up and play the part of *Yachties*. Just before dark, I hop into the dinghy wearing make-up, long white pants, a silk navy strappy top, and heels. Of course, I have to take the heels off to get in the boat and then I must put my foul weather jacket on to keep the salt water spray from soaking me, and let's not forget that whatever hair I had styled earlier will not matter one bit because by the time I get there, it will be blown all around anyway. It is tough to be girly.

As we tie up, we are greeted by a young man wearing board shorts, flip-flops and a long sleeve T-shirt. He has white blonde hair and a day-old shave. "Sure is chilly," Pete comments. "We wouldn't know we were even in the Bahamas." He agrees and tells us that they get a couple of days a year like this. He directs us to the clubhouse and tells us to go ahead and make a drink. The bartender whose name is Stuart, isn't here yet, but he will join us shortly. Pete knows the way as he explored all of this earlier today.

I step inside and pan the room from side to side. It comes right out of the pages of Architectural Digest, chic West Indies Island Décor. Lots of framed pictures of families give it a homey feeling. Pete goes behind the bar and makes us a drink. This would never happen in the states. Through the game room, we enter the great room where the dining room tables are already set with linens, silver and polished stemware. The look-through fireplace breaks up the space. The living side has several seating areas and a sweeping deck overlooking the sea. What a find amongst the deserted islands! This is not at all what I expected. With our drinks in hand, we are immediately drawn outside where the sun has set, but remnants still light the sky. Dusk and dawn are my favorite times of the day. The glow hangs so perfectly in the horizon. Who owns this place? It is a home, not a hotel. My mind goes wild, imagining all kinds of scenarios.

Tapped back into reality, Pete guides me back to the game room to meet our dinner companions, a very preppie group. They are dressed straight out of the Izod and Lilly catalogs. Did they decide to come here this year rather than summer on the Vineyard as in years past? This is the last night of a week-long stay. Introductions are made. We learn they are from Atlanta and are having a bit of a reunion. They are just as curious about our story. We chat away like old friends.

Stewart is behind the bar now with two little towhead kids in pajamas. We are introduced to his sons, two-and-three-years-old. He talks to them like they are adults. His wife joins them. She is young and thin with blonde hair and has a look of casual elegance, clearly comfortable in her role. Old money, I guess. We learn that Stewart's Dad, Stu, built the island from scratch. He shows us a laminated article about the island and another one from when they were featured in Coastal Living. Stewart and his young family have been living on the island for several years and plan to move back to their other home in Miami in April at the end of the season. It will soon be time to get the children in school.

We meet an older couple from Washington who are very interested in sailing. They have subscribed to yachting magazines for years but never owned a boat and don't know the first thing about it, but they want to learn. I tell them they should hire someone like Pete to take them out on a few trips to show them the ropes. He is a great teacher and has lots of knowledge. They pelt Pete with questions and he is happy to have all the answers. He is in his element. He looks proud, admired, promoted, and appreciated.

Tanned and relaxed, Pete is different than when we first started out on our journey. He even has a preppy look tonight wearing a dark blue pullover sweater, khaki shorts, loafers without socks, and fifteen or so pounds lighter. Being the admired yachtsman is a long way from the hate and turmoil of a failing marriage and the hurt of a divorce.

Pete and I are seated at a table for two as are the other couples while the big party of eight is joined by Stu, the owner. The food is exquisite, the service gracious and attentive. How quickly I have forgotten how I *do* like the finer things in life or at least I appreciate them, like grand hotel lobbies, 600 thread count sheets, pressed linens, polished silver and porcelain tea cups. Just before coffee and dessert, a warm gooey chocolate-something topped with raspberries is served, I excuse myself.

Passing by the big mirror in the ladies room, I catch a glimpse of myself, pausing long enough to scan my reflection in the mirror. That's the old me, wearing perfect make-up, hair twirled up and tussling down, tanned in a cute outfit, wearing an air of confidence like I was born with it instead of self-assurance being something I worked at for years by painstakingly watching and copying the way other ladies carried themselves and the way they spoke. Is this the person I want to be, or is it the vagabond girl who needs nothing but two suitcases, a computer and an adventure? Who do I want to be? Who am I?

Sunrise over Pig Island, how fabulous! Another chilly, windy day greets us. We will be here for at least one more day waiting for the weather to clear, so we go into town looking for a fuel filter. Something is wrong with our dinghy, it won't plain. It just can't get enough speed; our little eight horsepower engine seems only to have three horses working. Empty handed, we return to the boat and decide it is a movie kind of day. We turn the main salon into a movie theater by putting the table down, creating a big sofa pit, hooking the computer up to the flat screen TV, making popcorn and watching *Last Holiday*. Hunkering down for another rough sleepless night of rocking and rolling, we hope the anchor won't slip.

# Chapter 26

## *Island Hopping - Bahamas*
## *January 2007*

Another cold front is moving in, which means the winds will blow from the north and the water will be rough, so we duck into Sampson Cay Marina for a night or two adding six miles to our count now totaling 521 miles.

We wake to 69 degrees, 59 wind chill with winds of 20-25 knots out of the north. The cold front definitely moved in. I just didn't think it would be so cold in the islands. Apparently, the real island weather doesn't come until we cross the Tropic of Cancer. The Dominican Republic, Puerto Rico and beyond will have the *real* tropical weather.

It is still a bit windy, but we decide to go ahead and move to Black Point Settlement, a real town only about an hour away. We need to gas up and maneuver off our dock and onto the gas dock. The wind is pushing us hard against the gas dock making it easy to dock, but it won't be easy to get off. We take twenty-two gallons of diesel at $3.34 a gallon. The dockhands push hard, Pete revs the engine, we scrape hard along the wooden dock and the rub rail becomes a scrape rail. The real worry is trying to clear the multi-million dollar yacht, Mustang Sally, directly in front of us. We rip the yellow man-overboard gear right off the side, but do manage to narrowly miss the yacht.

Arriving at Black Point Harbor, we choose an anchorage amongst the other twenty-some boats. We dinghy in to check out the town and on the way, pass by Lioness. We are happy to know they are here and look forward to seeing them.

The grocery store we find is a small shack with a few shelves, a couple of bins with produce, a made-for-home floor model chest freezer filled with baggies of unidentifiable meat, and just a few toiletries behind the counter. The clerk is a very elderly lady in a brightly colored muu-muu. We are looking for chili powder and ask for it. She doesn't have any, but another couple that is shopping tells us they have extra and would be happy to give us some. Just a teaspoon in a baggie will do. They tell us to stop by their boat, Te ur. We are not sure what to make of them. They are dressed in African print baggie clothing. He has a full long beard and her gray hair is styled in cornrows with beads hanging down her back. Pete remembers them from another island, but I don't.

We walk further along and find Lioness, or Keith and Karla, using the Internet at Lorraine's Restaurant, a hole in the wall. The place is a little concrete square block building with a few plastic chairs and tables. An upright cooler sits off to one side and another small room with a desk houses the computer. Free Internet is available for diners. Lorraine comes out of the kitchen door, drying her hands, and tells us to help ourselves to a drink since she is in the middle of something, and will be out it a bit. We should go behind the bar and make our own drink!?! She is the local entrepreneur who owns and runs the restaurant, has some real estate rentals and takes orders for baked goods. Lorraine also monitors the VHS radio and is a big help to the boaters.

It is a happy reunion. Keith and Karla are sitting with another couple on the boat, Just Now, and they know me. "You are Barbara Singer." I am dumbstruck. The new couple is from Burnt Store marina, the harbor where Pete lived and I worked. Chatting away like old friends, we decide to all have dinner together tonight at Lorraine's. What a small world.

On the way back to our boat, we stop by Te Amour, a funky, old school boat with a dark green hull and beige canvas trim and a row of colorful flags that line the mast all the way to the top. A big Canadian flag hangs from the back of the boat. We are greeted warmly and invited onboard for cocktails. An interesting couple, they are high school sweethearts, married for some thirty years with three grown children. They live in Nova Scotia, own and run a campground in the summer and take off on their boat during the winter. Jan is the hunter in the family and shows me her spear gun. Cameron's amazing watercolor paintings decorate the main salon. They have been sailing for seventeen years. They strike me with feelings I can't quite explain. They definitely march to the beat of a different drum. Back in my old life, I probably wouldn't have given them a second glance, but today I am drawn to them. I read once that interesting people usually have a colorful past. There is something about them that just plain old feels good. When I started on this journey, I made a conscious decision not to judge and already I am reaping the rewards.

We go back to Lorraine's, meet Lioness and Just Now, and enjoy a wonderful home-cooked meal of fish. We joke, laugh and tell stories. Our table of six are her only customers. The camaraderie of the boaters really makes the trip. Having just arrived today and after too much wine, we have a hard time finding our boat in the anchor parking lot. It is pitch dark tonight and all we can see are anchor lights that look like stars. We must pay closer attention to our location before we go off in the dark next time.

We are down below, just waking up and having our morning coffee, when we hear a dinghy motor coming closer and a shout, "Good Morning Ooh La La!" Back on deck we find Jan and Cameron who tell us they are going into town for breakfast. We haven't eaten either, so we invite them to join us. "Turn off the engine, Cameron," Jan shouts. She is loud and boisterous and he is quiet and gentle. His easy smile and warm eyes speak volumes.

Pete, Jan and Cameron are sitting at the table while I am in the galley whipping up bacon, eggs, and toast. We talk about our kids, college and travel. Like a thunderbolt, she turns to me and says, "Yeah, the biggest problem today is the kids get out of school and have no job." I must get going on this internship thing for Brittany who will be finishing her third year in a few months. This is the last summer before she graduates and her last opportunity to do an internship if she doesn't go to grad school. I am sure she will, but an internship is her best chance of getting a job right out of school.

With breakfast on the table—a feast to behold—we all join hands and give thanks. For the next two hours, I am totally mesmerized by the stories Jan tells of their colorful life. They lived on the Red Cross Mercy Medical ship that sailed up and down the African border and helped the natives. They lived onboard with their three children who were schooled on the boat. They were paid $500 a month and were provided with room, board and medical care. The ship would come into port where people were lined up for medical and dental care. Some had walked for days. The boat was about 500 feet long and had some 200 beds and several operating rooms. Jan worked in the food service and Cameron was a mechanic, but everyone helped care for the people when they were in port.

When they had a chance, the two of them took the boat's motorcycle and went off into the back country to explore. Some people thought Cameron was Jesus Christ. He has the look and certainly has a kindness about him that I would imagine Christ had. I hang on every word. Now that's living and experiencing. Could I handle the rawness of being so close to poverty and death? Would the joy of knowing I helped someone outweigh the sadness of loss? It all so much to think about. Later I would go on the Internet and check out mercyship.org.

That afternoon, we take our bikes and go into town to explore, riding along country roads dotted with shacks, peddling hard. It seems like everyone is sitting in the doorway of their homes, weaving straw into baskets, listening to religious radio programs, or at least the old people are. We see the school children, about ten of them, all dressed in clean and pressed uniforms, walking home for lunch. The men are huddled around a TV set at the bar watching an old American Western, but where are the women? At home with the babies, we guess, but we pass the houses and see no small children running around.

Missing my own child so much my heart hurts, I make it my mission to call her. Yet this is no easy feat as most phone booths are deserted. We stop at several establishments and try to call with no answer. I feel like Brittany is not answering on purpose. Later, I find one that actually works and to my shock, she picks up. We chat away. I push her about going to see the intern guy. She promises she will. We talk until my calling card runs out and we get abruptly disconnected.

We arrive at Lorraine's to get the bread and she tells us it may not be ready yet, but we should walk to the house behind the restaurant and talk to her mother. Her mother's house is not a shack, but a sturdy concrete block home. We knock and she invites us inside.

Lorraine's mom must be seventy-or eighty-years-old and is a tiny little thing, but strong and sharp as a tack. We go into the modest kitchen and there is the bread, about five loaves, cooling on the counter. She drizzles coconut on the top to be able to determine which one is regular and which one is coconut. On the stove, I notice a big pot of what I think is oatmeal. When I ask her about it she says, "No that is the coconut."

"Really, I inquire, how do you make that?"

"Well first you pick the coconut," she starts to explain.

I burst out laughing. I am thinking you take a cup of butter, a little sugar, add some coconut and stir till it boils. Not go out and pick a coconut!

I look around Lorraine's mom's kitchen. The stove and refrigerator are modern, but the cabinets are simple shelves without doors. They have been here for a very long time. Next to the back door that is wide open and has a direct view of the ocean only a few feet away, is the VHS radio. She loves to listen to the boaters talking back and forth, and of course, is always listening for a call for help. She tells of different times when boaters were in trouble and how she and the locals all rushed out to help. The radio is also how she takes the orders for bread. I don't see a regular radio or a TV. She is sweet and kind and seems very content with the life she has lived. Happy to share her stories with us, it seems she truly wants us to learn about her life, and we are eager to hear.

Today I will eat healthier, exercise, not drink so much, learn Italian and not get any more bruises on my legs, so lovingly called boat bites. Everyone seems to have them. I don't know how we get them, but we do. We have been on the boat one month now.

We wake to cloudy, breezy, chilly, 72 degrees and eat coconut bread toast for breakfast. Later we move to Lee Stockton Cay to visit the Caribbean Marine Research Center. The center is closed because of no funding from the US, we are told. Two people live here now, but they can have up to forty scientists. They study breeding and habitat patterns for grouper and conch. I am not reading the guidebooks anymore. Expectation leads to disappointment. I am not listening to the weather report either. It's just too frustrating. The water is cold and so is the air, but we snorkel anyway. I see an octopus and giant starfish. There are hundreds of starfish. I wish I had a wet suit.

There are lots of new boat names coming across the radio, like Caribbean Dream, Sweet Sensation, Steadfast, Akunamatada, Abracadabra and Here's To Us.

We meet our only neighbor in the harbor. John is a single-hander and this is his fifth year alone. He was a steeple horse farmer from Delaware. His story seems strange—he is a bright man with a colorful past. I guess he may be hiding from the tax man. Anyway, he joins us for cocktails and brings popcorn sprinkled with Old Bay seasoning. This becomes our new favorite thing.

I am reading a book given to me last year, *How to Be Like Women of Influence* by Pat and Ruth Williams. He was the General Manager for the

Orlando Magic Basketball team. The book is a biography of twenty great women of the 20th century, like Anne Frank, Margaret Thatcher, Oprah, and Golda Meir. One thing they all had in common was that they were relentless in their efforts, worked long hours and were excellent communicators. They wrote letters and gave speeches. They were totally dedicated. It gets me thinking about the purpose of my life and what is yet to come.

We decide to pull up anchor and motor around to Rat Cay. It was rough in our little spot last night and we didn't sleep much. Today it is cloudy and windy. We are hoping for the sun to come out. I am tired of cold and cloudy days and running from or waiting for weather. Some cruisers have been coming only to the Bahamas year after year. Could I do it, the same place? No, I am impatient to see more, and I need warmer weather.

We dingy to shore and meet the family onboard Contented Turtle. Originally from Virginia, Mom, Dad, eight-year-old son, cat, and dog live onboard full-time. This is their fourth year home-schooling Rudy. They just stay around the Bahamas.

Today I have been working below on the computer too long, and get a little nauseous. The boat is rocking too much to stay below. Rolling is when the boat moves from side to side; rocking is when the waves hit the boat from front to back. Rolling is worse than rocking.

I take a big blanket and go up on deck and curl up with a new book I picked up at one of the book trades. I am amazed where my mind goes with endless amounts of time. Most of the books in the trade bins are romance stories or John Grisham novels. No one reads serious stuff out here. No self-help books. Is that because they are no longer in the race and don't need to change, improve, evolve? They are happy?

We stay on the boat all day until 4:00 p.m. then decide to walk on the beach and listen to the surf. We are treated to a perfect sunset and moonrise as the clouds finally clear to let a brilliant full moon sparkle on the water. I skip dinner, fall asleep on deck and awake around 3:00 a.m. to a bright sky. With a full moon, there is way too much energy in the air to sleep. It is February 1st and time to pay bills. I start thinking of things I need to do back home like Brittany's internship, taxes, letters of recommendation and my stuff in storage.

# Chapter 27

*Georgetown, Bahamas*
*February 2007*

It surprises me how much I like being on the water at night. The moon is big and bright. I get out my computer and write until sunrise and the moon is still out when the sun arrives. Did someone forget to tell the moon to go down? Isn't it supposed to go down before the sun comes up? Didn't he get the memo? I never knew the moon and the sun do their own thing and have their own paths. The moon is on a twenty-eight day cycle, just like women. See there, everything changes. We humans spend so much time and energy trying to keep things the same when the truth is, the minute we have something, it starts to change—like babies, relationships, and jobs. It is supposed to change, like the ebb and flow of the tide. Wow, how far away from natural biological rhythms am I?

At last we sail into Georgetown, the end of the line for most cruisers. There's a whole community here. For some, it is their winter destination and they will stay for six months. We anchor out, amongst the 233 other boats. The local VHS Channel is 68 and everyone listens to the morning *net* at eight. If someone has something they want to say or sell, they request it by giving their boat name and when the announcer calls their name, they speak. After the program, there is a flurry of calls responding to the messages. Everyone hears every conversation. Channel 68 is the hailing channel for Georgetown, then side conversations are moved to another channel, but if I want to hear what they are saying, I just switch to the channel they indicate.

I love seeing the names and ports-of-call of the boats, and there are lots of new ones here like Bad Boy, Raising Hell, Free@Last, Sound Waves, The Kids' Money, and a catamaran called Bad Kitty. Te Amour is here. We dinghy into town to do laundry and check out the grocery and liquor stores. First we drop off our laundry, which means carrying big black garbage bags slung on our backs like Santa Claus down the street to the coin-operated laundromat. We find Maria, who will gladly do our laundry and have it finished before five. It costs $23 for four loads, plus $7 for the detergent and a tip.

When we pulled into the harbor earlier, we saw Lioness anchored. We radio to them and invite them to go to the Chat 'N' Chill on Volleyball Beach. It is the cutest open-deck place right on the sand with the best sunset view. We meet up with Keith and Karla along with other cruisers. For some, it is their first voyage like us, and for others their seventeenth year. Everyone is relaxed and friendly. We end up staying for dinner and eating melt-in-your-mouth ribs cooked on a big outdoor BBQ. The water is flat calm and makes for an easy dinghy ride and restful sleep. We need it.

We wake about 6:00 a.m., in time for sunrise, to find everything damp/wet inside and out with 100 percent humidity. Even my make-up brushes inside my make-up bag are wet. This is where I draw the line. Pete spends the morning working on the dinghy while I write. It seems like the engine isn't getting enough gas. We picked up some parts yesterday at a little hardware store and are hoping a new fuel filter will do the trick.

By afternoon, we decide to move to the marina and dock so we can get electricity and water. Our batteries don't seem to charge fully and then quickly go dead even though we barely have anything running. One overnight plug-in should get us back to whole again. We move to a very worn out dock, but a bargain at eighty cents a foot or $30 a night. Without first putting shoes on, I jump off the boat to tie down the lines. The wood on the dock is very old and splintered, and in a few minutes I manage to get the mother of all splinters. I don't need a needle to it get it out, I need a pliers. Fortunately, it is in the pad of my foot and doesn't bleed much, but makes a huge gouge that leaves me sore and limping. I broke the rule: Wear Croc's at all times.

That night we meet up with Jan and Cameron and some of their friends who brought bongos onboard and want to find a band. We hop into a cab and go to the fish fry, a series of shacks by the sea where the locals go. They serve food, drinks, and supposedly have a band tonight. The shacks are rustic, but the DJ is jamming on an open-air deck right by the ocean. The moonlight is dancing on the water as though it wants to be part of the party. Food aromas waft over us and we go in search of whatever it is that smells too good to pass up. Pete and I share delicious shrimp curry over white rice. Our hefty island chef is embarrassed as we go on and on about how delicious her food tastes. The music gets louder and faster as the night goes on. We, white people who can't dance, are sharing the floor with the clearly rhythmically gifted locals. The drumming gets louder, bringing out our native instincts, and soon we turn into howling, jumping, crazy people laughing until we can't breathe. It's definitely time to go home. We walk to the marina while the others go get their dinghies to ride out into the harbor to their anchored boats. The boats are our houses and the dinghies are our cars. Just as we are settling down in bed, we are serenaded by a dinghy full of drunken sailors. What fun! We are sillier now than when we were teenagers. Can we get arrested for drunk dinghying?

In the morning, we awaken to meet our new neighbor on the dock, a single-hander who lived most of his life in Alaska. We discover we were at Chub Cay with him—he remembers me as the girl who wanted to watch Oprah. On the radio we hear Coco Loco (Trish and Jerry whom we met in Marathon) calling someone. I guess they are still together and made it to Georgetown. We radio them and agree to meet at the St. Francis on Redshanks Island for the Super Bowl Party tonight. I am excited to see them and hear all about their journey.

I start reading a new book, *You Can Have It All*, by Arnold Patent–1988, a metaphysical book that teaches about the laws of the universe and creation. Without realizing it, this little book will become my guiding light. Having time to read is such a luxury.

We get out our collapsible bikes and take a ride all over the island. The outlying areas are not much better cared for than the little downtown, and not very inhabited. The bikes seem to peddle harder each time we get them out. Maybe the salt air is affecting them. We spend the rest of the afternoon washing down the boat, removing visible chunks of salt that have formed on it. The cockpit needs a good scrubbing.

We learn that Bambi can jump off the boat at high tide. Any other time, the boat is three feet lower than the dock so she can't make it, but as the tide changes and the boat gets level with the dock, she decides to go exploring. Unfortunately, we discover this before she gets off the long series of dock and onto land and beyond. I wish she would run away.

After exhausting all options with repairing the dinghy, Pete realizes there is a secondary hull and the boat is extremely heavy when we launch it on shore and try to pull it out of the water. So we decide to hoist it up out of the water and open the plug in the bottom to see how much water is in there. We are shocked when we can barely crank the wench to get it out of the water. So when the back is just inches out of the water, I jump in and swim over to release the plug. Water gushes out for what seems like forever, at least a hundred pounds of water we guess. With the plug back in, we put the engine on and take her out for a test spin, and to our surprise, we plain right out of the shoot. All the fixing and looking for parts when our dingy had simply taken on water and weighed too much to get going. Amazingly simple. Our dinghy is such a pain.

A very sad looking boat with four motley Bohemian Gen-X kids onboard comes in and docks nearby us. They have dreadlocks and are wearing long gauze skirts. Two girls and two boys, I think? I am not sure what country they are from because they are flying a black flag. After filling their water tanks from the dock, they ask us if we have an extra sexton. Sexton, who uses that anymore? But what that really means is, they don't have GPS and are navigating like Christopher Columbus did. We don't have one, but would have gladly given it to them. They also ask if we know anything about fishing. We can't help them there either. We are in the middle of our dinghy job when they come by and they are gone before I really have a chance to talk to them. I am dying to know their story and why they named their boat, written in sprayed-on graffiti style letters, Pestilence.

Before dark, we make our way to the bar to watch the Super Bowl. We aren't exactly sure where it is and want to get there before it gets too crowded. Lioness comes with us. We are perched on a deck, high on a hill, sitting at a table outside, under the stars with what ends up to be about a hundred other yachties. We meet up with Trish and Jerry. He has spent many a winter at Georgetown, so it's like old home week for him. Trish is loving the cruising life and told Jerry he is stuck with her. She even called home and put her condo up for sale!

TV monitors are strategically placed all around the restaurant. The crowd roars with every touchdown and reacts to the commercials, and let's not forget the great halftime show by Prince. It is an exciting evening. More than once I lay my head back, look up into the star-filled night and put out a prayer of gratitude. I never thought this is where I would be for Super Bowl 2007. The dock has turned into a dinghy parking lot with about fifty boats that all look alike. It's totally dark when we weave our way home afterwards in a sea of anchor lights.

The next day I get a disturbing email from Brittany. She wants to take a year off from school and go back to Rollins and finish there. I spend all day trying to find a pay phone that works and call her, walking forever only to discover the phone isn't working, or the ones that do work have a long line of people ahead of me. I send a ton of emails with no response. When I finally get a response, I get a one liner from her, "Forget it, that email was five days ago." I am crushed. I spent the last two days worrying and trying to talk to her and then, just like that "forget it."

We do a big grocery shop and spend $200. We still have pretty much onboard, but everyone says the same thing, "Buy it when you can, you never know."

As we are putting our groceries away, we have visitors who have come to ask us about our bikes, which have been chained to the dock for the last few days. They ask if we have a permit for them. "Permit? No, why?" I ask.

Apparently they took their bikes off their boat in Nassau and were told by a government official that they needed a special permit to ride around on them. I never heard of such a thing, but then again, Nassau is very busy and the last thing they want is a tourist getting killed on a bike. The driving there was similar to a major city and the streets were very narrow. We invite them onboard.

This is their first year too. They bought a brand new trawler, named Carpe Diem, decked it out with satellite phone, TV, all the latest and greatest, and have had nothing but engine trouble. They are from North Carolina, sold a business and everything they own, and have one sixteen-year-old daughter at sleep-away boarding school. Hmm. Why didn't I think of that?

I want to spend sunset on Stocking Island at Volleyball Beach reading the Cosmo Pete picked up for me. He paid $8 for it! He thought "The Bible," from the movie *Legally Blonde*, might cheer me up. I spy a hammock with my name on it. It was a hard day being so worried about Brittany, not being able to talk to her, running all over town trying to find a phone, and then getting her shitty email. So now it is time to chill. We run into Contented

Turtle. He remembers us and I remember their little boy and big dog. What a small world? Too many margaritas later, it's time to call it a day.

Overnight the winds pick up to forty knots and pound on the swim platform at the stern of the boat at my head. It sounds like someone is hammering the boat with a sledgehammer, or is that pounding in my head? In the night, we convert the salon to a movie theater and both sleep out there. This is the cold front moving in that we have been waiting for, so we can move on to the Turks and Caicos Islands. We wake to cold, rain, wind and clouds. I am over the weather and ready for something else. I wonder if it would have been better to hoof it to the Leeward Islands where it is warm all the time, and do the Bahamas on the way back in April when the weather is warm, and all this cold front business would be over. To pass the time, we watch three movies, *Casino Royale, The World's Fastest Indian* and *Paris When It Sizzles*. We can be electricity hogs because we are plugged into the dock. We even have microwave popcorn. The microwave is a big electricity burner and we can only use it when the engine or generator is working. We don't leave the boat all day.

Jan comes by to deliver a going away present she made for me. She knows we are leaving tomorrow for the Turks and Caicos and they will be heading the other direction. She needle-pointed a book marker that uses flags to spell out our boat name, laminated and all. I am touched by her kindness. We are kindred spirits. She is wearing a broad rimmed straw hat to which she has attached the head of a lobster she hunted. She's one of a kind. The first time I saw her, I judged her as *way out there* because of the wild African prints and hair braids. "No one I would want to hang out with." Oh, how wrong I was. She calls me Barbie. The only person who ever calls me Barbie is my Mom. I am just three years older than Jan's daughter.

We are up early, showered, and plan to shove off by 10:00 a.m. I make one last effort to reach Brittany and we finally get to talk. I have twenty minutes left on the calling call and we talk until the phone cuts us off. She sounds okay, just a little lost and needs her mom. I try to remember what it felt like to be twenty. I also understand the pressure she feels to make a decision about what she wants to do with the rest of her life, when I am forty-five years old and don't know what I want to do with the rest of mine! I just want her to have more choices and opportunities than I had. Maybe she should take a year off and work for a non-profit in a third world country, or maybe she should get her undergrad from Emory and do her graduate work at NYU and become a legislator and make a real difference. Which one makes a *real* difference?

Or maybe I should.

We go by Lioness and wave goodbye and shout to Te Amour as we pass them. It is sad leaving our friends. Georgetown is called Chicken Harbor because most people don't go farther than this. I am eager to get to islands where people live and villages are filled with local color and customs.

It's a great day to be on the water. Blue skies, puffy white clouds, light breeze, and deep blue water make the trip a postcard day. We pass a beautiful old school sailboat going the other direction with all four burnt orange sails out, strutting her stuff like a peacock. The sun shines down our happy little boat, bobbing in the waves with tropical music blaring. Until, at 3:00 p.m., Pete turns around to discover the dinghy is no longer being towed behind us. Oh my God, this is not good. We try to remember what time we last checked it. We have to go back and get it. We have to have a dinghy. Fortunately, we took the engine off and have it mounted safely to the back of the boat. I was the one who cleated off the dinghy. I was the one who didn't want to hoist it on the deck where it would be secure because it is such a pain in the neck. I was the one who complained that Pete re-does every knot I do, and I am not doing any more if he's going to come after me and change them. I am the one who is responsible for losing the family car! Hopefully we can find it. If not, will we be able to buy another one and how much will that cost?

Pete says he is the Captain and he is the one ultimately responsible. He makes the final call. Either way, we have just made a two-thousand dollar mistake. The good news is, no one got hurt and the wind is blowing toward the land and not out to sea. We have a good chance of finding it. We will backtrack the thirteen or so miles to Georgetown. If we can't find it, we will get someone to take us out in the morning in a dinghy and get much closer to shore. It will take us until dark to get back to Georgetown and anchor.

No luck finding the dinghy. We radio to the local dive shop and see about hiring a skiff to take us out in the morning. They tell us to call at eight. Our call to the dive shop puts out the red alert to Georgetown that a cruiser has lost their dinghy.

By chance, we anchor next to *Te Amour*. They heard our call and say they know someone who has a forty horse power dinghy. We should call them. We are exhausted and decide to give it a break for tonight. Pete fires up the grill and we make steaks and Portobello mushrooms on the BBQ. We aren't under any time restrictions.

First thing in the morning, we hear on the radio that someone found a dinghy. Our hopes are quickly diminished when we learn it is not ours. During the morning net, we put out a call for help and get lots of offers. Someone has a dinghy for sale if we don't find ours. Jan introduces us to *Where To?* He's got the dinghy with a big engine. We explain we lost ours between here and twelve miles out. He motors over in their dinghy called *Been There* in less than ten minutes with charts and binoculars in hand. I stay behind to man the radio. In less than half an hour, Jan calls to invite me to go to town. I need eggs. We can take the hand-held VHS radio so we can still monitor it. She radios to Cameron, "Te Amour, Te Amour, this is *Me Amour*. Barbara and I are going to shore. Be back in an hour." They have a different name for their dinghy too. How cute!

I come back with $50 worth of groceries. How does that happen? I decide to make brownies for the victory party, certain they will find the boat. We go to Te Amour to bake and check out Cameron's watercolors. He is quite good. His subject is the majestic old school yawl with all fours out in full bloom. We passed it yesterday and apparently it came right through Georgetown.

At noon we get the call. They found it! Everyone can hear the news and there is lots of hooting and hollering going on. We can hear the whole boating community cheering and honking. *Been There* says it was eleven miles away and just a little damaged.

Sound the Alert! Party on the Ooh La La tonight. Lots of well-wishers stop by, but we eventually settle in with eight people onboard. *Where To?* are both retired acrobatic pilots and met each other through flying. They are traveling on a green and yellow trawler. I make champagne cocktails from the recipe we got while dining at the Columbia Restaurant back in Florida. In our celebratory state, we come up with brilliant names for our dinghies, *Spotted Cub* for the Lioness and *Viola* for the Ooh La La.

In the dim light of dawn, we pull up anchor at 6:00 a.m. to a big orange sky, and make our second attempt at the fifty mile run to Rum Cay. This time the dinghy is secured to the forward deck. Jan paddles over in her dinghy to bring me a book she wants me to read. I just started *The Glass Castle*, but am happy for new material. As we pull up anchor, she serenades us from her deck with all four verses of a song.

As serendipity would have it, Lioness is sailing with us. They made their repairs to their boat and Keith told his job offer to wait. They told us that watching us leave yesterday really got them thinking about what they're doing and why they came here. They wished they were going with us. So when we returned yesterday, they decided they wanted to go to the Turks too. We motor sail for ten hours, arriving at 3:00 p.m. in time to snorkel. I make tacos for the four of us and we hit the hay at eight o'clock.

We wake at 12:30 a.m. and pull up anchor at one, with a full day of travel ahead of us. The beautiful night sky is filled with stars and a half moon shimmers its glow across the water. I stay up until two, then sleep until Pete wakes me at six to take over. Lioness stays next to us all night. The morning greets us with an awesome pastel purple sunrise at 6:30 a.m. Around eleven o'clock, the Bahamian Defense Ministry radios us to inquire who we are and where we are going. Keith thinks it's a joke. "Give us your boat name, home port, last anchorage, destination," the official-sounding voice says. Keith responds with some cheeky comments until Pete cuts in and gives the official answer. After that, we switch to another channel and Keith said he thought it was us being silly!

By afternoon, we cover seventy-nine miles and reach our destination for the day, Atwood harbor, another deserted cove. We hop in the water and find the best snorkeling of the entire trip, so much wildlife and living reefs all so close to the surface. We see two turtles, giant stingrays, coral towers, and even a shark! Later that night, we walk along the beach and for the first time in my life, I see glow worms, little microscopic creatures that glow a neon green light when you brush against them or, in our case, step on them. This only happens during a certain moon and has something to do with their breeding cycle. I imagine I am interrupting their fun! There are thousands of them along the water's edge. We decide to make a fire and hang out on the beach for the evening. During our wood collecting efforts, we find all kinds of debris, make our own version of *Wilson* from the movie Castaway and tell stories of what we think living on a deserted island would be like.

Around the fire that night, Keith shares his story of having just recovered from heart surgery. That was the catalyst for their selling everything and making this trip. It's funny how life-changing events push us down the path. Pete's push was a divorce and mine was Tom's death.

Another early morning wake-up call, this time 5:30 a.m. A glorious red sunrise is complimented by a bright half-moon. The weather is sunny, the sea is calm and the wind is fifteen knots. We motor sail most of the day, putting out the jib for a little extra speed. Anchor up at seven and we reach Abraham Bay by sunset, covering another fifty-seven miles. The little town of Mayaguana has a population of 262.

We spend a quiet evening on the boat and have dinner with Lioness. We are tired. Bambi has a sleep-over with Jake, Lioness's cat, and falls off their boat. No harm done, but she clearly doesn't like being in the water.

# Chapter 28

*Provo, Turks and Caicos*
*February 2007*

By 6:00 a.m., the anchor is up and we radio Lioness to confirm they are clear to go. Another full day of sailing is ahead of us. The winds are not in our favor, so probably more motoring than sailing. As soon as we get out of our protected cove, the water gets rougher than we thought. Once again confirming what I already know—weathermen lie. After some 250 miles of travel in the last four days at six miles an hour, and three books later, we are happy to be pulling into Sapodilla Bay on Caicos Islands. There are eight boats already anchored in the milky aqua cove—new names we haven't seen before like Money Pit, Captain Ed, and Northern Goose. The Caicos are a collection of islands and we have landed on Providenciales or as the locals do, "Just say Provo Mon, don't hurt your tongue."

Provo is a very developed island. A building boom has put them on the map for tourism. According to the guidebooks, it all started in 1966 when the government allowed a group of investors to lease/purchase some four-thousand acres on the Providenciales. The seven investors, or the seven dwarfs as they were called, arrived in Provo on a boat of the same name. Two of the investors were Theodore Roosevelt, III and Richard DuPont. Part of the agreement with the government was that the developers had to dredge Sellar's Pond and create a channel to the sea, build a road to con-nect the three existing settlements or towns, construct a hotel and jetty, and employ a certain number of the local population. This was all completed within five years. That opened the door for the boom to begin. Resorts, ma-rinas, restaurants, condos, residential projects, dive operations, a casino, a posh golf course, and several shopping centers have sprung up with no end in sight. This is truly a cosmopolitan island where native Turks and Caicos islanders, Haitians, Dominicans, Americans, Europeans, Canadian expatri-ates and a variety of other nationalities and cultures live peacefully together.

Some people think it's too commercial and the Leeward Highway feels more like a suburb of Florida than a Caribbean Highway. I am looking forward to civilization and a lively nightlife.

By the time we are anchored, the sun is just starting to set. We decide not to go to land. Customs is closed, so we raise the yellow quarantine flag, make a rum drink, and enjoy the evening. Lioness joins us for dinner and a movie.

I am so looking forward to going ashore and seeing all the glamorous resorts, having lunch at a charming seaside restaurant and doing a little shopping. I dress in a not yet worn pale blue halter dress, white wide brimmed hat, big movie star sunglasses, white deck slides and a native straw bag thinking this attire is appropriate.

Bambi got sick yesterday and threw up. She has been moping around ever since. A day on land should set her straight. We try to take her off the boat when we can, but she comes back full of sand spurs. They jab our fingers when we try to pull them out of her fur, and of course, you take your life into your hands when you mess with Bambi. She will take it for so long, then she growls or snaps at you to let you know she has had enough. Worse than that, she always seems to leave one or two of the spurs in my bed. They are unbelievably painful.

Keith and Karla pick us up in the Spotted Cub. Our dinghy hasn't left the deck where it is securely fastened since we got word of strong winds. There is no chancing letting that thing get away from us again. If it ever leaves the boat, it will be tied securely with two lines from now on. We all go to shore, including Bambi. Our first stop is the immigration and customs office. Apparently we go to them. Just as we slide onto the beach, we are greeted by a tanned and buff young man wearing only board shorts. He is GR from Daytona Beach. What a small world! He is on a boat named SanSan, and has been anchored here for three weeks and is going completely stir crazy as he waits for sails to be sent from the states. GR knows the island very well and is eager to give us all kinds of pointers. "Rent a car, it is way cheaper than a taxi," he explains. "Things are very spread out." He is on his way into town and agrees to walk with us and show us where the customs office is located.

Walking up the sand beach and onto a dirt road, we are quite a band of tourists, Keith and Karla, Me and Pete, Bambi and GR. It is hot, dry, dusty and long. Not what I expect.

"How far is the town?" I ask.

"About seven miles away," he explains.

"What!!??!!" I gasp.

"There isn't really one downtown," he explains. "It is very spread out. The customs office is just down the road, but you'll need a car to get around. The people on the old sailing vessel Liahana can arrange one for you. They will send a driver to the beach to drop off the car. That means we will have to walk back to the boat to get a car. This does not make me happy.

We walk along chatting and finally come to a T in the road. Ahead of us is a huge shipping yard filled with big metal containers, dust, tractor trailer trucks coming and going, dust, cranes, dust, fork lifts roaring and beeping when they back up, dust and all surrounded by a chain link fence. GR says he is going left into town and we should go right to a security shack. They will direct us to the office inside the shipping yard. This is crazy. This is how they greet tourists? Where is the steel drum band? Where are the rum drinks with umbrellas? Where is the fanfare? We dodge our way between the moving pieces of heavy machinery to find the beat-up concrete block building of immigration.

I can't help but make fun of how ridiculous this is. So I break out in song. "Green Acres is the place to be, hard living is the life for me." We all crack up. Instantly I am nicknamed Zsa Zsa. We step into the small, air-conditioned (thank goodness!) office and go up to the counter. I take off my sunglasses throw my head back, hold out my hand and say, "No paparazzi please." We are a mass of giggling and silliness. The young dark customs agent doesn't quite know what to make of us. Even though he tries to maintain his position of importance and authority, I do catch a slight smirk here and there. We are brash Americans pelting him with questions, making fools of ourselves with our naiveté. He hands us the documents to fill out, but only has one pen, so I reach in my bag and pull out my red jewel-encrusted *special contract signing* pen, which quickly becomes the autograph signing pen. Again with all the Hollywood glamour I can muster up, I say, "Who shall I make it to, Darling?" We all fall out into laughter, this time including the agent. With all the forms completed and $75 per yacht paid, it is time to get the stamp in my passport. In anticipation, I take my fist and fake stamp four different documents and announce, "There now, finito." We have gotten completely out of hand.

Outside, Karla insists on getting a photo of Zsa Zsa and her dog walking through the shipping yard. A young construction worker in uniform even comes over to shake my hand and poses for a picture. We have lost all sense of decorum.

Back at the guard shack we wait about ten minutes in the hot sun for the Hertz courtesy van. Every big rig must stop at the shack and have their documents checked. It is very busy and each truck that passes by kicks up more dust and revs the engine to put it into first gear.

At the Hertz counter, we continue with our charade. What has gotten into us? Is it being on land, being in quasi-civilization, getting a car? What? Our rental car is a gray four-door compact-something with a missing hub cap and a nasty scrape over the passenger rear tire. The steering wheel is on the correct side, but the cars drive on the left-hand side of the road. Pete volunteers to take the wheel. As we leave the parking lot, he puts on the turn signal and the windshield wipers start going. An easy mistake, but when it happens over and over, we tease him about it. "We've got the cleanest windshield on the island, but six people have rear ended us." We start out fine until we get to the first traffic circle. Are you kidding? What are they thinking? Were these installed by the lobbyists for the taxi companies? We can't do them right in New Jersey, how are we supposed to do it with everything opposite. I cover my eyes with Bambi's paws and Pete goes screeching around, weaving through the traffic.

Pete is a natural. "This is a piece of cake," he says. "I am a left-handed dyslexic. Driving in the states seems backward. I have finally found my home." Even with a rum drink under his belt, he is a better driver than any of us. Listening to Caribbean Rock on the radio, we go flying down the one main highway that is marked in yellow on the map. "Follow the yellow brick road, ha-ha. Follow the yellow brick road, he-he." We sing at the top of our lungs. We have completely lost our minds. One of us spots an Internet place and Pete whips the car into the parking lot. We all climb out and I starting kissing the ground. "I made it. I made it. Thank goodness."

Next, we pass a marine supply store and make another unexpected two-wheels-on-the-ground turn into the parking lot. Lioness needs some stuff and I want to get a courtesy flag. It's a fun custom that whatever country we are in, we fly a small flag of that country from our mast. Some boats have lots of them. Pete wants me to keep them as a memento of the trip. The Turks and Caicos flag has a flamingo and a blooming cactus on it. The country is actually named after the cactus because the bloom looks like a Turkish fez hat.

We have lunch at a very American Restaurant, Calico Jack's, in a little shopping center that has a bank, camera store, and Internet shop. We take a table outside and are soon greeted by a young white kid. He is the manager from Canada and has been on the island for three years. We also meet a young man, a Brit, who sells ads for a local real estate magazine. He used to work on the Cayman Islands, but they have priced themselves out of the market and with all the changes in the banking laws, offshore investors have moved on to other islands. It appears to be the Turks and Calicos' turn at the trough.

I make a phone call from the store next door. Now this is more like it. In a nice air-conditioned office, the friendly store owner hands me a cordless phone and tells me to just dial one and the number. It will be sixty cents a minute. After searching all over the island to find a working pay phone and trying to use a calling card, I discover that a $10 card actually got me just three minutes after Cable and Wireless phone company charged its access fee. What a rip off!! Imagine all the poor immigrant workers who have left their families behind to come and work construction to pay $10 for three minutes just to say hello and tell their loved one how much they miss them. To my good fortune, Brittany answers and we talk for a little while. The crisis is over. She sounds good. Of course, everyone typing away on the five computers can hear every word I am saying, but still much better than a hot pay phone for $3.50 a minute.

It is Valentine's Day morning and I prepare a special anniversary breakfast of mimosas and eggs benedict on the deck for Keith and Carla who were married three years ago in Belize. They come over at 7:30 a.m. We get up early now, the sun rises at 6:30, although the pre-sunrise at 6:00 a.m. is better and Chris Parker, the radio weather guy, comes on at 6:30 and Caroline, the weather girl from Nassau, comes on at 7:00 a.m. We are usually beat by 8:00 or 9:00 p.m.

Later we are off in the car to run to the grocery store, liquor store, and fish market laughing like joyriding teenagers. We can't help ourselves. When we get to the store, I decide to leave my big purse in the car and take my zip lock plastic bag that carries all the important stuff. Everything that leaves the boat goes in a plastic bag or it will be sure to get wet. My new "purse" is instantly dubbed "zip-lock Gucci."

The market is a big, clean, brightly lit IGA that has everything. The prices are higher than at home, but not outrageous. In the liquor store we meet a friendly police officer in a very impressive uniform. We chat awhile and learn where the fish market is. We tell him we are surprised how hard it is to find fish and he informs us that most of the locals are descendants of African slaves and prefer pork and chicken. Like Americans, most people we have seen are overweight.

The fish market is a find. The island style lobster processing plant is in full swing. A narrow trough, about ten feet long and filled with water, is the work station for six men wearing big white waterproof aprons and muck boots. They are cleaning the lobster and dropping the tails in one bucket and the rest of the carcass in a wheel barrel. A huge scale weighs the catch, the first one is sixty-five pounds. You can imagine what that means at $16 a pound for the tails. We take some pictures and a ten-pound box of tails with us. That's about thirteen tails.

We spend the next day snorkeling and running the roads. We actually find a farm that raises conch. The man who owns Conch World came to Provo some twenty-five years ago, wrecked his wooden boat on a reef and stayed. He is a marine biologist from Mystic, Connecticut who started the farm a few years later. We learn that thousands of eggs are hatched at one time, but few make it to adulthood. A baby conch actually grows its own tiny shell and is about an inch long at three-months-old. They harvest two-year-olds that are about three inches long and three-year-olds about four inches long. They stop growing at ten-years-old. The biggest ones are twelve inches long. There are trays of circulating water stacked on top of each other in row after row of barns that house the different ages. The conch is attached to the shell and they never leave it since it grows as they grow. They make the shell by mixing sand with salvia. They look like a snail with one claw, that they use for movement. They don't really do anything but lie on the bottom of the ocean and eat algae. Occasionally one will move an inch or so.

Oh, but they do mate, shell attached and all. Our guide actually shows us Sally first. He holds up a slim covered old shell and says she is about ten-years-old. In just a few seconds, she slides her whole body out of the shell, exposing this fleshy mass and lone claw that looks like a giant shark's tooth. Our guide points out a single vein on the side of her body explaining that's how you can tell she's a girl. Next is Jerry. He does the same thing, except immediately, we can tell he's a boy. He has a long, thin, black tubular vein dangling down most of his body. This organ can stretch up to one foot long and can grow back if for some reason it should get cut off. Take that Lorena Bobbitt!! For the rest of the day, Jerry is our hero. Go Jerry. Go Jerry.

By afternoon I am ready for a nap. Lioness needed some repairs to the trampoline on their boat, so we dropped it off in the morning. It will be ready in a few days. We won't be able to move anyway because a cold front will be moving through for the next few days and the winds will be strong, making the water too rough.

I skip dinner and go to sleep early. I am exhausted. Why is it that I feel like I must go, go, go? Is it because I have a car, or because I am on an island with life? I wonder.

I wake in the night with my throat on fire and incredible sinus pressure. I stay in bed all day. A storm is rolling in, so Pete puts the dinghy on deck and later, goes off exploring with Keith. I spend the day re-reading *Having It All*. It explains how laws of the universe work. About how thoughts can be turned into action and how creation happens. It is so clear and enlightening to me. I understand! It is an unusual treat to have the boat to myself. I am enjoying the time alone until I get unexpected little visitors.

Two adorable little blonde girls about seven or eight-years-old come rowing over on their little dinghy. They have braided necklaces and bracelets incorporating seashells and are selling them. In perfect English, they ask if I would like to buy something. I am much more interested in them than I am in their wares. Before I get to ask, the handheld radio one of the girls is holding squawks. It's their mother, making sure they are okay and being polite. She tells them to come home. Standing on deck, I watch these two little girls with braided ponytails row away. Who are they and what are they doing here?

Even though I don't feel well and would love to spend the day lying around the boat, I know this will be my last chance for a few days to talk to Brittany. So I radio over to Lioness and let them know when they go back for their laundry, I want to go along. Pete decides to come too. They tell us about their rough night. Somewhere about 5:00 a.m., they were awakened by a loud bang. An old dilapidated wooden boat that was anchored in the harbor broke loose and rammed into them. It was still dark and when they went on deck to see what happened, the flashlight and noise woke their neighbors and they came out to help. They pushed the old boat off of them and let it wash onto shore. They had no damage, thank goodness.

We stop at two different phone booths with each one having at least two phones and none work. *Cable and Worthless* strikes again. Surely the airport will have a working phone. Squealing through a few roundabouts and dodging other cars, we find the airport. There is a fee to park. Why must everything be so difficult? I am hot and cranky. Even if Brittany does answer her phone, which I know she won't, I am not exactly in the best frame of mind to be the supportive mother. We park and go inside. The terminal is busy. After finding the phone and dialing that long distance access number, then my credit card number, and then Brittany's number, I get voice mail, leave a one-minute message, and hang up. I just want to go back to the boat and lie down. Dr. Phil, this isn't workin' for me.

Next we pick up the laundry. Karla paid $13 in advance for two loads to wash and dry. That was not for the lady to fold it, just to use the machines. Some of the clothing isn't even dry, so Karla will have to hang them out when we get home. It is Saturday, so everyone is here. At 7:00 a.m., there is a line out the door. Yesterday, everyone was at the bank cashing their paychecks and today, the big line is at the Western Union, sending money back home. There is plenty of work here with all the hotel and condo construction. With a work permit, people from Haiti and other islands can come and support their families. There are more immigrants with work permits on the island than there are natives.

Once back on the boat, we girls decide to watch *Under the Tuscan Sun* and the boys go exploring. When they return, they tell us about a Mega Mansion that has its own island complete with tennis courts and its own swinging bridge. We hop in the dinghy for a look.

The place is amazing with one huge house that rambles on forever. Security cameras are perched on high poles surrounding the exterior perimeter, not of the house, but of the island. The terra cotta tile roof gives it an Italian villa feel. I can see a glass enclosed work-out room. All the patio furniture is draped in white sheets, which tells us the owners are not in residence. Who owns this place, a movie star or maybe some corporate giant?

We invite GR and Nate from San San for cocktails at five. We have bumped into them in the last several days, but never really got to hear their story. We do know that they ordered sails from Sarasota, Florida five weeks ago and are having them shipped to Provo. They have been here for three weeks. The sails are on the ground as of yesterday, now they are trying to get them out of customs before the weekend or they will have to wait until Monday. They are going stir crazy hanging out here. Having only rented a car for a day or two to pick up supplies, walking has become the answer. So much that they walk seven miles each way to eat pizza. That means about an-hour-and-a- half each way! "What else do we have to do?" Nate says, "Besides, we need the exercise."

GR, who seems to be in his thirties, is the captain and owner of the boat, and Nate just got onboard in Nassau. He bought the boat after a deal to buy a business fell through two days before the closing. The business seller, age seventy-three, died and his nineteen-year-old wife decided not to sell. So GR made an offer on three different boats, cash and closing the next day. He readied the boat and left last fall. He always wanted to island hop in the Caribbean, so he took a disappointment and turned it into an opportunity.

The boat is registered in Daytona, Florida where GR got started. This is great because that is where Karla and Keith are looking at getting a job. He has lots of useful information for them, especially that they need to get on a waiting list right away for a boat slip. GR knows the guy running the marina and will email him tomorrow. He started out his journey with another friend, and his girlfriend and her four-year-old daughter onboard. Neither of those worked out, so he met Nate who was on another boat and they hit it off; Nate *jumped ship* and is now sailing with GR.

Twenty-six year old Nate, grew up *off the grid* in Vermont with his mom, so he is used to alternate water and electric systems. He went to school at

University of Colorado, Boulder and moved to Massachusetts to meet his cousin and ready a boat for a round-the-world trip that they have been planning since they were kids. After months of preparation, they start with several others onboard for the first leg, and after a few months having only made it to Nassau, Nate's cousin decides he wants to be the only one to complete the round-the-world and Nate will have to get off before the end. Nate was stunned and disappointed, but as fate would have it, he joined up with GR and is still going. It looks to me like GR could be talked into a round-the-worlder. I admire both of them. So young, with such a great sense of adventure and lack of fear. I ask Nate if he has read anything good lately. "Yes," he says, "I just finished *Conversations with God.*" Wow, that was a life-changing book for me, but I was forty when I read it. He is light years ahead of me.

As they say goodnight and climb into their dinghy, they invite us to come down to the beach for a bonfire. We are tired, but all agree we can't miss it. So after dinner, we go to shore and help feed the already big fire. Several others are around the campfire, so introductions are made. We meet Sara and John who live on a thirty-two foot sailboat called Liahana, which is Hawaiian for The Promised Land. They are Mormons from Austin, Texas and have been anchored here for nine months and live onboard with their five children, age's four to eleven. The two little girls selling jewelry are their kids. She home-schools them and for punishment the kids have to swim laps around the boat! They have no electricity or refrigeration, being vegetarians, it's not that bad. They used to eat fish until the eleven-year-old boy started crying when they filleted a fish he just caught. He couldn't understand how it was okay to kill a fish, but not a cow. So they decided to skip the fish thing too. They use oil lamps for light, hand pump for the toilet, gas for cooking, and laundry is dipped in the ocean off the back of the boat and hung on the sides with clothespins. The nearest grocery store is five miles away and they have no car, so they walk or ride their one bike. Their budget is $250 a month. Sara tells us they could never have gone from a regular house to this without having lived with the Amish in Ohio. They want to start a church here and learned it will take another year or so. Their engine is broken, so they can't move anchorage. The dinghy is a little wooden rowboat. They do have another dinghy, a small wooden sailboat like a sunfish, but from a hundred years ago. They took the little sailboat on *vacation* a few months ago. The seven of them climbed in and went around the island to a little cove and camped out under the stars. I listen to their story in sheer amazement.

Bad weather is expected to roll in today, so it looks like another boat day. Just as well because my cold has moved into my chest and I sound like an old lady who smoked three packs a day for twenty years. The big event of the day is our visit to SanSan. I am surprised to see a very clean and organized boat. The main salon is sleek and minimal. They show us how their windmill works and explain how they have all the power they need. I also get a lesson on the Skype phone and how they can talk anytime via computer for free. I go home with windmill envy and start cleaning up our boat.

The cold front finally comes and goes. The winds have stopped; it is now very dry and 73 degrees. I go for one more walk-run for exercise. Our last errand of the day is to go back to customs and get our exit stamp for a whopping $15.

Goodbye Caicos. Hello Turks.

# Chapter 29

*Grand Turk Island, Turks and Caicos*
*February 2007*

On the road again, just like the song, but we are not on the road. It feels good to be in open water again. We pull up anchor at 9:00 a.m. and motor sail all day, arriving on South Caicos clocking fifty-one miles. It was a rough ride with six to eight foot seas. We are the only two sailboats anchored. Beaten up and exhausted, I make lobster risotto for all of us and call it a day by seven. We will go to town in the morning and see about getting our five-gallon bottles of water filled and head out again by 11:00 a.m.

Cockburn Harbour is a very industrial town. Not much of a dock to speak of, not that it matters for the rusty old boats tied up to them. Pete and I ride in with Karla on Lioness's dinghy. Ours is such a pain in the neck to load on and off the boat. They have davits that hook onto the dinghy and pull it up, leaving it hanging out over the back. We have to take the engine off, take the fuel tank and hose off, bring it around to the side, hook it to the spinnaker pole, hoist it up, flip it over, which is not an easy feat, and tie it down. Then do the reverse, every time we want to go out for a spin. It's okay to leave it down for short hops, but we no longer tow it from behind since we lost it in Georgetown.

We find the all-in-one store just a short walk from where we docked the dinghy. Here we find water, a fairly decent grocery store, international calling, gas pumps, and the place to pay your cable and wireless telephone bill. The locals are very kind and helpful. I make a call to Brittany and the conversation flows easily. I am so grateful for the light-hearted chat. More than anything else, I want her to know I am on her side and I am her greatest supporter. Our last few calls felt more like we were adversaries than allies. I need to add this to my gratitude cards.

Anchor up and off to Grand Turk Island, world famous for diving. Keith and Karla are avid divers and brought their own gear. After a five-hour motor dead into the wind again, we anchor just off the sandy beach of a charming little town. From the boat, we can see a red and white church and cute pink building that we find out later is the library.

Karla stays onboard while we ride into town on the Spotted Cub with Keith. It is already 4:00 p.m., but he wants to make a quick run to the hardware store. We are no sooner on the main street through town when a band of school kids in neatly pressed uniforms walked by. I ask them if anyone speaks English. In all my travels, I have found I have a better chance of asking the younger people since they usually have to learn English in school.

Looking at me like I am crazy, they confirm that of course they speak English. I am dealing with teenagers, I forgot. They tell us where the hardware store is and say they are going that way. I compliment one girl on her choice of sunglasses, which happen to be very similar to mine. One of the girls likes my bright pink Crocs. She wants to get a pair in purple. I tell her how to order them on the Internet. As we walk along, I realize I am in the middle of this pack of kids, mostly girls, and I blend right in. I am the same height as they are. We chat like old friends. Pete and Keith follow behind us, amazed at the way they accept me so easily. They say things to shock me or see what my reaction is and I laugh at them, letting it be known they can't pull the wool over my eyes. They are curious what it is like to live on a boat, and I want to know how old they must be to drive and who has their license. They must be fifteen to learn and sixteen to drive. Most of them can drive, but driving and getting a car doesn't seem to be a big deal.

Another boy is listening to an I-pod. I ask what kind of music he likes and if I can have a listen? He says I won't like it. He, like every other teenage boy in the USA, is listening to rap. I ask them about Brittany Spears and prom. I learn that they wear floor length dresses, any color, but bright ones are the most popular. They don't have to have a date, they can go in a group. High school and college are right here on the island, so they don't have to go anywhere. They have all been to the USA, mostly to somewhere in Florida. Their parents either work or own a business in the tourist industry, like a dive shop or a restaurant. The kids want to be doctors and lawyers, one girl, the self-professed leader of the group, wants to be an entrepreneur and make a whole lot of money.

We walk the mile or so to the hardware store and they deposit us right at the front door. I try to say their names, but they are difficult to pronounce, so each one makes up a short name I can say. We say our goodbyes and just like that, they are off, a band of kids in school uniforms walking down the street.

We get what we need at the store and get back to the boat just before dark. Karla is making dinner tonight on the Lioness. She kept Bambi on the boat with her all day today so that Bambi and Jake could bond. After dinner, Karla decides to comb out Bambi. Her hair has grown a bit and I think Karla is missing the hair salon. Considering Bambi's mood swings, I admire Karla for trying. To all of our surprise, Bambi likes it and actually becomes very playful, more playful than I have ever seen her. She loves being the center of attention. She is cute when she is clean and fluffy, and the way she cocks her head when we talk to her is adorable. Maybe she just needs a little more attention.

With the morning pretty well shot, we decide to take the bikes into town while Keith and Karla go diving. Commercial dive boats are already tied to buoys just a few hundreds yards from where we are anchored. We are in twelve feet of water, the buoys are in thirty feet and just out from there is *the wall* that drops off 800 feet. This is *the* place to dive.

We peddle all around the island. My bike seems to be pedaling a lot harder than Pete's. I am the athlete and am huffing and puffing going up and down minor hills. I stop to make an adjustment, but it doesn't change anything. They are more work than they are worth. We ride past the police station, some rundown shops, the local housing—ranging from good, bad, and ugly pink flamingos—the old cemetery, and the salt ponds.

History tells us the island was used to make salt for over 100 years. Water drains from the ocean into shallow ponds, then evaporates and that's how they make salt. We can still see the intricate dredging system and an old windmill. I guess they used the same technology as the Dutch and the Romans before that. Turkish salt is still known to be the finest. Who would have guessed?

The downtown is adorable and the oldest part is walled on both sides with a full canopy of mature trees offering lots of shade. Here the street is dotted with 100 year old buildings, now little dive shops, and charming bed and breakfasts. We check out the local watering holes with their oceanfront decks and open-air bars, each one offering more local color than the last.

At the Sand Bar, we order two beers and meet our young bartender. I learn Anna is from Canada and this is her sixth year on the island. We have met a lot of Canadians in the islands. I wonder if it is because it is so cold there most of the year, or if socialism makes it easier to give up the rat race and choose again. We are having a nice visit until a little rain comes. The wind is going to change directions in the next few days, and our little anchorage will be exposed to the northerly winds and will no longer be calm like it is now.

"You don't want to get caught like that big catamaran did last week," Anna says.

"What cat?" Pete asks.

"Didn't you see it?" she asks. "A storm came up out of the north. We told them, in English, to move the boat, but they didn't. Then someone went out and explained it in Spanish, still they didn't move. When the storm came in, it was smashing their boat against the concrete wall and the owners came running out of the hotel and tried to keep the boat from hitting by pushing it away with their feet. A surge came and lifted the boat and it came crashing down and pinned the guy's leg. It didn't pinch it off completely, but it was clearly crushed. The locals drug him to shore and made a tourniquet until he could be airlifted to Jacksonville, Florida for treatment. We heard his leg couldn't be saved."

Later we see the boat. The hull is completely broken apart. Even from far away, we can see it was severely damaged. We all agree, move when it is time. Don't mess with Mother Nature.

At The Turks Head Inn we meet Sandy and her sister from Key West, originally from Australia. They bought this big beautiful historic building right on the water for less than a million dollars. They moved here when Key West out-priced itself in the real estate market. Sandy said it is a great place to live. It's safe, friendly, and if something happens, the police know who to go to. She picked up most of the furnishings on e-Bay and they did a lot of the restoring themselves. When she bought it, the building had been subdivided into single offices for offshore banking, but they put it back to its original glory.

It's getting to be 5:00 p.m. and to our disappointment, the Poop Deck Bar and Museum are closed. We decide to go back to the boat and get ready for dinner. Rather than break down the bikes and load them onto the dinghy, we just push them into the bushes. We have locks for them, but left them on the boat. We weren't planning on leaving the bikes anywhere. We are coming back first thing is the morning and it is already dark. They should be fine.

After a casual dinner onshore, we come home to find Bambi eagerly waiting for us at the bottom of the steps. She doesn't like being below and we rarely do it to her, but tonight it was rolling and chilly. Without realizing it I forgot to close my cabin door, something I have been doing ever since she peed on my bed. I guess she was pissed because tonight she pooped on my bed. Too bad such a lovely evening ends on a bad note. Too bad my decision to pay more attention to Bambi just got tossed overboard. I don't like her and wish she wasn't onboard. Onshore, everyone thinks she is so cute. I have tried to give her away several times, but she is not my dog. We are back to just tolerating each other.

At 8:00 a.m. we decide that Bambi needs to get off the boat, so we dinghy to shore to discover our bikes are gone. We should have gone back and locked them up, but we didn't. There is lots of activity on the street. Today is the inauguration of the newly elected premier and there will be a parade and ceremony. Maybe the police moved the bikes to get ready for the festivities. We report the missing bikes to one of the many uniformed police on the street. They won't be able to do anything about it until after the festivities, but they know where the boat is anchored and the most likely thieves so they will reach us by VHS radio if they come up with anything.

Just as we finish our lunch, the storm clouds build and the wind picks up. We make a mad dash to the boat and quickly get the dinghy loaded. I don't have time to dive and we still haven't heard from the police about the bikes. Oh well, if that is the worst thing that happens to us, we will survive.

Lioness has a little trouble getting their anchor up, but after Keith dives down and loosens it, we are off to Luperon, Dominican Republic about 100 miles away. It's an all night run and we hope to arrive at 8:00 a.m. About fifteen minutes out, we get a call from the Turks Police. They have located our bikes. We can't go back now, so we tell them thanks, but to donate them to a family that can use them.

As we roll along, bobbing with the waves, I remember something I read just yesterday that one of the laws of the universe is we get everything we want. It may not be what we think or in the right package, but the clearer we are, the clearer the universe will deliver our desires. Our thoughts are pure creative energy. Did I wish our bikes to go away? What a pain they were, I thought. Loading and unloading them. They were heavy and got sand all over the V berth. Mine peddled hard and the seat didn't come up high enough. I was the one who suggested we leave them in the bushes. Did all those thoughts cause the bikes to be taken away? During my morning meditation/gratitude, one of the things I pray for is to totally understand the laws of the universe and to fully and completely be aware of creation. Does it happen like this? Do I really get what I want every time? Did I really wish the bikes to be taken away? Did I wish for Tom to go away? Did I ask for the universe to open a door to a new life, and without realizing it, another door had to be closed. Is it really this basic? And are the results delivered so quickly? It seems so swift and sometimes incredibly harsh. Is this what is meant by "every opportunity or hardship has the answer within it and we have asked for it in some way?"

After sunset, I go below to make dinner. While I am frying up the hamburger, I start to feel a little queasy. It is a bit hot and loud with the engine on full speed. By the time dinner is ready, I am ready to barf. Now I get sea sick? I have been on the boat almost two months. How strange. The sea is rough and it is dark outside. I pass a bowl of chili up to Pete who is at the helm, and tell him I am going to lie down for bit and see if sleep will make me feel better. When I awaken an hour later, Pete is down below putting the chili away. The boat is on auto-pilot and Bambi is at the top of the stairs, sniffing around, hoping for a treat. I go to the bathroom and Pete warms some chili for me. With the kitchen secure again for more rough seas, we both go up to the cockpit.

"Where's Bambi?" I ask. She is usually tucked in behind a cushion or in a little nook behind the captain's chair.

"I don't know," Pete says, "She was just right here a minute ago."

We start to call her name looking for her.

"Did you take her down below?" I ask.

"No," Pete says. We lock our harnesses to the jack lines and go out on deck. Pete's on one side, I am on the other. We are frantically calling her name. Maybe she went out to pee and got stuck under the upside down dinghy. The boat is rolling side to side at a forty-five degree angle. Neither of us ever saw her leave the cockpit. I look out into the dark rough sea while holding onto the rigging as the wind whips all around. If she fell overboard, we will never find her.

"We have to go back and do a search and rescue," I shout to Pete. "Radio to Lioness. They are about a mile or two behind us. Maybe they will see her."

"It's too late," Pete shouts back, shaking his head. "We don't know how long she has been out there or where she could possibly be. It is almost impossible to see a person, shouting and waving their arms, let alone a little dog. She's gone."

We work our way back into a silent cockpit. Neither of us says a word. We are both thinking of her watery demise. How hard did she swim? How cold is the water? How long did she last? How much did she suffer? I look out into the blackness. The sea, she takes no prisoners. I could have been nicer to her. So she had a mean streak? Everyone gets a little testy now and then. I know I would have preferred to live without her, but drown in the ocean? That is just horrible. And then it hits me, MY thoughts create MY reality. I didn't wish Bambi dead, but I did say at every chance I got, that the dog really should go. She bites people, she peed and pooped on my bed, she turns into the devil when food is involved. This whole meditation thing has gotten out of hand. I didn't wish for Bambi to drown or for the bikes to be stolen.

Does this mean if I ask for a thing or situation, if I don't take action when given the situation, that the universe steps in and gives it to me anyway, even if it's not at all the way I wanted it to happen? If I had given Bambi away to a loving family or we sold the bikes, they would be gone from me rather than being taken away. I have been asking for divine intervention to get the result I want. Good things happen all the time, just not in the package I hoped for like getting fired and the next day going to Atlanta to find out I can get more financial aid because I don't have a job. I got to go on a trip with Dad to Alaska because I didn't have anything to go back to in Orlando. Moving to a town that I have been to once in my life where I know no one, only to meet a man with a sailboat who would love to go island hopping around the Caribbean. These are all things I asked for, yet they didn't come exactly like I thought. I didn't like getting fired even though I was miserable. I didn't like having Tom die and Brittany move out of state, leaving me with no reason to stay in Orlando, but it did start me on an incredible journey. I did choose to be a server at the marina bar near where Pete *happened* to be living. Why did I get that job rather than one of the others I applied for? I got what I wished for every time.

My thoughts create my reality. I asked to be aware of the power of creation, and now I fully understand the responsibility that goes with it. I must guard my words and thoughts as though it is a life and death situation because it is. I must think about this more.

I turn to Pete and tell him I am sorry. He is sorry too. Here we sit in our little cockpit, in a boat in the middle of the ocean, in the darkness with our regrets. I tell Pete to go below and get some sleep. I know he won't be able to, but he needs to at least rest. It is going to be a long night. I will wake him at two o'clock.

There is another flotilla of boats about fifteen miles ahead of us. I can hear them on the radio. There are four boats in the group and they are also heading to Luperon. When they call to each other on Channel 16, the hailing channel, then move to another channel to talk, I listen. They are twenty-seven miles out from the shore and are being pounded with rain. That means when we get up there, in about two hours, we will get hit too. I radio to Lioness and tell them in case they weren't listening. Karla is at the helm. I decide to wake Pete at midnight so we can take down the main sail and get ready for the squaw. At midnight we turn on the deck lights, steer straight into the wind and Pete climbs out on the deck, harness on and hooked to the jack line, to let the main down while the boat rocks and rolls. I am at the helm and watch Pete getting thrown from side to side. We have already lost one tonight, please hurry up and get back in the cockpit. He is struggling and cursing. I don't know if that is cursing because we are in trouble or because he is frustrated. I try to stay calm. I can't help nor can he hear me even if I do call to him. Worry is wasted energy.

He finally gets the sail down and we are back on course. Pete goes back to sleep and the plan is that I will stay up until 3:00 a.m. or until the rain starts. We never hit the rain. I guess in an hour or two, the storm moved out of the area or dissipated. At 3:00 a.m., we change places and at six we are both up, coffee in hand, ready to anchor in a new country. As the sun comes up, we can see the cloud cover all around us. Everything is damp, even without looking at a gauge, I am sure it is 100 percent humidity. With landfall in sight, we should be in the harbor by 8:00 a.m.

# Chapter 30

*Dominican Republic
February 2007*

Between the bands of rain, seven boats arrive in the harbor along with us. There is quite a commotion in the channel leading into the harbor as a boat has run aground, and lots of other cruisers have come out to help get it loose from the sandbar. Someone from a dingy is shouting to us. It is Nate and GR from SanSan. They beat us here.

The harbor is full of other boats, so after we find a spot to anchor, we fly the yellow quarantine flag and go below to sleep. After a nap, I climb up the ladder, pop my head out of the cockpit and look around. "Hello Vietnam!" is the first thing that comes to mind. We are anchored in a cove surrounded by lush green mountains dotted with palm trees. The heavy rain coming down is running off into the harbor and a mud line is drifting across the water, making the whole port a murky chocolate brown. It feels completely different than the Bahamas.

Soon there is a knock on the side of boat. Immigration has arrived. We are surprised they came to us, especially in the pouring down rain. We are instructed to go to the blue trailer at the government dock and pay $25 for a stamp, get a tourist card and an agricultural clearance stamp. We are also told to put our *international trash* in a special dumpster by the dock. So later when the rain stops, we dingy to shore, take care of business and walk around the little town of Luperon. It is very poor, but happy island music is playing from every business. The people are pretty with dark skin and light eyes. They are clean and nicely dressed. We walk past the hair salon where loud gas-powered generators are running outside on the sidewalk. We learn the power goes out regularly, especially in the hair salons because of the heavy use, so in order not to lose business, they run the shop with generators during the power outages. We see advertisements around town boasting this innovative benefit of the salon.

That night we go to the marina dock and find a big thatched roof open-air bar and restaurant that is the headquarters for the cruisers. We have dinner with Lioness, SanSan and Lone Star, a new boat from Texas. We manage to stay dry even though there is a major downpour going on all around us.

In the morning there is another knock on our boat. This time it is Handy Andy. He is the floating gas station and hardware store. He wants to know if we need fuel or water or any other supplies. We order what we need and he goes to shore and brings it to us. He is very friendly, speaks broken English and has huge muscular arms. I am amazed when he returns with ten-gallon containers full of gas and water and proceeds to lift them by hand effortlessly from his boat to ours and then, using a giant funnel, pours each one into the proper tank. I watch in awe as he lifts one container after another, his dark black skin glistening in the sun.

Last night we were told about the flea market at the marina dock on Sunday mornings, so we go check it out. Cruisers and local businesses bring all kinds of wares to sell and swap, artists sell their crafts and the restaurant makes a buffet brunch complete with Bloody Marys. We meet all the other cruisers and lots of ex-patriots. I am surprised how many have made the Dominican Republic their home. Some have been in this harbor for years, others return each winter year after year. We meet Dori on the sailing vessel Sol Y Mar, who has been living onboard full-time for three years now. She is down to one storage unit after starting out with three. We also meet Trudy and Guy onboard Abracadabra. They are retired from Florida and traveling on a trawler.

In the afternoon we go back into town to drop off some laundry. We have two big garbage bags full. There is a self-service Laundromat, but we feel like we should help out the local economy and let the ladies wash it for us. We walk down a dirt path to a shack that is barely standing with a muddy creek running behind it. "She's not going to wash it down there is she?" I ask Pete.

Apparently she understood what I said and motions for me to come inside. There she proudly points to a washing machine with rollers on top to squeeze the water out. It's a bargain at four loads for $20. That is until we are walking back later and I see my panties hanging in a tree drying. I feel bad. I would have given her $20 not to wash my clothes.

The next day we are off on a little day trip organized by Jose, the local tour operator/hustler. He has arranged for a van to drive us and four other couples to climb the waterfall and visit a botanical garden.

The waterfall is amazing. At first, I think I am in over my head when we are outfitted with helmets and heavy-duty vests, but it turns out to be fun climbing through the rushing water over huge boulders in the thick forest. I am amazed at how tropical and lush it is.

With luck and grace on our side, we are in the country on the day of the big festival—New Years for them, I think. Again, we hop on a bus, much bigger this time, arranged by Jose. Like a bunch of overgrown children, we laugh and drink the whole way to La Vega and back. The festival is like Rio or Mardi Gras with a parade filled with colorful outfits, floats, and music. We eat and drink our way through the carnival.

The following day, Pete and Keith are working on the boat and Karla and I talk about Brittany and the situation. She thinks I am holding on too tightly, that I must release my desire for the outcome and trust in Brittany and the universe that she will find her own path. I write a new gratitude card about Brittany and carefully add it to the others.

Keith isn't feeling too well and has an upset stomach and diarrhea so Karla and I volunteer to go to shore and buy some medicine. We find the pharmacy just fine, but all the medicine is kept behind the counter and we must ask for what we want. That's not the problem. The problem is no one speaks English. Laughing like schoolgirls at the thought of who is going to demonstrate through sign language what we need, I step up to the plate and volunteer. First I rub my tummy and make a bad face. The pharmacist in her clean white coat shakes her head knowingly. Then I hold up one finger, like wait just a minute and fake throwing up. Very sympathetically, the pharmacist says, "Oh."

Then I turn to Karla, who by now is totally cracking up but doing the best she can to hold in the laughter, and ask if she wants to take over for the diarrhea section of the show. She is laughing so hard she can't even speak, so I turn to the professional behind the counter and making a very uncomfortable face, rolling my hands indicating there is more, I turn my rear-end toward her and motion stuff coming from my ass. The pharmacist returns the painful face and shakes her head knowingly while Karla goes outside and bursts out laughing. The pharmacist opens a box that I can't read, cuts three pills from the foil strip, and sells them to me for one dollar each. She writes on a piece of paper "1-24." I hope that means take one a day and I hope that she sold us the right medicine, or we could kill Keith. Once out in the street, Karla and I are a complete mess. I tell her she owes me for my grand performance.

⚜

Today is our biggest adventure yet. The four of us have rented scooters to drive to Isabella, a beautiful beach about twenty minutes away. We pick up our Rent-a-Wreck scooters in town and head out. Pete has the map, but I am sure I heard Jose say we should make a right turn leaving the Marina dock, which is in the other direction. According to the map, we should turn down a little road just out of town. Well that little road ends up being a washed out dirt/ rock road. Pete is sure this is right, so we keep going. Soon we come to a shallow, but rapidly flowing, muddy creek. Here we find two men and a makeshift raft onto which we proceed to load the scooter and rider while the men, one on each side, guide us across. It's a crazy fun adventure and everyone we meet tells us we are going in the right direction. After an hour of bouncing along on a dusty dirt road in the middle of rural farmlands and ramshackle houses, my scooter dies. I try to kick start it, but nothing. I am cranking it with my foot, looking down and before I know it a whole herd of cows is passing me on both sides since I am in the middle of the road. That takes the cake. "Can't you see I am a little busy here?" I shout to no one in particular.

The locals come out of the woodwork to help. Some walk, some are on motorcycles, and one guy even comes by on horseback. How do they know we are here? They turn the bike upside down and replace the spark plug for a whopping $2. I clap and cheer when the bike starts up and everyone thinks I am silly. The people look at me strangely, but I am probably the only person they have ever seen with blonde hair and blue eyes, or maybe it is the hot pink Crocs. We are very low on gas, so another man brings us gas which is sold by the El Presidente beer bottle. We fill our tanks and are off again. At 3:00 a.m., we give up and turn around, never finding the beach.

Back on the boat, I get a great email from Brittany. She loves her classes, has made some new friends and is getting involved in promoting baseball on campus by starting her own website and blog. Karla was right. Look what happened the very next day after I wrote the gratitude card. Wow, the universe works so fast.

Lael sends an email asking about my plans for the summer. I write back and tell her that I must give it more thought.

On another day of sightseeing, we hire a driver to take us to the big port town of Puerto Plata. The man is driving crazy and after barely missing hitting a donkey, we make him pull over to buy beer. After finally arriving in town on a beautiful coastal road, we tour the Amber Museum and have lunch in an old Colonial style restaurant. I didn't know anything about amber, but quickly learn that the Dominican Republic has some of the world's biggest mines and it is really not a stone but petrified tree sap. Some of the most valuable pieces have insects suspended in the clear golden stones. It is actually very light.

Before we leave town, we decide we must take the cable car up to the top of the mountain. At the top, there is a beautiful lookout and park, so we brave the ride up and look around.

Today is our last day in Luperon and all tanks are full. We have a great fish lunch with Lone Star and their friends, a couple on the sailing vessel Moonsail, at a restaurant owned by a French couple with a German waitress. We get our departing stamp at the commander's office and mail our postcards.

At the marina dock, we meet the sailing vessel Santori. A retired professor from North Carolina, Worth has been a single-hander for three years now, and is planning to sail around the world after his daughter graduates from college in May. He is looking for a first mate and invites me to come. I take his email address.

At dinner, we learn that Lioness is heading back. Frustrated with minor problems, they are not having fun and are both tired and ready to go back. They will come with us to Rio San Juan tomorrow, but then head back. They still have a month and will dive in the Turks, and then go back via Jamaica and Grand Caymans.

We make the all night, fifty-four mile run to Rio San Juan under a light cloud cover, big moon and a little fog. The morning is spent resting and then we dinghy into town with Lioness. The locals come out to greet us. They are friendly and it is cleaner than Luperon. We have nicknamed Luperon, "Leprechaun," since Keith never pronounces it right, and Puerto Plata became "porta-potty" for obvious reasons. We find a lovely little white hotel called Bahia Blanco with yellow and white awnings and a killer view of the sea. We stop for a drink and learn the rooms are $17 a night. At the bar, we meet two young biologists from Seattle. They are working on a government-funded project.

For our last supper together, we grill burgers on the Lioness. At midnight, we pull up anchor and motor sail fifty-six miles to Puerto Escondido arriving around 10:00 a.m. Our running total for the trip is 1,176 miles in fifty-nine days.

This, by far, is the most majestic tropical cove yet. It really looks like a faraway landscape with high lush green mountains dropping straight into the emerald green water. The surf crashes against the rocks while palm trees sway on a sandy beach that is sprinkled with thatch roof huts and old- fashioned fishing boats. Paradise! It could be Bora Bora.

Anchoring is a little bit tricky. We certainly don't want to break loose and hit the side of the mountain. There is one other boat in the cove, the sailing vessel Blue Jay with three kids in their twenties onboard. The real fascination is the local men net fishing. There are two little boats strategically set along the mountain with several men in the water slapping it, chasing the fish right into their nets. Before long, they are rowing over to us, offering to sell a big round of fish to us for $15. After we buy the still alive fish, we discover that neither of us has ever filleted a fish. I decide to give it a try, but when I slice it open it flops around. It is hard to enjoy it for dinner with that scene still running in my mind.

In the morning it is time to move to Samana, a little port town at the east end of the island and the staging area for our big twenty-four hour pass to Puerto Rico. We leave our little private paradise at 3:00 a.m. because the water is calmer at night. Blue Jay is already gone. We hardly get five miles out when there is a bump and the engine drops in RPMs. Not good. Pete goes below while I take the helm. I have no control without the engine. The transmission fluid is low, so he adds some. In the dark, he puts up the sails in case we lose the engine completely. After ten minutes, we give it another try. The prop is spinning, but the speed is just not there. Rather than take a chance and make the six-hour run, we decide to turn around and go back. The motor works a little, but rather than risk burning it up, we try to do without it. With the wind as our only power, we are barely moving and I can't really steer. Just yesterday, I was saying that I thought we would sail more and how much fun it would be if we sailed more—never realizing what I was telling the universe to do. Now that we are sailing, I want to go back to motor sailing. We will have to wait until sunrise to anchor, so we just putter around at sea for three hours and then anchor at first daylight.

At noon, Pete puts on snorkel gear and dives under the boat to discover we picked up a crab trap and the rope is all tied around the prop. The cage is gone but the rope is not. Pete gets most of the rope off, but is exhausted, so I give it a go. It is hard to hold my breath, dive down under the boat, and cut away at a nylon rope that is wrapped so tight that it has now become a solid ring. Pete is bleeding from scratches on this back from the barnacles growing on the bottom of the boat. We stay onboard for the rest of the day.

# Chapter 31

## *Haitian Refugees – Dominican Republic March 2007*

Our second attempt to move to Samana is gratefully uneventful. As we round the last cape and head for the harbor, we are joined by two huge cruise ships. We give way. They anchor out and lower the tenders. We hear the local officials hailing them on the radio and preparing to board. This is a big whale-watching place. Samana is a town built into the side of the mountain with buildings stacked on top of each other with an amazing view of the sea. It reminds me of Positano with the scooters zooming around, but the palm trees and the constant beat of salsa blasting from every open-air bar give it away. This is the Caribbean, not Italy.

In the dinghy headed toward the docks, we stop by sailing vessel Blue Jay to say hello and tell them the story of our day-late arrival. A man aboard the sailing vessel Sea Bound waves good morning, so we stop by. He has been here three weeks and gives us the lay of land. "The cruisers meet up for happy hour at the blue tent over there everyday at 5:00 p.m.," he says, pointing to the street along the ocean. "Why don't you join us and meet the others?" We will.

We go first to the *commandante* to check in and get a paper. Even though we already did it for this country, we must check in and out of every port. Again, no one speaks English, so this should be good. We are greeted by the friendly smile of a pretty young girl wearing a green army uniform, black jump boots and perfect make-up. She is sitting behind an old beat-up desk, typing on an antique manual typewriter, ribbon and all. She is expertly clicking away, filling in blank spaces on a standard form, using a black sheet of carbon paper to make a copy of it. Next to her typewriter is a little bottle of white-out, just in case. I feel like I am on a movie set, in a war room telegraph office in the 1940's until I notice a silver laptop, next to another manual typewriter on another desk. There is an electric typewriter on the floor in the corner under some papers. Boxes of old documents surround it. Electric typewriter, now that adds a whole new set of problems.

She asks us a few questions, which we don't understand. Drawing a picture always works. She wants to know if our sailboat has one hull or two. We laugh at how simple it is. Thank goodness I don't have to do the diarrhea pantomime again. She likes the name of our boat. Every official does. It looks funny written, but every time we pronounce it, they repeat it smiling, raising their eye brows and shaking their heads with such gusto. Ooh La La! It sounds intriguing. We get the stamp, and to our surprise, we pay no money. All this checking in and out and filling out forms is useless. Nothing will become of any of it. It is usually all about collecting the fee.

We walk around the town, immediately getting away from the waterfront and all the *fake island* stuff set up for the cruise ships. It is hot, and the streets are busy. Big buses are lined up along the oceanfront, waiting to whisk tourists off to the waterfalls or deserted beach for a BBQ. We pop into a little dark and dingy grocery store. Pete is looking at the bottles of rum when the clerk comes over and shines a flashlight onto the label so he can read it. Either the electricity has gone out or they don't want the expense of the lights.

There is a lottery stand on every corner. These little booths don't sell anything but lottery tickets. We have seen them everywhere, even in the backcountry the day we took the scooters. We still can't figure out how much it costs or how much they can win, but it seems very popular.

Next, we go into a house wares and clothing store. Again it is so dark I can barely see. Clothing and merchandise are piled everywhere. The jeans don't have any tags, so I can't tell if they are new or used. Funny thing, at home we want them to *look* used, but we don't want them to *be* used. I ask the clerk the price. Jeans are $5 and a cute top is $2. In the back of the store other clerks are folding clothing that just arrived. Huge white canvas bags are piled on the floor. They are unpacking Ralph Lauren Polo and Tommy Hilfiger shirts. These have labels and tags from stores we recognize from home.

We learn from one of the cruisers that clothing is very cheap here. American stores and Goodwill send all their leftover merchandise to Haiti, and the Haitians sell it to people in the Dominican Republic for money to buy food. We are told that there is a Goodwill store here if we need some boat clothing. One day a yachtie spilled red wine all over his shirt, so he walked down to Goodwill to buy another one and thinks he bought back the same shirt he donated in the states.

We go to search for some lunch. There is supposed to be an open-air market in the center of town, so we head that way. We walk past several restaurants that smell good, but are too seedy for me. We are greeted warmly by the locals. It is hot and the street is getting dirtier the further we go. The market is more than I can take. I desperately try to get past the smell and the filth. Produce stands are blended in with groceries, art, stereo speakers, clothing and food vendors. A butchered chicken is hanging from an overhead hook and another one, skinned, is laying on the counter, bloody and covered with flies. Next to that, a man is selling saddles. Fifty pound bags of assorted dry beans are rolled open and lined up. Rice is sold this way too. I walk around the back of a food vendor to watch an old lady stirring a pot of some kind of stew and then serving it over rice. It smells good, but seeing her *kitchen* and wondering how long the buckets of meats have been sitting out, I can't do it. I turn to Pete and say, "I'll have an order of E coli with a side of Salmonella. Let's head back toward the water and the *fake island* restaurants. This is a little too real, even for me."

We do buy some great looking red apples from a sweet old lady. As I walk away, I notice this sticker on one of the apples says "Product of Washington State." Imagine that.

We climb to the top of a hill following a narrow winding street and find a lovely restaurant with an outdoor table set with crisp linens. We have found a Chinese restaurant with a view of the sea and a much-appreciated breeze. After a couple of glasses of wine, I decide I could get used to this.

Could I really? I mean, could I really live here all the time. It is a tropical paradise. We learn a very nice apartment with a swimming pool rents for $450 a month. We know food and household help are inexpensive while phone, TV, and computer are available via satellite. A scooter is perfect for transportation and the island is big enough and has lots to see. There is plenty of nightlife and enough tourists and cruisers coming through to keep it interesting.

But it's poor. Could I get past the filth and squalor? The people seem happy. They do not beg or accost you with their wares. They don't walk around in despair. They work, they carry their babies and say hello to us as we pass by. So it's not Beverly Hills or New York. Now there's a thought. It's not New York. I have seen filth and squalor in New York City the same or worse than here. It's just that it is not right up against the grandeur of Park Avenue and Trump Towers. Do the Dominicans know they are poor? Or are they more content because there is no disparity? Everyone is poor. We have not seen many TV's. Only one or two and they have been in American-owned bars. I don't think the locals have it. If they don't know what the rest of the world has, does that make it better? If we got away from the trappings and treadmills of America, would that make it easier to live here? And why do I want to get away from something so many others are dying to get to?

At five o'clock, we meet up with the other cruisers at the blue tent. It is one of many outdoor bars lining the waterfront street. The *restaurants* are portable carts like we use for carnivals and fairs. Plastic tables and chairs are set out on dirt or stones and plastic tarps serve as protection from the rain and sun. The air is filled with salsa music. Men are huddled around tables, intensely concentrating as they slap down the domino tiles. We learn they bet on the games. It is the Dominican version of Poker.

We are introduced to the group, Peter and Don on sailing vessel Sea Bound, Beth and John on sailing vessel Snoopy, and Bruce and Sue on sailing vessel Wood Wind. Sea Bound has been here three weeks. Don owns the boat and has lived onboard for twelve years. He found Peter, a very accomplished captain, on an Internet website that's like a dating service, but matches crew with captains. (www.7knots.com). Peter is from Nova Scotia and tries to get on a boat in the islands for the winter. He has hopped aboard several times now and he says, "They always work out."

Snoopy lives onboard full time also. They just came to Samana after living in Luperon for three years. Unbelievable to me! Luperon was super poor and the harbor had brown muddy water. The tide doesn't pull the water out to sea and with all the boats anchored, I can just imagine the condition of the water. At other harbors and anchorages, when it got hot, I just jumped in the water to cool off, but in Luperon we had to get off the boat in the afternoon when it got hot. We meet several other yachties that bought houses up in the hills just outside of town and made it their permanent home. Seeing Samana, I would never choose Luperon.

John, onboard the sailing vessel Snoopy, was the Handy Andy of the harbor before Handy Andy. He took fuel and water to the boats, cleaned the bottoms, and helped the yachties with mechanical problems. He is wearing a T-shirt that says 1-17-09. I ask him what that means. "It is the last day President Bush will be in office," he says. "They are selling like hot cakes in the states and I had this one made here in the Dominican Republic."

Anyway, the sailing vessel Snoopy has a great story. They honeymooned in the islands and went out on a sunset cruise on a thirty-foot sailboat that the captain actually lived on. They were totally intrigued and went home to Erie, Pennsylvania and set up a seven-year plan to live on a boat in the Caribbean. As the time came near to put the house on the market, they were sitting in the bar where they got engaged and a man stood up and asked if anyone knew of a house for sale on Mulberry Street. "Why Mulberry Street?" Beth asked.

"Well, I am getting married and the only way my fiancé will move here is if she can have a house on the water," he explains.

"Forget Mulberry Street," Beth says. "I have a house for sale with a great view of the water." The next day he came over to look at the house and bought it. Hmm!

Then I chat with Sue on Wood Wind. They live in Gig Harbor, Washington. She is a school teacher and her husband Bruce is an artist. Unlike most boaters, they keep a home in the states, but spend a lot of time on the water. This is their tenth year. We learn that we are traveling in luxury compared to them. They don't have any refrigeration onboard. She has a two-burner stove that operates with a kerosene alternative and no auto-pilot. They do have solar panels to make enough power to run the VHS radio. The little black and white TV they had onboard died and they haven't replaced it. The kicker is that there's no toilet, just a bucket that gets tossed overboard.

They brought the boat down along the California coast and through the Panama Canal, then across Caymans, Jamaica and then around to the Dominican Republic. Just last week, they were off the coast of Haiti, near Monte Cristo, and were both down below when Sue popped her head up for a check and sees something in the water. Using the binoculars, she sees two people shouting and waving as they cling to the tip of a sunken cigarette boat.

Bruce and Sue had just been discussing what they would do if they encountered refugees. The Haitians are so desperate to get off their island, they will do anything: risk their lives, even kill. If they step foot on American soil, they can stay. If the coast guard or other officials catch them in route, they send them back. All they have to do is get on another island—any island—and find work, legal or otherwise. They send most of their money back to their families in Haiti via Western Union that takes a 10 percent fee, while working on getting immigration papers and trying to eventually get the rest of their families out of the country.

Sue and Bruce had just heard about the situation in Haiti, that people get on boats that are oversold where thirty-three people show up for a boat that has thirty seats, and three are shot to death right on the dock. The *smugglers* are always looking for boats and money on the ocean. Traps are set up where someone pretends to have a problem to lure boaters, and then others come out of nowhere and overtake the vessel. I knew about *pirates,* but I thought they wanted fast boats and fat fisherman flashing cash, not a slow- moving sailboat with live-a-boards, but I certainly never considered desperate refugees.

Immediately, they get on the radio and give a frantic *Mayday-Mayday* call for help. Surely, the Haitian or Dominican coast guard can't be far away and in a fast boat, they will be here in no time. "*Mayday-Mayday.* Man overboard. Sunken ship. Two people in the water." There is no response. "Where the hell is the coast guard? Why aren't they coming? My God, these people could die. *Mayday-Mayday.*"

This time there is a response, but it is from another cruiser. "Give us your coordinates," the voice says. "How far offshore are you?"

The other sailboat is too far away to help. Almost an hour goes by when they realize no one is coming. "What is going on? Is this a trap by smugglers? Do the officials know they are Haitian refugees and they don't care about these people?" It is all too unbelievable, too horrible to even think about. They must be saved, and they must be saved by Bruce and Sue.

They maneuver the boat and get close enough to throw out a line and get them onboard. The man is severely burned and the woman is in total emotional shock. They are speaking Creole, a blend of French and Spanish, so quickly and panicky that Sue and Bruce can't understand anything other than "quatro-ocho, quatro-ocho." The lady keeps shouting "forty-eight, forty-eight." They give them blankets and something to drink and try to give first aid from the little kit they have onboard. The toothpaste size tube of burn cream barely covers a fraction of his severely burned arms.

It isn't until they get to shore and find someone to interpret that they learn there were fifty people on the boat when it exploded while they were refueling, and forty-eight people burned to death. They had been stranded for three days. Sue is weeping as she relays the story to me, struggling to get the words out. The pain is still fresh and raw having just happened a few days ago. I am bug-eyed and speechless. Tears are rolling down my cheeks, too. I can't get my head around the words. How can we treat each other this way? We are all people and in one stroke, we could be the ones born in Haiti and not in the USA. Dear God, something must be done about this!

CNN and MSNBC have contacted them for interviews. They become reluctant celebrities. Bruce says Sue has been handling most of the interviews. She is much more diplomatic about what happened. He is just plain outraged.

On the way back to the boat that night, Pete and I talk about what we would do in a similar situation. We would do the right thing. We would have taken them onboard even if it meant risking our own safety. We would not have let them suffer. We have all heard about pirates and the inherent risks of being out at sea alone, but we are talking about someone's life.

It's not until the second night that I learn that Bruce was commissioned by a Florida restaurant chain to do all the artwork for the menu and the interiors. He is quite a famous Caribbean artist. When the company learned that they have a sailboat and island hop, they decided to add their travels to their website and have Sue and Bruce send in a weekly update.

"The restaurant chain is headquartered in Orlando. I know people who work for them. I hope they are completely freaked out about what happened and use their resources to take on this cause." I write down the website and later, follow the link to Bruce Smith's Voyage. This horrific tragedy is documented on their March 2nd posting.

After a sleepless night, it's finally morning. Why do we hate the Haitians and why isn't someone helping them? I go to shore to use the Internet while Pete meets the dock hand he has hired to clean the barnacles off the bottom of our boat, and swim down to the propeller to get the rest of the crab trap rope that is still wrapped around it.

I find a little office supply store that has four computers at one big table. The cost is 70 pesos an hour, or about $2. All the computers are being used, so I wait. The people at the workstations are white. I suspect they are boaters, but maybe locals or ex-patriots. Having a computer and Internet service would be quite luxury here, I think.

My turn comes and I log on. It's all in Spanish, but I have used the computer so much that I know what to do even if I can't read it. I just have to remember the order of the buttons. Like cut, copy and paste. Just like a traffic light, red on top, yellow in the middle and green at the bottom. I pull out my travel stick and can't figure out where the USB port is, so I ask for help from the lady sitting next to me. She doesn't speak English, only French, but she understands what I need. She is using a travel stick too and together we figure it out. Let me get this straight, I am using a Spanish computer, sending an email in English, and getting help from a French lady. I love this!

I meet up with Pete and we stop at a cute little restaurant just a few blocks from the ocean. The outside tables have red and white linen tablecloths. I didn't realize it was Italian until the server passes by with a huge plate of homemade pasta. I am not much for pasta, but that looks really good. Of course our server doesn't speak English and page after page of the menu is only in Spanish. I know people in Florida complain about signs being written in Spanish and business being conducted in Spanish, but right now I would be very happy just to be able to order some food. I do understand pizza, not my favorite, but at least I know what I am getting. I usually just order fish, but we have had so much of it lately. "No pizza," she says. I know I should learn Spanish, but I am too busy learning Italian. I have been doing my Italian language lessons on the computer and now I am trying to communicate in Spanish. Good God, no wonder I am so mixed up. I will just stick to a smile and sign language. It has always worked for me in the past.

Our cute young server calls over the owner to help take our order. He speaks Spanish and Italian, which is of no help to us. At the table next to us are two businessmen. They hear us and offer to help. They are Italians that live here on the island and speak English. "You really need to learn the language," he says. "It's not hard. It's similar to Italian." Easy for him to say, he has been speaking multiple languages since he was a child. He is fluent in Italian, English, Spanish and French.

Why is it so difficult for me to learn? Americans really need to teach other languages to kids when they are young. It sure seems like other countries are way ahead of us. Trying to learn a language as an adult is tough. On the other hand, in Europe, different countries speak different languages. It would be the same as if the people from each state spoke a different language. Most Europeans speak multiple languages and many speak English. And not long ago when the immigrants came to the United States, they were forced to drop their home tongue and adopt English. Parents made sure their children only learned English so they would fit in.

Even my parents speak Pennsylvania Dutch, a dialect of German, but it was never taught to the children. My parents were teased mercilessly when they went to school and didn't speak English, and they were never going to let that happen to their children. Imagine being five or six-years-old and going to school and being taught in a language you didn't understand. It still happens today in our country. Only it is English being taught to Spanish-speaking children.

After a rest on the boat and happy hour at the blue tent with our friends, we decide to find the pizza we weren't able to get earlier today. Sea Bound recommends some place around the corner, so we give it a try. We pass through an iron gate and walk down a narrow alley to find an adorable outdoor Italian restaurant. Under the thatched roof, there is a little garden and some tables covered with red and white checkered tablecloths and lots of candles. It is very dimly lit and we don't realize that the electricity is off until we see the chef making pizza at the outdoor oven by candlelight. I need to use the restroom, and our server walks with me outside in the dark to a separate building. She leaves me there to grope my way back inside.

We learn our server is the wife and owner, and the pizza maker is her husband. She is Dominican and he is Italian, living here just three years. We are very interested in them and in true Italian style, he comes to our table and joins us for a glass of wine. In broken English and Italian, we talk. He is interested in life on the boat and about sailing. When the electricity comes on, he pops in a DVD and there on the wide screen TV is Elton John in concert. Back to the 21st century! The pizza is great. I think the artichokes make it.

That night as I lie on deck and look at the lights of the harbor town, pondering what the chances are of us eating in two Italian restaurants in the same day in the Dominican Republic, I think it's a sign. I have been thinking about what I will do next when I get off the boat in about a month. My original plan was to go to Italy, but I really like this boating thing. Pete will need crew to sail back to Florida or just stay on an island. I could stay on longer, but what about Italy, my beloved Italy? Talking with the pizza guy tonight made my soul stir. There is something there for me. Now is the time, Barbara. Keep moving and keep it light.

We spend our last day in Samana exploring in the dinghy and beachcombing. I find lots of sea glass, more emerald than sea foam green. Lots of plastic and styrofoam litters the shores around the harbor. We really need to come up with biodegradable alternatives. Plastic and styrofoam take thousands of years to decompose; even the harsh sea water doesn't break them down. It is sad to see paradise ruined with trash. We lounge and hang out on the boat. Tanned and rested, we gear up for our next big move.

# Chapter 32

*Puerto Rico*
*March 2007*

With twenty-four hours of motor-sailing in front of us, we take turns at the helm doing four-hour stretches. As soon as we cross into US territory, we are buzzed by a low flying coast guard helicopter. I guess this is our welcome home. After 148 miles, we drop anchor just after 6:00 p.m. and in time for a great sunset. The trip was uneventful during the calm moonlit night.

In the morning at seven, we pull up anchor and move forty-four miles to Ponce Yacht and Fishing Club. We called on the radio and they know we are coming, but we still circle for an hour before they give us a slip number. We are barely secure when the Immigration Officers board our boat and ask to see our credentials.

Later we go inside to the marina office to register and to my surprise, on the line above us in the registration book, is SanSan. I didn't know they were here! After a real shower in the bathhouse and looking human again, we radio to SanSan to discover they are on the next dock over. GR and Nate come over and introduce us to the reason they have stopped at Puerto Rico: their respective girlfriends have arrived. We meet Jen, Nate's girlfriend from Colorado and Jessica, GR's girlfriend from Florida along with Jessica's daughter, precocious four-year-old Gia. Jen hasn't sailed before, but Jess and Gia have lived onboard SanSan before. We have a lively visit, catching up on all the adventures.

That night Pete and I get dressed up and take a cab into town for a lovely dinner at a local fish restaurant. I didn't expect to have such luxury. The next day we play tourists. The downtown is clean with architecturally interesting buildings, a church, a cool fountain, unique fire station and an art museum. After another great luxurious meal at Marc's Restaurant inside the old charming Hotel Melia, we rent a car and go to a Sam's Club type warehouse place and buy way more supplies than we need.

Back at the marina office, I fax a letter to one of my renters, arrange to have a hot water heater replaced, buy my return ticket to Atlanta and tried to arrange for FedEx to deliver my mail. I feel invaded with all this business. Buying the airline ticket makes me sad. I don't want to think about it being over.

In the morning, we push off at 9:00 a.m. to clear sunny skies, but no sooner are we out in open ocean when the waves kick up. No matter how much Pete studies the weather faxes and tries to predict the winds, it is impossible to be certain. We are taking thirty knot winds straight on the nose. The fourth anchor attempt holds and we set in Puerto Patillas just in time for another pretty sunset. I finish downloading all my and Pete's music CDs onto my I-pod library. I curl up with a new book, *The Biography of Walt Disney* and welcome a quiet evening.

The next day we move another forty-three miles to Vieques Island. The eight hour ride is rough with four to six foot seas. We are happy to anchor in a quiet secluded cove in blue water surrounded by mangroves.

To our surprise, late in the afternoon we see two kayaks coming toward us. We are far from any town and haven't seen another boat in hours. Where did these people come from? Through the binoculars, we can see a man and boy about ten-years-old in one boat and a teenage boy in the other. They are coming right toward us. They don't look like trouble, but we discuss what to do just in case. When they arrive, we learn that they are from Philadelphia and are staying in a little resort near by. They got disoriented and are struggling to get back before dark. The man is eager to call his wife and let her know that they are okay. They are hot, tired and thirsty. We help them onboard and give them some water and the phone. After his wife learns they are okay, she yells at him for scaring her and taking such a foolish risk. Pete shows them on the chart where we are and they decide that they will not get back before nightfall, so Pete volunteers to take them back in the dinghy and tow the kayaks. The boys are grateful not to row anymore. They take the handheld radio with them and I stay onboard as mission control.

I enjoy the evening alone on the boat, play some classical music and write a new gratitude card about being a writer. I open the zip lock baggy where I keep my cards and read each one slowly out loud, feeling the words and what they mean to me. I am so grateful for so many things. I read old pages from my journal and am amazed at how many of my dreams have come true. I am totally aware of the power of creation. Me and God/The Universe together are unstoppable. Oh, what I have experienced!

Darkness starts to fall over the little secluded harbor. Relief washes over me when I see the portable bow light of the dinghy and know that Pete has safely returned.

I am excited about today's twenty-one mile move to Culebra. We are up early and on the move when we pass a sailboat unusually close to land. Pete radios to the sailing vessel Alma and we learn that he ran aground last night and is stuck. He has been trying to radio for help but can't get a signal. He is an older man single-handing. He fell down when he hit, but isn't hurt—just a little bruised and shook up. Pete keeps radioing to the coast guard and when we get out to sea a little bit, we reach them. Before they find out if the man is okay and his exact coordinates, they ask if he damaged a reef. I realize this is important too, but how about human life?

Culebra is the island I visited just after Tom died when I tried to get a caretaking job there. I am happy to show Pete the lay of the land, especially the fabulous beaches. Just as we are coming into the harbor, we hear Trudy and Guy from Abracadabra on the radio. What a pleasant surprise. We call them and arrange to meet tonight for the band and big St. Patrick's Day party at Iguana's. The bay is bigger and nicer than I remember, so is the town. We walk around and check it out.

The next afternoon, we rent scooters at a little place next to the airstrip. Pete is interested in the planes and how the airport works. We ride out to Zoni Beach and the world famous Flamenco Beach with some of the most beautiful crystal clear water we have seen yet.

# Chapter 33

*St. Thomas, US Virgin Islands*
*March 2007*

Today is a day of serendipity. I've been reading about the laws of the universe and debt. The way we feel about the debt and the person we owe the money to directly affects the flow of money and energy into and out of our lives. I am thinking I don't have any debt except mortgages on property, but I will always have them, so I don't really consider them debtors.

Then I remember that I still owe my Dad $1250 from Alaska. After we got back and my credit card bills came in, I had everything figured out. I owed him. Well I went flying off to ski and then jumped on the boat so fast, I had every intention of paying him, but I just didn't. And in some ways, I guess I just thought that he should forgive it, but that is not my decision to make. I was clinging to some unpleasant memories of the trip and let that overshadow so many awesome memories. I even have a check or two with me on the boat and now I am in a US territory and can mail it to him safely from here.

I make the decision to *gladly* give him the money and mentally go over the best parts of the trip. I even look at the photos from Alaska again, which are stored in my computer. It makes me happy. When we go to shore today, I will buy an envelope and stamp and mail the check. This has been on my mind for several days now.

Charlotte Amalie is a bustling harbor town. The cruise ships are lined up along the big docks, small boats like ours dot the blue water and seaplanes land just off shore. Ferries honk their big horns when they pull out, headed for St. John just a few miles away. Like all cruise ship towns, jewelry and other duty free shops abound. Our goal is to get away from here as quickly as possible and see the *real* town. We head for the famous ninety-nine steps that lead to the pirate's fort high up on the hill.

Along the street, we pass a Rastafarian dude dressed in a Jamaican style poncho and dread locks, leading a donkey whose hooves he has cleverly painted to match the donkey's red lipstick. To finish off the photo you can take with him for just a few dollars, the donkey wears giant green sunglasses and opens his lips for a toothy smile for the camera.

Down the street a bit, we see a big muscular black man dressed in the costume of an African warrior, feathered head dress, face and body painted, holding a shield. He too is posing for pictures for money, but strangely enough, he is carrying an overnight express envelope, not Fed Ex, but the US Post Office. I comment about the envelope and ask if he is the delivery-man. I am expecting a package being sent from the States today, my three months worth of accumulated mail, and maybe that is my package. He is not the deliveryman, but he's headed there right now and we can follow him. He stops to pose for the tourists, but catches up to us on the street. No sooner do we round the corner than there is the post office. Yes, a big, grand US Post office. Great, I will go inside, buy an envelope and stamp and take care of business first thing this morning.

Inside, the line to see the postmaster is very long and evidently the post office doesn't sell envelopes, just special mailing and fancy ones. Well, I'll just buy a card in a gift shop and surely, someone will have a stamp. Outside, our African warrior friend is working the crowd for photos and we hear his story. He is saving his money for an airline ticket to Canada. We tease him that it is really cold there and he will need more clothing than he is currently wearing, which right now is a Speedo under a feather skirt. Pete takes my picture with the warrior in front of the post office holding the overnight letter.

We cross the street and walk past two or three jewelry stores when I see a staircase in the alley leading up to an art gallery. "Let's pop in here," I suggest. The gallery is large and airy. I am immediately drawn to the Haitian Art; maybe that is the way to help them, through art. We are looking at a painting when a lady comes over to us and asks if we are on a sailboat. We turn around and to our surprise there is Teri Jones, the artist onboard the sailing vessel Sea Otter. Pete bought a piece of her work in Luperon several weeks ago.

We chat like old friends and learn all about her journey here. We saw Sea Otter in the harbor, but didn't remember who was onboard. She works and paints in the gallery for a few months each year, but this year she is staying longer. I pick out a card with a colorful Caribbean scene. It is perfect for my dad, adding a little joy to this transaction rather than the *strictly business* envelope I originally intended to send to him. We walk around and Teri is very knowledgeable about the artists. I love hearing their stories.

Out of nowhere, my phone rings, a sound unfamiliar to me since it has only rung once or twice in the last three months, but it works here and hoping to talk to Brittany today, I slipped it into my purse. It is Bernie Salerno, a mortgage broker and member of the club I used to work for. I haven't heard from him in well over a year.

"Barbara Singer," he says. "I can't believe I am actually speaking to you. I thought surely I would get voice mail. First, where are you? Italy?"

"Not yet, but I will be in May," I tell him. "No I am in St. Thomas, island hopping on a sail boat for a few months."

"Well, aren't you a lucky girl?" he says. "By the way, the reason I am calling is that I have this new mortgage product that will take ten years off a thirty-year mortgage using the bank's money. It's not for everyone, but I think it will work for you."

Mortgage? This guy calls me out of the blue and wants to talk about mortgages? How bizarre? I tell him I'll be back in town the last week in April, he can call me then. It isn't until I am lying in bed that night, listening to the water lap against the boat that I really get what just happened. *Before* I even had the check mailed, my other debt was addressed. A messenger was sent to help reduce my mortgages. Is this really the way the universe works? It is way too easy.

I pay for the card, buy her last stamp, fill out the card, enclose the check and practically jump up and down when I drop the envelope in big blue mail box. Now, where are those ninety-nine steps anyway? The little town is darling. Dripping with history, Dutch influences are everywhere in the charming little nooks, and loaded with character. I love old, especially old bricks, old windows and old doors. Here, I am especially interested in the wood of the hurricane shutters. I guess they are hundreds of years old. The ticket to tour the Pirate's Tower also includes tours of three other homes, the 1829 Hotel and the Pirates Inn Hotel, all built into the side of the hill. We climb up steep stairs and walkways for a trip down history lane. Old Island ladies greet us at each house and give us a little history. The furnishings are made of the finest

Virgin Island Mahogany, which is a rich dark brown, different than Barbados Mahogany that is also beautiful, but much lighter in color. The seats are made of cane and the pieces have an easy curving line that reminds me of the sea. The wood is hard, too hard for even a termite. We are told the antique dealers go crazy for West Indies Furniture and now I understand why.

The art in the homes is a mixture of old and new. Our guide points out a particular piece and explains that it was done by the "Father of Impressionism," Camille Pissarro. He was born here on the island and painted some scenes of the harbor back in the 1850's when there was nothing here, just natural landscapes and maybe a building or two. *A Creek in St. Thomas* is painted in muted shades of green and brown, but it is the detail of the tiny palm trees and grassy banks that is particularly striking.

We stroll along and enjoy the gardens drenched with blooming flowers. When we are standing in the living room of the last house, soaking up the sweeping view of the blue sea through giant doorways, I notice a painting. It is another Camille Pissarro. All the brilliant colors of the island, the flowers, the sea, the sky and his works are done in sad browns and greens. "Remember, Impressionism, 1850's," I think to myself.

We stop for a beer at the 1829 Hotel Bar. It too is old and full of character. An ornate old backgammon game decorates each table. Supposedly this is the home of the World Championship of Backgammon. Our bartender tells us to have a seat outside on the verandah and he will bring our drinks. This is the first of many times we will experience the easy, slow-yourself-down style of island service. He brings our drinks and graciously pours them into frosted mugs. He is from Nevis, but has lived here for twenty-six years, he tells us proudly in his deep Island accent.

We find our way through winding streets of old houses and buildings looking for the old Synagogue with sand floors. Some buildings are charming, but some are ready to fall down, hurricane or not. We pop into anything that looks like a grocery store hoping to find big hard salty pretzels, peanuts in the shell and Twizzlers red licorice. We don't find any of those things we are craving, but Pete does find a fifth of rum for $3.50 not some off-brand, but the real thing. We bought some in Puerto Rico for $7 a bottle and thought that was a bargain. He's going to buy a case before we leave.

We trudge up a hill so steep and narrow that we have to jump out of the street and into the doorways of houses to get out of the way of the cars. They are revved at high RPM's to make it up the hill. We miss the entrance of the church because we are so fixated on the construction work across the street. A cool old brick building that long ago was painted pink is now being covered by stucco, and a modern round porthole window has been added. The *new and improved* building will be cute, but knowing what they are covering up makes it all wrong. Where is the historical society? The one that I had a love-hate relationship with when I renovated houses back in Florida.

We huff and puff all the way to the top to realize we must have missed the synagogue. I spy a cute art gallery and an old bed and breakfast, so we will have to come back this way. Now we are really determined to find the synagogue. Back down the hill, we find the entrance, plain as day. We go inside the open doors, melt into a pew, and soak up the history before our eyes. Built in 1823, the sand floors are a reminder of the Jews who had to hide the practicing of their religion by holding services in cellars, and the sand floors helped muffle the sound of the prayers. Baccarat Crystal chandeliers hang from the ceiling over dark wooden alters and pews. What a special place.

We meet the clerk in the gift shop. She is from New Hampshire and moved here five years ago. She stays for ten months out of the year. Originally she intended to rent, but quickly realized that was not cost-effective, so they bought a little place on the point. "If the cliff goes, so does my house," she says, with a carefree gesture. It has turned out to be a great investment. What she misses most is fresh fish.

"Fresh fish, you live on an island surrounded by water. What do you mean?" I ask.

"The water is shallow and most of it is protected natural park reefs, so there are no commercial fishermen here. The seafood comes from Florida," she explains. We are amazed at this, but have found it to be true on our entire trip.

As we say our goodbyes, she recommends we go to the Camille Pissarro Gallery. He is the famous artist from the island. Oh yes, the painting we saw in the other house. We climb back to the top of the hill and pop into a lovely gallery and then work our way down the other side. The steep narrow street is lined with white buildings. With the blue sky above and the vivid blue of the sea peaking out between the white buildings, I am reminded of Greece—blue and white everywhere with an occasional pop of color from a bougainvillea plant. I snap picture after picture. I love digital. I can take all the photos I want and edit later. Although my trusty old Cannon takes better photographs, it's big and bulky and takes film. In my old life, boxes of photo albums filled every bit of space under my bed. Feng Shui says it's bad to keep stuff under your bed. I thought it kept my memories alive.

After several attempts, we locate the gallery, only to discover it is closed for lunch. It's two o'clock so we decide to have lunch too and find the local Caribbean spot, Cuzzin's, packed. It's time to have a drink, check back on the gallery, and after that, we'll try the restaurant again. By then, it should have died down a bit. We find an outside table in a little alleyway shop and order rum smoothies. Our server is a crazy girl who is coming and going and talking to everyone who passes by on the street. She is carrying supplies from another shop down the alley. Dressed in an apron, Converse high top sneakers, baggy pants, and backward baseball cap, she is clearly wired. She's friendly and buzzing all around and we are amused by her. As we pay the bill, we tell her we have been waiting for the Camille Pissarro Gallery to open. She says, "Oh, you need to see Cody. Before you go back up there, let me check next door, I think he is in the restaurant. They also display some artwork down there." Back in a flash, she escorts us down the street and introduces us to Cody, the gallery owner.

Tattoos cover most of the skin that peeks out of his wife-beater shirt that is covered in paint splotches. His twenty-something body is long and lanky and red dreadlocks are tied back from his face and dangle down to his buttocks. They remind me of the roots of the mangroves we dinghied through on Shroud Cay, growing all twisted together. His barely-there scraggly facial hair around his mouth is accented with five lip piercings, two on the bottom, two on the top and one just under his nose. A three-inch long goatee completes his unorthodox look.

His eyes are kind and he greets us warmly. We look at the art on display while he pays his bar tab. We follow him back to the gallery as he chats along. He is very well spoken and his knowledge of the great Camille Pissarro impressive. Pissarro studied in France and Argentina with many of the other famous impressionists like Monet, Renoir, and Van Gogh. He is remembered as the one pushing the others. It is said that he was quoted saying, "I knew that Van Gogh would be great or go mad, but I didn't think both."

We climb the three flights of stairs for the second time today to get up to gallery. The trip up is less than impressive, but once inside, we are overwhelmed with color and find the gallery full from floor to ceiling. Even with all the beautiful paintings to look at, I am still drawn to the 200 year old floors and old brick walls. Cody guides us to a display honoring Pissarro and points out the intricacies of his works. I ask him which one is his favorite and he is clearly stumped. Hasn't he thought about this before or does it change with his mood?

Then he proudly shows us his own works. He draws and paints, but music is his real love. His current band isn't playing anywhere yet, so we can't watch him play the drums. He belongs to a group of drummers who meet every full moon. There are twenty regulars, but others are welcome, and sometimes the number swells to seventy-five people. What is it with drummers and artists? That's what we did in Matlacha—a group of drummers met every Friday and on the full moon.

Cody is not related to Pissarro, but his mother took over the shop from the previous owner and when his dad died, Cody came to St. Thomas to help his mother. That was five years ago when he was fifteen. This talented, brilliant young man is twenty-years-old! He is doing what he loves and expressing his talents so early in life. Good for him. This is another law of the universe.

*Doing what you love, what you are naturally talented at doing,*
*puts you in alignment with the universe*
*and immediately the infinite supply of energy is available to you.*
*You feel the aliveness that comes from having*
*the unlimited energy of the universe flow through you.*
*This aliveness influences the energy signals you emit.*
*People and circumstances that support you, are drawn to you*
*like a magnet.*

Thank goodness I didn't judge him or write him off as some weirdo, druggie loser and miss this delightful encounter. And thank goodness I didn't judge our crazy server who introduced us. In my old life, I would have treated her very differently, but she is the one who is alive, full of energy and *being who she really is.*

I pick out my absolute favorite Pissarro print and have it rolled in a tube. We purchase a few postcards of the other paintings. Wrapping up my purchase, Cody looks up at me and points to a print behind him. It is of a young waiter wearing a white shirt and a chauffeur's cap. "That's my favorite," he says. "I have a giclee of it that Janine, the artist, embellished for me, adding some purples and blues." I had long forgotten that I asked him which one was his favorite, but he was still pondering my question.

As tradition dictates, I get Pete to snap a photo of Cody and me. Whenever I buy art, usually in a foreign country, I take a photo of either the artist or the person in the gallery. There is something really special about the relationships surrounding art.

As we go back down the stairs and alleyway that lead back out to the tourist's shopping Mecca, the marketer in me immediately takes note of how to get traffic up into the gallery and improve the visual path upstairs. Hang some art on the stairway walls, add flowerpots, add a water fountain on the landing, and for goodness sakes, add some music. Get people in the mood to buy. Build some excitement as customers ascend. Make a T-shirt, "I made it up to the Camille Pissarro Gallery." When I come back here, I will work at that gallery. It has the right vibe.

We go back to Cuzzin's Restaurant and have the place to ourselves and we revel in our good fortune. I think back about the day and how the universe works. Today was not a strange series of coincidences, but a day created with awareness.

Two days later when my packet of three month's worth of mail arrives, I find a letter from my old company informing me that I never cashed a check from several years back, and I need to claim it before it is turned over to the Treasury Department. I am confused by this since I have auto deposit. Anyway, there is $575 just waiting for me to collect. I opened the flow of money and it came to me like a magnet, and so very fast. The speed with which things happen is amazing to me.

I also receive the latest issue (March/April) of Veranda Magazine. I love a new magazine, it is like opening a present. I love the smell, the feel of the pages, and most of all, the feast for my eyes. I am very visual, so the perfectly photographed scenes of table settings, furniture, flowers, art, and designer homes provide a feast for my eyes. I always start at the beginning and carefully study each page, soaking up the colors and highly stylized ads for jewelry and home furnishings. And then, right there on page fifty-eight, I see it. I do a double take. A beautiful impressionist painting with bold letters across the top *PISSARRO, creating the impressionist landscape* splashed across the page. Seven pages of art and a story that keeps me glued. The article says his work will be on display at three major galleries for the next year. The collection brings together forty-five pieces from major museums and private collections from around the world, and it's the first exhibition to focus solely on the revolutionary landscape paintings of Pissarro created between 1864 and 1874.

I had just finished telling Pete, after we visited the gallery in St. Thomas, that I want to learn more about Pissarro, and I wondered why he is not as famous as the other painters he hung out with. Ask and you shall receive. When the student is ready, the teacher will come. All things are available to us, all we must do is just slow down enough to see it. The signs and teachers are always around us, we just overlook them.

Do we all see the world the same way? Is red the same to me as it is to someone else? When I look at an abstract painting the artist describes as a beautiful bouquet of flowers or a playground full of children swinging and jumping rope, I don't see that at all. I see colors and movement, but no flowers or children. I know what I see, but what do others see? What does the world really look like? Am I missing most of what happens? The law of the universe says slowing down and listening to your inner voice or *the God in your heart* is the way to really get in touch with the universe. Oh my, there is so much to learn.

The next day, in a newspaper from St. Johns, I read my horoscope for March 21, 2007. It says, *Sagittarius, the familiar can appear extraordinary. After years of soul searching, your boat may be coming in fast—very soon. You may not recognize it at first. When you sweep out the last of the dust, you wake up and smell the roses. Your intuition is at an all time high. Use it!*

Wow, I am blown away. I have been reading about the laws of the universe, and part of it talks about how our intuition is our connection to the infinite intelligence. Whenever we want to know what to do next, just ask. The universe is willing and gives us signals as to what is best for us to do next. If we listen and follow its guidance, our lives will work perfectly. From the vantage point of infinite intelligence, all variables can be seen. If we ask, the answer to which variable is best for us will be sent to us through our intuition. Infinite intelligence can be called God and intuition can be called gut feeling. It is really nothing new, just presented in a way that is more palatable to me.

In the Dominican Republic, I was trying to decide what do to next after the boat trip is over. I am supposed to spend May in Italy and try to start with the villa rental business, but I feel turmoil between my new business partner and me. It doesn't feel right. Maybe I should bag Italy for this year and just go on to Aspen. Then in one day, I have lunch and dinner in an Italian restaurant and the owner joins us at our table for a glass of wine.

A few days later when I get to Puerto Rico and my phone starts working, I have a message from my friend from Aspen. When am I coming out? He would be happy to see me. Is this the sign? My soon-to-be business partner emails me about my plans and I tell her I am up in the air and will need to really think about it. I am getting conflicting messages. What should I do?

Then it clearly comes to me. I am thinking about not going to Italy because I am scared. Things are not in a neat little package. When I really listen to my heart and review my Betty Boop Journal, circa 2005 and the things that I had written, I know what to do. Western Europe is really calling to me. I even had maps of Europe in two different journals. I may not stay in Italy the whole summer, maybe go to Vienna, Prague, Budapest or even keep going to India, Katmandu, and Bali. These places are all on my A- list.

Once I make the decision, the universe rallies around me. Standing at the navigation station on the boat, I get on the Internet and find a furnished room to rent near Florence for the month of May, perhaps longer, so I send an email. I look at Eurail passes and hostels all over Europe. As I look around the salon of the boat, I see a novel I have yet to read, but brought onboard entitled, *1000 Days in Tuscany,* another book, *Living Abroad,* and yet another title of a light-hearted novel called *Faking It.* I actually have to chuckle out loud. *Fake it till you make it.* Isn't that a slogan from one of those self-help/motivational things I've studied over the years?

I go online to buy an airline ticket to Italy. Wow, the prices are through the roof so I work every angle I can think of, like flying out of different airports and using big carriers going into big cities. British Airways has always been the best from Orlando. I do find something from Philadelphia to Rome. My family lives near Philly so I could visit them. I could take a train to Florence quite easily. It is still $800, which still seems too expensive. I email my prospective new business partner to see if she knows of any better options. Her response is short and distant. She used frequent flyer miles. The exchange rate is poor and no, she doesn't have any info on Eurorail passes. I'm not feeling the love. We haven't talked in person for several months. We played phone tag and never got together. As I have learned from the book, *The Four Agreements,* don't assume and don't take it personally. Let it go, sleep on it and I will feel differently in the morning.

I do feel differently in the morning. I get a response from a website called sublet.com. It's a site that posts all kinds of rooms for rent and apartments all over the world. The room is available! It is just a few minutes walk to the bus, and a twenty-five minute ride to the city and train station for 350 euro a month. My heart actually flutters when I read the room is available and I can have it. I don't need to start a business to live in Italy, just go. The universe rises up to give me my heart's desires. Is this really how it works? It is too easy!

In the clear of the morning when I do my best thinking, I realize that I too have air miles. I had forgotten all about them. I was saving them for an emergency ticket home from the islands if things got sticky. I won't be needing that, so I call Capital One. I have enough miles to buy a ticket for $910, so I buy a ticket departing May 1st from Philadelphia to Rome via London and returning September 1st to Philly. I will have to buy a second ticket from Orlando to Philly and back, but I have made that trip many times and I can get it for about $200. I make my return to Orlando October 1st so I can spend a month with my family. September is a great time of the year to be in Pennsylvania. All I have to do is figure out how to wire some money to the lady in Italy to hold the room. I'll spend next winter in Aspen and stay through the summer if I like it. No point in zigzagging all over the place. There now, it is done.

# Chapter 34

*Foxy's – British Virgin Islands*
*March 2007*

Today is a day we have been anticipating for the entire trip, we are moving to the tiny island of Jost Van Dyke and going to the world famous Foxy's. Pete has been talking about it since we started planning the trip. He came here some ten years ago when he chartered a sailboat. "I've got to take Barbara to Foxy's," he has said at least twenty times. "I have a dinner a reservation at Foxy's." When other cruisers asked how far down the island we were going, Pete would always say, "At least as far as BVI, I have a reservation at Foxy's."

We motor into the already crowded harbor called Great Harbor. For such a small island, it sure is popular. According to the guidebooks, it has a worldwide reputation for great beach parties and no matter where in the world you are, there will always be someone wearing a Foxy's T-shirt or hat.

It is after 3:00 p.m. by the time we set anchor and have our traditional rum drink. I pass and opt for club soda. Ever since Brittany called and said that she had some plans for me when I get to Atlanta and there are some friends of hers who want to meet me, I decided I better reel it in a little and get a handle on my eating and drinking.

We dinghy to the dock just in front of the building that houses the custom's office on the bottom and police station on the second floor. Both have porches. What a cute little town. Well, I wouldn't call it a town—one sand road runs along the beach and is dotted with a couple of shops and restaurants. We go straight to customs and present our passports and documents for the boat. The officer is eager to get finished as he needs to catch the ferry home. He doesn't live on the island. I tell him he looks like Arsenio Hall and he gets a big laugh out of that. I clap my hands when he puts the stamp for the BVI's in my passport. He thinks I am silly until I explain that collecting stamps in my passport is one of my favorite things in life. With our forms complete, we move to the outer office where another officer signs the papers. Two children play in the office and the older one tries to put the little one on the lap of the officer. The little one has small sections of hair combed into squares and then braided into little sticks standing straight out. Her dark skin against the red shirt she is wearing is delightful as she carefully walks around, a skill that appears to be newly acquired. The officer, Dad I guess, is clearly unhappy with this, but in a gentle thick accent, he says, "Why do you do this now? I am working here." The children go outside on the porch and play and wait. When it is all said and done, we pay about $40 to enter the country.

Now it is time to explore. Pete is eager to show me Foxy's and to check on our reservation we called in by VHS radio earlier today. "Let's sightsee first, then head down to Foxy's," I suggest. So we walk down the sand road toward the church I was looking at through the binoculars from the boat. It is yellow with red shutters and doors, made of concrete block and built in the 1700's. It was cuter from a distance. The doors and windows are open and we see some children, but we don't want to disturb them, so we don't go inside. We continue to walk past a couple of little open-air restaurants, snapping a photo or two. It reminds me of Ambergris Caye in Belize, except they have cars here and in Belize everyone drove golf carts. An old school pickup truck pulls into the street and waits for us to pass. I snap a picture of it and the driver stops to say hello. He is Vinny from the Corsair's. He says it's been a crazy day and he is going home for a quick shower before the dinner crowd. Normally they are open all day so he invites us to come back for dinner. We stroll along, admiring this picture-postcard street and view of the palm trees lining the beach. There are two guys under a tree, one in a hammock reading and the other one playing a drum. Tied to the tree is a white baby goat on a bright pink leash. I do a double take. Yes, that is definitely a baby goat on a leash. I walk up to the young man and ask if I can pet his goat. He says it is not his, but yes I can.

Then he says it's really a sheep. This is not the first time this conversation has come up. If it were a sheep, it would have wool; goats have hair similar to a dog. We were told that it is too hot for sheep to have wool, so they have adapted. I think it is folklore and someone is pulling the wool over our eyes. Wool. Oh, well.

We work our way down to Foxy's, walk in and check out the place. It is just as colorful as Pete said. The open-air restaurant and bar has sand floors and every inch of the ceiling is covered with signed T-shirts, hats, bras, panties and business cards. Some look like they have been here for a very long time. Except for a couple that is milling around and two guys at the bar, the place is empty. The stage has a drum set and some speakers on it along with a black barefoot mannequin playing a guitar. "That's Foxy," Pete explains. "I never met him, but they say he still comes around." I walk around a little. It is too cute.

Pete orders two of Foxy's private label draft beers and we see our boat name in the reservation book on the bar. The lady behind the bar is tallying up receipts. She has us down as La La, not Ooh La La. Our name confuses everyone until they understand it. We just laugh and leave it alone. Seven-thirty tonight, and looking forward to it.

We get our beers and look for a good place to sit when I spy a hammock just across the road by the beach. We take our picture in front of the Foxy's sign next to the hammock and then climb in. It is big enough for two, so Pete gets in looking one direction and I look the other. We rock gently back and forth, listening to the melody of the gentle surf with a light breeze rustling the palm trees. Sand blankets the ground all around us. Paradise. We are the luckiest people in the whole world. This is Foxy's. We made it.

When our plastic cups are empty, I volunteer to go to the bar for a refill. Pete says he wants something with rum rather than another beer. I walk up to the practically empty bar and stand in the open space between two men. The bartender comes over and I order a beer and something fun with rum in it. The bartender makes a few suggestions when the man on my right suggests what he is having. He rattles off the list of things in his rum drink and I tell the bartender I'll have one of those. The man on my left walks away and I chat with the rum guy. He is from Texas, just got off a boat and has taken a hotel room. The boat was not as comfortable as he had hoped since it has no air conditioning or toilet. He came here to dive. On the bar in front of him sits a pack of Parliament cigarettes and a lighter. Old man cigarettes for such a young guy, I think. He barely looks thirty-years-old, but it is hard to tell his age with the dark week-old stubble on his face. I tell him that I am on a boat too. We left Florida on New Year's Eve and have been island hopping the whole way down here. We had to come to the famous Foxy's. "Have you met him yet?" I asked.

"No, I have been here three weeks and never saw the guy," he answers.

I pay for my drinks and just as I turn to walk away, another man comes up from behind and makes a big sweeping motion around the neck of the guy next to me.

At first it looks like a surprise greeting, like the way young men punch or hit each other in a tough-guy kind of greeting. The rum guy grabs his throat and says, "What the fuck?!" He pulls his hand away from his throat and sees the blood. He jumps up from his seat at the bar and just looks at the guy, stunned. "You cut me?" The other guy, a young islander with puffy hair on top, just stares at him. "What the fuck, you cut me!" the rum guy shouts. He turns to another man sitting under the shack next door and shouts, "Your brother just cut me!" He starts shouting, "I need a hospital! Where is the hospital?" He walks quickly down the street, heading the 200 yards or so back toward the police station.

I grab the drinks and quickly go back to Pete. My eyes wide open in shock. "What happened?" Pete asks.

"Didn't you see that? The guy just got his throat slit. I was standing right there."

"No," Pete says. "I didn't see anything from here. I just heard the guy shouting."

We are both stunned. And then, nothing happened. No police, no ambulance, no sirens, absolutely nothing happened. Three men come casually strolling out of the restaurant and are talking quietly in the street. They light cigarettes. They point at me, but we can't hear what they are saying. It must be drugs, we guess. He obviously knew the guy. We decide if the police don't come, it must be local island justice.

Minutes after the attack, the calm serene scene we were just experiencing returns. We lie in the hammock with our drinks and watch the palm trees sway in the breeze. The empty restaurant is as picture perfect as it was before. The building next door has T-shirts and other tropical wares displayed on the front porch. We are frozen. It is like it never happened. After at least half an hour, we go inside the shop, buy a shirt with the Foxy's logo on it for Pete and a Foxy's hat for me. Everyone must have at least one thing that says Foxy's on it.

We walk back to the dinghy dock by the police station and pass by a pickup truck backed into the walkway. I notice his license plate and snap a picture. I have been taking pictures of the license plates in all the different countries. The owner of the truck shouts angrily at me, "What are you doing? Why are you taking a picture of my license plate?"

"Oh, sorry, I just never saw plate like this before. I will erase if I you want me to."

"Just go on, this is not the time or place for that." I walk past him, the truck and the lady with him. As we walk down the dock, I turn to Pete and say, "Welcome to Jost Van Dyke." What was that all about?

Back on the boat, we chill until it is time to go to dinner. I think about what happened. It did really happen, didn't it? I didn't imagine it. It was totally surreal. Where did the guy go? I never saw a weapon. I don't know what he cut him with. He wasn't really bleeding that much. When the jugular gets cut, doesn't blood spurt out everywhere? Did the guy mean to scare him or kill him? Where are the police?

At 7:30 p.m., we dinghy to the other dock closer to Foxy's and get a table right in front of the stage. A man is playing the acoustic guitar in Jimmy Buffet style and the place is filling up as we order drinks and dinner and listen to the music. Then in strolls the Famous Foxy. He is an old Island man, barefoot with rolled up dirty white pants and a T-shirt. His dark face is covered with a scraggly gray beard. He is jovial and dancing whimsically. He takes the microphone, tells a joke or two, and invites his guests to come dance. He says he is too old to sing and play the guitar, but he can still come out to have some fun. The dance floor fills up, the crowd is getting loud and the food is fantastic. It seems like another normal day at Foxy's. Did it really happen?

The only thing unusual is that there are three Swat Team police standing by the hostess stand. They are dressed in camouflage pants, black jump boots and light flap jackets. Is this usual? They must know who we are. They know our boat name. We checked on our reservation minutes before the attack. They know the eyewitness had a reservation. When we looked in the book, there were only about six or eight reservations for the entire evening. Wouldn't you think the cops would go to each table with a reservation and ask if they had been to the restaurant earlier today?

When the last song is over, we decide it's time to go. The crowd thins out quickly and we dinghy back to the boat. By now we are getting good at navigating in the dark and finding our floating home. What a day. Ever since being on the boat, time and days and perspective have totally changed. Three months is a long time to be away, to be remote, to be out of touch. Maybe I am losing it. Maybe I should just be grateful that I didn't get hurt. Should I go to the police and tell them what I saw? What happened to the guy? Is he still alive or was someone else waiting for him to finish the job? If it was a drug thing, I don't want to get involved. I also don't want get caught up in something that could be way more involved than I think. What if we get held up here for days? I go to sleep that night with more questions than answers.

In the morning, Pete wants to go into town for breakfast. Maybe we'll hear some scuttlebutt on the street. We'll just listen and try to learn what happened. I am unusually busy on this particular morning. Normally I start my day by writing or reading my meditation/gratitude cards. But not today. Today I want to be busy, so I get the bucket on a rope and wash the deck with sea water. There is sand and footprints all over the place from last night. So I scrub the deck and drink my coffee. Pete asks several times if I am ready to go to breakfast, but I keep puttering. Finally, I throw on the white pants I wore from the night before and roll them up, slip on my pink crocs and sunglasses and announce I am ready to go. I think I combed my hair. Oh, well.

We dinghy to the dock by the police station and see three men standing out on the second floor balcony talking. We walk by and I hear them talking about the attack. "Walk slowly," I whisper to Pete, "Listen to what they are saying."

"He was talking to a blonde lady from Florida," the man said. "You are not doing your job if you don't find her. She has been on a yacht for three months and she is out in that harbor somewhere."

We stop under a tree next to the police building and move in closer, hiding under the brush. My heart starts to pound. We strain to hear.

"He wasn't doing anything when it happened, he was just sitting at the bar talking to that lady," the man pleaded. "You know who did it and you can't cover it up."

What should I do? I ask myself. I don't want to ruin our trip. I don't want any trouble. A man could be dead and I am the only one who saw what happened. Surely the bartender saw it. He was standing right there too. Do the right thing Barbara.

Then it hits me like a ton of bricks. I am no better than the sailing vessel Wood Wind when they floated by the Haitian refugees waiting for help for an hour, but too scared to take them onboard. I thought that what they did at first was deplorable. I chastised them. "If I saw people clinging to a sunken boat out in the middle of the ocean, I wouldn't have hesitated to have helped them," I'd said. And now, here I stand and I am hesitating to help this man.

With eyes wide and a mouth so dry I can barely speak, I turn to Pete and in a hushed small voice say, "We should go talk to the police."

"Are you sure?" Pete says. "You have no idea what you are getting into, but it's totally your call."

"We need to do the right thing," I answer in a low tone, knowing the seriousness of the situation.

We come out from behind our cover and walk a few steps and then up the staircase leading to the balcony. The men are standing outside—one Islander wearing a police uniform, a white man wearing a baseball cap, little round glasses, and a white T-shirt with a big red dive flat on it and another Islander man with a beard, wearing a well-worn shirt.

"Hello there," I greet them. They all turn and look at me.

"Is there something I can help you with?" the officer says, annoyed with my presence.

"Yes, I am the blonde lady from Florida."

The three of them are stunned. Colin, the white guy, says, "Praise God. You are here. I can't believe you are here." He is trembling, his lip starts to quiver and his eyes well up with tears. I want to hug him and comfort him, but I don't. "Thank God you are here. We were just talking about you and then you appear out of nowhere. It's a miracle."

"Is he alright?" I asked.

"Yes, my friend Chris is lying in a hospital in Tortola with a fifteen centimeter cut in his throat and thirty stitches. He is an emotional wreck. He begged me last night not to leave him, but I had to come back here to my family and business. He was a hair away from hitting the artery and dying, and now they are accusing him of getting into a fight and that the guy who cut him did it in self-defense. The guy who did it is Foxy's son, a known schizophrenic. He said Chris's cell phone told him to do it. It kept telling him to cut his throat. He should never have been allowed on the street. There is plenty of money for him to be taken care of in an institution, but nobody does anything about it."

The words keep spewing from Colin's mouth. "And now, people are trying to cover it up and make it look like Chris was the one at fault." His voice cracks as he relays the details. Colin is clearly on the brink of falling apart. "My friend comes here for a vacation and now he's lying in the hospital totally freaked out and told not to move or it could kill him."

What am I hearing? I can't think fast enough to understand what I have just heard. A random attempted murder of a tourist by a local mental case and a police cover up? My head is spinning as I try to absorb the insane story I just heard. An attempted murder at the famous Foxy's Restaurant by Foxy's known psycho son? This could ruin Foxy's and tourism for the whole BVI's.

"Surely, the bartender saw what happened," I said. "He was standing right there. You did talk to him?" I question, directing it to the cop.

"He didn't see anything," the cop said. "His back was turned."

"Like he is going to say anything and jeopardize his job. He works for Foxy," Colin jumps in. "He's not going to say anything. He's got one of the best jobs on the islands."

Oh, my God. It is a cover up. No one saw anything but me? In a stunned but firm voice, I say, "Well I saw what happened. There was no fight. The guy was sitting at the bar when another man came up from behind him and slit his throat. I didn't see a weapon but I saw the blood."

"He had a piece of broken glass," Colin adds.

"It happened very fast," I said. "He made a big sweeping movement around the guy's throat. Then the guy jumped up screaming at the man, 'You cut me, you fucking cut me!' He turned to another man sitting under the shack next door and said, 'Your brother fucking cut me!' The guy wasn't bleeding a lot when he walked down the street holding his neck shouting, 'I need a hospital. Where is the hospital?'"

The three of them look at me, each one with a very different expression. Colin is relieved, the cop is very serious, and the other man has the look of *there's going to be trouble.* The officer says "I will need you to make a formal statement."

"Yes, of course, I will," I reply.

"Come in and sit down," the cops says. Colin stands in the doorway and listens and the third man leaves. "Let's start at the beginning. Where do you live? What is the name of your boat? When did you arrive on Jost Van Dyke?" the cops asks.

Colin keeps going on about how things get done on an island. "You should be doing your job, and now you can't cover it up. You should have found her. For crying out loud, she was sitting on a boat in the harbor since yesterday and you guys couldn't find her?" The cop is clearly annoyed with Colin and tells him to be quiet and let him do his job.

I turn to Colin and say, "Tell Chris that I am sorry we didn't help him get to the hospital. It all happened so quickly and we were scared. It was totally surreal. We should have done something to help him."

"Well you are helping him now," Colin said.

The officer shoots Colin a hard look. "I am trying to get a statement here," he says in a disgusted tone. "I am getting confused with all the chatter. Now, if you don't mind. Please keep quiet."

"I have to go anyway," Colin says. "Look, I run the dive shop, please stop by and see me and my wife when you are through here. I really want to talk to you." Pete gives him our boat card with email addresses and Pete's phone number. Colin can't thank us enough for coming in. Chris will be so happy when he finds out.

The officer looks relieved that Colin has left. "I am sure you are doing your best to find out what really happened," I assure him. "He is just upset. He is scared for his friend. I am sure you will do the right thing." The cop seems to appreciate my kind words.

I continue relaying my story as the officer writes it down. The phone rings and the officer pick's it up. "Yes, Mr. George, I am doing everything I can, sir. I am getting the statement from the lady from Florida right now. Yes, sir. Yes, sir. Good bye." The cop hangs up. I don't like the idea that someone from the outside knows I am in here. My guard immediately goes up.

My statement is two pages long. He reads aloud to me the printed statement at the top that says the information I have given is true and that if I lie I can be arrested. He is very formal about this. He asks if I can read his handwriting. It is very neat. "Read it carefully," he says, "Then sign the bottom." Just as he hands me the document, another man rushes up to the door. He is clearly out of breath from running and appears to be agitated. The officer gets up and goes out on the porch with the man. I start to read the document when suddenly, I am gripped with fear. Who is this man? What does he want? Could I be in danger? Colin is gone and Pete and I are alone in the police station with the cop. Who was just on the phone? I move my chair from next to the desk where my back is toward the door to where my back is facing to the wall.

"Listen to what they are saying," I whisper to Pete. We are quiet and strain to hear. Something about a check and contact her before she leaves the island. Okay, breathe. Calm down. I am letting my imagination run away. Read the statement. I read it out loud to Pete. Everything is correct except the report says the man who did it was white or clear skinned and so was the victim. I never said the color of either man. I am shocked. The man that did it is black and Chris is white. It was Foxy's son. Foxy's son is a very dark-skinned Islander. Did the cop try to trick me and hope that I didn't read the statement carefully? Thank goodness for the interruption and the extra time I got to carefully read the statement. Then the reality runs through me like ice water in my veins. Oh my God, Colin is right. It is a cover up. I turn to Pete and ask, "What should I do?"

If I point this out, the cop will know that I caught him. If I don't say anything, I am lying and surely not helping Chris. Pete shrugs his shoulders. When the cop returns, I calmly point out the error. He strikes through white and writes black above it. I initial beside the change. He has me sign the document and print my name at the end of the second page. I am getting a sinking feeling. My stomach is doing a flip-flop.

The officer says, "Now you can go on and enjoy your breakfast." We had been discussing whether we should eat or just pull anchor. Pete hands him a boat card and I add my cell phone number to it. The cop doesn't think we will be contacted again. We say our good-byes.

Back down on the sandy street, we head toward the restaurant. No one is on the street but us. Out of nowhere, an Islander comes walking fast behind us. He comes up on my side and I cross over in front of Pete and push Pete between me and the man as he walks by.

"Watch out," I whisper to Pete.

"What's wrong." he says.

"Didn't you see that guy? He came out of nowhere?" I am shaking, white as a ghost. I grip Pete's arm. "Let's skip breakfast and get back to the boat. If you don't mind, I'm scared and just want to get out of here." We pull up anchor and go. The farther away from the island I get, the worse I feel. The reality of the events of the last few hours is crushing me.

Am I in danger? Will they be looking for our boat now? Wait, they don't know our boat. They think we are on the La La. The cops know our boat is the Ooh La La, but Foxy's doesn't or is Foxy and the cops the same thing? My head hurts. I think I am going to throw up. I need to know if we are in danger. I didn't get the officer's name, all I can remember is the #37 on his shiny silver badge. I didn't get a phone number. I didn't even get a copy of my statement. That was really stupid of me. I didn't get Colin's last name or the name of his shop or a phone number. I don't know Chris' last name. What is wrong with me? If I have the chance to meet Chris, I will. Not like when I gave CPR to the man in the park. I was freaked out and glad that he survived, but I didn't want to meet him. Was it because he was homeless? Was it because he looked so much like Tom? Was it because I had a chance to save someone when the only person I really wanted to save was Tom, but my pride stopped me? Meeting Chris is for the sake of his recovery, not for me. He must know what really happened, what I saw.

I have a friend who lived on St. Croix for ten years, and he knows how the islands work. He may even know Foxy. I turn on my cell phone and pray I have service. I do, thank goodness. No answer, so I leave a message. In a few minutes Brandon calls me back. I tell him the short version of what happened and ask if he knows Foxy, and if he thinks I am in danger. He doesn't know Foxy, but he knows a guy who does. He will call him and find out if I am in danger. "Don't tell him my name or the name of my boat," I plead with Brandon.

"I won't," he assures me. "I know you are scared, but look man, you were in the wrong place at the wrong time or the right place at the right time depending on who you are." Interesting choice of words I think. My morning meditation card that I have been reading for over two years now says *I am in the right place at the right time. Everything is happening just as it should.*

The next call I make is to my former husband, a cameraman for ABC news in Orlando. We haven't spoken but a few times since our divorce five years ago, but he picks up. I am very serious and skip the small talk, getting to the purpose of my call. I relay the story. "It is another Aruba scandal. It's big, I'm telling you and you can have the story." He gets a pad and pencil and writes down all the details. "Call me as soon as you have anything. Watch the wire service and find out who owns Foxy's. There is a lot at stake here."

We arrive at our next stop, Green Cay, a famous white sand patch of an island with one palm tree and great snorkeling. We drop anchor and load our snorkel gear into the dinghy. The sun is out, we are surrounded by other boats, and I am going to snorkel in one of the most sought-after places in the world. It is awesome. I should not be having this much fun when someone is lying in the hospital a millimeter from death. It is so surreal. When we finish and start loading our gear back into the dinghy, I look up to see the Ooh La La. Oh my God, there is a dinghy tied to her. Someone is on our boat! Oh, my God, they found us! It is not the police. Then I realize, I am looking at the wrong boat. Get a grip, Barbara. Stay calm. You are far enough away. No one is looking for you.

I finally get a return call from Brandon. His friend in St. Thomas says that we should get off Jost Van Dyke as quickly as possible and just stay quiet. He doesn't think anyone will come after us, but we shouldn't draw any attention to ourselves. The more I think about it, the madder I get. I don't want to be the one to ruin tourism for the BVI's, but I don't want someone else to get their throat slashed either.

We arrive at Soper's Hole Marina and take a mooring ball. Pete decides that staying in a busy marina, close to lots of other boats is the safest bet. The little marina village is adorable, but I am in no mood to shop. The first place I see is Serenity Day Spa. Pete suggests a massage to help me relax and is happy to turn me over to the little Indian girl running the place. "I'll be back in an hour to pick her up," he says. I have been holding back the tears all day and behind closed doors, lying naked on the table, I succumb. The tears trickle down my nose and I try not to make a fool of myself, until the girl leans down and whispers, "It's okay to let it out. Whatever it is that has you trembling should come out." I am no longer weeping, I am sobbing. Long deep breaths calm the waves of emotion that erupt from my core. The masseuse starts with my feet and legs and stays away from head and heart—unusual, but wise. There is way too much energy going on up there. Finally I relax into slow deep breaths. She is very good. My massage is over and I dress and go find Pete at the bar. "You look a little rough," he says.

"Yes, I would like to go back to the boat and take a nap," I answer. "I am exhausted."

I sleep until 7:00 p.m. We go to dinner at a lovely little outdoor place with a balcony overlooking the harbor. The food is great, Pete has lamb chops and I have curry shrimp. Twinkle lights glow all around us in the restaurant and on the water. Again, I feel guilty for having so much pleasure when all in the world is not right.

Morning comes with overcast skies and a light rain. We make the eight-mile run to Road Town, Tortola, the capital and town where the hospital is located. Surely here we can get the newspaper and see if anyone has heard anything. I don't even know Chris' last name. I can't just walk into the hospital and ask to see Chris, the American who was brought here from Jost Van Dyke two days ago after getting his throat slashed.

We radio to the marina to see if a slip is available and then motor in to Dock A9 where I throw the bough line to the waiting dockhand and then run to the stern and throw that line. By far and away, this was the easiest, most uneventful docking yet. We go to the office to check in and I head for the dive shop to try to find out the name of the dive shop on Jost Van Dyke. The girl behind the counter doesn't know of one, so I flip through a magazine that says there is no dive shop on Jost Van Dyke. I check the copyright date, 1997. Just old, I think. She pulls out a little local guide and starts to look at the ads. "Here it is," she says. I ask her if I can keep it but she says it is her only copy, so I write down the phone number and email address.

As soon as I am on the boat, I use my cell phone to make the call and get a recording that says my service can't complete the call. Oh well, we are going into town and I will make the call, check my email and buy a local paper. I need to know what has happened in the last twelve hours.

We go directly to the Safeway grocery store and buy two papers, the daily and the bi- weekly. NOTHING. Not a word. I am not as surprised as I am disappointed. Next we go to the Internet café. I explain that I need to make this call to Jost Van Dyke and the girl behind the counter dials the number. A lady answers the phone.

"Is Collin in?" I ask.

"No, I'm sorry. He is out for the day."

"Is this his wife?"

"Yes it is."

"Well, uh, hello, I am Barbara." Remembering what Brandon told me, don't bring attention to yourself. Keep a low profile. The Internet café is crowded and the phone I am using is right on the counter in the middle of the place. Everyone can hear each word I am saying.

"I am the lady from Florida. I was wondering what Chris' last name is. I am in Roadtown and thought I would go see him today."

"Oh, you are the lady trying to help us, of course," she says. "His name is Godson." Her accent is so thick I can't understand.

"Could you spell that for me? Is there an H in there somewhere?"

I repeat it back to her and finally understand his name.

"What was the name of the Officer?"

"The man in charge is Clark."

"And what is your name?"

"Andrea, Andrea and Colin," she answers.

"Good, I am getting the information I need," I tell myself.

"Chris is not in the hospital anymore," she says. "He went home this morning."

"That's great," I reply. "That means he was okay to fly."

"He went by air ambulance. His father wanted him out of the country as quickly as possible."

"Was there an arrest?" I inquire.

"Yes," Andrea says. "The sad part is there is no facility on the islands for a man like that."

"What was the man's name?" I ask

"Christian."

To myself I think, "Oh my God, it was Foxy's son."

"Good, that is good news," I tell Andrea.

"Chris was in a hurry to get home. I am sure he will be contacting you by email as soon as he can. Thank you for helping."

I am relieved as I hang up the phone. A quick check of email and voice-mail on my cell phone shows no news is good news. It is over. Thank goodness. Part of me wants the fight, feeling that this should not just be brushed aside, and part of me knows that it is a terrible tragedy for a family, even if it is a famous one. It is not for me to decide.

I never hear back from my ex-husband. Some things never change. I reached out to him and he let me down.

# Chapter 35

## British Virgin Islands
## March 2007

We spend the rest of the day being tourists in Roadtown, Tortola. The town is cute and the shops are busy as a big cruise ship has come in this morning. A light rain blankets the town as it did yesterday. We have not had rain at all on the trip other than the day we arrived in Luperon. Deciding that we must have a rum drink in the famous Pusser's Bar, I take Pete's picture in front of the building. He is becoming quite a rum aficionado.

We pop into several galleries since I find art so much more interesting than jewelry. Pete comes over and says, "You have got to see this." He guides me over to a small display in the corner of a tiny room and there is a Pissarro print. "Spooky," he says, "You are way too spooky." At first he thought the stuff I have been reading and talking about was New Age and weird. Then when things started to happen like Bambi, the bikes and Brittany, and he saw the results, he became more open to it. Now he says, "Say nice things about Pete. Pete is a good guy."

Not only do we find the painting we bought from Cody, we find some new prints too. We are discussing the prints when the ladies behind me gather in closer to see what we are looking at. I ask if they have been to St. Thomas yet and explain about the gallery and how Pissarro was born there but studied with the other great impressionists of the time. I relay what little I know about him, but they are so impressed by his story that they buy a print.

Pete just stands back and watches the show. "You are amazing. You are selling art in a gallery you don't even work in. You can sell."

"That is one of my talents," I tell him. "I didn't learn to sell, I was born to sell." Another law of the universe is *use the talents you were born with and you will discover the purpose of your life here. You don't learn talents, you just have them and must be willing to express them freely and openly and then you will be in line with all the energy of the universe.* I guess selling is one of mine. And art, well I do love art.

It continues to rain and after a drink or two, I am ready to go back to the boat and take a nap. We spend a quiet rainy night on the boat but with air conditioning! Thank goodness. When it rains, we have to close the hatches and windows and then it gets really hot and sticky. We are docked and have electric hook-up, a treat we haven't had for about a month. I open all the closet doors and drawers and try to dry things out a bit. My phone works and we have Internet.

I lie awake in bed as morning comes through the small windows of the boat. I regret being so hard on Gary. Maybe it is not newsworthy. Maybe it shouldn't be in the news at all.

Pete goes to the dock master to get water, gas for the dinghy and check out. I stay onboard and lock myself in, something I have never done before. I still feel a little uneasy about things and think Pete has been gone a long time. I fill out the postcards I bought yesterday. Just as I finish, Pete comes back with a fresh haircut.

"No wonder you took so long, I was beginning to worry," I tell him.

"No reason to," Pete said. "I picked this marina because it is home base to the Moorings, one of the biggest, most prestigious charter companies in the islands. I knew security would be good here. I brought you the newspaper," he says, plopping it down on the table. "It came out today, but there isn't anything in it about the attack. That was the first thing I did," he adds. "I wanted to make sure we didn't have a reason to hit the road in a hurry."

I start flipping through the paper, thinking he might have missed something. Instead, I turn to the horoscopes and read mine. It was like a slap in the face. I couldn't believe what I was reading.

Sagittarius- *You are making many enemies, Sagittarius, and it's time to step back. Contrary to what you believe, you don't know it all. Therefore, be a student instead of a teacher.*

The words sting as I read them again and again. I don't know it all. Today I will get my meditation cards out and go back to studying the book on the laws of the universe and how things work. I do have a lot to learn. Was this a message from the Infinite Intelligence? Who am I making my enemy? It's time to reel it in, so I turn off the computer, the phone, and the air conditioning. I go on deck to air that is stifling, thick and muggy. Back to reality, maybe air conditioning isn't such a good idea.

For the next week we island hop. We sail to Norman Cay and visit the William T, a famous bar that is actually a boat floating in the sea. You get a free T-shirt if you jump off the top naked.

A new day brings rain and clouds, making it a perfect lazy day. Pete works on the water pump while I read, becoming a student again. In the afternoon we move to Cooper Island and snorkel caves with bright colored coral growing on the rocks. I get a blister from the fins. Two new bruises are added to my legs after slipping twice on the boat because I didn't wear shoes.

Our next move is to Marina Cay. We climb to the top of the hill to visit the house that inspired a famous movie from the 1960's called *Virgin Islands* starring Sidney Poitier. I nap while Pete tinkers with the generator.

We sail another nineteen miles to Virgin Gorda in winds of twenty-five knots with six to eight foot seas. It is very rough. We have lunch at Saba Rock and a drink at Bitter End, and another one at Last Resort. Pete wants to be able to say he had a drink at every famous watering hole.

We take a taxi to Spanish Town and get high on the hillside to see amazing vistas. From here, we walk all the way to the Baths and climb all through the strange tunnels running through ancient volcanic rocks being shaped by the swirling water. We even stop for a drink at a cliff-side bar, Mad Dog. The day ends with a five-star dinner at Biras Creek Resort. It boasts it is the top-rated chef and restaurant in the BVI's. Rumor has it that Catherine Zeta Jones and Michael Douglas are regulars.

We make another hop to Trellis Bay on Beef Island for the full moon party, which has been highly promoted in the guidebooks. I love a full moon and fire, so I am really looking forward to it. We arrive first thing in the morning and find all the mooring balls are already taken. I guess we are not the only ones who know about tonight's party. We find a spot to anchor after several attempts and finally settle in.

Once on shore, I find a pay phone and call Brittany. She totally dumps on me, telling me how angry she is at me for leaving her and how selfish I am being. She hates that she must worry about my safety and says how much it upsets her that I may be in danger. If Bambi drowned, I could too. If some man got his throat slit, I could too. She feels alone and that I have abandoned her. I am her only family. She doesn't like not being able to call me when she wants to talk to me and whenever I call her, it is to tell her what to do or relay some tragedy. Why can't I be normal like everyone else's mom? She is worried that I am unstable. I hang up the phone completely deflated. I feel like someone punched me in the stomach and I never saw it coming.

My next phone call is to Debby, my best friend. She will know what to do. She listens to me and responds in that wonderful tough-love way of hers. "Barbara," Debby says, "It's the same story, just a different day. We have heard it all before. Brittany is struggling as a young woman learning to be on her own and when things go bad, you are the easiest target." I only have myself to thank. I did spend my whole life making her the center of my universe and now things have changed, and she doesn't like it. Who wouldn't feel left out?

I tried to get her to come on the boat for a week or two. She could have flown to any island and we could have picked her up, but she didn't want any part of that.

I am not her only family, but all my relatives live in Pennsylvania, and her real dad moved out of state when she was three and moved back when she was sixteen. They rarely saw each other during that time. After that, when they did see each other, she would come home frustrated and usually in tears. I did hoard her when she was little. I thought I was protecting her and keeping her from hurt and disappointment and now, it does feel like I am her only family. Gary drifted out of the picture after our divorce. I understand that she feels alone.

I let that one phone call eat me up. I turn and churn our conversation, or should I say my beating, over and over again in my mind. I feel sad and mad. Maybe I should just go home. I am angry at myself for allowing Brittany's words and feelings to rip my heart out and ruin this day, and all the other days that there have been calls or emails like it. The more I think about it, the worse I feel.

The airport is right next to the bay where we are anchored. I keep watching the airplanes and wonder where they are going. Should I be on one of them? And go back to what? Orlando or move to Atlanta to be close to Brittany? What good is it going to do for me to be in Atlanta when she will want to be with her friends, not me? Should I stop living my dream so she can have the *idea* that her mom is neatly tucked away somewhere?

We walk down the beach and take a seat at a Tiki bar on the beach. The owner of the bar called De Loose Mongoose lives on a boat and is from Bermuda. I want his life. Does he have worries and if so, what? Which palm tree to tie up the dinghy to? What should the drink of the day be, a rumrunner or a margarita? My heart is heavy.

At midnight, we go back over to Fireball Beach and watch the giant old rusty mooring balls being floated out into the water. Designs have been cut into each ball and wood slipped inside now making the flames lick through the art. The beach is packed and everyone is dancing to the Reggae band. I think drumming would be better, but the party is great. I read just the other day that *disappointment comes from too much expectation.* Just let life unfold as it does, stay in the present moment and don't miss one little thing.

I fall asleep the minute my head hits the pillow, but by 3:00 a.m. I am awake. Moonlight hits my face when it shines through the little window as the boats swings, securely anchored. I lie there thinking of Brittany. Am I being selfish? I pull out the book, *Having It All,* and look for some insight about the conflict between Brittany and me. *Harmony: When we attract a person who acts less than lovingly toward us, that person is showing us a part of ourselves we do not love and accept. The universe in its infinite wisdom, is giving us the opportunity to see a part of us that we are hiding from ourselves.*

What am I hiding from myself? Is this who I am? I want to have that wonderful happy-go-lucky relationship with my daughter that I had before—before Tom, before Alaska and before the Ooh La La. It is not the adventure or moving that scares her, it is the fear of her mom being out of control and leaving her behind. I am being out of control because I lost control of my life? Am I afraid of being left behind? Again?

Tomorrow will be a new day. We'll move to Leverick Bay, the most Eastern part of the BVI's and stage for the jump to St. Martin. The BVI's are beautiful. We added fifty-five miles to the log book island hopping here, for a total of 1,679 miles trip-to-date.

# Chapter 36

## Expired Passport – St. Martin
## April 2007

I set the alarm for midnight and we pull up anchor. We have a fourteen hour motor-sail to St. Martin tomorrow. The only thing between us and there is eighty-five miles of open ocean. Pete takes the first shift, midnight until 3:00 a.m. and I will do the second. My rest is totally fitful in the rough water. I rock and roll in my bed, stuff falls off the shelf, and bottles clink with every wave. The door to the engine even swings open, allowing its roar to invade my room and make me get up to re-latch the door.

At 4:00 a.m., I wake and look at my watch. I yell up to Pete at the helm. "Why did you let me sleep so long?" He knew I was tired yesterday and thought I could use the extra rest. I grab a Diet Coke from the fridge, something I never do, but it is easy caffeine, put on my foul weather jacket, long pants and harness and climb up the stairs to the cockpit. I let my eyes adjust to the darkness. "Anything going on?" I ask Pete.

"Not much," he says, "A big tanker went by and so did a cruise ship." I scan the 360 degree horizon and see nothing but open ocean. The course is set on the GPS, straight line for the next ten hours. I think I can handle that. "Go get some sleep, Pete."

It is dark but light at the same time. The full moon is backlighting big puffy clouds. I can easily see the cloud formations against the dark black sky, and there is enough moonlight to see the swells that kept me from sleeping. Waves are hitting the boat on an angle from just off the port side of the bow, making the boat sway and rock rather than pounding directly on the bow, creating that horrible thrashing we had on other rough nights. Still, I know that the water is being forced in reverse into the bath sink and head, letting seawater and other gray water splash all over the bathroom. With each rough crossing, I do a full cleaning of the heads and floors. I don't want to track that gross water all over the floors and carry the germs from our feet to the sheets. Besides, the boat smells nice after a good cleaning. I am surprised how dirty it gets. I use a dustpan and brush to sweep the floors, or a little mini vacuum only when we are on a dock and have electricity.

I chose the second shift so I can see the moonlight on the water, the pre-sun and sunrise. This is one of my favorite things. Tonight the moon is going to tease me and not let me have the full exposure although it does make for an interesting sky. There is plenty of light. I watch the water dance in the wake of the engine and bask in the glory of moon reflecting on the water when a cloud so kindly moves out of the way.

When I first started this journey of self-discovery, one of the books I read said: in order to find out what your true talents and passions are, write down everything that you love. Some of mine are collecting stamps in my passport, moonlight on the water, listening to the ocean, grand hotel lobbies, fireplaces, walking city streets, exploring other cultures, helping people, ethnic food, elegantly set tables with fine white linen, crystal and china, fresh flowers, piano music, room service, learning new things, enjoying a cup of coffee in a featherbed and a new magazine. If I put them all together or even a few of them, then this is what I should *do* with my life. I ponder this as I ride the waves, alone in the darkness. This little boat is the only thing on the ocean for as far as I can see in all directions.

I am strapped behind the helm and rock back and forth with the swells. My legs are a little sore from my run yesterday. I decide a little stretching is in order, especially since all I have to do is hold the position and let the boat do all the work. I stand at the helm with my legs spread wide and do side-to-side lunges. I haven't formally exercised in months. I know I am going to have to hit it hard for a few weeks when I get back. I realize I can also do abdominal crunches by rocking my legs across a bench. Actually, just holding a sitting position and adjusting myself to the rocking of the boat is like doing crunches. Wow, three hours of crunches and lunges, at least it is a start back into my fitness routine.

I remember sitting on the porch of the tree house last spring and for months every morning, I would get up, read, pray and try to understand my purpose and what I should do with the second half of my life. I was in the ray. I was in the light. I couldn't wait to get up in the morning, put on my white robe, get my coffee, and go sit on the swing to read, learn and then watch my world unfold. Each day was filled with energy and excitement as I watched what I was learning turn into reality. Like the book says, "Playing the spiritual game is all there is. Once the game is understood, the material world will just fall into place." In the days on the porch at the tree house, I wasn't exercising like a crazy woman, yet I felt strong, healthy and lean. I do recall wondering when my body would turn to mush, but it never did. The body requires so little, mostly not to be abused. Look at the yogis, they are lean and toned, and don't punish their bodies. The spiritual game is all there is.

After an hour or so, the sunrise show begins. First, the pre-sunrise. I think of it as the opening band before the headliner, or foreplay. The only trouble is, sometimes the foreplay is better than the real thing. It's the anticipation, the hinting of what is to come. The only way to tell is to let it play out, to wait and see. First there is just a tease of a glow on the horizon. I play a game with the sun and place a little bet. I guess the exact place the sun will rise on the horizon and lock it in on the compass. Then the glow turns into a pastel shade of yellow, then orange and pink. Beautiful pink, it is the best of all the colors. It gets brighter and richer and lights up the white clouds in the sky behind me. The black sky turns to blue and the shadows of clouds now turn pink. As daylight comes, the water totally changes. The reflection of the pink clouds on the dark water looks like a thin film of oil covering the surface. Swirling and dancing, it plays with me. The sun comes up big and fast. The colors disappear quickly into the whiteness of the sun and brightness of its reflection on the water. No afterglow, geez. I guess that means the only thing left to do is light a cigarette. Oh, I forgot, I don't smoke. And on top of being over way too quickly, the sun won the bet. It didn't rise where I guessed it would. I will have to stick to my original theory: pre-sunrise is usually better and lasts longer.

Another day and I get another chance to see my world unfold before me. It will soon be 100 days on the water. When I went to Alaska with my dad, I kept track of the days by numbering them, day one, day two because I knew we would be gone for forty-two days. I will fly back on day 104. It has gone by very quickly and it has been everything I wanted it to be and more. We have gotten further than I thought. I am excited about going to the Leewards. We have traveled much more luxuriously than I thought, eating out more and doing more touring. We have been fully stocked and have purchased whatever we wanted along the way. Pete has been very generous. I wonder what is coming next for him. At times, it felt like he was on a rampage to live, feel and experience everything, like he was in some kind of hurry, like he knows his time is running out. Is this his last hurrah and I don't know it, or is this the universe telling me that this is the way we should all live? Life is short. Should we live like time is running out and be in a hurry to experience all we can? When we talk about what he will do after the trip, he has no plans. Will he stay in the islands and find work? Will he go back to Florida or sell the boat? Even getting someone else to come onboard to make the trip back has not interested him. I don't want to leave him stranded. I have been the one pushing him to make arrangements.

I wish I was staying onboard, but my plan to be with Brittany for her birthday is set. So is my commitment to be in Italy for May. I wish I were staying onboard at least to get the boat back to Florida by June. Could I live onboard forever, I mean as a lifestyle? Have a million dollar view that I can change whenever I want? Would I need to change and to keep moving, or would living onboard become like a house after a while and I would get up and go to work like before?

I definitely love being on the water and in nature. The beauty and isolation far outweigh the inconveniences. I like being on the go and changing harbors. I wonder if that would stop after we have toured the whole line of islands and then the need for conquest would halt. Would changing anchorages happen seasonally rather than every few days? Would I want to live on a boat if I had a job and went to work every day? Do I overlook the hassles because I am on an adventure of a lifetime, or would it still be fun if it was my permanent home? I don't know the answers and I won't find out this time around. I am getting off in a few days to go on to the next adventure. Perhaps those are questions for Pete, not for me.

Just then, Pete stirs on the couch below. He pops his head into the cockpit and asks if everything is okay. "Uneventful," I report. After a while, I can smell coffee brewing. He joins me at the helm and we welcome another day. Immediately he notices Saba Island on the horizon. I never see landfall and he can spot it so easily. It is an island about thirty miles south of St. Martin, but much higher, that is why we can see it before St. Martin. We enjoy our coffee as two spunky little dolphins jump out of the water at the side of the boat. In unison, they jump and swim hard to play in the wake, just off the bow. What a delightful greeting to our new country.

Just after noon, we motor into the harbor. There is a bridge we must pass under in order to get into the lagoon and it opens on a schedule. The next opening is 5:30 p.m., so we decide to anchor outside and take the dinghy into customs, then move the boat later. After filling out the forms and paying a whopping $10, I get the stamp in my passport. I look at it carefully. I want to embed in my mind how happy that little stamp makes me.

The island is divided into two countries—St. Martin, the French side and Sint Maarten, the Dutch side. We clear customs on the Dutch side. St. Barts and Guadeloupe are also governed by the French. Going from side to side of the island is much like crossing the state line, a non-event.

There is a charming story about how the division of the island took place, although totally unsupported by historical fact, but it goes like this: The French and the Dutch were so civilized that, rather than fight over the island, they had a Frenchman armed with a bottle of wine walk in one direction, and a Dutchman equipped with a flask of gin take the other. Where they met became the boundary. The French ended up with a bit more because the gin was stronger than the wine and slowed the Dutchman down.

In the early days, the island was important to the Dutch because of the salt ponds in the southern part, which is why they settled that half. St. Martin was successful for a time as a producer of tobacco and then sugar. When the sugar market collapsed, in an attempt to stop the downward spiral of the island, the island became duty-free. It worked and quickly became the Caribbean's biggest shopping mall.

We hop on a dollar bus, like a mini van, and head to Phillipsburg, the capital. Here is where all the great shopping, and beaches are and where the big cruise ships come in. We spend a delightful day popping in and out of shops and art galleries and have a cool drink on the second floor balcony of a little pub. The view is spectacular. The blue water stretches out as far as we can see, and the beach is covered with brightly colored umbrellas arranged in neat rows. It reminds me of the French Riviera. After a delicious Indian lunch, we decide an afternoon of lying around the boat is in order. We decide to go out late for dinner and try to catch a band and enjoy the nightlife. I start a new book, pop in a lively CD, and take my lounger up to the foredeck. This is paradise.

After a slow-moving morning, we move the boat a whopping six miles to Phillipsburg harbor to buy gas. Pete dinghies to shore to check out the gas situation and buy a new waterproof camera. Last night when we returned to the boat, I dropped my purse into the water, ruining the camera and my cell phone. My bag was barely in the water a second and both the camera and the phone were in a zip locked baggy, not zipped tight. I have been so careful the entire trip with my cell phone, rarely taking it off the boat. It is my everything. It has all the phone numbers, passwords, codes, addresses etc. I haven't been able to hot sync it to my new laptop, so I am totally freaked out about losing all the data. I would never even think about taking it off the boat, but I was so desperate to talk to Brittany, I took a chance and lost. She never did return my calls anyway. This is the third camera that got ruined. Saltwater is a killer.

Later in town, we are drawn to the most delightful outdoor restaurant when we see a huge bowl of fresh mussels go by and our taste buds come alive with the aroma of garlic. We linger at the menu board until Francoise, a very French waiter, comes over and insists we sit and eat. He waves his hands around and speaks French so fast that neither of us can keep up, nor do we care that we have no idea what he said, but we are definitely having lunch here. He dramatically pulls out my chair, kisses my hands, tells Pete what a lucky man he is and claps his hand for someone to come and bring up water and bread. He speaks English too, of course, and tells us he is the only person working today and he is very busy, but he will try to give us the best service he can. "Bring us the wine and an order of mussels," Pete tells him and we will worry about the rest later. I think Francois must be Italian. No, he is definitely French, he just flirts like an Italian. The day is glorious. Warm sunshine, cool breezes, and we are sitting on what feels like the French Riviera sipping a lovely Bordeaux. How lucky am I?

We hop back on the dollar bus and travel further out on the island to the charming seaside village Grand Case. Open-air restaurants spill out onto the sea, each one more chic and inviting than the last. Our tummies are too full to eat, but we walk along admiring how French each quaint little place is. I like it here. It really feels like we are in a different country. Oh, we are.

It is about two o'clock on Saturday afternoon before Easter Sunday. We just anchored in the turquoise harbor of Gustiva, St. Barts after moving fifteen miles. This is the island of the rich and famous. It is an adorable little hilly town with red roofs popping out of lush green vegetation. We dinghy into town to find some lunch, clear customs, see about getting some gas and use a computer. After tying up, we walk down the dock past mega yacht after mega yacht. Each one has an elegant boarding bridge decorated with planters and monogrammed rugs, and of course, uniformed staff waiting to assist their well-heeled clients when they return from a day of sightseeing.

We are surprised to find the customs office closed, but figure they are taking the weekend off for Easter. No gas today or tomorrow either. The airport, however, is definitely open. Small aircraft cut so close to the top of the mountain, they look like they are sure to crash. I can't imagine putting the runway so close to a tall mountain, nor can I imagine how quickly the plane must descend on the other side.

After lunch, we stroll along the streets and pop in and out of one charming chic boutique after another. We climb the stairs to find a little shop with several computers lined up along the wall. I open my email first and read a discouraging letter from Brittany. She doesn't think I should come for her birthday, she is still mad at me. The letter is long and cuts like a knife right through my heart. God, I hate this. I feel like the bull in the fight arena, running angrily, not knowing where to really direct my anger. I am in pain. I want to attack, but I don't know to whom or where to direct it. We really need to get this whole thing straightened out. I print out the letter so I can read and re-read it. I torture and re-torture myself. I also reply back, telling her I am coming and attach my original flight information. We just need some face-to-face time.

I go online to purchase a ticket from LIAT Airlines (Leeward Islands Air Transit). We decided yesterday to take the next few days to get to Antigua, and that I would fly out of there on Friday, the thirteenth. A bit creepy I know, but I need to file a tax extension and meet my other connection, and of course, be in Atlanta to celebrate Brittany's twenty-first birthday. Pete thinks that this is a good harbor for him to stay in for the two weeks or so until his new crew can fly in. I purchased my ticket from Puerto Rico to Atlanta weeks ago in order to get a better rate. We didn't know how far we would get and didn't want to be locked into a certain destination. Between weather and boat problems, it was way too difficult to hit the mark. As I sit here, filling in personal information, I pull out my passport and type in the number and expiration date of April 10, 2007. I look at the screen. What, that can't be right. I look at my passport again. Oh, my God. That is this year, wait a minute, that is this month. Oh, my God, my passport is expiring in three days! This can't be right.

How can this be? I have shown my passport at least a dozen times in the last few months. I looked at the dates before I left. I swear it expires on October 4, 2007. As I stare at the document in disbelief, I see how the numbers are written backwards, like in Europe, with the 10-04-07. At any rate, with my mouth hanging open, I show it to Pete.

"Look at this expiration date," I tell him.

"How did that happen?" he asks.

"I don't know, but we better find out what to do," I respond.

I buy the ticket and we get the phone number for passport services from the website. We need an international calling card to use the pay phone, but everything is closed for today. Nothing left to do but climb on a bar stool with a view of the harbor and the mega yachts, and drink a lovely bottle of French wine for six euros. This is the life.

Two o'clock and the cabin is stiflingly hot. No air is moving at all. I take my blanket and pillow and quietly climb up the stairs to the cockpit. The night is still as golden lights twinkle all over the hillside of Gustiva. The water gently rocks the boat to and fro. The moon is bright and only about two-thirds full; a few stars are out and the others are being blocked by the clouds. The most interesting objects on the horizon are the lights of the boats. The mega yachts anchored are like mini cruise ships. All decks and the water around them are lit up, but it is the tall ships that shine the prettiest to me. A single line on every crossbeam of the mast, and the cap of the anchor light at the top. These huge sailboats look like a tall building standing alone in the night. How much electricity does that use up, all those lights? What kind of generator and battery system must it take to make all that power? They are in a whole different league.

I wonder why they are anchored out. We saw so many of them docked with their elegant ladders and uniformed staff. Then it occurs to me, if they don't have any paying customers onboard, there is no reason to be on the dock. If the staff needs to get to shore, they can dinghy in. It is probably several thousand dollars a night to be docked. Earlier today, we guessed that it took about eight people full-time to run a ship like that.

But at this moment, it is not my problem. My problem is that the real world is crashing down around me so fast I can't breathe. I am scared out of my mind. How could things go from paradise without a worry in the world, to my daughter's mad and doesn't want me to come, my phone and all it's data doesn't work, my passport expires tomorrow and I haven't locked in Italy? Breathe and calm down. Take it one thing at time. How did I get so *out of one with the universe* so fast?

The law of the universe says: *Over-thinking or over-analyzing something takes the energy away from it. Release and trust.*

Everything can be fixed. Right now the most important thing is my passport. I have three choices. Get on a plane on Monday and fly home. I will get on the Internet or go to the airport in the morning and find out what can be done. This would mean walking up to the airport and buying a one-way ticket from St. Bart's to Atlanta, just call it a day. God knows how much that would cost. I could fly the same carrier and try to use my existing tickets, just pay the change fees. I would need to pack up everything tomorrow, taking only the bare minimum and leave the rest behind and have Pete ship it later.

Pete, what about Pete? I would be totally leaving him in the lurch. St. Bart's is not a place he wants to stay. It is very small, too small really, with barely any services. He needs to go back to St. Martin or go on to Antigua. Either place is somewhere he has a chance to be with other cruisers and either hang out for a few weeks and wait for someone to fly in, or find crew to hire. St. Martin is closer. We could go there tomorrow and I could fly out on Monday.

My other choice is to just go home as planned. Use the tickets I already bought and deal with the expired passport in Puerto Rico. I cannot be the only one in the world that this has happened to. Antigua probably won't notice my passport has expired and I will get stopped in Puerto Rico. It is a US territory and a big airport, surely there is an embassy or something like it there. I do have until Friday to get the situation straightened out. I just need a one-week extension. Then I must quickly get it renewed before my May 1st flight to Italy.

Or I could just stay onboard. No one has ever checked the dates on my documents. I just don't have to go through customs anymore and ride back to Florida on the boat. We would be back in June. I could change my ticket to Italy. That would take care of Pete's problem, too.

I need to straighten everything out with Brittany, file my taxes and fill out forms for Brittany's financial aid. My phone doesn't work and I have no phone numbers for anyone other than the few I can remember. Time is running out. I am panicking. Don't pile it all on top of each other. Breathe. You will figure it all out in the morning.

Easter Sunday and we are up and in town early. I want to get a jump on the day. We will call the Passport Emergency Office and find out what to do. We will get online and see what flights are available from here or St. Martin. A decision must be made today.

I know it is only 8:00 a.m., but there isn't a soul around. It is a ghost town. Even around the harbor, there are only a few old men sitting along the docks. We find one shop open and decide to get a French breakfast of cafe au lait, pastry and quiche and let some time pass. We find a charming shop where the deli cases are filled with platters of freshly made salads and whole roasted chickens piled high. Beautiful pastries and desserts, too pretty eat, fill the shop along with bread, beautiful bread of all sizes and shapes. Everyone coming and going speaks French. It really is charming here.

We buy a phone card from the shop and walk across the street to call the passport office. It is busy. I try several times and realize it is the phone, not the number. We walk to another phone and try again. Dialing the access code, then the pin number, then the country code, then the area code and phone number, to my delight, I get through! Now I am in automated phone hell only to discover that this number doesn't handle my type of issue, it is for missing persons outside the U.S. I try and try to get a human being, without luck and use up half of my calling card. We need to get to a computer and get the correct number to call. Nothing is going to be open until noon, if at all on this Easter Sunday.

After wasting the morning, the only thing left to do is to go to the airport.

Surely we can get Internet there and I can check on some flights. We walk to the taxi stand and ask how much to go to the airport. He says $20. "That's ridiculous," I tell myself. "It's just around the corner." He sees the look on my face and says, "I know it's a lot, but it is Easter Sunday." I would go find someone else, but Pete says okay. We climb up a very steep hill and our taxi doesn't sound like it is going to make it. As we come over the crest, we see a very short runway directly at the foot of the mountain that ends right at the ocean. Dear God, the planes come right over the top of the hill and drop down fast and stop hard before falling into the water. And I thought Aspen was a tough approach.

The airport is a little strip of open-air counters for air and rental cars. One restaurant and bar is our only hope for Internet. Pete sets up shop there while I go find LIAT Air and see what arrangements I can make for a flight out for tomorrow.

No LIAT counter, no Internet, no English, but I do find an irritated Frenchman who doesn't want to be working today. We find one kind counter worker who lets us use her phone and computer, but nothing pans out. I leave two messages for friends in the US, hoping they can make some calls tomorrow. We learn that the islands celebrate Easter Monday too, and again everything will be closed.

Frustrated and exhausted, I decide we have spent enough time and energy on this project. By the time the wine and calm from the glow of the lights from the mega yachts reflecting on the water takes effect, I decide we should just proceed as we planned. I will fly out of Antigua, change planes in Puerto Rico, and be in Atlanta by Friday night. What is the worst thing they can do? The island people won't check my expiration date and if they notice it in Puerto Rico, I will already be in US territory and I am going home anyway. My passport will have expired three days earlier, not three months or three years. I decide to just wing it.

Let's just proceed as planned. I will fly out from Antigua on Friday. There, a decision has been made and I will put it out of my mind. We are sitting in a lovely restaurant and dining on fresh mahi-mahi and melt-in-your-mouth sea bass served over risotto. We call it an early evening. I am exhausted, not feeling very chic amongst these beautiful people. I feel fat and I am worried about getting home and what I am going home to. And oh yeah, where is home anyway? With that in front of me, I try to enjoy the last few days of the trip.

Monday, we spend a lazy day on the boat, then snorkel and dinghy to the beach, play in the surf and lie in the sun. Tomorrow morning, we will move to St. Kitts, then on to Antigua. We wake at our usual time, have coffee on the deck, and pull up anchor at 8:00 a.m. I stay below to write since the water is very calm. As I recap the last few days and really think about what is happening, I completely change my mind. Wing it!!!! Have you lost your mind? I ask myself. Get stuck out of the country with an expired passport? A few years ago, it wouldn't have mattered much, but now with all the tightened security. Wing it!!! I don't think so.

I go up to the cockpit to talk to Pete. He says he will do whatever I want. We have only traveled about an hour and if we turn around now, we can go all the way to St. Martin and be there by noon. The airport is right next to the harbor. We can dinghy to it. Pete assures me that this must have happened before, and he thinks they will give some type of temporary document and send me on my way. It may take some time, but there shouldn't be a problem if I am on US soil in Puerto Rico. Yeah, easy to say, he is not the one with an expired passport.

"I am sorry, Pete, but I want to go back today," I tell him. "Let's turn around." Being very understanding, Pete turns the boat around and we head back for St. Martin.

I have three hours to pack and store my stuff so Pete can return it to me later. I drag out my two tote bags and try to decide what is vital. I am going home today, this day, the 100th day of the trip. It has a nice ring to it. It must right.

I am so sick of wearing the same clothing that I take only a few pieces to wear in Atlanta until I can get to my storage closet in Orlando and replenish my wardrobe. I throw in notebooks, music, electronics, toiletries and supplements. I have to go through everything as we have it all mixed up. My mouth is dry and I am sweating. I am sad and happy at the same time. We will not have a chance for a proper celebration. I don't want to open the bottle of Champagne that was bought for this occasion, as I know I will be all weepy and I need to have a clear head for the task at hand. I need to change my LIAT to a flight today to Puerto Rico, then do customs and change my Delta ticket to Atlanta from Friday to Tuesday. Then get my feet on the ground in Atlanta today, call Brittany and tell her what time to pick me up at the airport, and hope she shows up.

When we arrive in the harbor, Pete circles around looking for the best spot to anchor. Sometimes he finds a good spot on the first time around, sometimes it takes half-an-hour. He is going to be in this spot for two weeks. Please hurry, please hurry, I say to myself. It is noon, I have plenty of time.

After we set anchor, Pete puts on a clean shirt and throws my bags into the dinghy, and off we go through the inner harbor and around to the other side where the airport is located. Our dinghy is barely moving with the extra weight of my luggage. Can we go any slower? To my dismay, there is no dock for the airport, only a private one for an abandoned restaurant several hundred yards from the terminal. Loaded down like pack mules, we walk as fast as we can to the terminal. Why didn't we take a taxi from the bridge? We would be there by now and I wouldn't be schlepping all this stuff down this hot dusty road. I don't say a word. Be gracious. Pete has bent over backwards to get you here.

Once inside, we split up to see what arrangements can be made. Delta doesn't fly out of this airport and there is no one at the LIAT counter. Then Pete points to the reader board. American Airlines direct to Atlanta leaving in one hour. I run to the counter and the girl tells me I missed the one-hour check-in deadline. I beg her to get me on the plane. I don't have any luggage to check. I can go directly to the gate right now. She makes a call and relays the instructions from the person on the other end of the phone.

"You can buy a ticket and get on this flight for $1072," she says.

I turn to Pete with an expression on my face that I can only imagine looks like.

"Whatever you want to do, Barbara," Pete says.

I turn to the counter girl and say. "I'll take it. Get me on that plane," I say.

Complete and total relief washes over me. I am going home today. I will be safely back in the USA and I will see my daughter in just a few hours. Everything is going to be all right. I'll get my phone fixed, do my taxes, do the financial aid forms, fix things with Brittany and send the money for my room in Italy. Everything's going to be fine.

We walk quickly to the security checkpoint and I turn to Pete to say goodbye. "I am sorry things got so crazy at the end, but this has been a trip of a lifetime and I can't thank you enough. You are a good man, Pete, and I wish only the best for you." We hug goodbye. "I'll see you back in Florida in the fall," I tell him. I turn and ride the escalator up and wave goodbye to Pete as he stays by the turnstiles. He looks shell-shocked. These last few days have been a bit crazy. He's going to be fine. I think he was hoping for a different ending.

Finally at the gate, I find a seat and catch my breath. Pete is on my mind. Knowing our time together was coming to an end, we talked a lot this week about the trip and how it all came together. He gave me a trip of my dreams and I gave it to him too. He gave me freedom from worry of money and I gave him his confidence back. He thanked me for trusting him. He became very emotional when he thanked me for never second-guessing his boating skills, his navigational skills, his weather calls and so on. I tried to be a good first mate. He was the captain and called the shots. If he said we pull up anchor at 2:00 a.m. and move, we did. If he said we wait another day for better weather, we did. I was happy to cook, make drinks, and entertain.

He thoroughly enjoyed having other cruisers onboard and I was happy to be the hostess. We seemed to gravitate toward the younger cruisers and often referred to them as the kids. Pete was well-liked by everyone we met, and they respected his opinion and knowledge, which he gladly shared. He is a very social and amiable guy, he just didn't know it. He thought he was shy and an introvert, yet he would often strike up a conversation with strangers before I would. Admiring and complimenting him on his social skills was just what he needed.

I think that in the beginning he would have liked it to turn into a romantic thing, but after we had a talk about it, he was a complete gentleman and I was very respectful to him and never stepped out of line where other men where concerned. For all intents and purposes, we appeared to be a couple.

As far as sex goes, after being on the camping trip with Dad, there was no way I was getting on a boat without *packing*. Before the Alaska trip, I never gave it a thought. I was always with a man. My Dad didn't take his eyes off me for one minute, sex outside of marriage was a sin and he was going to have none of that, for him or me. It got so bad I was scratching on every tree in the forest. I was better prepared when I boarded the Ooh La La. One of my long standing mottos on the subject is "All a girl needs in life is a Rabbit and a trust fund."

"Flight 1582 to Atlanta now boarding at gate nine," the loud speaker calls. That's me. I should call Brittany and tell her what time my flight gets in. I go to the pay phone to see about making a call. The operator tells me it will be a $5 access fee and $3 per minute for international. I can't charge it to my cell phone and there are no collect calls permitted to Brittany's cell phone. Well, that decides it, I'll wing it. I will just take a taxi from the airport to her apartment and surprise her. Hopefully, the surprise will soften things between us.

A few minutes later, I am seated on the plane and we are airborne. I can feel the landing gear going into the compartment below. Wheels up! I don't know why getting on an airplane makes my heart sing, but it does. My heart could just burst. I am a be-jumble of emotions. Excitement and anticipation, fear and worry, loss and finality. The burdens of *life's stuff* are looming over me as I repeat to myself, "I am open and eager to see what comes next."

Before I know it, the flight lands. At customs, I ask what would have happened if my passport were expired. I would have been given a warning or been detained for further investigations, and at worst, missed my connection. Unless of course, the ticket agent noticed it and they are instructed not to let anyone board without proper documents. It would have all been straightened out in a few days.

# Chapter 37

*Brittany's 21ˢᵗ birthday*
*April 2007*

I am happy to be on the ground in Atlanta, even though it is freezing cold. It seems like an eternity until I am in the taxi headed for Brittany's apartment. I hope she is home and I hope she is happy to see me. Thank goodness I sent her so many postcards from the trip and I have her address memorized, because that—along with every other important piece of information—was lost in my water-soaked phone. The cabdriver is sweet and together we find her apartment just around the corner from the Emory Campus. "I will wait for you in case she is not home," he says. But I am not worried. I can see the light on in her third floor bedroom window.

I drag my heavy bags up the endless steps and plop them down on the floor in front of her door and knock. She swings the door open and stares at me in shock. "Mom. Oh, my Gosh! My Mom's here!" she calls back to someone in the apartment.

"Surprise!"

Seth joins her at the front door. "Hey, are you supposed to be here today?" he asks.

"No, I am a little bit early, I hope that's okay," I answer.

Brittany is still in disbelief, but she is happy to see me. All the worry about our reunion swirls out the door along with the chilly night air. We hug and kiss while she tries to get over the shock.

I open my bags and find her presents and we chat about everything. They want to know details about the trip and I want to know about their classes and what's going on. We talk while I sit on the floor in her room. Then her roommate, Sam, comes home with his girlfriend. I meet everyone. I am surprised how much they know about my travels. Brittany made it seem like what I was doing was so weird and *out there* that she didn't want anyone to know, but we all laugh and I tell stories. I am exhausted and set up shop in the living room and sleep on the couch. They go out to do whatever it is college kids do after midnight.

In the morning I wake about 9:00 a.m. and try to be quiet, not sure who is home and who isn't, so I pull out my computer and get to work. Express passport renewal is number one in order to get it back in time for my trip to Italy. Second is sending money to Paola for my room in Italy. I made a list of what needs to be done, but today it is Brittany's day. Not yet her birthday, but that doesn't matter. Hours pass and I am starting to wonder if she is even in her room.

I go for a jog around the neighborhood or should I say more like a walk, huffing and puffing up and down the hills. I can't get over how green it is and how beautiful all the flower-filled yards are. I also can't believe how out of shape I am. When I return to the apartment, I look for a scale. None to be found. I really want to know just how out of shape I am. I knew when I hit the ground I would really need to suck it in for a while, but it would be really nice to know what my starting point is.

It's eleven o'clock in the morning and Brittany is still not up. I shower and get ready for the day. Then I remember a parenting book I read a long time ago. It said that teenagers and young adults learn best between the hours of 2:00 p.m. and 2:00 a.m. If a parent wants to have a meaningful conversation with their kid, they should set the alarm for midnight and poke around the house and act like they can't sleep. Never talk to your young adult about anything important before lunch.

She gets up about noon and walks slowly into the living room to find me busy at work behind the computer. With bed hair and disheveled pajamas, she points her finger at me and says in a not quite awake tone, "You are here. I wasn't sure. I thought maybe I dreamt it." It is one of those great moments I never want to forget!

For the rest of the day, we do what girls do best—we go shopping. I really want her 21st birthday to be special. She has already picked out several items and we breeze through the mall. After shopping, we go for Vietnamese noodles and then back to the apartment. She has classes on Wednesday, so I can use her car. Her refrigerator is empty, so is her gas tank and the cartridge in her computer printer, not to mention a funny grinding noise when I hit the breaks in her car. I have a whole new list of things to do and am happy to do them. We all need our moms sometimes. I still need mine and reach out to her when things get upside down.

The days fly by. Brittany has school and spends hours in the library coming home well after midnight. I run errands, take the car to the shop and wait for it, and I watch TV. Yes, I admit it. I watch TV and every movie she has in the house. I suck up all the junk I can absorb. Funny, in my old life I rarely watched TV at all. I was too busy *crossing things off my list.* She can't believe how much I sleep and that I don't mind staying around the apartment so much. It is paradise to me: land, TV, Internet, and phone. I even make a fire in the fireplace on one particularly chilly, rainy day. Brittany told me later, they had never made a fire before.

She likes the smell of food cooking and has become quite a chef herself. I pick up all the ingredients to make her favorite childhood dish, chili, and one night teach her how to make it. She is quite pleased with the results.

I barely eat and exercise everyday, and I can feel my body coming around. I haven't had a drop of wine and don't even miss it. One day I ask Brittany if she has a scale. "Dear God no, what kind of inhumane torture would that be?" she says throwing me a glare of pure distain.

"Look, I didn't ask if you had a meth lab in the basement, I just asked if you had a scale," I respond with a chuckle. She probably doesn't weigh a hundred pounds.

Her much anticipated 21st birthday finally arrives. She has planned a small dinner party at a hip restaurant in the city with about ten of her friends. I am up and out early for the last trip to the mechanic and plan to stop and pick up a few little things she can open at the table. I want to get the latest abdominal workout to hip hop, but when I stand in front of all the movies to choose from, I see *The Notebook* and remember her saying it is the best movie ever and the two actors are dating in real life. Then I see, *Super Size Me*, another of her all-time favorites.

I also wanted to have a champagne toast for her at dinner, but learn that most of her friends are not yet twenty-one, so remembering her saying that her favorite drink is a White Russian, I opt for a bottle of Kahlua instead. I do get a cake and candles, which Seth will sneak into the restaurant ahead of time. I spend the rest of the day cleaning her apartment, borrowing a vacuum from the office and getting my stuff packed for my morning flight to Orlando. When she gets home from school, there is a giant singing balloon and a funny card waiting for her. She is so cute coming through the door.

All she really wants to do for her 21st birthday is go to the grocery store and buy a bottle of wine, and charge it to her debit card. She has a fake ID and can buy wine, but has to pay cash since the names don't add up. So Brittany, Sam and I hop in the car and go to the grocery store. She walks up and down the aisles of wine bottles and to my surprise, is quite knowledgeable. Of course, I have to take pictures of my sweet little girl, who was born weighing a whopping five pounds just twenty-one years ago today, getting carded at the grocery store. I wouldn't miss this moment for the world. I take pictures and she rolls her eyes.

All the worry, frustration, and anger I felt coming from her before never appear. All the things I wanted to fix never needed fixing. Perhaps after she released them onto me, she was free of the pain and then it was my burden to carry them or not. I created the *monster*. For all intents and purposes, she is an only child and was raised by me alone. I was her everything, and when I didn't behave the way I have always behaved, she lashed out. She doesn't have anyone else to turn to. I thought I could be her everything, but I was the one who changed. I have the choice to accept the burden or let it go. I am teaching her how to treat me, what is acceptable and what is not. I must try to let my head make the decisions, not my guilt. Parenting is always a challenge. Somehow, I thought I was finished, but now I think I will never be finished. It just changes.

We drive to the party and I am so happy to see her surrounded by her friends, smiling and laughing and being comfortable in her own skin. Everyone is taking photos and passing them around for the others to see. No one is ordering a drink but Brittany. They are really serious students. This is a serious school. A 3.8 GPA doesn't just happen. She orders a fun specialty drink from the menu. I think the cake might embarrass her when they bring it out, but I am happy to see that she is truly pleased. The whole restaurant sings to her. Even the table next to us sings and says, "Oh look, she is turning twenty-one." It really is a big deal. She cuts the cake and hands out the pieces. When she opens her gifts, she turns to me and says, "You were listening to me. I didn't even tell you I wanted this CD or that I like Kahlua."

"I do listen little one, it just took twenty-one years for us to start hearing each other," I reply. "A real gift is giving someone something they will enjoy without them even having to ask."

After dinner some of her friends come back to the apartment and I stand in the doorway of her room and watch the girls as they all pile onto her bed. They are huddled around her laptop looking at Brittany's page on *Facebook* to watch her age turn from twenty to twenty-one. They are giggling and laughing looking at the pictures. As I stand in the doorway, I can feel the energy and love in the room. They are young and beautiful and have their whole lives in front of them. Each girl's face is fresh and has no lines. They are naïve and untouched by the traumas of life. They have stars in their eyes and they dream big dreams. How wonderful.

My, how this room has changed. It is almost one year ago to date that I first walked into this empty blank slate. One year ago, I drove away without a plan. Funny, I still don't have a plan, but I am not the same girl I was a year ago. My, how I have changed. It has been a wild ride. I couldn't have planned it any better. Tomorrow I am getting on a plane, and in two weeks getting on another plane bound for Italy for the summer. I too have my whole life ahead of me and I dream big dreams. Whatever happens, happens. Be brave. I am in the right place at the right time and I am open and eager to see what comes next. Even when it's bad, it's still all good.

# Chapter 38

*My Beloved Italy*
*May 2007*

This time when I am dropped at curbside check-in at the Orlando airport, I am not weeping. I am open and eager to see what comes next for me. My agenda is not very clear other than I just want to experience the Italian lifestyle and live. I fly out on May 1st and return September 1st to Pennsylvania and back to Orlando on October 1st. I have decided from now on I will fly on the first day of the month, hoping it will be easier for me to remember the dates. My overnight flight to London leaves from Philadelphia at 7:00 p.m., and there I will change planes and go on to Rome where I will take a train to the town of Arezzo in Tuscany where my new landlord, Paola, will meet me. The apartment is about half-an-hour from the train station in a small ancient walled village called Foiano della Chiana. Honestly, I haven't even looked these places up on the map. All I know is that I will be living in Italy, about an hour from Florence, for the summer. I got goose bumps the day I read Paola's ad for a room for rent. There I was standing in the navigation station of the boat somewhere in the Caribbean, planning my next move and the ad popped up on the screen of Sublet.com. Paola explained to me later that I never asked her any questions that her other houseguests asked. Do I have a private bath, do you smoke, and how many other people live in the house? Do you have any pets? I just emailed her and said I definitely wanted the room for May, maybe longer.

I wasn't able to send her money via Western Union back in March. By the time I got money from the ATM, which came out in the currency of the island I was visiting, changed into euros, and paid the western union 10 percent fee, I had very little left to wire. I explained by email that I was living on a boat and I would be back in the states in mid April and would send her money then. She was okay with it. She also worked on a boat as a chef for the summer and took it as a good sign. Normally she would not risk holding the room without money, but for some reason, she felt good about me.

I am carrying two huge suitcases, but this time, they represent the future. I will be here for four months and I want things. I am probably bringing more than I need, but after being on the boat I want more clothing options. My new room will be my only home. It is different than knowing I have a place to go back to, yet I am okay with this being "homeless." It is almost a year now that I don't have a permanent place. I guess knowing that I can always go back and put things together again makes it all right. Or maybe knowing it is not there at all helps me to continue this vagabond lifestyle. Either way, I am comfortable with my choices and make the journey with peace in my heart. No tears this time, only a free light spirit and hope.

For whatever reason, I defer from my usual international overnight travel method, which is buckle up immediately when the flight takes off, put on slippers and a blanket, take a sleeping pill, put on a blindfold and neck cushion and sleep until I hit the ground. For some reason, I choose the movie instead, a delightful story of two women who swap houses for Christmas, one in England and one in Los Angeles. They both need change and I find it a lovely tale. The movie tells me something I need to hear. Just another sign from the universe that I am in the right place at the right time and information and encouragement are given to me exactly when I need them. Why did I choose to watch the movie rather than sleep? The signs from the universe are so subtle. In my old life, I would have missed it because I had a plan and I was working the plan. Now, I have no plan to speak of, but the universe does.

After changing trains in Rome's main terminal, I board a train for Arezzo. My original train is cancelled, so I take an alternative train that is slower. After three hours, I find myself standing in front of the train station with my luggage, waiting for someone to approach me. It is chillier than I expect. I need a jacket. It occurs to me that I never told Paola what I look like, but there aren't too many other travelers with such a large amount of luggage. I take my newly purchased international cell phone from the box, put it together and to my surprise, I get a signal. I locate Paola's phone number and dial. Her pleasant voice answers the phone and she tells me that her friend, Anna, is on her way and will be there in a minute. She will drive me to Paola's house, where she is waiting for us.

After just a few minutes, a smiling Anna greets me and we load my bags into her tiny car. She speaks just a little bit of English and I speak no Italian, so the ride is quiet. The countryside is simply lovely. It is May, the fields are freshly plowed and I can see neatly planted rows of young plants just starting to grow. I am really in the countryside, complete with rolling hills and farmland. It reminds of Pennsylvania without the cows.

Finally I arrive at my new home and Paola comes to the car to greet us. Both ladies are middle-aged and we are all mothers of children in their early twenties. They are artists and make jewelry, paint and write together. Both are Bohemian and have a comfortable style about them. We are instant friends. Paola speaks English, along with four other languages, so she interprets for us while we eat the lovely meal she has prepared. She grew up in Brazil and has really led a life of following her heart. She is very international and has quite a music collection that reflects her eclectic style. This building was her grandmother's and she used to come here during the summer as a young girl. Much later, she moved to Italy, bringing her two daughters and now she has lived here for about ten years. She is happy to have me stay with her. I think life got quiet for her after her daughters moved out on their own.

She thought I would be older. She knows that I am forty-five-years-old, but she is surprised when she meets me.

"It is because I have turned around and I am now going in reverse," I explain.

"What do you mean?"

"I decided when I turned forty that every year from now on, I would subtract one year rather than add. So, I am now thirty-five-years-old and next year I will be thirty-four. I had my daughter when I was twenty-five and devoted the next eighteen years to her, so I have decided that the next eighteen years are mine."

This gets a big belly laugh from Paola. It is the first of many *Ah-ha* moments for her.

The third floor apartment is plain but cozy and homey with terrazzo floors. Many things are from Paola's grandmother. One big wall is covered with hundreds of photographs stuck to cork board, wonderful memories of a full and rich life. My room is simple and plain with a desk and high speed

Internet connection, a single bed, a big armoire and a futon. This will be home for the next month.

After a big meal and lovely welcome, I excuse myself to sleep. I can barely keep my eyes open. The time change in Italy is six hours ahead of the US. I drift off to sleep around 8:00 p.m. I think I adjusted to the time change just fine when I wake at six o'clock. Last night Paola lowered the exterior shutter on my window, making my room completely dark, so the sunshine and street noise wouldn't wake me up. When I open the shutter, it is very bright outside. Blue skies, warm sunshine, chirping birds and just over the tree tops, I can see the brick steeple and bell tower of the church across the street. I love hearing the bells. I want to make a CD of bells. Strange for 6:00 a.m., but what do I know—until I take a closer look at my watch, it is actually 12:30 p.m. The hands on my watch are straight up and down. I am looking at it upside down! I slept for sixteen-and-a-half hours! Impossible I think, until I wander out into the living room and find Paola. She went out earlier this morning for fresh rolls and has a lovely breakfast waiting for me. It would have to be lunch, but she doesn't mind.

After breakfast/lunch it is time to explore my little town. Paola has taken the day to spend with me. We walk from our little apartment down a wide tree-lined street, past a little coffee bar and other charming shops into the main square. There is a fruit stand and little market, a flower shop, two hair salons, a butcher, two bakers, two gelato shops and several restaurants with outdoor dining. We pass through a big thick wall into the old section of town. I love walking through the winding narrow streets, something I will do many evenings. It is chilly and damp, but very green. She said yesterday was 75 degrees, but today is 50.

"There is no night life here," Paola explains, "and unfortunately, the last bus from Arezzo leaves at 8:30 p.m., so if you want to stay in town, you must get a ride home or stay overnight." Clubbing and partying is the last thing on my mind. After six weeks in the RV and 100 days on the boat, I have gotten used to quiet and isolation. Besides, this is what I asked for…isn't it? I will be here for the month of May and then move to Florence. I don't have a place there yet but I am not worried. The right place will come.

I am farther away from Florence than I thought. Foiano della Chiana is a lovely little town. I am closer to Florence than to Rome and very near Cortona, where *Under the Tuscan Sun* took place and close to Montepulciano, one of my favorite towns. Everything is accessible by train or bus and I will become an expert at the schedules. I think I will also become an expert at body language, although, in a different culture, even that is different. I think people are always yelling at each other because they are so passionate when they speak. I even think they are arguing when they are talking about the weather.

I knew coming here was right from the moment I saw Paola's ad on the Internet. It was the sign I was looking for. Just get to Italy and sort the rest out later. I have finally learned that blind faith goes a long way and too much planning sucks the energy and fun right out of the cosmic experience. Just let things happen. This location is perfect for my intention here.

What is my intention for Italy? I just want to live. I want to know or experience what it is about Italy that has drawn me here. I have visited many times before and each time I wanted more. Is it the lifestyle, the people, the food, the landscape, the language, the history or the architecture? I don't know, but I came here to find out.

It is very important to have an intention, or in my old life, I would have said, "Know your outcome." The universe can't bring you what you want if you yourself don't know what that is, or worse yet, you give out mixed signals. Get clear about what you want. If you want potato soup, focus and ask for potato soup. If you are wishy-washy and say, "Oh let's just see how things turn out, or today I will wish for this and tomorrow I wish for that," you will get vegetable soup. There will be potatoes in there, but a little corn and peas and carrots too. Then you say, "*Somehow* I didn't get the potato soup when that is what I really wanted." You don't have to *make* the soup, you have to *ask* and *believe* that potato soup is yours, just as though you ordered it from a menu and the server will bring it to any minute now.

This Italian lifestyle, what is it that is so different from our American lifestyle? One of my Italian friends who owns a leather shop in Florence once explained it to me this way. Understand that you are in the same business as your father. If you are born in the leather business, you sell leather; if you are born into the restaurant business, you are a restaurateur. The next thing is your house. The house you live in is given to you by your family, or you live with your mom and dad, even if you are married. Your grandparents or uncle probably lived in it before you, and your kids or cousins will live in it after you. If you need a bigger house, you trade your house with someone else in your family. There is no need to remodel or upgrade or invest a lot of time and money into your house, because it is not really your house anyway. Everything is old. It came with furniture and it will go with furniture. Cars are a method of transportation, not a status symbol. If you live in the city, a car isn't even necessary. So after career, house and car, what is left? Family. And that is why life revolves around relationships and eating. So much time and attention are given to eating.

This notion of enough is never enough and get ahead, get ahead, it doesn't exist. Italians dress impeccably and wear major designer names, but they don't have twenty pairs of jeans or twenty designer purses or twenty pairs of shoes, they choose one for the season and that is what they wear, and they wear it all the time. It is not uncommon for an Italian woman to wear the same outfit two or three days in a row. The next year, they buy something from the new collection. An Italian's entire wardrobe could fit into a standard American coat closet.

Paola and I run errands. We go to the bank, the post office, the grocery store and pay the phone bill. This takes most of the late afternoon. The shops close for lunch and re-open around 3:00 p.m. until 7:00 p.m. There is a line for everything and no one is in a hurry to do anything. "It's Italy," Paola says with a shrug. Once back at home, we cook and talk. Why it surprises me that we have so much in common, I don't know. By now, I think I should know the universe would put me in the right place. We talk about children and men and dreams and travels and life. She is a wonderful cook. We discover that we even like to eat the same kinds of food.

As evening comes, I settle into my room. I ask Paola if she minds if I re-arrange the furniture. Of course, she doesn't. Later, when she comes to my door, she has big smile on her face. "I am happy to see you are planning to stay for a while," she says. "I forgot that this is your only home and you need to make it feel like it belongs to you." Then she sees the little pink and green sticky notes I have placed on the mirror. "What are these?"

"These little notes are for me to remember who I really am. They are daily, constant reminders that my life can be anything I want." She goes over to the wall and reads each one out loud.

*I am in the right place at the right time.*
*Be Brave*
*All good things are coming to me now.*
*Life is meant to be fun and I am willing to enjoy it.*
*I am a child of the universe and abundance is my birthright.*
*I am always Joyful, Grateful, Loving, Accepting and Abundant*
*I am rich, well and happy*

Then I show her my index cards as I carefully take the worn cards from the plastic baggy. After being on the boat, I learned the importance of keeping everything in a plastic baggy. Some cards are two-years-old now. My wishes and wants have changed over time, but I love reading the old cards and know that those dreams came true and that this is how the universe works.

She is very familiar with the ideas, and I think she has lived an authentic life. She just got off the track along the way. Over time, I would learn that my purpose here was to wake her up, to breathe some life and energy back into her that somehow got lost along the journey of life. Sometimes we just get tired. Paola is only fifty-three-years-old and has a lot of living to do. It is not her time to rest yet.

Then I share *The Secret* with her. She has not heard of it, so I explain. It is a book written by Rhonda Byrne, a lady from Australia. She has taken important information about how the universe works that has been available to us for centuries and put it into a book that everyone can understand, even someone who is totally new to the metaphysical world. She focuses on the Law of Attraction and explains how we have attracted everything in our life and how we can use this law to create the life we have always dreamed of living.

Rhonda appeared on Oprah when I was on the boat and I got so many emails from friends who saw it and wrote to me to tell me that I was living *The Secret*. All the things I had read and all the *crazy* things I spoke about were part of *The Secret*. Ask the universe, believing that I am a child of God, and I receive whatever I wish for. *The Secret* even includes creative visualization, putting pictures on a wall of everything we want, or simply seeing our vision, helps to make it real. I used to have such a wall in my office, and often taped things to my computer and sure enough, they would materialize in my life.

When I returned from the boat, I watched the video and got the audio CD's. I would be happy to give it to her as I have so many of my friends'. I also have it on my I-Pod and listen to it daily. It is my daily dose of inspiration and a gentle reminder that the world is mine and all I have to do is ask, believe and receive. It is that simple. We are the ones who complicate it.

That night, I send an email to some friends back home telling them I have landed in Italy. Most didn't know that my next move was to come here. No nightlife, no TV, no one who speaks English, except Paola, my landlord/ roommate. Thank goodness, I have high speed Internet in my room and plenty of time to read and write.

The next morning when I wake, it is chilly. I pile all the blankets I can find in my closet onto my single bed. I even wrap a quilt around me when I sit at the computer. I try to dry my hair with the hair dryer from home using the adapter I brought to plug in my computer. To my shock and horror, it goes puff and a little smoke comes from the plug. I ruined my adapter! So I quickly run into town to see if they sell anything that will work. It is the only way to use my computer. Fortunately, they have what I need and I purchase it just minutes before they close for the day and the rest of the weekend.

The next day I take the bus to Arezzo to the Antique/Flea Market. The town is packed. Paola and Anna have a booth selling handmade jewelry and abstract paintings. They stayed in Arezzo last night and will stay tonight to avoid traveling back and forth. The outdoor market goes from 8:00 a.m. until 8:00 p.m.

Arezzo is quite a well-known town. It is the birthplace and home of many famous paintings by Piero della Francesca (1450-1550). There is a special traveling exhibition going on now. First, I visit the most famous chapel, which houses his amazing works, and then I walk up the steep hill to another church where I catch a wedding party just emerging from the giant front doors. The bride is dressed in a typical gown and the groom is in a military uniform. The crowd around them is well-dressed even though some are in jeans. Inside, the little side chapel where the ceremony was held is decorated with huge flower arrangements. To me, the side chapel is more beautiful than the big church. It is full of huge Roman sculptures, giant candelabras and religious objects, but the best part is a blue and white ceramic wall mural depicting Mary with child. It looks more like an antique store than a place of worship. I could spend a whole day in this single chapel.

Lastly, I walk to another section of town for the art exhibit. I spend hours carefully studying the faces and the style of the works. These paintings are 700 years old, yet they tell the same stories that are being told today. I think about the childhood game of whisper down the lane and how in a few people the story can get grossly changed. What must have happened over hundreds of years? I guess the story hasn't changed, because we have the pictures to keep it accurate. I buy postcards of my favorite paintings so I will remember my visit here, just like I have done many times before. I have a little collection of postcards of precious works of art.

In between the art, I poke my way through hundreds of booths of art and antiques. I have the whole day to do as I please. I love not having to hurry, to sit when I want, to eat gelato when I want. I successfully get myself to Arezzo and back and enjoy having the apartment to myself for the evening.

When I check my email, I have received one from a former associate of mine from the Citrus Club. She is surprised that I have landed in Italy. She tells me that she visited Italy last summer and went to a charming little winery and if I get to Tuscany, I should try to visit.

Actually she wrote: love ya. . . . if you get to Tuscany, go to the I Selvatici winery and ask for the owner Giuseppe Sala . . . after Bobby and I went to Italy last April, he came to Jacksonville to do a wine dinner for us. Then went on to Citrus to do one there . . . he is great fun (very good looking, single, etc. etc.) . . . or email him at info@iselvatici.it and let him know you are coming . . . the winery is small, but high quality.

"If I get to Tuscany," I think. "I am in the heart of Tuscany. Great, just what I need," I discount her words. I really appreciate my friends trying to help me get on with my life, but oh dear, a handsome Italian winemaker. A man is not the answer and besides, he is probably old and doesn't speak English and I don't know Italian yet. I just got here. I want to write and be still. I came to Italy to find myself and to listen to my inner voice. I am finally comfortable in my own skin. I like who I have become. I am really okay with the way things are. But … it could be fun.

Tomorrow there is a little festival in my village featuring antique cars. I can only imagine what that means here. In the USA, we are proud of 200 years of history, but what does antique mean in Italy?

My legs are tired from all the walking, but they will be beautiful soon. Everyone walks everywhere or they ride bikes, even the old. I love how older couples dress so nicely and walk arm-in-arm. No one is fat, even though they eat pasta and bread at every meal, and now I know why. Even the girls pushing strollers with new babies are slim and are wearing tight jeans. They wear great shoes too, very few sneakers and I love hearing the heels on the sidewalks. I will have to work up to this. I am not yet Italian.

I have decided that teeth are important and someone needs to clue in the Italians. They have terrible teeth and everyone smokes, so they are yellow too. Yuck!!!

I take the next few days to get acquainted with my village, my new home and the time change. I walk or ride Paola's bike everywhere. The view is amazing from every window of my house. There is a little terrace off the kitchen with a sweeping view of the countryside and another terrace, a bigger one, off of the living room, which faces the street. Here is where I have my morning tea or as Paola teases me, my American coffee. Although, truth be known, she would rather have American coffee than Italian coffee, which is actually Espresso.

The sun is warm during the day, but at night it is chilly. I sleep in every warm thing I brought and pile the blankets on so high that I have trouble rolling over at night. This is on top of the fact that I am sleeping in a single bed and think about falling off anyway. It makes for weird dreams. The heat for the house is a type of portable heater, but we are out of fuel and summer will be here soon, so no reason to fill it now.

Having nothing to do is totally decadent. I sleep when I want, eat when I want and do whatever I want. Time means nothing. Even the calendars are different. Our calendars are shaped like a box and divided into sections with days across the top and weeks listed by rows. Not here. Here the days are just listed in a long row. Since I haven't learned the Italian words for days of the week yet, I find the calendars very difficult to read. I can't group the weeks together. Over time, I learn to love to see the calendar this way. I find that a long running list of days is really the way life comes anyway. What a paradigm shift.

I ride the bike through the countryside. I love the rolling hills and farmland. I peddle through Pozzo della Chiana which means *the well of the river,* old, old, old and dripping with charm. I fly down the hill from one walled village, ride through miles of countryside and climb up a hill to another. I roam the streets, listening and watching and breathing. I am the luckiest girl in the whole world. Look where I am. I will never *settle.* Whoever said the expression, "You made your bed, now lie in it," should be gagged and bound. I realize that consequences come from actions, but what about choice? Because things didn't turn out with Tom the way I thought they were going to, doesn't mean that I have to lie in an empty bed/life and suffer for all of eternity. I can choose again. This is what I choose. I feel so free and light walking along, alone and so content.

Never again in my life will I fill my basket with crap and not have room for the good stuff. It is like having a basket of rotten eggs, thinking that these eggs are better than no eggs at all. Once they were fresh and new, but now they are old and way past their prime. Then someone gives you golden eggs, but they fall out of your basket and onto the ground because you don't have room for them, yet you keep walking along, wondering why your basket stinks. If I had stayed in my old life, I would not be here right now. I could not have my old life and my new life. I had to get out of my own way and let the new come. The old was blocking the new. The thing is, I had to empty my basket and let it be empty while I got out of my head and inside my heart to find out what kind of eggs I wanted next. When we hold on to the old, we never move on to the good stuff. Change is good. Let life flow. I spent a whole lot of time and effort trying to stop change and the tighter I held on, the more I squeezed the energy from bringing new life to me. Everything changes. It's natural like a flower, the moon, the tide and the weather. That is the irony of it. Someone needs to tell someone!

It rained for a while today. I will be happy for warmer weather and blue skies. The countryside is delightful. I hate to admit it, but as I was riding along today, looking out over the green patchwork fields, admiring the neatly planted rows of corn, it occurred to me, it looks just like where I grew up back in Pennsylvania. I never wanted to live there, and spent my whole life somewhere else without my family close by. Have I come all this way to realize that I love the countryside and being outside in nature is all there really is? Could this be what I love about Tuscany? It can't be. It must be the Ferraris.

Only a week goes by until I email Giuseppe. It goes like this:

> Dear Giuseppe Sala,
> I am a friend of Susan Greene from Florida and used to work with her at the Citrus Club in Orlando. I understand you are a famous wine maker and quite handsome, according to Susan. I am in Tuscany for the summer and would like to come to your vineyard to meet you.
>
> I am currently in Foiano della Chiana, just outside of Arezzo. Where are you? And what would be the best time to visit? I trust you speak English as I am very slowly learning Italian.
> Looking forward to meeting you,
> Barbara

He replies:

> Dear Barbara,
> Thanks for your message and your compliments...eheh, I'm not so famous like Susan say but I will be very glad to receive your visit to my winery.
>
> Foiano della Chiana it's about an hour from my winery, we are situated on Chianti Hills...do you have car? Anyway, this is my cell phone and you can reach me anytime...please give me a call and I will explain you how you can arrive here..338 103XXXX.
>
> I hope to hearing from you soon . . . my best
> Giuseppe Sala
> I Selvatici Winery

So I call him. We chat easily. He is charming and I love listening to his accent. He speaks excellent English and explains to me that he is nearby the train station of Montevarchi which is half-way to Florence from Arezzo and easy enough to get to from Foiano. I should come on a day he is not busy with tourists coming for a wine tasting. I am not going to be a big buyer for him since I have nowhere to ship the wine.

He tells me to call when I am ready to visit and we'll make the arrangements. I am here for the whole summer, I tell him. There is no rush. We say our goodbyes. I hang up the phone. I like the way I feel.

Just a few days later, I wake up and think I want to visit that winery. I call Giuseppe and tell him I want to come today. He says that he has a few other appointments, but if I could arrive at 11:00 a.m., he can arrange to pick me up and drive me to the winery and then back to the train station again. So I walk to the bus stop, ride to Arezzo, take the train and arrive by 10:00 a.m. Knowing I am early, I decide to take a coffee.

I walk into the little bar in front of the fountain by the train station, appropriately named Caffe Fontana. I order a cappuccino from the handsome young man behind the counter. To my surprise, he asks me in clear English, where I am from. Is it that obvious I am not a local? I guess not, with blonde hair and blue eyes and a deep tan from being on the boat. I tried not to tan. Each morning, I brushed my teeth and lathered on 45 SPF sunscreen from head to toe, but there was no getting around the sun. Ever since I returned from the islands, everyone has guessed that am from Florida or California. Today I am wearing a white T-shirt and pink floral Lilly skirt and my favorite Tommy Hilfiger high heel sandals. Without realizing it, I dressed the part.

"I am American, from Florida," I tell him

"Really," he says. "I have been to Miami. I have friends that live in the states and I went to visit them a few years ago. I would like to go back."

I extend my hand, "What is your name?"

"Fabio," he answers.

Fabio! You're kidding. Do people actually have that name? This is right out of a movie. Of all the names in the world, his is Fabio?

"Well, hello Fabio, I am Barbara."

He has a delightful shyness about him. He is curious to know more about this stranger who just walked into his bar, but I sense a certain feeling of politeness that doesn't allow his questions to flow freely. He expertly prepares the best cappuccino in all of Italy. The froth is so creamy it tastes like warm ice cream, one I will come back for again and again.

Fabio asks, "Are you here to go to the Prada Outlet?"

"No," I reply. "I know the only *real* Prada outlet is in Montevarchi, but no, I am here to go to a winery."

"How long will you be in Italy?"

"I am here for the summer." I answer, happy as a schoolgirl on recess.

"You are so lucky to have such a long holiday. And what do you do for work that allows you to stay so long?" he asks.

"I am a writer." There, I said it out loud, for the first time. "I am writing a book."

"Really?" he says with a raised eyebrow. "I couldn't write a book. How do you do it? I mean, where do you start? How do you know what to write?"

"I just tell a story. I write about what I am thinking about at the moment." I explain.

"What is the book about?" he asks.

"A novel, well actually it's a memoir, about my life. I have lived a really crazy life."

"You are so young to write a book about your life," he says.

"I am not so young, but actually I am only writing about the last few years." I ponder about this after I finish my cappuccino and go back out into the sunlight. It has been a crazy last few years. Before in my old life, I would work to make something happen. Now, I don't have to work at anything, I just live. It is much more fun this way. This game of life doesn't work at all the way I thought. Life is meant to be easy and abundant. Being aware of this and operating from this vantage point changes everything.

I walk into the town's main piazza and stroll around window shopping. It is darling. A little before eleven, I phone Giuseppe and let him know I have arrived.

"Great, give me ten minutes and I will be there," he says.

"How will I know it is you?" I ask.

"I will be driving a grey Audi station wagon. How will I know it's you?" he adds playfully.

"I am blonde," I reply.

He is personally coming to get me. I am impressed and a bit surprised. I thought for sure he would have some staff member come to get me. I would learn later that he was expecting a typical older American lady and that he expected to *waste a day*. He has seen enough American tourists to get the picture. When I told him I was blonde, it did pique his interest a little. She could be fun.

Time passes quickly as I watch the hub-bub of comings and goings at the railway station. Several old men are sitting on the benches next to me in the shade, chatting. I have no idea what they are saying so I play a little game and make up their conversation. Before I know it, a grey Audi station wagon pulls up and out comes Giuseppe. He starts to walk toward me. That is *not* a decrepit old wine maker, I think. And later I learned, he thought, "That is not a middle-aged, out-of-shape American lady," and maybe he wouldn't waste a day after all.

He is 100 percent Italian, dressed in a fabulous blue and white linen shirt, perfectly fit Diesel jeans, tan ostrich shoes, Prada of course. He is smooth and confident as he strides right up to me and greets me with a kiss on both cheeks. His tussled dark hair is short with a little bit of spike over the crown, just a hint of rock star. Designer sunglasses hide just enough of that cocky bad boy charm. He is lean with broad shoulders, making his shirt fall perfectly over his slim hips. He looks like a teenager, but he is definitely a man.

The ride to the vineyard only takes a few minutes and the scenery is amazing. I learn that he was born here and grew up on the winery. He is well traveled, loves Japan and Thailand and lived in California for a few years and worked for Robert Mondavi, but this really is home. We ride along a very steep curvy road, winding through deep woods and then travel down a gravel lane, past rows and rows of vines to a group of old buildings. The winery is surrounded by sloping hills and big green mountains off in the distance. It is breathtaking. I am the luckiest girl in the whole wide world. Look where I am.

My host shows me to the tasting room and moves smoothly around, preparing glasses and bottles of wine. The tasting room has been added in the last few years. Floor to ceiling windows let the amazing view captivate the tourists who make the trek into the Chianti Hills to drink the wine. Giuseppe rolls through the tasting with pride and skill. This is not his first time.

First we taste a slightly chilled, crisp clean white. It is so fresh, it barely has any color, not at all like the caramel, buttery Chardonnays I used to drink. It has been so long since I had *my* chardonnay, I have practically given up white wine completely. I have learned that I enjoy a much bigger range in palette of red wine, so even if I am not familiar with it, I have a much better chance of enjoying an unknown red than a white.

Then I taste a 2002 Chianti. I am pleased to see that he is pouring one that is five years old. It is a reserve. Quite lovely, smooth, rolls over the tongue nicely, not too fruity or young.

Then we try the Super Tuscan, the one I am looking forward to tasting the most. I like a big bold red without the tannins. They do settle down after the bottle is open and the wine is allowed to breathe for a little, but a Super Tuscan made with Sangiovese grapes shouldn't have tannins at all. The bottle says Cardisco, a word I am not familiar with. Giuseppe explains it is an ancient medieval word that means Sangiovese, the only grape used to make this wine.

Also on the label is a drawing of a crest of Napoleon. When I ask about the symbol, he tells me that his great grandfather, six generations ago, fought with Napoleon and was given a war medal, and that is a drawing of the medal. Then he moves to a drawer and takes out a little box and a framed certificate and shows me the actual medal and a document signed by Napoleon himself. He explains that it is very special and the Louvre in Paris calls each year trying to buy it. History! I am holding history right in my hands.

The he explains that his family is most famous for the Vinsanto, a sweet desert wine made from grapes that have been laid to dry into raisins before being pressed, and then the wine is kept in barrels above the ground for seven years so it will be exposed to the change in the climate. The barrels are made of five different kinds of wood. Vinsanto means Wine of the Saints.

Ten years ago, Giuseppe and his dad, Fausto, opened an old barrel of Vinsanto that his grandfather made that had been in the attic for forty years. They thought that it would be bad, but from the moment the cork was out, they knew they had something precious. Because of the sediment only 135 or so small bottles of 1958 were made. Today only a few remain and sell for 600 euros a bottle.

I am delighted when he takes a small precious bottle from a little hidden cupboard and tells me that 1997 is his best year and there are only a few bottles left. It got a ninety-eight rating from Wine Spectator, my first clue that he is famous. He pours me a taste. It is golden and thick in the small glass. It is like nothing I have ever smelled or tasted before. Although it is rich and full like a brandy, it's not alcoholic—something like a Port, but so much more. It is complicated and earthy. There are so many things going on inside my mouth and my mind.

He must prepare for a couple who will be arriving in a few minutes. He asks if I would mind waiting while he does the tasting and then we can go have lunch. I am surprised when he suddenly has time to have lunch with me, an unexpected treat.

"That's very kind of you," I reply, thinking he is being nice to me because of Susan, "but it's not necessary."

"No, really, I would like to take you to lunch, it's just that I have one more appointment. Make yourself at home. You can look at the chapel and walk around."

"The chapel?" I inquire.

"Yes, it is inside that door right there," he says, pointing to one of the doors on the nondescript building next to us. "Just go inside, the door is not locked. That is the chapel where my parents where married and I was baptized. A priest used to come from town every Sunday for the employees, but not anymore. Anyway, come back in about an hour," he instructs me.

I stroll across the gravel driveway and gently open the door. Sure enough, there is a tiny plain little chapel with white walls, a couple of pews and a little altar complete with a cross and two big candlesticks on a little table with a linen table cloth. I take a seat and let the comfort of this little sacred place wash over me. I imagine all the wonders of life that happened here. This building must be 200 years old.

I wander around the other buildings and walk down the lane and mostly take in the vista and imagine what it must be like to live here. Does he take it all for granted? Has it become old hat or does he really get it? I sit on a hillside and soak up the sun.

Soon he finds me and sits down next to me. In an almost dream like state, I turn to him and ask, "Do you get it?"

"Do I get what?" he asks.

"This, do you get where you live?" I ask again.

"Of course, I was born here." He answers with complete confidence in a thick accent.

He needs to take care of a few things and tells me to follow him. We walk up to the farm house and as we go inside he calls out for his mother. "Mamma, Mamma. Come inside and meet my mamma," he instructs me. We walk through a small reception room and into the cozy living room filled with old dark wood furniture and a well-worn dark green sofa. Crystal and china are displayed in the hutch. The room is filled with years of trinkets and memories. Giuseppe rolls up the shutter and flings open the window, flooding the room with light and an amazing view of the valley and town off in the distance.

Soon his mother, Carla, arrives and introductions are made. She is a modern-looking woman, except for the apron, and has stylish short blonde hair and blue eyes. She doesn't speak English, so Giuseppe explains to her that I am from Florida and that I know Susan. She offers me coffee and I accept.

While she is gone, I notice a pair of bronze baby shoes on the sidebar. I learn they are his. He is an only child and lives here with his mom and dad. He is thirty-two-years-old, has never been married and isn't interested in having children. His parents have lived in this house for over forty years.

Carla returns with a little tray, neatly stocked with everything I will need for my coffee, I mean espresso. We chat briefly as Giuseppe does the interpreting. She is warm and friendly and seems to enjoy the tourists that come to the winery. I couldn't miss the ease with which they talk to each other and the comfort and warmth of their home.

Back in the car, we drive on the winding road, traveling up and down the hills. There are a lot more hills and trees than in my town. He expertly maneuvers the car from one crazy hairpin curve to another. As we talk, I learn that he was just in the states a few months ago to do some wine tastings, and he did a dinner at the Citrus Club where I used to work. He knows everyone: Hank, my old boss; Traci, the member relations director; and Frank, the chef. He was traveling with Claudio, his friend and chef who has a Tuscan cooking school and restaurant. He stayed at the Westin Grand Bohemian Hotel. I am shocked that we have so much in common. He came to my club just months after I left.

He is very athletic. He is a Super G downhill skier, loves motorcycles, fast cars, has over 600 jumps from an airplane and loves the night life. He even served two years in the military, which is required by all Italians. He tells me stories of wine events he has been invited to by *Wine Spectator* magazine. He has led a full life and likes adventure.

We arrive at a little restaurant down a dirt road, definitely off the beaten path. Pitena, which I would nickname Vito's Place in honor of Vito, the owner. As a matter of fact, I don't think it is a restaurant. As we pull into the parking lot, it looks more like a park with an outside dining pavilion. We have a wonderful lunch and chat like old friends. He is intrigued by my stories of life on the boat and where I am going next. I am so full of hope and joy. I have just started on my journey and am so excited about all that is to come.

After a two-hour lunch, while we are having coffee, Giuseppe offers to drive me back to Foiano.

"Really, it's not necessary. I have taken up enough of your time," I protest.

"It's okay," he says. "We will arrive quickly because I can take the autostrada."

I am enjoying his company and would love to have a whole hour to observe his profile and delicate Roman features. His face looks like those I have seen in the paintings I have been studying ever since I arrived here in Italy. The paintings are hundreds of years old and yet, right in front of me, is the same face. That is pure lineage, not like in the melting pot of America. This man is pure Italian. He looks like a young Stallone. He is so handsome, I am sure he has girls lined up around the block.

The drive back to Foiano is easy and pleasant. He drives very fast on the highway and gets right up behind other cars that are going slower than we are. He passes and shifts gears with complete control. I don't flinch or comment on his driving. "He does this everyday," I remind myself. "I am just along for the ride." This is one of those moments when I tell myself to adapt to my surroundings. If I want to be a local, then do as a local. It's not a big deal. Besides, if I don't look at the road, I can study this delightful object of art sitting next to me.

On the highway, we pass an accident off on the shoulder of the road. The cars are very mangled. "Mamma Mia!" he exclaims, looking at the wreckage.

"Momma Mia," I think to myself, "Do they actually say that?" The answer, I would learn later, is yes and they say it often!

When he stops the car in front of my apartment, I thank Giuseppe for such a lovely day and especially for driving me all the way home. He asks me what I am doing for the weekend and I explain there is a little festival in my village on Saturday and Sunday. He says he must work on Saturday, but maybe he will come for the festival on Sunday. I am surprised.

"Really, you want to come?"

"Yes, I will call you in a few days," he says.

"Great. That would be nice," I tell him. After the traditional kiss on both cheeks, I get out of the car and open the gate. I turn around to wave goodbye, but he is already pulling away.

That night as I lie in bed, I recount the day. What an interesting and surprising day. He is sweet and charming and so very polite. What a lovely way about him. He is so handsome, fun, and young. Is he entertaining me because I am alone, because I am a friend of Susan's, or because it is Italian hospitality? This will require more thought. And think about him, I did. For now, be grateful. I am the luckiest girl in the whole wide world. I am in Italy. I visited a small family winery and peeked inside history. I am discovering a whole new world and I am not afraid. I am not lonely or scared. I am open and eager to see what comes next. I am in the right place at the right time.

In the morning I send an email to Susan. Mr. Yummy, that seemed to sum him up.

To: Susan Greene
From: Barbara Singer
Date: 05/11/2007 02:31PM
Subject: Mr. Sala is Yummy

i met Giuseppe today. what a delightful man. we had a great day at his vineyard and he is coming to my village for a festival on saturday.

Thank you so much for the introductions.

i love it here!!!

Barbara

I go for a walk to the Piazza and watch all the families out and about. Later in the day, a bike race goes by my window. The weather is still cold so I putter around the house, drinking tea and reading the only English books Paola has, *Oh, The Places You'll Go* by Dr. Seuss, which should be required reading for anyone on a spiritual journey. On her bookshelf, I find "*The Devil Wears Prada*" which I have already read and have the movie. I read it again anyway. No, let me rephrase that, I devour it like every good book.

I settle into the Italian lifestyle. We take the trash to the dumpster instead of the garbage truck coming to us. These big containers are strategically placed all over town and the garbage is separated for recycling. No microwave, I love it for health, but hate doing the dishes all the time. We have no hot water in the kitchen because it is broken and no dishwasher, so we heat water on the stove and wash the dishes by hand. We automatically fall into a rhythm of taking turns without ever discussing it. Paola likes having another mom in the house. We know what needs to be done and just take care of it. It is like we were sisters once.

Another day passes, storm clouds roll in again, but little rain or thunder. I spend most of the day wrapped in a blanket typing away on my computer in my room. Only the ringing of the church bells reminds me how fast the time is going by.

The next day is market day. I love how all the vendors come to the piazza and set up little tents and sell their wares, everything from pots and pans to panties and candy and don't forget fresh meat, produce and flowers. It is more of a social event than a shopping day. I love how the children are adored. A young mother can barely push the stroller a few steps without a *Nonna* (Grandmother) or someone stopping to pinch her baby's cheek, or rub its chubby little leg, including men. In the bakery, the little ones each get a slice of bread rather than a cookie. The children are truly adored here and somehow everyone has time to let it be known.

I pick up bread, parmesan, mozzarella cheese and some fresh tomatoes. No need for basil as we grow our own on the terrace along with rosemary and sage. Now I really know why the Italians are so skinny. They eat the same food again and again. How many ways can they eat tomatoes and white flour—both, according to my nutritionist, are terrible for me and my blood type. How many ways can they use wheat: bread, pasta, pizza? After how many years of eating the same thing does a body know exactly how to digest it? And additionally, it is grown in this town. It grows with the same sun and air that they breathe. It grows from the same ground they walk on.

Not like in the US; one day we eat Thai, the next day Indian, the next day grapes grown in Chile or oranges from California. We give our bodies so many different things to eat from all over the world that it is no wonder we have poor digestion. This is why we have aisles and aisles of medicine for poor digestion. Italians eat only what is grown in their area and what is in season. In summer they eat melon and zucchini, and in fall they eat porcini mushrooms. Another reason Italians are skinny, is uncooked oil olive is sprinkled on everything.

I go into the soap store as I call it. In the US it would be like an Eckerd's or CVS. I need shampoo. I go up and down the rows of beauty products and laugh when I notice that there are many boxes of hair color, but only two shades of blonde. I guess it is not very popular here.

Back at home, Paola and I listen to Pink Floyd and the Beatles while we cook dinner. I find this comical. I ask her if she is playing it for me, but she says no. She has the most amazing collection of music. I especially like North-African Groove and Middle Eastern with a techno beat, something new to download onto my I-tunes.

After dinner we decide to watch a movie. Paola doesn't have a DVD player, but I can play them on my computer. I tell her I have the movie, *The Devil Wears Prada*. She says her daughter sent her the book and she would love to watch the movie. She is enjoying speaking English and is happy to watch the movie without the words being dubbed over in Italian. Evidently there are professional voice-over talents who are celebrities because they sound like certain American film stars. Who knew?

The little festival in my village is a disappointment. I am not sure if it is because of the weather or if I didn't go at the right time. There are a handful of funky little cars but the Fiat 500 (*Cinque Cento*) is my favorite, a little car that looks like Fred Flintstone should be peddling it. They were made for about fifty years, but discontinued some twenty years ago. I also think it is funny that the scooters are called Vespas—which means wasp in Italian—and the funky little three wheel cart, something between a riding lawn mower and a mini pickup truck, is called an ape or bee. I think they are called wasps and bees because of the little buzzing noise they make. And of course, there is a wedding in the church. The couple is adorable and they drive away in an old white Volkswagen Convertible Beetle decorated with ribbons and sunflowers. They look like hippies: she is a flower child and he has long hair down his back. Both are wearing white from head to toe.

So when Giuseppe calls on Saturday night to make plans for Sunday, I tell him the festival is not so fun and we should probably find something else to do. Not to worry, he has a program. He will pick me up about 11:00 a.m. I should bring a swimsuit, or swim costume as it is called in Italian, and a jacket.

He has made plans to go to Galenda, a charming little country estate that has been converted into condominiums. It is a cluster of old stone farm buildings situated on top of hills with a sweeping view of the countryside and vineyards, complete with a swimming pool and an old millstone. Giuseppe's friends, Stan and Patsy from Colorado, own two of the condos. They won't arrive for another few weeks, so they gave Giuseppe the keys and told him to use it whenever he wants. They also own the company *Italy by Vespa* and bring tourists to Tuscany to ride Vespas from hill town to hill town. What fun!

Giuseppe picks me up before lunch and we ride to Montevarchi and then onto Radda in Chianti and then to Galenda. I had driven through this area some years before and remember circling Radda in Chianti on the map as one of my favorite villages.

Even though the nights are still cool, the days are warm as the sun bathes over the fields. When we arrive, Giuseppe suggests we lie by the pool for a little while and relax, then take a little ride on the Vespa. Here are the first tests of my new-found freedom. Go to the pool and wear a bikini in front of man who has the body of a teenager. Ride on the back of a Vespa and trust a virtual stranger. Life is meant to be fun and I am willing to enjoy it. Relax, just be. Don't over analyze everything, it sucks the energy right out of the moment. So from this moment on, I am totally at ease. We change into bathing suits and go to the pool.

I am so in the moment and so happy, my heart could burst. I can't believe my good fortune. I am in the heart of Tuscany, lying by the pool at a beautiful private country villa with the most awesome vista, with a fantastic glass of wine in my hand, sitting next to the fun-loving Italian man who made it.

Later we take a red Vespa out of the garage and go for a ride. The roads wind through wooded areas, and then around another curve is a vista of the Chianti wine country that takes my breath away. We are not far from my village, but oh my, it is so different with more hills and sweeping vistas. I love my village with all the farmland, but this, this Chianti countryside calls to my soul. It feels so good to me. I can breathe.

I love riding on the back of Vespa, holding on to Giuseppe as we sway from side to side along the winding roads. The sun is warm on my back. I love the wind all around us. I miss riding my Vespa that is back in a garage somewhere in Florida, and my little sports car with the top down. I rarely drove it any other way. I love being outside in the sunshine with my hair blowing. I am totally at ease. Pinch me, is this really happening? I am riding on the back of a Vespa in the middle of Tuscany with a man, who I am learning, is just as beautiful on the inside as he is on the outside. Can it get better than this? With my arms wrapped around his torso, I give him a little squeeze and say, "Thank you. Thank you for bringing me here."

"You're welcome," he says, then reaches back, placing his hand in the crook just behind my knee, just a little touch to let me know that this is real and I am not dreaming.

We spend the rest of the day riding along and talking and telling stories. I learn he is a thrill seeker. He loves to go fast and loves the adrenaline rush. He was on the European ski team. He loves a party and hits the club scene hard. He had long hair until just a year or so ago. He lost two of his best friends to accidents. It changed him. Life is different for him now, something I understand intimately.

I tell him about my travels in the camper and on the boat. I tell him about Tom dying and how I willingly became homeless. I tell him about other trips I have taken and talk about my love of travel and how I will winter in Aspen this year. I explain how I plan to stay here for May and move to Florence for June. In July, I may travel around a little and then for August, I found a place in Malta.

"Rather than going to Malta, you should go to Monte Argentario," Giuseppe says.

"Really, where is that?"

"It is the Italian coastline about two hours from here between Florence and Rome. It is still Tuscany," he explains. "Porto Santo Stefano is the most famous town. I used to go there every summer when I was younger."

"What is it like?" I ask.

"Beautiful blue water, cliffs with a view of the sea and several islands to visit by boat," he says. "I have the license to drive a boat. I have a license for everything you know," he teases.

All too soon, the day is over and once again we pull up to my apartment, but this time he pulls into the parking lot across the street and turns off the car. Still in the driver's seat, he turns to me. He looks directly into my eyes. His eyes are the most unique color of gold with little brown specks in them, sometimes they look more greenish when he is wearing an olive colored shirt. But in this moment, they are an intoxicating shade of golden brown. I follow his gaze as his eyes move across my face, up to my hair and back to my lips. His long beautiful eyelashes blink sleepily. His cheeks are slightly pink from the sunbathing earlier today.

He leans closer to me. "I want to see you again," he whispers, as his lips brush ever so lightly across mine. Up until this moment, I didn't know he was interested in me this way. I was just taking the day as a complete joy and a stroke of good fortune. I was just being myself and treating Giuseppe as a friend. We kiss. I am caught off guard by this kiss, but oh my. I have heard the stories of what fantastic lovers Italian men are and that kissing is a national pastime, but I have never experienced it. But this kiss, oh my, this is a kiss to be savored. I close my eyes and let the flood of emotions wash over me.

I draw back from him and slowly open my eyes. Oh dear, where did that come from I think to myself. But the look on his face seems to express what I am thinking. Another kiss like that and neither of us will be going anywhere.

"Well, I guess this is goodnight then," I say, taking a slow deep breath.

"What are you doing next weekend?" he asks. "I don't know my work schedule yet, but I will call you."

"Okay," I respond. "I would like that very much."

I get out of the car and dreamily walk to the apartment and up the three flights of stairs. I undress and climb under my mountains of blankets and shiver until I warm up. My head is swimming.

I sleep until 10:00 a.m., totally decadent. I feel so free and light without a schedule. I go online and copy down conversion charts for miles, pounds and money. I need to learn my numbers. I need to learn Italian. I have a small phrase book, but it really isn't helping. I thought I would learn the language just by being here, but that is definitely not happening. Also many people speak English. They just take one look at me and start speaking English.

It is afternoon by the time I leave the house. Today I decide to ride the bicycle to Lucignano, a little walled village at the top of a very long hill about five miles from my village. There is a very important church (*duomo*), as always, at the top of the town. All the important buildings are at the highest point, for protection, I imagine. I have to push the bike for the last half mile or so, something that was shameful in my Ironman days. I justify this because I have no gears on this bike. As I am trodding along, I imagine what beautiful legs I am going to have and how fast I will fly down this same hill on the way home. It is sunny and warm and the vista is beautiful. *Bellisimo.* I love Italy. The little town is adorable. I love walking around the old winding narrow streets. I find a charming restaurant with an outdoor terrace. I am too late for lunch, but must remember it when I come back. Instead, I wander into a little bar and order a slice of pizza and a glass of wine. I find a seat at a table outside and take it all in. I am living in Italy! Am I dreaming or is this really happening? The shopkeeper brings me the slice of pizza and in English (of course), asks me where I am from. We chat briefly. I enjoy my very late lunch. Still hungry, I order a sinful looking pastry and cappuccino. If he didn't know I am American before, he does now. The cappuccino comes out with a design of a flower made from chocolate in the froth. It is too beautiful to drink. The German couple next to me orders one too and she takes a photo of hers before she drinks it. We laugh with each other in spite of ourselves, just happy to be here. It is after 6:00 p.m. when I head for home. I love biking and almost make it up the hill to Foiano without walking. Next time, I will make it all the way, I tell myself.

I have fallen into a lovely routine. Sleep late, have tea on the terrace, walk to the bakery for a roll, add a little cheese, tomato, fresh basil and olive oil. Then I write for a while, go for a bike ride somewhere, come back, write some more or play on the Internet or read. I love to walk the tiny streets of the old section of my town and listen to the families. I imagine what they look like and what they are talking about. Then I walk home and climb into bed. I fall asleep around midnight or one, something I never did in my old life. Back then, I was in bed by nine so I could get up at six and go to the gym.

I love having nothing to do. I never thought I would say that, but it is totally delicious. I am not in a rush to do anything. I have all day to do whatever I want. I eat when I am hungry, I sleep when I am tired. I even nap. Me, Barbara Singer napping? I would have never guessed it. Time means nothing. I am shocked how quickly the day goes by. It stays light until almost nine, so it is no wonder that it's after midnight before I think about going to sleep.

On Tuesday, Giuseppe calls me. He asks if I have plans for Wednesday night. I do not, on Wednesday or Friday or any other day for the rest of my life.

"I would like to come to Foiano and we can go to dinner," he says. "I don't want to wait until the weekend to see you." He is so sweet in his honesty. I love the way he knows what he wants and just says it. It is his combination of boyish charm and manly confidence that rocks my world. I am flattered that he can't wait until the weekend and we agree to dinner.

This time when I am getting ready, I know it is a date. Eager anticipation makes me think about what I am going to wear and how I want to fix my hair. This time it is I who feel like a teenager. It seems like an eternity by the time eight o'clock rolls around and the downstairs' bell rings. I buzz back and wait for him at the top of the stairs. This will be first of many times we laugh about my living on the top floor of a building and making him climb the stairs, out of breath, to come see me.

When he reaches the top, he greets me with a casual Ciao Bella. Then an extra long gaze into my eyes turns into a slow light kiss. As we pull away, I give him *the look* of "don't start something you don't plan on finishing," and he returns with a look of "be careful, you are starting something." We both giggle like kids and I usher him into the house to meet Paola.

He is smooth and talks easily with her. He is light and funny. They both speak Italian, so I can only judge the conversation by body language. Something I think I will perfect by the end of my trip.

We decide to walk to a little restaurant around the corner. I have been past it many times, but never went there and Paola knows the owners, so she calls ahead for us. It is a big old house with a restaurant on the first floor, guestrooms upstairs and lots of outside dining. It is too cold now to eat outside, so we go into the main dining room. I am totally surprised at the elegant décor and the vista behind the sweeping sheer drapes. We sit on big white padded Parson's chairs. The music plays, the wine flows and Giuseppe orders a wonderful dinner for us. I want him to choose so I can try new things. We talk and laugh and eat. When it is time for coffee, I suggest we walk into town and take a coffee there. I want to savor my dinner and the wine before a coffee.

Outside the night air is cool, and Giuseppe helps me wrap my pink pashmina around my shoulders. I look up at him to thank him and he takes my face into his hands. And then, a kiss, a kiss that takes my full and undivided attention. One kiss that is a thousand kisses at the same time. A kiss so light and gentle that his lips are barely touching mine as he explores every part of them. I let my head fall back and my mouth open just enough to let his tongue slide inside. A touch, a press, a lick. It is all too yummy. My heart starts to pound and I can feel a wave of passion roll over me. We kiss again and again and again.

Strolling the tiny streets of my village, I show him the places I like to walk the best. Usually I am alone when I walk past the doorways, especially at night when the families are home. I can hear the plates clanking as they make dinner and talk. But tonight we are arm-in-arm, walking in unison, holding each other, kissing. It is one of those moments I will never forget.

We wander into the bar on the corner of the piazza and order two coffees, which are actually espresso. Giuseppe is surprised that I order coffee. I have decided that if I am going to live here, I need to do as the locals do. Then he tells me that Italians only drink cappuccino before lunch and espresso the rest of the day. At 7:00 p.m., I should drink an aperitivo like champagne or a light white wine. I shrug my shoulders and give him the *I didn't know* look. He kisses me and smiles with that wonderful sheepish grin and says, "Don't worry, I will teach you everything you need to know." The look that follows is more telling than he intends and he blushes.

We walk slowly back to my apartment. Wrapped together, stopping every few feet to kiss and adore each other. The stars are out, hundreds of them. "Look, aren't they beautiful?" I comment. "I love looking at the stars. There is a saying I have been repeating ever since I was a little girl. Whenever I see the first star of the evening come out, I say this little poem for good luck:

*Star light star bright, the first star I see I see tonight.*
*I wish I may, I wish I might. Have the wish I wish tonight.*

At my apartment door, we say our goodnights. We both know it is not appropriate for me to invite him upstairs. He asks me if I will come to Galenda with him for the weekend. I smile and tell him I would love to. "It will be worth waiting for," he says. "This weekend will be magical." With those words, I climb the stairs to the apartment alone, so happy my heart could burst. As I prepare for bed, my phone chirps. It's a text message from Giuseppe: "Sweet Dreams...Kisses." That night I can barely sleep a wink. Pinch me, I must be dreaming.

Thursday and Friday, I am off on the bicycle to explore villages in my area. I love riding. I loved it when I was training and I love it now, doing it for pure pleasure. I feel like I am really part of the land. I can smell the grass or hear the tractors or hear a dog barking. I love the sunshine on my hair and in my face. My legs are getting stronger and I don't have to walk up the hill going back into Foiano. Every old walled village is built on the top of the hill so enemies could be seen for miles away before an attack. But to me, it means that just before each town, there is a big badass hill I must climb, including the one back home. The one leading back to Foiano is particularly long with a few steep parts for giggles. Back in the day of training when I was first learning to ride the bike, my trainer would tell me to let the bike do the work. Now, riding a bike without gears, that means let my legs do the work. It's okay. I want beautiful strong legs. I have been off the boat for almost a month now and have gotten my shape and weight pretty much back to normal.

I decide the bus schedule is too difficult to get to Cortona, even though it is only twenty-seven km or about fifteen miles away, so I decide to take the bike. I figure it will take about an hour or so to get to Camucia, the little town at the bottom of the hill, and then I will take the bus up to Cortona, much too long and steep a trip for the bike. To my dismay, when I pull out in the morning, I have a flat tire. Strange, but I push it to the gas station just a ways down the street. Let's see now. How am I going to explain this to a man who definitely doesn't speak English? This should be good. Actually, it was much easier than I thought. All I had to do was point to the flat tire and he pumped it up but that didn't do the trick. I have a hole that needs to be patched. As kindly as he could in Italian and sign language, he gives me directions to the tire place.

I push the bike down the hill past the bus stop, up the hill to the corner, make a right and down the hill, not really sure what I am looking for. Just when I am ready to give up, there is a garage. A young man in a greasy one-piece uniform doesn't speak English either, but I get my message across. He takes great care and detail in patching the tube and putting it back on the rim and back on the bike. In my cycling days, I could have patched that tire and been back on the road in less than five minutes. But I don't have a patch kit, and I am in Italy. An hour later than I planned, I am back on the road to Cortona, and it only cost three euros to fix my tire.

With a conscientious decision that I am not in a hurry and that the ride is part of the adventure, I enjoy the hour-long journey. Camucia is bigger than I think. I find the bus stop where I can lock the bike and for one euro, ride the bus up the three-mile hill to Cortona. The bus won't arrive for another forty-five minutes, so I poke around the shops and eat a gelato.

It is lunchtime when I finally arrive at my final destination, and what a treat. I have been to Cortona before, but it didn't sing to my heart like today. I love wandering up and down the old narrow streets. The views from the various lookouts around town are amazing. We are up very high and I can see for miles around, even Lake Trasimeno, off in the distance.

In one of the shops, I am greeted in perfect English by a lovely young blonde girl. We chat for a while and I learn she came here with Georgia State University a few summers ago. They have a big summer program in Cortona and lots of students, professors and their families take over the little town. Anyway, she fell in love with an Italian guy who plays in a band and after graduation, she moved here to be with him. How cool is that?

The main piazza has a church with a big sweeping staircase that the locals and tourists use as a gathering and resting place. The shops that line the piazza are right out of a movie set. I wonder if they actually shot parts of *Under The Tuscan Sun* here. After climbing in the heat to the very top of the town to see the church, I am ready to take refuge in an air-conditioned museum that houses a famous painting of the Immaculate Conception. I purchase the English language audio guide and take my time. This lingering over each painting is pure joy. I love being able to spend as much time as I want, noticing all the tiny details, especially of their faces.

On the way back to the main piazza, I walk past a hostel so I stop in. It brings back a flood of memories of when I back-packed across Europe for six weeks back when I was just finishing college. I also search for the restaurant of Massimo and Daniela. They are friends of Paola's who used to have a place in Foiano, but sold it and opened a new place here. I actually walked right by the restaurant when I first arrived. It ended up being near the bus. Anyway, Massimo speaks perfect English and his restaurant is totally chic and modern, not at all what I expect. I sit at one of the outdoor tables and have a glass of wine and soak up the moment. So this is where Frances Mayes', author of *Under the Tuscan Sun,* dream came true. Italy really is a magical place. I make the return trip home by retracing my steps. It is by far my most grand endeavor on the bike.

Giuseppe calls me every day now just to talk and see what I am doing. Then he calls me again each night to tell me good night. It is absolutely the sweetest thing in the world to me, that each night when I go to sleep, I am tucked into bed like a child, with a kiss and a wish for sweet dreams. In between, he sends me little text messages just to tell me he is thinking of me. I love that. Is this what they mean by Italians are wonderful caring people because they are so loved by their mothers? I am not sure, but I do know I can get used to it.

In the morning when I wake, my legs are sore. It is something I know well from my old days of training. Ouch, good morning legs. I spend the day on the Internet looking for a room to rent for June in Florence. I listen to Michael Bolton's Vintage CD over and over. It is chilly and storm clouds move in, but there is very little rain. The tolling of the church bells tells me that time is passing. I make a list of all the little towns I want to visit before I move on.

I buy the tickets for the bus at the Tabacchi, the official store that sells controlled items like cigarettes, lottery tickets and stamps. The little old man who works there takes delight in pretending he doesn't understand what I want. Then I go back to the apartment, ask Paola what I am saying wrong, and return again to purchase the correct ticket. I am determined I am going to get him to be nice to me.

At first I stay close to Foiano, but as time goes by, I get more brave and understand how the bus and train schedules work, and I start to go further. I pack essentials for the day, which include digital camera, I-Pod, cell phone and a bottle of water. I feel like Brittany with all my tiny gadgets. Today, I set out for Montepulciano and Pienza. I must ride the bike to the little town of Sinalunga, only three miles away, where I get the bus. I don't know the timetable, but I am starting early enough, so I should be fine. To my dismay, I have another flat tire. Again, I push the bike to the repair shop and find the same young man who repaired it before. This time he decides I need a new tube, so he fixes me up for seven euros. I peddle to Sinalunga only to discover that I missed the last bus for today. So I buy a panino, a sandwich made of fresh crusty bread, one slice of prosciutto, one slice of cheese and no condiments. I sit on the park bench and eat. I decide to go home. I am tired and feeling just a bit cranky. I stop at the corner market and buy a bottle of wine and crawl into bed with my computer to watch a movie. I fall asleep and wake up at 10:00 p.m. Paola has been home for hours and has started to worry about me.

"Is everything okay?" she inquires.

"Yes, fine. I just needed a day in bed." I stay up most of the night writing. Time is so strange here.

Friday night finally comes and I am counting the hours until Giuseppe picks me up. By the time we arrive, the sun is setting over Radda. We stop to pick up a few things at the corner market there, take a quick coffee and watch the sun go down over the patchwork hills of Chianti.

At Galenda, we open a bottle of Giuseppe's wine and he cooks pasta for me. We are in the kitchen together and chop and kiss and cook and kiss and talk and kiss. In advance, he has thoughtfully brought everything we need to make our dinner: most importantly, fresh tomatoes from his mother's garden. I carefully set the table, using all the fun Ikea plates and goblets. I brought my computer, so we listen to great music and eat. Every candle in the place is lit. It is after midnight when we finish our meal.

He comes out of the bathroom with a beach towel slung over his shoulder and holds out his hand and says, "Come with me."

"Where are we going?" I ask.

"Come with me, I want to show you something."

He takes my hand and we go outside into the cool night air and walk down a little path between the buildings. The crickets are chirping as my eyes adjust to the darkness. I can see the blinking of fireflies. I catch one in my hand and show Giuseppe.

"What do you call them in English?" he asks.

"Lightning bugs or fire flies."

He says, "In Italian, they are called *lucciole*."

I explain that when I was little girl, we would catch a lot of them and put them in a jar and shake it to make a homemade flashlight. He tells me that when he was little, the kids would catch them and put them under a jar and leave them on the table overnight. In the morning, the bugs would be gone and a few gold coins, like pennies, would be left in their place. The gold of their lights turned into gold coins, kind of like our tooth fairy.

We walk past a little structure housing a religious statue, *Madonnino* in Italian. I love them. They are all over Italy. I would like to have one in my home someday. I ask Giuseppe what Saint he would choose if had to pick one to put in a prayer house. He looks at me with the most bewildered face. "What do you mean, babee? You don't pick one, they are already in there." I just laugh.

Giuseppe leads me further down the path and between the rows of grape vines. There he puts the towel down and we lie on our backs and look up to see the stars. Yes, the brilliant luminescent stars. There are millions of them. The sky looks like a diamond encrusted bracelet. Some stars are bright, some so tiny they are barely there.

"What is that little thing you say when you look at the stars?" he asks me.

"Star light, star bright, the first star I see I see tonight. I wish I may, I wish I might, have the wish I wish tonight," I answer.

"What do you wish for?" he whispers in my ear, kissing me softly.

"I wish for you to make love to me."

And so right there in the vines, on this cool summer evening in May, we make love, so sweetly, so tenderly and so passionately. I let myself fall. I let the defenses down. I want to feel everything. I want to be in the moment. I am alive.

For the rest of the weekend, we barely leave the apartment, only to swim and ride the Vespa. We make love in every room of Galenda. The bed is new and doesn't yet have the frame, so it is two single mattresses pushed together, propped up with crates. We laugh as the mattresses get pushed apart and our body parts fall down in between them. At one point, the whole mattress starts to fall off the makeshift frame and we slide to floor, laughing all the while.

One night after dinner, we decide to watch a movie on the living room floor. All the furniture has not yet been delivered, so we drag the comforters from the bedroom and spread them out on the rug and make a bed in front of the TV. I make popcorn and Giuseppe starts the movie, but before long we forget about the movie. We are so in the moment of passion that neither of us notices the blankets are gone and the new rug is so course that Giuseppe's knees become a combination of carpet fur mixed with little bloody scrap. The scabs on his knees will be a little reminder of our weekend for many days to come.

As the morning sun starts to peek through the shuttered window, there is just enough light for me to see the beautiful silhouette of the man sleeping next to me. His skin is so fair and delicate. Little laugh lines draw from the corners of his eyes. A five o'clock shadow outlines his face and strong chin. His hair is all tousled. He has gotten too much sun on his chest, making his skin glow against the thick black chest hair covering his muscular pecs. The rest of his body is smooth and shapely. I let my eyes slide down the curves of the muscles on his arms, down the side of his long lean torso, over the hump of his perfect little tush and down his long shapely legs. He truly is a piece of art. A sculpture. My very own David. The glow in the room of the morning's first light casts such warmth over our little hideaway. I lie awake dreamily letting my mind soak up the still life painting in front of me.

Later that morning, I put on a new matching bra and panty set that I just bought at the weekly market. I sneak into the kitchen and attempt to make coffee. I am standing in front of the stove waiting for the coffee to gurgle, when Giuseppe comes up from behind me. "Good Morning, Babee," he says and starts kissing the back of my neck and shoulders. He is not shy as he cups my breasts and then slides his hand across my stomach not stopping until he has reached my most private spot.

"You can't touch me there," I say.

"Yes, I can. Remember, I have the license," he whispers playfully.

I arch my back as my body rises up to met his. He is at full attention.

"It's morning, Babee," he says. "Excuse me. I am always this way in the morning."

"Oh, Love, you don't ever have to apologize, especially for this," I say as I reach around and touch him. And in a moment, my bra is on the floor and my panties are wrapped around my ankles and I am sandwiched between the fire on the stove and the heat of his naked body behind me.

It is nearly lunch by the time we are riding the scooter along the picturesque roads. We are headed for Radda for a real coffee and as we enter town, we can see the Vespa tour group all out on the street, getting ready to start their ride for the day. They are standing in front of one of my favorite hotels in the countryside, Hotel Vignale. It is a lovely four-star property filled with antiques and little sunny rooms, each with a fantastic view. It is built on the slope of a hill, so every level has a sweeping view of the valley. The dining room is on the next level down and looks like a wine cellar with its brick ceiling with additional seating on the terrace. But the best part is the swimming pool with its bright yellow umbrellas and chair covers, backing up directly to a big drop-off, opening up to a view of the vineyards. It is old, elegant and dripping with character.

We pull up in front and are greeted by Maurizio, Giuseppe's friend, and the tour guide.

"This is Barbara," Giuseppe says.

"Oh," Maurizio replies, "She is the American writer from Florida?"

"Yes. Yes, I am the American writer from Florida," I answer. Wow! I have always been a reader not a writer. I have always been the mom, the membership director, the athlete, the neighbor, the friend, but never the American writer from Florida.

Because I don't know what to do or even how to say it, I follow. For the second time in my life, I don't lead. I didn't know what I was doing on the boat either, so I followed and what a lovely adventure unfolded for me. I don't know the best place in town to eat, I don't know the best tomatoes, and I don't even know the right way to cook here. Everything is different. So instead of controlling and *managing* my world, I just live in it. I discover that following is much more fun than leading. I discover I love to be taken care of. I discover that Giuseppe thinks of everything and I don't have to. All I have to do is enjoy. And be grateful.

I don't even have to speak at times. If I don't understand or we are making arrangements and it is not what I want, he can read it in my face. "What's happened?" he asks. "What do you wish for?" I am oblivious to the fact that the less I do, the more he likes it. It's crazy to me. The world I grew up in was do more, be more. I don't even call him. I let him call me. I'm not even sure why, other than he is so attentive about calling me that when I think about calling him, my phone rings. All I do is radiate joy and revel in the moment of my pure bliss.

On Fridays, I take the bus from my village to the train station in Arezzo where I take the half-hour ride to Montevarchi. I enjoy a coffee with Fabio and wait for Giuseppe to pick me up, then we take the scenic ride to Galenda and spend the weekend, and on Monday morning, I make the return trip.

One day, Giuseppe arrives at the train station wearing an orange sweatshirt that says Bora Bora. I can't believe it. "Have you been there?" I ask.

"No," he says, "but I would like to."

"It is the most beautiful water I have ever seen, and I can say that because I am a bit of an expert on that subject. We can go there someday if you like," I offer.

"Yes, I would like that," he says. "But first we must go to Monte Argentario, to the seaside, and then I want to come to see you in Aspen this winter."

I love that. Here is a man who loves to travel and make plans as much as I do. "We are so lucky," I tell him. "We can do anything we want. We can choose anything!"

"You know I can ski," he says jokingly.

"Yes," I reply.

"You know I used to race super G." he says, throwing me the bait.

"Yes," I reply. "Do you know I can ski too?" I ask him.

"Yes," he says.

"You know I am an Ironman."

"Yes."

"Twice." I say, accepting his challenge. I love that he is competitive, like me. He is so much like me it is shocking. His birthday is one day away from mine, December 19th. I never knew a man who was a Sagittarius. He is the male version of me—happy, optimist, fun-loving, competitive, loves to travel, energetic and social.

A few weeks ago he got an I-Pod and asked me if I would put some music on it from my computer. When I asked him what kind of music he liked, he told me to load everything we've been listening too, to just put on whatever I want. I loaded the songs and in a few short weeks I find him singing along. I love to check the I-pod to see what he is listening too. Josh Groban, Bob Marley and Nora Jones are his favorites. I asked him one time if he knew this music from before. He didn't. He had heard their names, but never the music. I loaded my entire "favorites play list" and he loves it all. Not possible. Giuseppe just goes for something full speed ahead. He said once that it is better to live a short life as a lion than a long life as a sheep, and I couldn't agree more.

⁂

On one of my return trips to Cortona, as I board the bus in Camucia, I notice a heavy set lady with long dark hair, red lipstick and very pale skin asking the bus driver a question in English. She sits near me and we start to chat. She lives in California and came to Italy on a bit of a whim, as most of us do, I have found.

When we arrive at the top of the mountain, I invite her to join me for a drink at Massimo's place. We sit and chat for a while. In the most serendipitous way, I learn she is an astrologist and Tarot card reader. I knew I met her for a reason and the reason is to help me understand a dream I had just a few nights ago.

"I had the most incredible dream," I tell her, "and I want to know what it means and how I can have it again. I dreamed that I was in the ocean, just floating there alone, and a huge ship came up to me and its enormous bow came right over my head. Just when I thought it was going to run me over, I started to swim and got pushed away and out of the water by the huge surf of the bow. Then before I knew it, I was flying through the air up, up, away from the ocean so high into the air that the earth looked like a globe. The best part was the feeling of flying. It was pure euphoria: the air rushing past my skin, my hair and my face. I felt totally exhilarated and then I woke up. I tried to go back to sleep and get that feeling of complete exuberance back, but it was gone. What do you think it means?" I ask her.

"It's simple," she says. "The world belongs to you. The whole world is yours. You can do with it what you want."

"Really! It that what that means?" I exclaim, completely happy with the answer. Then I tell her about Brittany and ask what I can do to fix our damaged relationship. To my surprise she says that every soul comes here with something they want to experience and the universe, in its divine wisdom, places that soul in a family or in a situation so that *thing* can be fully experienced. Brittany may have felt abandoned even if I stayed in my old life and remained married to Gary, and if not, she would find a way to feel abandoned through another set of circumstances. The best way to understand what a soul's purpose is on earth is to do her astrological chart. Then she starts to tell me about houses and other things and I get a bit lost, but it certainly gives me something to think about.

I tell her that I am going in search of Frances Mayes' real villa. Her eyes get big and I think she is about to fall off her chair. "Really! Oh my God, that is my dream. I would love to see it."

"Well, you can come along if you like."

So together we go walking out of town, into the hilly countryside to find the villa. It doesn't take long to realize that my new friend is out of shape and having trouble keeping the pace. I don't know how far it is or if we are even going in the right direction, but I don't think she is going to make it. How sad, I think, a little hike in the hills has her heaving for air and all red in her face. She is shocked to learn that I am only eight years younger than she. "Come on sister, what are you doing with your life?" I question her. "You have a whole lot of living to do. You need to get in top shape. What are you waiting for? Start living your dreams now. You know what you need to do, so just get on with it."

I volunteer to go ahead and make sure we are navigating correctly and then return to get her. Within the hour, we do find the house, and to me, it would have been worth walking all day to see. It is not the house in the movie, but the real villa she lives in, even to this day. Rumor has it that she doesn't really live here anymore, that so many people disturbed her that she bought another villa nearby and is planning to turn this one into a bed and breakfast. How? This is her home. She created it with love. That is obvious.

It is more beautiful than I imagined. The house itself is boxy, but I love the rose-peach color and all the green shutters. The gardens and the walled terraces leading up to the house are over the top. All the flowers are in full bloom, cascading down. At the bottom of the hill, the gate is closed and next to it is a little prayer house that holds a porcelain statue, some flowers in a vase and a few other trinkets. There is a little note tucked under a candle. I take it out and read it out loud.

*Dear Frances Mayes,*

*I finally made it to Italy, all because of you. It is more wonderful than I imagined. Now I can really appreciate it the way you do.*

*Betty Smith, Pleasantville, NJ*

Tears well up in my eyes. I understand. It wasn't Frances Mayes or *Under The Tuscan Sun* that drew me here. I have been coming to Italy long before that, but I get it. Live your dream. We do share a common love for all things Italian. I carefully fold the note and slide it back into its original spot.

We take photos of each other in front of the prayer house and more photos of the house and gardens and linger for a while. We are like two kids on an Easter Egg Hunt who just found the first prize egg.

I am off to find the monastery of the monk, St. Francis, who spent ten years in a tiny room. It is just a few miles from here. I leave my new friend to slowly find her way back to town, and I head in the other direction. The monastery is a much longer walk than I anticipate, so after my visit, knowing I must ride my bike some fifteen miles home, I decide to hitch a ride. I know!

I am crazy! I strategically choose a lovely German family with three children driving a mini-van. I think they are harmless enough and a single woman on foot with a little backpack is equally harmless. They are happy to drop me back in town and I make my way home to Foiano. As I lie in bed that night reviewing the day, I know I am a lucky girl. Today I fulfilled another life-long dream.

This weekend at Galenda, Giuseppe's friend Antonio joins us for a swim at the pool. He is about forty-years-old, single and owns a clothing manufacturing business. He speaks English and is great fun. For the first time, I hear him call Giuseppe, Guisey. Giuseppe is actually Joseph, so Guisey is like calling him Joey. They have been friends a long time and both grew up in Montevarchi. At the pool, Giuseppe offers wine to the other sunbathers and before you know it, they have an appointment to come to the vineyard for a tasting. For the girl that Antonio thinks is particularly cute, we decide to leave a bottle of white by their door for her to try later. Watching Giuseppe talk about the wine and share it with total strangers is pure delight. He is in his element. The love and the passion can literally be poured from his veins. How wonderful that he knows his gift.

Later that night, after dinner and after Antonio has gone home, I draw a bath for us. I light some candles and slide in, calling Giuseppe as though I have a problem and need his help. He comes to my rescue and sees the trap and falls right into step. He undresses and joins me in the big tub. We laugh and splash each other. I even snap a photo or two. It gives a whole new meaning to "a picture is worth a thousand words."

It will soon be time to move to Florence. I have been on the Internet looking for rooms to rent. I have appointments to see three places. Bright and early in the morning, I walk to the bus stop, go to Arezzo and make the one hour train ride to Florence, getting off at the last stop. On the ride I think about my intention for my stay here. It is art, music, history, language and architecture, Italian style. As we pull into the train station, called Santa Maria Novella named after the oldest church in Florence, I chuckle to myself at how many times I have passed through this station and the wonderful memories it holds for me.

Armed with a bus ticket, a map and a couple of addresses, I go in search of my new home. I am shocked at how easy it is. The first place I go to I learn that the room is probably not available, but she has a friend nearby who does have a room available. She offers to drive me to the other place. We are greeted by a friendly older lady who shows me the room. It is connected to her house, but has a separate entrance and little pantry/kitchen and bath that are for the use of the renters. There are three bedrooms in this little *side house*. The room is small and very austere with two singles beds, a desk and closet. No paintings on the wall. It looks like a Romanian orphanage with its simple black iron headboards. And did I mention it is right across the street from the train tracks? Where is the Italian splendor?

Next, I go to Eduardo's house. His apartment is near Piazza Della Liberta on a wide tree-lined boulevard. He is at work, but the girl who is currently renting the room will be home and has agreed to show me around. I ring the bell from downstairs and Maria buzzes me in. I am out of breath by the time I reach the top floor of the building. She is standing in the doorway, waiting to greet me. To my surprise she is Mexican, studying in Italy, then moving back to Germany where her fiancé is waiting for her. I love this. She is sweet and friendly. She shows me the little room that is available, the bathroom I will share, the non-existent living room, which is more like a foyer with a sofa, the big well-stocked kitchen, and the best part, the terrace, which sits just over the tree-lined street.

Lucky for me, I can ask all the important *girl* questions from someone who lived in my *future* shoes. She tells me the neighborhood is safe and she walks home at night without a problem, the location is great, wireless Internet in my room and most importantly, thirty-five-year-old Eduardo is a perfect gentleman. He is easy-going and smart. He works days and goes to University at night and takes classical guitar lessons. The place is quiet and I will have it to myself a lot. Seems great, but I am hesitant to live with a man I have never met. Don't ask me why, after having lived with Pete and Buddy, neither of whom I knew either.

The third place is about ten minutes further away from the heart of the city. It is in a lovely residential neighborhood near Piazza Della Cure. I have difficulty finding it, when finally, Gretchen the landlord, comes out into the street to meet me. She is a young thin German girl who came to Florence to study for the summer. The apartment is a series of small rooms with no real main living area. It has a small kitchen and one bath we will all be sharing. She just found out that she got the internship she was looking for, and will be moving to Switzerland on July 1st. That works great for me. I am only here for June, maybe more, but I'll see. Of the four bedrooms in the house, two are available, so I can choose. Her boyfriend shares her room with her and the other one is rented to a guy from London. She doesn't think she will rent the other one since she will only be here for another month or so. One is bigger than the other, but the small one has a window that looks out onto the small lawn and courtyard. There is a little garage that has been converted into a one-room studio rented by another German student and friend of hers. The courtyard needs some attention, but I think I will enjoy mowing the grass, trimming the bushes and planting some flowers. It is so incredibly hot that I think having the garden is a must. The best part of all though, is the al fresco on the ceiling. It is pink with birds and flowers. It has a big bed that I can imagine myself lying in all day while staring at the painting on the ceiling. Actually the bed takes up the whole room except for a little desk, chair and an armoire. As I walk down the hall to leave, I step over a big pile of a dog, Bagley. He is a friendly old golden Lab. I think we will become friends and we will go for walks all over the city. I decide to take it. The rent is 450 euro, about $600. She doesn't want any money now, so I tell her I will see her on the first of the month.

There now, it's all settled. That was easy. I got myself to and from Florence, navigated the city and found myself a place to live. Oh, how I can't wait to live in Florence, another life-long dream coming true.

Before I leave town I pop into a little shop selling Murano glass from Venice. I want to get a new ring to replace the one I broke on the boat. I had been wearing it for over a year when I broke it snorkeling. I got stuck in a strong current and pulled so hard on a rock that I broke the ring right off my finger. It was red with gold flecks and all the customers back at Portobello's would always comment on it. I bought it in Venice, but my replacement will come from Florence. The shopkeeper is a fair-skinned, bald, blue-eyed man in his late fifties. I am taking my time, enjoying all the pretty colors when two American ladies come into the store. They are speaking English, so I ask them where they are from. "Florida," they reply.

"Really, me too." I tell them. "Well at least most recently." They are from Ft. Lauderdale and I tell them I was living near Cape Coral before I got on a sailboat and went island hopping for the last 100 days. They are intrigued and we chat away like old friends.

"So what are you doing in Florence?" they inquire.

"Well, I am living in Italy for the summer and just rented an apartment for the month of June. I am going to Italian language school," I explain.

"What a cool lifestyle. Why are you doing this?" they ask.

"Because I can. I have no husband and my only child is in college in Atlanta, and I have always wanted to travel and live abroad." So there, I think to myself, because I can! That gives a whole new meaning to "when life gives you lemons, make lemonade." They are amazed. Alone, you are doing this alone? "I am not alone," I explain. "Strangers are just friends I haven't met yet."

I tell them about my ring and they don't know about Murano glass. I give them the short version of how the glass in made on a little island in Venice and there are little pieces of gold inside. I truly want them to know that these are little pieces of art. It is just like working in the gallery back in Matlacha. They end up buying a lot of jewelry. After they leave, I turn to the shopkeeper and tell him I just can't decide between this ring or another one. He quickly takes both rings from me, carefully wraps them up and puts them into a bag and hands it to me.

"There, my gift to you."

"Gift, why?" I ask.

"For letting me watch you tell your story and selling all that jewelry. That little thing that just happened was magical."

"It's true, my story," I defend myself.

"I know," he says gently, "I can tell by the sparkle in your eyes." He hands me his business card and says if I want to work while I am here, I should come see him. I look at the card.

"Thanks Liugi."

"Be careful," he says in a protective fatherly way. "This city is filled with people who will try to take advantage of a girl like you."

"Thank you, but don't worry, I'll be fine." I have a well-trained badass guardian angel, Gabriele, who has been given a real workout since he was assigned to me last year, I say to myself. Later when I move to Florence, I run into Luigi several times during the next month. He always has a big hug and an offer for a coffee, a glass of wine, or a roll in the hay but I always just go on my merry way. And what a merry way it is, indeed.

On Wednesday night, Giuseppe comes to Foiano for dinner.

"Where do you want to go?" he asks.

"Let's go to that little outdoor place I found in Lucingano," I reply. "I think I can find it again."

"If not, I know a wonderful little pizza place." Giuseppe says. Great, and just like that we are off to the little ancient walled village next to mine. As we near the town, we are surprised by all the cars. They are lining the street for miles. There must be something going on, we decide. Not to worry, we find a place to park and walk. I am not prepared to walk as I am wearing heels and a skirt. The tiny streets are packed with people and we don't find the restaurant I remembered, but we find the pizza place Giuseppe knows. We go inside where it smells wonderful. We order two beers and a pizza for each of us. Tonight I learn that Italians drink beer with pizza, not wine, and the pizza has a very thin crust, so each person orders their own. It is the size of a large dinner plate, but not so doughy and filling like in the states. The place is full of patrons, but we are in no rush. After a while I hear a steady drum beat coming from the street below the window. We ask our server what is going on. We are told it's a parade. Tonight is the beginning of the Festival of Roses. "You have got to be kidding," I think to myself. Just like a few years ago and the Peach Festival in Lunda. That was the year fourteen girls rented a villa, and on our first night there we stumbled upon the Peach Festival—straight men wearing tights and medieval outfits parading through the streets. The night that sweet, newly divorced Mary Beth got kissed by one such young stud in a dark doorstep as the rest of us spied on them from behind the fountain in the piazza. The wonderful memories flood back. That was the trip that Tom died.

But this is now, and I am here and this is the Rose Festival in Lucingano. I go to the window in the restaurant and lean out on the two-foot-deep windowsill and look down onto the street. There it is, the parade, complete with costumes, floats, musical instruments…the works. What a lucky girl I am! Giuseppe calls me back to the table when our food arrives. When we finish eating, we walk out onto the street, mingle in with the crowd, watch four elaborate floats go by, and of course, the Rose Princess. I can't see because I am so short, even with heels. Giuseppe expertly guides me here and there, trying to provide me with the best view of the parade. "I wish I were tall," I tell him.

"Amore, (my love in Italian) just like the Vinsanto, the best wine comes in the smallest bottle, delicious, complicated and to be tasted in small portions."

My head falls back against his shoulder as his arms wrap around me and we watch the festivities unfold right before us. We stroll in the crowded town, arm-in-arm, kissing and just being in new love. That night after he drops me at home, he sends me a text message. Sweet dreams Amore. I drift off to sleep, the luckiest girl in the whole wide world. Someone does really need to pinch me, because this is bigger than I can imagine, and I have a really big imagination.

Late one night I am on the Internet, just playing around and I see a link to learn Italian. I have been here for what, three weeks now, and I don't understand anything. I am not learning to speak Italian. I need to go to school and why not while I am in Florence? By morning, I have chosen my school, Istituto Italiano. It starts on Monday, June 3rd. I hope there is space available. It cost 500 euro for a month. I send an email and get a reply that space is available. Housing is provided if I need it, which I don't. Wow, for another 500 euro, they would have placed me with an Italian family that doesn't speak English. For 1000 euros, anyone, any age can come and live in Florence for a month and go to Italian language school! Within the hour, I am confirmed. Stefano writes that I am all set. "See you on the first day of school." Is it really this easy? It can't be.

Tomorrow I move to Florence, so I spend the day walking around my village. I really love it and will miss it. Maybe I will come back for July or August. For now, it is time to move on. I really found peace here. I found strength and courage I never knew I had. I found out I am okay with being alone. I have explored this whole area by myself and I enjoyed it. I am so grateful to be happy, healthy and whole. My legs are strong and beautiful and I no longer have to stand up to ride my bike back up the hill to Foiano. I am in top condition and my body responds to the needs I put on it. All that crazy Ironman training has come in handy.

I love being in the countryside. Somehow it feels like home. It's crazy that I never wanted to be in the country when I was growing up in rural Pennsylvania, and now I am so at home here. I don't know what to do with this. Is being a farmer of dairy, corn and tobacco that different from being a farmer of wheat, olive oil and wine? Why is this so chic and my kind of farming so unromantic?!

Giuseppe is coming and he will drive me and my two bags to Florence. He is so yummy and fun. Paola is making a farewell dinner for us. Like a true Italian, when I move, I will take my basil plant with me. How can I eat sliced tomatoes laced with olive oil and salt, if I don't have fresh basil leaves to chop and sprinkle on top?

I can't believe my luck. No, let me rephrase that, I am the luckiest in girl in the whole wide world and I know it. All good things are coming to me now. I am in the right place at the right time. It's all good.

# Chapter 39

*Florence – A City of Art, History and Language*
*June 2007*

Today I move to Florence. I can't believe it is really happening; I have always dreamed of living in Florence. It is a city that has everything: art, history, music and architectural brilliance. After visiting many times, I can't believe I am really going to live there.

Around 10:00 a.m., Giuseppe struggles to lug my big, fat, heavy suitcases down the three flights of stairs. "What do you have in here?" he asks.

"My rock collection," I tell him with a straight face.

He looks at me with that sweet face and I can literally see him translating what I said. I love to watch the light bulb go off, and then he comes charging over to me to tickle me and kiss me and let me know he appreciates my joke.

We make the one-hour drive to Florence. He knows the way by heart. It seems odd to me, but why wouldn't he know the way. He grew up here and I am sure he came to the city many times to come to the clubs and hang out. Gretchen knows I am planning to arrive by noon or so. We find a parking spot and I take one of my bags with me. This time when we arrive, the place looks totally different. The kitchen is small, very cluttered and dirty, and my room is so crowded with furniture that I can hardly move around the bed. I guess I was so focused on the ceiling that I forgot to look at the floor, which today looks filthy. Anyway, after putting my suitcases in my room, we go to the living room where I introduce Giuseppe to Gretchen. Along with Gretchen, we find four other young men huddled around a laptop trying to get the wireless connection to work.

They are all students, two from Australia and two from London. No one is Italian, so we speak English. Although I think it could be fun living in an *international dormitory*, I want to have the Italian experience. I do feel a bit like I have walked into a den of wolves with my five male roommates. I am the new kid, but they are new too. When I came to look at the apartment, there were only three people living here, now there appears to be seven including me. Remember, we will be sharing one bath. I am a bit overwhelmed by the whole situation, but it is the dirt I can't get over.

The look on my face is all Giuseppe needs to understand I am feeling a little apprehensive about the whole situation. He too is not comfortable about the arrangement. Once outside, we both burst out laughing. What was I thinking when I picked this place? I still have Eduardo's phone number programmed in my phone, so I decide to give him a call and see if his room is available. The problem is my school starts on Monday and Maria isn't moving out until Thursday.

So I give Eduardo a call and he tells me the room is still available and he doesn't mind me coming on Monday, but he will have to call Maria and ask her too since we will all be sharing the bathroom. He is downtown shopping with his girlfriend, Riana, who is visiting from Greece. They met in Florence, but she moved back to Greece after finishing University. They have been dating for about ten years. We arrange to meet them for a drink.

"Meet me in the Piazza Duomo. I will be on rail next to the golden doors of the Basilica," Eduardo explains. Get out! This is really what people say? Meet me in the Piazza Duomo! I guess it is like me saying to a friend in Orlando to meet me in front of the Epcot Ball. When we arrive, I recognize Eduardo from the photos in his apartment. Although he speaks English, he and Giuseppe talk to each other in Italian. As Giuseppe is explaining the situation, Eduardo's phone rings and it's Maria. She is fine with me coming a little early. I will sleep on the couch in the living room. For now, I can drop my two big suitcases off at the apartment, stay with Giuseppe for the weekend, take the train to Florence on Monday morning and go right to class. It's a little upside-down, but I am okay with it. The worst part is I must go back to Gretchen and tell her I changed my mind. "Why didn't I just choose Eduardo's place first?" I question myself. As we walk back to her apartment, I dread having to tell her. Then I remember that I am allowed to change my mind. This is my dream and I choose. It is not the end of the world. I haven't given her any money yet.

I go inside and find Gretchen in the living room with her boyfriend. I tell her that I changed my mind and I won't be taking the room after all. I hand her the keys, go down the hall, get my suitcase, and I am out of there. Now, that wasn't so bad. I didn't have to go on and on. I feel bad about leaving her hanging with the room and money but it doesn't seem to faze her. With that finished, we drive to Eduardo's and ring the bell. Maria buzzes us in. When we finally reach the top of the stairs, we are both out of breath. Giuseppe looks at me with that, "Dear God, what is it with your bags" look and I just shrug my shoulders. This time we just laugh, knowingly. Without realizing it, those bags are going to give him a real work-out before this summer is over.

With my living arrangements settled, there is one more thing to do before we leave town, and that is to find my school. I have the address and know it is near the Duomo. So off we go, holding hands, armed with an address and a little excitement. I feel like I am going to first grade, making a practice run the day before school starts. It has been a long time since I have formally attended school. I have taken evening classes for my real estate license and such, but nothing like this. We find the building and there on the marquee it says, Istituto Italiano Language School. I start Monday morning at nine, five days a week, four hours a day. This is really happening. All I can do is giggle like a schoolgirl, which I am. I am really excited about being able to communicate. I think it will change my whole experience. I want to be one of them, not an outsider. So it is settled, I have a place to live and I know where my school is. Now, it is back to the countryside to enjoy the rest of my weekend.

Monday morning, Giuseppe drives me to the Montevarchi station where I catch the train and make the one-hour trip to Florence, then walk another ten minutes or so to the school. My first day, I really do feel like a kid. I have a backpack and everything. I climb the stairs to the top floor of the building, which happens to be the fourth floor, and find the lobby overflowing with students. Most of them are young, college-age, but there are a few grown-ups like me. After I pay my tuition in cash, because no one in Italy likes to take credit cards, I am instructed to go to classroom C. There we have a briefing in English. I learn that most students have their housing provided by the school. Every day the school provides an activity for us. Today, at three there is a guided walking tour of the city. Although the students are from all over the world and speak many different languages, the majority are American college kids. This will be the only time we will speak English. From now on, it is only Italian.

We are divided into smaller classrooms of ten people. My teacher is Francesco, a pleasant man in his thirties. I am placed in a beginner class with five college students from the same school in upstate New York, three girls from Brazil (a mom and two daughters), an Asian man from Boston, and me. From the very first minute, I feel like I am behind. "Open your book to page three and Silvia, please read the first paragraph," Francesco instructs, all in Italian. I have no idea what he said so I look around and follow. To my shock and horror, Silvia reads the paragraph as though she has been studying it all night.

Am I in the right class? I thought this is beginner. The director of the school said I didn't need to know anything, not one word. Oh, this is not good. This is not good at all. I thought we would start with the alphabet, maybe counting or See Spot Run, but this, this is a full page of text. None of which I have ever seen before in my life. Why didn't I take some classes before? Why didn't I learn something before I arrived? What was I thinking? Please don't call on me. Please don't call on me. My mouth is so dry that I don't think I can speak English if he calls on me now.

At eleven we take a break. I fly down the grand staircase and bust out onto the crowded sidewalk, gulping in the air. I don't know if I need a cappuccino, a gelato, or a grappa, but I don't feel so well. I need something, maybe to be shot in the head. I wobble down the street and wander into the first coffee bar, which happens to be full of students. The café is buzzing and during the ten-minute break, I learn I am not the only one panicking; that everyone thinks they are in the wrong class and there are a lot of fun students from all over the world. Most speak English along with another language. I love how international it is.

Many students have made the trip alone and this is the first time they are meeting the other students. I think they are brave. One girl, Anna, is just nineteen-years-old from Lithuania and another girl, Adrianna, twenty, is from Mexico and there are a few grown-ups as well. Maniv, quite a fashionista I guess from first glance, a well-educated Indian man in his thirties, grew up in Toronto, but now lives in London. Christina is a single grandmother who was born in England now lives in Switzerland, but will be moving to Veneto, Italy. She is the housekeeper for a priest who is retiring and moving back to his birthplace. She has been to her new town several times to oversee the renovation of the house they will be moving into. I am proud of her for being so brave and agreeing to move to Italy.

So look at this. There are other crazy people in the world, doing what I am doing. It feels a lot like Alaska, when I was in Skagway. There are all kinds of people living all kinds of lifestyles that I have only dreamed about. They are not talking about it, but are living it, not dreaming about "someday I am going to"... but actually doing it. And here again, I find myself surrounded by people who take life as an adventure. The funny thing is, before I got started on this whole new lifestyle, I thought it was really difficult, but when I had no alternative, or I should say, when this was my best option, all the pieces fell into place. The only thing I had to do was let go of my old, worn-out life that no longer served me and go. Get out of my own way. It sounds so simple and it is. We are the ones who make the obstacles real and big. I look around the coffee bar and realize that at some point, each one of us sat at the computer and searched and found our way here. From all over the world, we all had the same dream and today, it is really happening.

With the break over, I find myself back in the classroom. I really want to learn. I really want to be fluent. Keep up as best you can, I coach myself. You will have plenty of time to sort this out when you get home. Thankfully, we do a mixture of reading, listening, exercise and working with a partner. My partner is Erin, one of the college students from New York, but she is in her late twenties and works full-time in public relations and goes to school at night. She, like me, doesn't speak another language and feels completely lost. This is supposed to be fun. She too, thought living in Florence would be all fun and games. Although she goes to the same school, she doesn't know any of the other students and being older and more mature, she hasn't taken well to dormitory living. Her light at the end of the tunnel is her boyfriend coming to visit for the last ten days of the month.

By one o'clock, my head is spinning so I decide to stay nearby rather than returning to the apartment and coming back later for the group outing. I pop into an empty classroom and review my notes. Two hours fly by and our small group of students is escorted out into the bright sunshine of this summer day and the heat of the afternoon. The piazzas are crowded as buses, cars, scooters and bicycles make their way between the throngs of people who look like foreigners. Lines of tourists who are waiting for their turn wrap around the buildings.

Our guide is a stylish lady in her fifties. She seems to be genuinely interested in sharing the history of the city, but I can't understand one word. Some of the students interpret for others, but I really feel sad that I don't understand all the knowledge offered to me. There really is a whole other world out there.

It is 5:00 p.m. by the time I make the fifteen-minute walk back to the apartment. I think it is a great location. The school suggested we get the monthly bus pass, unlimited riding for 50 euro, but I have already decided that I want a bicycle. I loved riding around the countryside and the freedom it gave me. This way, I won't have to wait for the bus and I can really explore the city. I saw a man renting bikes near the train station. Tomorrow after school, I will go to see him.

When I arrive at the apartment, I ring the bell downstairs. Maria buzzes me in. I hike the four long flights of stairs. Out of breath, I say hello. Maria speaks English, Spanish, German and Italian. I quickly learn that I have *language envy* because I am envious of anyone who speaks another language. I even look at the little Italian kids with jealousy and wonder if they know how lucky they are to be able to speak Italian. Why couldn't I have learned another language as a child? It would have been so easy to learn German or, for that matter, I should have learned Spanish. For twenty years, I lived in Orlando where Spanish is spoken everywhere. What was I doing? The more I travel, the more I realize that I do know the most universal language in the world. I am grateful to know English, but I also realize that I am handicapped not knowing other languages, as most of the world speaks several. Now I am living in Italy and I want so desperately to speak and understand Italian, but that alone is not enough. This is going to require some real work and I am up for the job.

Maria is really sweet. She is eager to go back to Germany where her boyfriend is waiting for her. She doesn't have the heart to tell her parents back in Mexico City that she is probably never going to live there again. She came to Florence to study for a semester. We are soon giggling like sisters. She offers to let me check the Internet, but I quickly realize that the keyboard is not the same, and memories flash back of sitting in the Internet café in the

Dominican Republic, typing on a Spanish computer in English, with the French lady next to me. It makes me laugh out loud.

Maria has a final meeting with her professor at school tonight and Eduardo is at music lessons, so I find myself home alone. I snoop around the apartment, reading the titles to his music and book collections and see what is in the kitchen cupboards. It is surprisingly well-stocked. The kitchen is bigger than the living room, which has become my bedroom. There is a TV in the corner, which I will learn never gets turned on. My big suitcases are stacked in the corner and I try to keep my mess to a minimum. The kitchen table becomes my desk and I get down to business. Before I know it, it is after 11:00 p.m. and I am exhausted. I put on my PJ's and lay out some clothing for tomorrow. Have I really been studying for over five hours? I re-wrote everything I learned today and looked up the definition of at least 100 words.

Giuseppe calls me to say goodnight. I tell him about my day, trying not to sound completely crazed, and he tells me about his. He is busy at the winery with tourists coming for a wine tasting. I am planning on going to see him on the weekend.

Each day I go to school and realize that I am getting further and further behind. I go straight home after school and study, go for a walk in my neighborhood, and then back to the books. I really like my teacher and the other students, but they seem to be picking things up a lot quicker than I am. What is happening? Most of the others speak a second language already—Spanish, Portuguese, or Mandarin Chinese. They already know masculine and feminine and how the words change when they are plural. I am starting at ground zero and the pace seems too fast. After the third day, I go to the office and request a private tutor. I can have an additional one-hour private lesson every afternoon. I just want to get some clarification in English. How do the rules work? Why are the pronunciations different when it is the same letter? And for God's sake, I am in the *beginner-beginner* class, right? Stefano, the director, is very understanding, and tomorrow I start my first private lesson.

As soon as my regular group lesson is over, I walk quickly to the train station to see a man about a bicycle. I am really excited and I hope he speaks a little English or this will get very interesting. With my translation guide in one hand and my cell phone in the other to call Giuseppe just in case, I am off. The man only rents bikes for a day and that times thirty days would be outrageous. He suggests I go to the bike shop and just buy a bike outright. So on a scrap piece of cardboard he draws a map for me. After a turn here and there, I find the shop with a sign on the door, "Closed until 4:00 p.m." I should have known better. Everything shuts down between noon and four. So I hurry back to school for my first private lesson.

Antonio is a spunky man with silver hair, although later I learn that he is the same age as me. Again, he doesn't speak English. After three days, I realize this is a complete waste of my time and money. I don't understand anything he is saying and worse, I think he is making fun of me. Finally out of pure frustration, I shout at him, "I don't care how many different ways you say it, I don't understand. I don't know that the ch in *chiave* (key) is pronounced the same way as *chiesa* (church) or *cinema* (cinema) from *centro* (central). They are all just words to me! I don't know where to start because I don't know any words."

And with that, he says in plain English, "Take your time, Barbara, you will learn. Italian is a difficult language, but I won't speak to you in English, only Italian."

And from then on we become friends, he pushes me to the breaking point more than once and I fight back the tears. I don't know what is more torturous, my group lesson for four hours or my one-hour with Antonio. Finally one day, he pushes all the books and papers out of the way and says in Italian/English, "Let's just talk. Forget about all the grammar and the rules. Why are you here?"

"Because I want to learn Italian," I answer.

"Why?"

"Because I love Italy, I want to live here and I need to be able to speak," I answer

"When did you arrive? When do you return? Why are you living here?"

"Because I can," I reply

"Where is your family?" he asks.

"My fiancé died and my only child is in university."

"How did he die?" he asks.

"He had a heart attack. It was very sudden," I explain.

"How old was he? How old is your daughter? How old are you?"

I tell him about going to Alaska and living on the boat. I learn that he is married and has two small children. He lives in an apartment near the school and doesn't have air conditioning. His wife is German, they are teaching their children English and German, and figure they will learn Italian when they go to grade school. He rides his bike to work. As soon as he finishes with my lesson, he must hurry and go to his other job. He has lived in Florence for twenty-some years and has seen the city change a lot. The tourists still come, but they don't buy like years ago. The city has become a melting pot and many of the shopkeepers are no longer Italian. This makes him sad. He wishes things were the way they used to be.

One day I come to my afternoon lesson and announce I bought a bike. Antonio is impressed and wants to hear the story. So, in broken Italian mixed with a few English words, I tell him that I went to the bike shop after school and told the man I wanted to buy a bike that is *vecchio* and *non caro* (old as in Ponte Vecchio or old bridge and not expensive). The man walked me through the shop and out the back door to a small parking lot where there was a row of used bikes. All were black except one: a purple girl's bike that looked like something right out of a Grace Kelly movie. It even came with a basket and a bell. He said it was 65 euros. Just to be sure I understood him correctly, I had him write down the price on a piece of paper which I have learned to carry with me at all times. "Perfect," I said, "I'll take it." We wheeled the bike out to the front of the store and I reached for my wallet.

"*Aspetta, aspetta.*" he said. (Wait, wait) He guided me over to a big display of locks. I did remember everyone telling me I must lock the bike, so I picked out one that matched the colors perfectly. "*No, signorina, non piccolo, grande. Due minute,*" he said, making a chopping motion with his hand. (No, Miss, not small, big. Two minutes and they will cut it). He pointed to the big heavy locks, so I picked one of those. Eighty-five euro later and I was out the door, thrilled with my new bike. Antonio is laughing the whole time I tell him my story, which takes up our entire one-hour lesson.

I really am a kid. I am so happy to be a student, riding my bike to school, wearing a backpack and doing my homework. I love taking my break with the other students and going to the activities the school plans for us. I even eat a gelato everyday after school. It is my little reward for surviving another day.

I ride all over the city. Nothing makes me happier than to be out, peddling down the narrow streets. I quickly learn that taxis and buses are the only vehicles that are allowed downtown, unless you live here and have the special permit that is required. Many streets are one-way, and God forbid I am coming down the wrong way when a taxi comes. It is like they have permission to hit me. They come flying at me, not even trying to make room to let me pass. More than once I have been brushed by a side-view mirror. So I learn to just stop if the road is narrow. For some reason, they don't seem to know what I am up to, so they slow down. And let's not forget the scooters. I love them, but I really must pay attention and stay out of their way. The bus drivers really are saints. There are buses everywhere, probably the most common form of transportation, and they mingle right in the tiny streets with scooters and bicycles and the thousands of tourists wandering aimlessly, not paying any attention at all.

The tourists are a problem for me too when I am on the bike. There are so many of them, and since there are so few cars on the street, the people walk everywhere. I quickly learn why I have a bell. It is such a gentle way of letting pedestrians know that I am coming. My little ring-ring alerts the passers-by and they move out of the way, sometimes. Other times, they step right into my path and I must slam on the brakes, which, by the way, don't work very well.

I finally settle in to my new room. There is a single bed on a futon-type bed frame, a desk, lots of shelving, and a hook for some clothing. My computer is up and running and I no longer have to look up words in the dictionary, there is this great website that does it for me. I get to spend my first evening with Eduardo who has been out every night since I moved in. So far I have only said hello and goodbye in the mornings, when he is leaving for work while I am making tea. He is dark, thin and very analytical and thinks a great deal when he speaks. He works in computers for a medical company. At first I am not sure if he is thinking about speaking in English, or if he is thinking about what he is saying. I learn later, that he is thinking about what he is saying and that *rush* is not a word in his vocabulary. I like him and come to appreciate the easy way about him. Anyway, he tells me that he will only speak to me in Italian, and even though I can't speak much, thinking in Italian will help. Thankfully there is no language involved in music. Eduardo plays the classical guitar. I love being in my room at night studying and listening to him play. If he is not playing, he is listening to wonderful classical music. I am the luckiest girl in the world.

Friday finally comes and I decide I need to move to a slower class, if there is such a thing. Back to the office I go to see Stefano. He hears my concern and knows that I am committed to learning, but I feel the pace is too fast. He explains that things will level out a bit after two weeks. The students who already know the information we have covered will now need time to learn new information. It sounds good, but whatever. I am embarrassed to take my note to Francesco and tell him I am moving classes and then I must walk into my new class full of strangers. I am learning Italian for me, no one else. I am the only one whose judgment really counts here.

By the end of the four hours, I realize that this isn't any better or worse, just different. They are covering material in greater depth than my old class, but no one is speaking. It seems to be a lot of book work. I don't know which is better. The real icing on the cake is that when we break into pairs, one person says a phone number in Italian and the partner has to write them down. I am paired with a lovely little old Asian lady whom I can't understand when she speaks English, and I certainly won't be able to understand her speaking Italian while deciphering some numbers. What am I going to do? Should I go back to my old class or stay in the new one? I decide to do nothing. Just go to Montevarchi to see Giuseppe for the weekend and chill. On Monday, I will decide what to do.

It's Friday night and I am having dinner with my school in some little restaurant. We meet at eight on the steps in front and all thirty of us walk to the restaurant. What a delightful time. We are all seated at big long banquet tables, and somehow I am at the *grown-up* table as opposed to the college kids table. We are supposed to speak Italian, but end up with a lively conversation in English.

Saturday afternoon I hop on the train and head for Montevarchi. I am so grateful to go out to the countryside. It is green and peaceful, and I can breathe. After I stop in to see Fabio and have the best cappuccino in Italy, Giuseppe picks me up at the train station and we spend the weekend in the sun by the pool and riding the Vespa. We watch movies and listen to music. I brought my school book and study when Giuseppe goes to the winery to do a wine tasting. Then back to the city on the Monday morning train.

It is hot. It is so incredible I can hardly believe that it is only June. What must it be like in August? No wonder everyone goes on holiday for the month of August. Florence is situated in a valley, so there is no summer breeze. Also, apparently it is built on swamp land that gets steaming hot in summer. I think additional heat is generated from all the hard surfaces of the stone buildings and roads with very few trees. Now, I have lived in Florida for over twenty years and I know hot, but this is crazy. Thank goodness my school has air conditioning, although most places do not. My apartment doesn't, so I sleep with the window open, which creates a new problem. Well, two new problems actually, mosquitoes and noise. After I have been bitten to shreds, Eduardo gives me this handy little device that plugs into the electric sockets and has a little vile of liquid that seems to do the trick. Why don't we have this?

I can hardly sleep with the heat, and now that the windows are open, all the street noise makes it even more difficult. Between the scooters and motorcycles racing down the street, the sirens blaring all night, and stressing about school, I hardly sleep during the week. It is after midnight when I finally fall asleep from pure exhaustion, after studying for hours. I don't know how the other students do it. They meet every night after dinner at ten on the steps of the Duomo, and drink and talk and decide what bar they want to go to. Sometimes they stay out until three or four o'clock in the morning. Youth is either wasted on the young or I am taking school way too seriously.

Everyone text messages in Italy rather than just calling. Texting is free and speaking costs money. No one has an answering machine. They see who the missed call is and then decide whether nor not to call back. My Treo from the states doesn't work here, so I have an Italian phone and phone number. I am completely retarded when it comes to texting on my *baby Italian phone* because I don't have a keyboard like on my old phone. Silly, I know, but it seems very archaic to me.

Thursday, we have made arrangements for Giuseppe to come to Florence and stay with me. I text message Eduardo and ask him if it is okay if Giuseppe spends the night. He replies, "Well that depends. If he wants to sleep with me, absolutely not, if he wants to sleep with you, that is something you must decide." I text him back, "Silly, of course I want him to sleep with me." He texts back, "Italian humor, get used to it."

Eduardo tells me I am saying Giuseppe's name wrong. "Excuse me?" I reply. "What do you mean?" He informs me that it is *Jew-sep-a*, not *Joe sep ee*. I understand what he means, because his childhood friends call him Guisy. (*Jew see*). So to avoid all the confusion, I decide to call him G. When I tell G about this, he thinks it is funny because I am pronouncing Eduardo's name wrong too, he tells me. His name is *Ed u ardo*, not *Ed wardo*. G says, "What is this Ed<u>w</u>ardo?" making it sound like he has a mouth full of marbles. To me, it all sounds the same, to them it makes a big difference. G scolds me that I don't listen, and in defense, I tell him that I am listening, but I don't hear the difference. It really does sound the same to me.

I have never thought about words so much in my entire life. There are so many small words in Italian. *Ho, so, e, fa* and so on, but then it occurs to be that English has just as many like *it, a, and, is*. With many words in Italian, just changing one letter changes the pronunciation inflection slightly, but completely changes the meaning of the word.

It is finally Thursday and G drives into the city to have dinner with me. He brings some wine and tomatoes from his garden and decides to cook pasta. We are just starting to poke around the kitchen when Eduardo comes home. They consult over cooking and which pots and spoons are best for what. Both men take their shirts off because it is hot, and they don't want to get their clothes dirty. They are talking and joking in Italian like old friends as I sit at the kitchen table and take in the scene. I am amazed at the wonderful way G and Eduardo get along. American men would never do this, especially strangers. There is no competition or jealousy between them, as a matter of fact, I wonder if I left, how long it would take them to notice I was gone.

We end up eating all together outside on the terrace. Because we are on the top floor, we have a little terrace big enough for a table and chairs, some plants and some lounge chairs. We are above the trees, so the terrace gets a lovely breeze. We eat wonderful pasta and drink the wine G made and laugh, then later listen to Eduardo play. Look where I am. I am the luckiest girl in the world.

Before the evening is over, Eduardo invites G and me to a little dinner party and recital he is planning. It is practice for the big performance at Fiesole he has coming up in a few weeks. Eduardo is very nervous about playing in front of an audience and his instructor thinks it would be good to practice in advance.

We spend our first night in Florence together. My new bed is really little and not very soft. G dutifully delivers my new comforter his friend picked up for me at Ikea, even though he doesn't understand why I want a big king-size blanket until I explain that I want to double it so it is twice as soft. Tonight I tell him about the story of the princess and the pea, and that I too can feel the tiniest lump and need a very special place to sleep. I can't tell if he doesn't understand or if he is not interested in my fable, but he seems less than impressed.

It is well after midnight by the time we go to bed. We spend hours kissing. I count the kisses I give him in Italian trying to reach 100. He loves when I pronounce my teen numbers wrong and have to start over. And he talks to me in Italian when we are making love. Before, I would hear the words and they were music to my ears. I didn't know what he was saying, and it didn't matter. Now I understand some things and other words I am trying to translate and get completely distracted. It is so hot in my little room that G stands in front of the open window to smoke and cool off. "I am wet," he says, rather than "I am sweating." He prefers to cool off naturally and slowly rather than use the fan. I lay all stretched out and satisfied on my feather bed and watch G's silhouette in the window. What a beautiful physique. I have always been an athlete and can probably name every muscle in the human body and how they fit together, each one with its own job and how poetically they overlap each other. How they get tiny tears when overworked and grow when they heal. I have found a new appreciation for the human body. This gives a whole new meaning to eye candy.

We spend what little is left of the night trying to sleep in my tiny bed, in my hot little room with all the noise of the city rudely interrupting us. We move from side to side, adjusting and re-adjusting our mingled bodies on a twin bed on the floor. Again, we get a bed that is less than adequate. We laugh out loud at our luck with beds. The truth is, we are so in love and so happy to be together, the bed is the last consideration. At 7:00 a.m., G's telephone alarm goes off, a silly whistling kind of alarm, and he gets up, dresses and tip toes to the door to make the return trip to the winery.

Later, when I check my email, there is one from him. "Good Morning Princess, I hope you slept well in your new bed, The King." He totally got my story and trumps me. He has advanced to King, skipping Prince completely.

That kickin' ass and takin' names rocks my world. I love that confidence. I love the playfulness. I love the delivery.

I decide that my time in Florence is going very fast and that I don't want to miss any of the highlights. Although I have been to the city many times before, there are just some things I must do again and again. I must see David. I must see the Santa Maria Novella. I must climb the stairs of the Duomo and walk to the Piazzale Michelangelo with its amazing vista of the city.

There are so many new things to see too. There is a Cezanne exhibit at the national gallery. I never really spent serious time in the Uffizi or the Pitti Palace Galleries. I love vintage clothing and have discovered that there are several amazing shops in the city. Shoes, shoes, shoes. And, *O Mio Dio*, (Oh My God) I almost forgot the shoe museum in the lower level of the Salvatore Ferragamo flagship store next to the Arno River. He was the shoemaker for all the big movie stars like Marilyn Monroe, and kept a foot mold for each actress, then made shoes specifically for her foot.

The designer shops with their chic windows line the streets. I am surprised to learn that the fashions are made in sizes two to twelve and a smaller set of sizes is made for the Asian market. There is no plus size. Plus is a small fraction of the world population and Americans are the only ones that buy it. How do Italians stay so slim and eat pasta and bread everyday?

The men are just as fashionably dressed as the women. The clothes are cut perfectly to fit broad shoulders and taper over slim waists. The pants have a narrow leg and fit snugly. Cool sunglasses, a great belt and shoes complete the outfit. The women are dressed in simple, but well-tailored clothing and add a well-placed accessory like a scarf or great bag. They all wear really cool, hip glasses.

No sooner do I put it out into the universe that my intention for living in Florence is art and music, than I am floating out of the Cezanne exhibit feeling like all is right with the world. I realize that I have just seen the most amazing works that I appreciate and am completely moved by the beauty of the paintings whose details I have just spent hours scouring, when a brochure is literally pushed into my hand by a street hustler. He is not promoting a nightclub but a classical music concert being held right here in the old cathedral-turned-concert-hall tonight, on Monday. They are having a concert on Monday? The tickets are only 15 euros and using my student discount, they are only 12 euros. I buy one without giving it the least bit of thought. I have my school book in my back pack, so rather than go home I just sit on the steps of this incredible building and study until eight when the concert starts. Dinner, well dinner will have to be a gelato. It is better than ice cream and comes in a zillion flavors.

I weep through most of the concert. The music swirls around my head, my heart and my body. The beauty of it is simply and totally encompassing. I have to remind myself to open my eyes. This is a *live concert,* but I find that I can listen better when I close my eyes and my only sense is hearing. I force myself to open my eyes and see the beauty of this ancient cathedral, the natural beauty of the marble floor and the lovely grain of the wooden pew I am sitting on. Then I look up and see the details of the stained glass windows, the ornaments of the altar, and all the works of art. It is sensory overload. I love it all. I don't want to miss one part.

Friday after school, I have a reservation to see David, at the Academia. I am so excited. He is *the* sculpture. My reservation is for 5:00 p.m. I made it for two people and ask at school if anyone wants to go. Luca, my Asian classmate, is eager to see the *unfinished* Michelangelo sculptures. We arrive to an unbelievable crowd. The street is jammed with people, three out-of-place giant black SUV limos and lots of security guards wearing funny earpieces. We get in the *reservations* line and discover that the people in front of us are here for a 4:30 p.m. entrance and are still waiting to go inside.

"What's happened?" I ask.

"Some celebrity is inside. They have closed the museum for their visit."

"Get out. They actually closed the museum? For whom?" I speculate.

"It's Cameron Diaz and Antonio Banderas. They are in Italy promoting the new Shrek Movie." Only in Italy I think. There is a fun buzz in the air. We are sandwiched between art lovers and star gazers. I can only see some heads rushing into waiting cars and others cheering. Then I get to go inside and have *my* visit with the famous David. We are instructed again and again, no photos. The flash damages the marble and every 100 years or so a major restoration must be done, sanding off just a fraction of this irreplaceable piece of art. This also means that the great sculpture will be covered with scaffolding for over three years during the careful repairs. Which means whomever visits during those years will miss out on the take-your-breath-away beauty of seeing him in full view as they enter the room. When a flash does go off, a security guard quickly rushes over and scolds the offender. It is clear to me that we are just passing through, but David is here to stay.

As luck would have it, or should I say, as the universe answered my request, just as I come under the spell of Michelangelo's great creation, an English-speaking guide brings her small group of VIP's right next to me. I saw them at the back of the huge line outside earlier, flashing some cash. They are definitely Americans. I hang on her every word. She passionately describes each detail of this great sculpture. Now I have seen him many times before, but listening to her makes him come completely alive for me. What a gift. What a pleasure. I am so lucky. When am I going to stop saying that I am lucky and *get* that this is how the universe works and that I have just finally figured this out? I am not any better or worse than the next guy, I am just tapped in. Tapped, like hooked into. Tapped, like on the head, hello or wake-up! It's like someone appearing and saying, I have always been here. I am so glad you have finally come over. This is the *best* and *only* game in town. Perhaps the awareness of my luck is my gratitude and I should remember to remember.

Just as I am having my little cosmic experience, a big ugly flash comes from the camera of the young man standing next to me. He is part of the tour. Our little heads snap in unison with whiplash speed to look at the perpetrator. Our guide looks like she has been shot through the heart. "What are you doing?" she shouts.

"Nothing," he replies with a shitty none-of-your-business attitude.

"Did you not hear anything I said about photographs?" she pleads.

"I'm sorry," he says, completely deadpan.

What a jerk. What complete disrespect. What lack of appreciation for the privilege he has been given. I want to slap him. How can he not know? This doesn't become apparent until after the commotion of the photo episode dies down when another young girl in the group, maybe twenty-five-years-old, asks our tour guide, "Who was David?" At this point the guide looks like she wants to faint.

"David. You know David and Goliath. David from the Bible. The stone, the giant. Good vs. Evil," the guide offers, attempting to draw some kind of recall.

Nothing. This beautiful young woman doesn't have a clue what the guide is talking about. Feeling completely foolish now, the girl says, "I am sorry, but I don't know who he is."

Then the beauty next to her says, "I don't know who he is either."

Dear God. Where does one begin? I have an instant flashback to the first day of language school. I knew I was coming to Italy. Why didn't I study more or learn to count or at least learn my alphabet? Why would someone come to Italy and not research who David was? We all start somewhere. And we are here and this is now. My heart aches for the tour guide.

The one piece of information that speaks to my soul is that in the pupils of David's eyes, there is a heart shape. I always thought that the empty eyes of great sculptures were creepy looking. The heart is the shape of courage. He needed to be courageous to go up against the Giant, and today we still give the purple heart of courage to heroes of war for being brave in the line of duty.

I also think it is interesting that David is not circumcised, even though he was Jewish. Today, my knowledgeable guide informs me that Michelangelo made the decision not to have David circumcised because he wanted him to be a symbol for all people, not just the Jews. When I tell this story to G later, his only comment is that he thinks his penis is small. That makes me *LOL* (laugh out loud).

Today is the halfway mark of my school and I must say, I can speak enough to communicate what I need, but understanding is really difficult. They speak so fast. It is difficult to speak Italian because as soon as I am struggling, they jump right in and start speaking English, or they take one look at me and start speaking English. I have also given much thought to the idea that somehow, I have convinced myself that learning Italian is difficult and that is the reality that is coming to me. As taught in *The Secret,* I attract my reality to me through my thoughts, words and deeds. Since I already know the language unconsciously, all I must do is remember it. How can this be? I am literally pushing it away from me by saying that *it is hard* or *I can't learn* or *I have a poor memory,* even though I want to know it. So I adopt a new mantra, "Learning Italian comes easily and effortlessly." I add a new sticky note to the wall along with all the others, and repeat it as I walk through my day.

Even though I love Florence, I don't choose to make this my new home. It is too harsh. There are hard surfaces everywhere, noise, and too many people. The city is so full of foreigners. Yes I, Barbara, a foreigner, am actually saying this. But coming off of two months in the RV, three months on the boat and one month of living in the Italian countryside, living in the city doesn't appeal to me like it used to.

That is not to say that I don't still love it here. I am taking every opportunity to soak up all the beauty that surrounds me. I spend hours and hours in the galleries of the Pitti Palace and the Uffizi. At first I would devour each painting and scour every inch, not wanting to miss one little detail, but after awhile I just let them come to me rather than my looking at them. Joy radiates from my heart. Sometimes I will catch myself staring at the beautiful frescoes on the ceiling, wanting to lie flat on my back and just look up. The rooms, floors and halls are so grand and ornate, I think they would overshadow the art, but they don't. I imagine what it was like to live in these great homes. Did they take it all for granted, or did the art make their hearts want to burst from pure joy? I stay until the last minute, then the guard ever so kindly, tells me it is time to leave.

On one clear day, I make the great climb to the Piazzale Michelangelo, quite a grand square with a vast overlook of the marvelous city below. I remember eating a farewell lunch at the ritzy restaurant up here with Debby one year. As I sit soaking up the sun and the view, I notice several chicly dressed people walking up the hill to a beautiful big church, so I follow. To my surprise, it's a wedding. Lots of people are standing outside on the church steps, waiting for the bride and groom to come out. I take a seat on the wall, out of sight and drink in the scene. The guests are well-dressed, and lively conversations flow while children run around playing tag. They must be important to be able to use this church. Soon a soft cheer rises up from the crowd and the bride and groom appear. He is dressed in a dark, well tailored suit and she is wearing a simple draped white dress complete with a floor-length sheer veil. They both have dark hair and eyes. They are young and beautiful and look so happy.

I stay until the group dwindles, and just as I am getting ready to leave, I hear the sound of Vespers coming from the church. It is 6:00 p.m. and the monks have come to offer their prayers. I walk slowly into the empty grand sanctuary and follow the all-male voices downstairs until I find a second small chapel below. Behind an iron gate are about twelve monks dressed in robes singing Bible verses in Italian. I slide quietly into a pew along with a handful of others. The room is cool and dimly lit with candles, their beautiful, humble voices stir my heart. I feel like I have slipped into a little porthole of heaven. For one hour, I barely move or breathe. I am so in the moment. When the others get up to leave, I do too, walking slowly through the main sanctuary and back out into the warm sun of daylight. This is Florence.

Later in the week, I have dinner plans with my friends who are visiting from the states. Giuseppe will arrive late, so I ride my little purple bicycle to the restaurant and he will meet us there. We have a lovely dinner and when it time to go leave, I ask G where he parked the car.

"It is very far away," he says. "Parking is difficult in Florence."

"It's okay, I will walk with you and come back after school tomorrow and get the bike," I tell him.

"Hey, let's ride the bike together back to the car," he suggests.

"We can't ride it together. Where am I going to sit?" I ask him.

He looks at me like I am crazy. "On the handlebars of course," he says.

"I can't sit on the handlebars, I have a basket on the front," I remind him.

"So?" he says.

When we arrive at the bike, he instructs me to sit on the handlebars facing him. "But I can't see where I am going," I say.

"You don't need to, I am driving," he says shaking his head. "Do I need to teach you everything? These American men, they know nothing."

So off we go, me on the handlebars with my feet on the rail between his legs, wobbling through the busy cobblestone streets of Florence.

At the first intersection, we stop and he leans forward to kiss me. "This is why you need to face me," he says with boyish glee. "So I can kiss you at every stop sign."

For the rest of the ride to the car, I don't care that I can't see where I am going. I don't care that the streets are busy and the ride is bumpy. I don't care that we could fall over and crash at any second. All I know is that I am riding on a purple bicycle through the streets of Florence on a hot summer night, with a beautiful Italian man that I am crazy about who stops about every block to shower me with kisses.

Either school gets better, or I just relax more and get into the groove. Some students advance, some were only enrolled for two weeks, and new students are added. Anna joins our class. She just graduated from college in Connecticut and is spending a few months abroad. She spent last summer in Morocco, a place high on my list. We hit it off right away and start touring the city together after school. One day we take the bus to San Gimignano, a wonderful old medieval walled village. By afternoon, we find a place to sit and eat cheese and salami, linger over a bottle of wine and discuss the meaning of life. We even find some old men to practice our Italian on.

I have gotten away from meditating and reading my cards, although I do still listen to *The Secret* on my way to school when I walk. I haven't experienced the nightlife much because I am so exhausted by the end of the day. I have worn out three pairs of sandals walking the cobblestone streets.

The big day of Eduardo's concert in Fiesole arrives. Fiesole is a beautiful little town high on the hillside overlooking Florence and is the home of his world famous music school as well as Leonardo DaVinci. Anna and I arrive early in the day to see the town, and then find the school that has an amazing sweeping view of the city. From the different buildings, we hear all kinds of classical music drifting out onto the lawn, violin, piano, wind instruments, and of course, classical guitar. We find the room where Eduardo will be playing. It is hot and very crowded inside, so we go outside and enjoy the grounds of this renowned school until it is time for his performance. He looks nervous when he enters the room, but once he gets started, the music flows effortlessly. I am so happy for him and so envious of his musical talent, although I know all the practice and time he has committed to his craft.

My last night in Florence, Eduardo, Anna and I walk to the Piazza della Signoria for an outdoor classical music concert conducted by Zubin Mehta. The Piazza is packed and we don't have the best view, but it doesn't matter because we came to hear the music. The full orchestra, in all their black and white glory, play to a grateful audience. Look where I am. I am in Florence with the replica of David towering over there, while the medieval castle of the Medici Family sits over here, and the moon and a handful of stars hang above. Dreams really do come true.

# Chapter 40

*Flying Solo in Sicily*
*July 2007*

The next day, G comes to the city to get me and my two big suitcases and drives back to Foiano and Paola's house. So down the four flights of stairs he lugs my heavy bags, and back up the three flights to Paola's house. I have made arrangements to stay with her again for the month of July. Although I plan be to traveling quite a bit, I still need a home base. I want to go to Positano and Sicily. She is happy for the company and the rent. On the drive out into the countryside, I notice the sunflower fields are blooming. I am happy to be back in my little village. Sunflower in Italian is *girasole* which means go around with (*gira*) the sun (*sole*). The face of the flower actually moves throughout the day to keep facing the sun. In the morning they look one way and in the afternoon another.

I am still undecided about what to do for August. I found a room to rent in Malta, an English-language island south of Sicily, but Giuseppe really thinks I should go to Porto Santo Stefano, so one weekend we drive to the seaside town, just two hours from the winery. The Tuscan landscape doesn't change much until we cross the bridge to the Island of Monte Argentario and start to climb up a little winding, hilly road and then, out of nowhere, pops the most incredible vista of a picturesque little cliff town dropping off into a harbor full of boats. "Now that's more like it!" I shout, adjusting my seatbelt so I can sit up and take it all in. "I had no idea Tuscany had this kind of coast!"

We spend the day poking around the town trying to get the lay of the land and checking to see if anything is available to rent in August. We end up wandering into a little real estate office near the ferry and meet Romano. We learn that he was born and raised here and is an old salty dog at heart. He is a big man with deep lines in his face from all the years of living in the sun. He keeps a little boat in the marina and every day in summertime, he closes the shop from one to four and goes fishing. He knows everybody in town. He is the unofficial mayor of Porto Santo Stefano and holds court on the porch outside his office every day with his buddies. He and Giuseppe hit it off right away.

Of course he has a place available for us, he tells Giuseppe in Italian. He hops on his scooter and we follow as he guides us to a little place way up a steep driveway. Once safely in the driveway, we climb the stairs of a little apartment building and stand on the terrace and look out at the royal blue sea. The view is breathtaking. The little terrace is filled with flower baskets hanging from the iron railing.

"We'll take it," I tell Romano, not even seeing the inside or knowing how much it will cost. There are two apartments to choose from: this one or a bigger two-bedroom unit next door. We decide on the smaller one-bedroom because it is newly remodeled and the view is better. Giuseppe will be able to take most of the month off from the winery because tourists don't come for a wine tasting much in August, but it is close enough for him to drive back when he needs too. Is this really where I am going to live, as a couple? I am open and eager to .... I am in the right place .... All good things are coming ... Yes, this is where I am going to live for August with this wonderful man.

Back in the hills of Chianti, it is festival time. Arezzo is having its big jousting festival. The main piazza is filled with sand and men in medieval costumes ride horses full speed ahead trying to hit a metal bull's eye with their long sword. The town is divided into four quadrants and each team has its own colors. The whole day is full of festivities including a parade and official ceremony introducing the teams. Anna and I take the train in the morning so we won't miss any of the events, and G will meet us in the evening for the jousting tournament. We are cheering for the yellow and blue team because G's dentist got us the tickets, and he lives in that neighborhood. So Anna and I each buy a scarf to wear with the team colors.

The parade is a-dream-come-true. It has it all—men in tights carrying colorful flags, horses, bands and women in long dresses that look like royalty. Where do they get these costumes? Do they own them? Does the town hand them out each year?

After being squeezed in a huge line, we finally take our seats in the grandstand. The piazza is surrounded by buildings and every window and balcony is overflowing with people and colorful flags. Before the jousting begins, each team performs a complicated flag throwing routine. It is right out of the movie, *Under the Tuscan Sun*. The crowd cheers as each team puts on their show.

Once the jousting competition starts, things get serious. The horses are nervous in the corral before they make the long run in front of the bleachers and loud cheering. Each team sends a horseman out, one at a time, for each round and points are accumulated by each team. The crowd waits for the official score of each horseman and goes crazy when it is announced. The young couple in front of us are screaming at the top of their lungs and jumping up and down when our team is ahead. Down on the stage, the team members heckle and taunt each other. In the end, our team doesn't win, but all the teams and the horses walk through the streets along with the huge crowd.

After a few days at home with Paola, I am off to Pisa where I will catch a flight to Sicily. This is my first *real, big girl, solo trip.* I am getting on a plane and flying to a new place and touring for a week alone, not like going to a conference or a spa or camp, or even renting a room for a month where someone is waiting for me. Even though Sicily is still Italy, it is like a different country because the dialect is so different. I am not going to meet anyone. I am really flying solo.

Trains, planes and autobuses, I have done them all again and again, so this time shouldn't be any different. I fly out of Pisa, of course I have to go early to see the tower. What a darling town and unfortunately, no one really goes there. Tourists go to see the tower and fly out of the airport. That's what I do too. My flight is at 6:00 a.m., so I stay near the airport. I find a tiny room for one person with a single bed and bath down the hall for 45 euros. I have air conditioning and a TV, with only Italian channels, but it is good practice for me. It is perfect. My cell phone alarm goes off at 4:00 a.m. and I get dressed and wander out into the dark, deserted street and cool morning air in search of a taxi.

Once at the airport, I check in carrying only a backpack. I am flying on Ryan Air, a local budget airline. My roundtrip ticket was a whopping 40 euro. Although the added charges double the price, it's still a bargain. I land in Trapani at eight and wait two hours for the bus to take me to the other side of the island. As I wait, I people watch and practice my Italian on unsuspecting travelers. I quickly realize that I am a target. There are too many offers for help, directions, or a ride to anywhere I want, including my final destination, Catania, four hours away. I understand I must be careful here. Once on the bus, I take the front seat so I have the big picture window and watch the world go by. The landscape is nothing like I expect. Passing through Palermo, a seaside city with miles of blue coastline, we drive through the middle of the island. Endless fields of yellow wheat, mountains, rolling hills and very few houses, stretch out for miles.

After the flight and a four hour bus ride, I arrive in Catania. So far, I haven't met any other Americans. I am so far from *home* now that most people think I am Swedish or from Denmark. I can honestly say that I am really comfortable in my own skin. The odd thing is, now that I have finally come of age in this solo game, I really miss G. I find myself thinking about him all the time. How funny this game of the universe works?

Sicily feels more like Greece to me and most people don't speak English. Most of the tourists are European and very few are American. Being a blue-eyed blonde is the most difficult part because I stand out completely and attract unwanted attention from the Sicilian men to the point of annoyance.

I finally arrive in Catania at 3:00 p.m., the broiling, hottest part of the day. At first the city seems very industrial as we pass by the shipping yards and warehouses by the port. The hostel is supposed to be a fifteen-minute walk from the bus terminal, so I go inside and get a map. The man behind the counter is very helpful and without knowing it, he will become my tour guide and I will come to him daily to buy tickets to the neighboring towns. The walk from the bus to the hostel is horrible. The heat, the dirt and the litter of the industrial street, and worst of all, the constant harassment of the passers-by, does not produce a very welcoming feeling. Just as I get rid of one unwanted man on a scooter, another one will drive slowly alongside me as I walk quickly, offering me anything I want. A blonde with a backpack is like a homing signal for Sicilian men. I can't get rid of one guy in particular who just keeps driving slowly beside me, speaking in Italian. I can't make him leave by being polite, but I don't know how to say *get lost* in Italian. I try to remember what G says to a driver who cuts him off or is going too slowly.

So there in Sicily, hot, tired and irritated, I say my first curse word in Italian. *Va fan culo* or fuck off. It works! The surprised driver speeds off. I finally turn the corner and enter into the ancient part of the city and a different world. I am overwhelmed by the huge, magnificent buildings. I soon find the Piazza Duomo and Piazza Curro so the hostel should be near. I find an abandoned building that used to be the Hard Rock Café of Sicily and the stinky ruminants of the morning fish market and then, at last, the hostel.

Happy to check-in and get rid of my backpack, I change and plan to head directly to the sea for a swim. To my surprise, in the girls' dorm I find Frederica, who also just checked in. Twenty-two and from Russia, she too is traveling alone and will finish her trip at her aunt's house in Amsterdam. We go to the beach together and stay until sundown.

I love staying in a hostel, just like I did twenty-five years ago. There are eight girls in a dormitory style room, so I choose the top bunk of one of the four single bunk beds. We have no air conditioning and a big bathroom down the hall for all to share. We can use the community kitchen downstairs and the refrigerator is packed with little packages of food marked with each person's name. One night I decide to cook fish that I bought from the market next door. Figuring out the stove and the whole pots-and-pans thing is more work than it is worth. I think I'll stick to eating on the go.

Each day a new young girl comes, and we sit up at night and share travel stories. The girls are from all over the world: Brussels, Finland, Spain. I am by far the oldest, but it doesn't matter. I have a good story to tell. The girls are surprised to find out that I have been officially homeless for over a year now. It still sounds strange, even when I say it. I have slept in a borrowed bed for so many nights now that I don't remember what sleeping in my own bed feels like, other than it was really soft. One night one of the girls asks me how old I am. "I could be your mother," I tell her.

"Get out!" she replies in shock. "My mother would never do this!"

I also discover I have very few needs. I look at my little backpack and think that the contents are all I will need for six days. The Italians do it. They have only a few really great pieces of clothing, but wear them often. It's not the lack of clothing that really takes me by surprise, it is the lack of beauty aids. I have now shrunk down my make-up and personal care products into one small zippered pouch.

I quickly explain to my new roommates that I haven't been traveling like this every night. My travels have been in chunks of time with a few months here and a few months there. Traveling, well touring, is very tiring. I have been traveling, but in a different way.

During the day, I buddy up with a girl and we go off exploring a town. One day, we climbed for three hours to see Mt. Etna, an active volcano. Smoke and hot air still come out of the top and out of other little holes, which we are standing on while looking over miles of black sand and lava rocks. It erupted in 2001, 1998, and 1983. I can't believe they let us up here to roam around freely.

One day I take a bus to Taormina, one of the most beautiful seaside towns of Sicily. I stroll the narrow streets of the city, window shop, stop for a gelato and then later an espresso. Another day I tour Siracusa, a beautiful old island town. I decide to take a boat ride and when the captain learns that I lived on a boat, he lets me drive. It is just a little putt-putt boat with about eight people onboard. From the water, the little town looks even more Greek.

Not as many people here speak English and I am happy to practice my Italian. As my first solo holiday comes to a close, I must make my way back to Trapani on the other side of the island. My flight is very early in the morning, so I need to sleep close to the airport. I don't have any plans, but I am sure something will fall into place, as it always does.

There is one more thing I want to see and that is the Greek ruins in Agrigento, so I hop on a bus and learn that it is a three-hour ride to get there, I will spend a few hours there and then back on a bus for a few more hours, ending up in Tranpani by evening. On the bus I sit in the front seat next to a handsome well-dressed man, Fabrizio. In broken English/Italian we communicate. When we arrive, his friend is waiting for him and they offer to take me directly to the ruins because they know my time is limited. I take the ride and they drop me right off in front. What good luck I have!

The ruins are a complete surprise. I had no idea they were in such good repair and so vast. It is hot and the walk is long and dusty in the clay landscape. I get the English language headset guide. There is so much in the world to see and to learn. I am amazed.

Happy to be back on the bus with air conditioning, I settle in for a long ride. At a rest area, I meet two young girls also traveling on the bus going to Trapani. They went to school together years ago and are taking a little reunion holiday. One girl is from Italy and the other is from Ireland. They are delightful, smart, and of course, both speak fluent English along with several other languages. We get to chatting and when they learn I have no definite place to sleep for the night, they invite me to stay with them, although they are not sure what their accommodations are like just yet.

When we arrive, we are delighted to learn that our little apartment is on the second floor above a wine and cheese shop on the main promenade overlooking the sea. Our balcony faces directly onto the harbor dotted with boats. Here we three toast to our good fortune and to new friends. Is it really this effortless?

One of the girls finds a pop radio station and we listen to dance music while we get ready to go out for the evening. According to the guide book, there is an ancient walled city nearby, so we decide that's where we should have dinner. Off we go in a taxi, zipping full speed ahead on narrow winding roads. As luck would have it, a big full moon comes out to shine on our path. Back in the apartment when the others have gone to sleep, I stand on the balcony and watch the moon dance on the water. Look where I am. At 5:00 a.m., I leave some money on the table for the room, sneak quickly from the apartment and go to the airport, heading back to Tuscany and back to G.

A few days later, I am off to Positano. I have been there before and list it as one of my favorite places in the world. Carrying only a backpack again, I take the train and then a bus on the winding cliff roads with major dropoffs that go straight into the ocean. The bus driver honks the horn on every hairpin turn. It is exciting and scary at the same time.

I have reservations at a hostel and once off the bus, I head up the hill to find my digs for the night. To my surprise, the hostel has a big terrace with a beautiful vista of the sea. They also have a little restaurant and bar that serves one dish a night for a whopping five euros. I check into the girls' dormitory and carry my sheets to room number six. There I find four bunk beds. Two are already taken, so I throw my bag and sheets on a top bunk, get my purse with my passport and money, and head out to explore the town. It is just as charming and quaint as I remember.

That evening when I return to the hostel, the terrace is full of faces from all over the world. I love this. I have a glass of wine and chat with other Americans from Missouri. In my room, I meet two sisters from England traveling together before one of them gets married next month, and two girls from Argentina and another from France. They think I am from the Netherlands. We chat in hushed tones because it is late and the rest of the house is quiet as people are sleeping. I stay for three nights at the cost of 20 euros per night.

In the morning I am back on the bus to Pompeii, the city that was covered by a volcanic eruption in 70 AD. I take the guided tour of this amazing lost city. Others on my tour are amazed when they find out I am traveling alone. "I am not alone," I explain. "I am here with you. Strangers are just friends I haven't met yet." I really do believe that 99.9% of the world is full of wonderful people, they just don't make the news' headlines.

On the train back to Fiona, I start to stress about money. I have my whole life to make more money. If something happened, I would spend it on Brittany or ill parents or even on my own illness, so why not spend on myself for pleasure. What is good credit for if I can't use it? Then I remember my little sticky notes. The world is an abundant place and there is plenty for everyone. Abundance is my birthright. Gandhi said, "There is enough for our need, but not for our greed."

I read a book once by Lynn Twist called *The Soul of Money* and she talks about using our God-given talents. Everyone has the perfect gift to give to the world. If each of us is freed up to give our gift, the world would be in total harmony. What is my gift? What is my intention for my stay in Italy?

When I return to Tuscany, my sister-in-law Patti comes to visit and we run the roads. I like playing tour guide. We go to Florence and the winery.

I also learn that one of the drivers who brings tourists to the winery met an American girl. Claudio was driving Megan, along with a group of other Americans, from Rome to Torre Guelfa Cooking School in Tuscany, and as they were riding along they hit it off. Before you know, Megan cancels the rest of her trip and spends it with Claudio. I meet Megan before she promptly goes home to liquidate everything and moves lock, stock and barrel. They marry, exactly to the date, one year later. Now there is a brave girl. It makes me think of a quote in an old journal. *Keeping your options open becomes a prison. You can never choose. You can never discover your destiny because you are afraid to totally commit.*

# Chapter 41

*Be Brave - Porto Santo Stefano, Italy*
*August 2007*

August 1st arrives and it's time to move to the seaside. G picks me up in the old farm pickup truck with a borrowed scooter loaded on the back. He comes upstairs to Paola's to get all my worldly possessions and drag the two suitcases and a computer down to the street, loading them into the truck along with a box filled with sheets and towels, another box with tomatoes, another with kitchen items his mom thinks we will need, and of course, a few cases of wine. We laugh at the sight of ourselves, but the scooter is perfect for the seaside and this is the only way to get it there.

G is really excited about the beach. July was such a whirlwind for me, I am happy to catch my breath. I am excited about the prospect of spending thirty days with G. The apartment and Porto Santo Stefano are cuter than I remember. We unload the truck and unpack. I open the box filled with sheets and towels and find beautiful freshly ironed white cotton sheets with little blue flowers. We push the two single beds together to make one big one. Of course, there is a Madonna over the wrought iron headboard. The first thing we do is try it out and make sure it is comfortable and doesn't make too much noise and disturb our neighbors.

By evening, we unpack the box for the kitchen and find a tray of homemade eggplant parmesan, several boxes of pasta, salt, prosciutto, cheese, bread and eggs. We also find fresh basil, zucchini and cantaloupe from the family vegetable garden. There is a whole box of fresh home-grown tomatoes. I also find a jar of Nutella.

"What is this?" I ask G.

"Nutella. You put it on bread. Haven't you ever tried it?" he asks.

"No, I've heard about it. I think it is like peanut butter, isn't it?" I ask.

"No babee, it's chocolate," he says shaking his head. "Must I teach you everything?" he teases as he comes over to give me little kisses all over my face.

For our first dinner in our new home, we make a feast. I set a big table outside on the terrace, light candles and open a bottle of his Chianti Reserva. The computer is playing Andrea Botcelli. G is in the kitchen making fresh tomato sauce for the pasta. I slice the cantaloupe and put the crusty Tuscan bread on a wooden board. We are giddy in our bliss and take pictures of the table and the evening as it is settling in over the sea. We toast to our first night in Porto Santo Stefano. I sip the wine, let it roll over my tongue, close my eyes, let my head fall back and take a long deep breath. I am so happy and content here in this moment. I slowly open my eyes and turn to G and say, "This is amazing. Who made this wine?"

With an embarrassed little grin, he says, "The King."

Yes, in this moment, he is the king and I am the princess. I am the luckiest girl in the world.

In the morning, I wake to the sound of a rooster crowing. I lazily open my eyes to see a dimly lit room with white walls with two colorful paintings on them. There is one floor-to-ceiling window closed with a dark green louvered door. I look around the room slowly and out loud, but not to anyone but myself, I say "Am I in Jamaica?"

"No, babee, you are in Italy," G says sleepily.

We discover it is just past 10:00 a.m., but with the shutters closed, we can't tell what time it is or if the sun is shining.

Snuggling close to him, I ask, "What shall we do today?"

"Let's go to the beach and swim," G says. "I want to get some sun, too."

"What if it's raining?" I ask.

"Don't you worry," he answers with a look that says it all, "I have a program for that." Then he gently kisses my nose and then my lips and then my neck and doesn't stop until I am totally satisfied. Making love in the morning is the best. A true luxury I never had time for in my old life. There was always something to do, somewhere to go or somewhere I was supposed to be. Staying in bed together until whatever time I want is new-found bliss.

Without a TV or books and magazines in my language, I have nothing to *do*, but to love G, listen to music, and read and write in my journal. Because of the language barrier, I have become very reflective. Rather than talking and communicating all the time, I am silent except with G. We have all day to lie in the sun, play in the water and explore the town. I no longer wear a watch because it scratches G. I took it off for him, but had no idea what a gift I was giving myself.

Another gift I received without even realizing it is the gift of music. Without all the other options of entertainment, we listen to music. The library on my computer is quite large and eclectic. I decide that the mornings are for classical, the afternoons for ethnic and nights for ballad singers, or I just let it play random all day. What a treat.

One night we go to a restaurant to eat fish. Being so near the sea, it seems appropriate. We hop on the scooter in search of Ristorante La Pace. Romano joins us since he is a friend of Roberto, the owner. The restaurant is on the second floor over looking the harbor with the adorable cliff town behind it. Our table is on the open air terrace. We sit down and Roberto hands us the menu. I am not sure if I missed something, but before I know it, plates of food start coming and don't stop. Apparently, the menus are just a formality, and the only thing to do is eat what is fresh, and Roberto decides what that is each day. First the antipasti, smoked swordfish, little fried fish balls, something like anchovies and a large bowl of huge fresh mussels in a wonderful broth. Roberto collects the menus and opens a bottle of white wine. He pours some for G to taste and when G gives him the nod, Roberto promptly tosses the cork over the balcony and onto the street below. He pours a glass for himself too and we all toast. We eat family style. Roberto and another woman wait on all the tables. He runs around the restaurant all night.

A new group of diners sits at the table next to us. Roberto hands them menus, and when it comes time for them to order, they start to ask a lot of questions about the food telling Roberto that this person is allergic to shellfish, and this person doesn't like fish and so on. Roberto immediately snatches the menus from their hands and tells them to go home and cook for themselves. Then he turns on his heels, goes to the kitchen and continues bringing big bowls of pasta to the other tables. The diners sit there perplexed until they get up and leave.

After a pasta course of fresh gnocchi, a wonderful lemon ice intermezzo and fresh grilled whole fish and potatoes, we are serenaded by Frank Sinatra. Roberto loves music and dancing. He plays it just for his new American friend. Each time he comes to our table, he takes another drink with us. After midnight, we roll out of the restaurant. The street is packed with people. Families with young children and old people are all out walking around. A band has set up right on the main piazza next to the harbor and starts to play. I feel like I am in a time warp, but am happy to walk off my over-stuffed tummy.

As the days turn into weeks, I realize I am living with an underwear model. G loves to walk around in his underwear. He waters our little garden and sweeps the patio in his underwear. He has a beautiful physique and now that he is tan, well, just that much better. One day we have no water and we can hear our upstairs neighbor, a pleasant woman in her fifties with teenage sons, out on her balcony talking to someone about the situation. G goes out on our terrace in nothing but his underwear and sunglasses to speak to her. After about ten minutes, I tell him that he will be out there all day talking to her if he doesn't put some clothes on. He is oblivious to the whole thing.

I do snap a photo or two of him standing in his BVD's on the flower-filled terrace with the amazing view of the sea behind him. Later, when I download the photo, I realize that he has the exact same stance as David. Michelangelo didn't carve David standing that way, but that is the natural stance of an Italian. I actually put the photograph of David and the photo of G next to each other and they really are standing in the same pose. Oh yes, I do love all things Italian.

One afternoon we hop on the scooter to do a little exploring. There is a long line of traffic waiting to get into the tiny harbor area so we, along with other scooters, drive on the center line as both lanes of traffic continue to creep along. I decide right then and there that I am going to be brave. Everyone else is riding down the middle. this is just how they do it here. I decide to be brave when it is time to snorkel in cold but crystal clear water. I decide to be brave when we hike down a forest trail and climb over rocks on the beach to find a secluded cove. I decide to be brave when we ride the scooter on dark winding cliffy roads at night when it is chilly. I decide to be brave and wear a bikini like all the other women, both young and old. I decide to be brave and make love with the lights on, even though he is younger than me. I learn how wonderful, fresh and exciting life is when I stop judging and filtering and just live.

I love that he calls home almost every day to talk to his parents, and the way he calls his mom Mamma. He talks to both his mom and dad each time and he says they are his best friends. He wants to know if it is raining. Rain is very important to the grapes. Hail is a big problem too. When the rains comes rolling across the Chianti hills, it creates big temperature changes which means hail. One bad hailstorm can ruin the entire crop in just ten minutes.

Tonight I sleep alone. G has to go back to the winery for a few days to do a wine tasting for some tourists. It is new to me. It feels like I must get used to it all over again. I try to be brave and be a big girl, but the truth is I miss him. Just when I thought I was used to sleeping alone, I have gotten used to being a couple. I miss the warmth of his long lean body sleeping next to mine. I miss the pillow talk in the morning. I miss knowing I will wake up next to him. In such a short period of time, I have grown to love everything about him. His sweet grace. He is farmer, yet a worldly traveler. He knows luxury, but could sleep anywhere. He is simple, yet complicated. He is young, but has lived a full life. He is like me in so many ways.

He makes sure that I have everything I need and reminds me that he is just a phone call away. I love the way he tells me to *be carefully.* I like being in our little hideaway alone. For three days, I putter around the apartment, ride the scooter, wash the sheets and wait for them to dry on the wash line. Every time I round the bend and see the full view of the harbor in front of me, I am reminded again of what a lucky girl I am. What good fortune I have. I am riding a scooter on the winding roads of this beautiful Italian sea coast with a view that is out of a travel brochure. I walk the tiny streets of my town. I am amazed that I can still spend an hour in a bookstore, even though I can't read the language. The only *must do* on my list today is at 4:00 p.m., really 1600. I must go online and figure out the balance of the tuition for the university for Brittany, then apply for a loan again to cover this next year.

I discover a completely decadent treat one night. I decide to watch a movie I brought from the states on the computer. I found popcorn in the market and thought it would be fun to have movie night alone. Without a microwave and butter, I will have to improvise. So I pop the corn on the stove and drizzle it with oil olive, then shave parmesan cheese on it and salt. Oh, My God! Rain starts to fall as evening comes. It's perfect, a movie in bed with popcorn and rain. Now, all that's missing is a glass of wine. I go to the closet and find only one bottle, his Cardisco. I can't drink this with popcorn. It is a sin. This wine, Cardisco, is a special Super Tuscan. This wine, G's Super Tuscan sells for $200 in California. He only makes 8000 bottles a year. I can't drink *this* wine with popcorn. I look around for some more and can't find anything else, so I open it, pour it into a glass befitting its honor, and toast to good fortune to myself in the mirror. I curl up in bed just as the first flash of lightning lights up the sky followed by a loud echoing boom. I love a good thunderstorm and I love the smell of rain, so I sit back and watch the show, inside and outside. There, on a warm summer night in August, I lie in a bed in Italy alone, watching a movie and drinking a very special wine made by a very special man, knowing that I am the luckiest girl in the world.

The following afternoon G returns and I run down the sidewalk through the little garden to greet him. He is wearing a pink T-shirt with a deep V-neck, exposing just the right amount of dark chest hair, and pink and green army print long shorts. No American man would wear that, but he looks great in it. This becomes my favorite outfit, or at least second favorite to the all white linen draw string pants and crisply pressed linen shirt. I help him carry in a new box of goodies from his mom. She is so kind and thoughtful. I love that she cooks for us.

We ride the scooter all over the island, zipping up and down the narrow streets. The road to our apartment is particularly steep and our little scooter struggles to get to the top. Each time we make it to the top, G gives it an extra goose causing the bike to lurch forward, making me hang onto him tighter and squeal with glee.

One evening we take a bottle of Prosecco or Italian champagne up to a high cliffy look out and sit out on a rock to watch the sun go down. From our little perch, we have an amazing view of the blue sea that stretches out for what seems like forever. The sky changes colors as the sun goes down, and the night air is chilly high on the cliff. We cuddle together to stay warm and then, just like in a movie, a big white moon rises over the mountain. It is huge and full.

"Did you know tonight is a full moon?" I ask G.

"Of course, babee. The full moon is an important time for the vineyard. We make special clippings by the light of the moon," he explains.

I have never known anyone one who keeps track of the moon other than me. This man works in nature. He can read the sky, the wind, the water and now me. As we ride home on the scooter, at each overlook I can see the moon glistening on the water. The night air is chilly so I hold on tightly to G. How lucky am I?

G loves American breakfast and I am happy to make it. He makes our dinner since we only eat Italian and even though I know how to cook, American-Italian just isn't gong to cut it. His cooking is simple and clean and everything tastes so fresh. He learned to cook from his mom who is an amazing cook. He wakes up hungry. I make eggs and toast or sometimes use leftover meat and cheese to make omelets. I make mocha on the stove in a little steel tank and a big mess in the kitchen. We linger over breakfast. I look over at the sink, full of last night's dishes and at the table full of more and ask G, "What time is the cleaning lady coming?"

"What cleaning lady?"

"Our cleaning lady, Rosa. In the US, everyone has a cleaning lady named Rosa," I tell him.

From that moment on, I am known as Rosa and he is known as Pepe, the gardener. When it is time to clear the table, we both call for Rosa to come from the kitchen. When I am washing dishes, he comes up behind me and kisses my neck and calls me Rosa. We laugh and joke with each other. He is so playful and clever even though English is his second language.

Not everything comes out just right. One day he asks me to crunch him.

"What?" I say.

"Crunch me right here," he says, pointing to a mosquito bite on his shoulder.

"You mean scratch me," I tell him. He wants me to correct him when he says something wrong in English because he wants to speak correctly, but some things are just cute, I never want him to say them right.

We have become good friends with our real estate agent Romano. We arrive at Romano's office to find his door open, the signal that he is home and available. He is always holding court. He knows everyone and everyone knows him. He has practically sold every property in the area and almost every customer becomes a friend. He has a full social calendar, going here and there and visiting old friends and new ones. He is young at heart and loves a party. He *is* the party, taking it from villa to villa. He even came to us one night and cooked some fish he caught earlier that day.

He is out front sitting with some other men. When we pull up, he introduces us to the others. He introduces me as the American writer from Florida, the sunshine girl. He calls me the light of the sun. "She is always happy," he says. That is my gift, my positive energy. A smile has a language all its own. It doesn't speak Italian or English.

Today he has invited us to go out in his little boat and eat ricci. I don't know what they are, but G is very excited about it and I am happy to get out on water. We bring three bottles of chilled Malvasia, the white wine G makes, three lemons and two loaves of bread.

Romano closes up his office. We hop back on the scooter and follow his scooter to the dock, passing the big mega yachts including the beautiful sailboat owned by the Tod's shoe family, and another dark hulled boat at least 100 feet long. We pass little restaurants and boutiques and finally arrive at Romano's little old fashioned wooden boat called a Lanca. Onboard, he takes off his work shirt and shorts and has his swimsuit on underneath. Before I know it, we are puttering along the shoreline looking up at the mansions hanging onto the cliffs. Romano points out Jack Nicholson's house and also shows us the one that Jackie O stayed in just after JFK was killed. Who knew this little, charming island was so famous.

Once we anchor, Romano puts on snorkel gear and jumps into the water with a bucket and a long pole. He is gone for a half hour or so and returns with a bounty of sea urchins.

I look at G. "Are we going to eat them? Raw?" I ask.

"You'll see. They are great. A real delicacy," he says.

Romano gets back in the boat and the party begins. Kneeling down, he takes an old scissors and cuts the urchins in half, and washes them out over the side of the boat. He instructs us to get the knife and cut the lemons in half and sprinkle a little juice on each one. Then we take a little chunk of bread and wipe the eggs onto the bread and eat it. This is one of those *Be Brave* moments. I try it and it is good. Not something I would stand in line for, but knowing that it is special and I should grateful, I eat them and drink a lot of wine. Later I learn that the urchins sell for $30 a shell in a sushi bar in New York City.

Tonight the moon is big. I sit on the terrace of our little hideaway and look up to the heavens. I am the luckiest girl in the world. I have made a habit of saying that because whenever I catch myself thinking, wow! I want to say thank you. It is my way of being grateful for the gift of this moment. Look where I am! How did I ever get here? I wonder about this often.

My friend Christy told me once after hearing my story that I have it much easier than others because I was forced to change. Someone else may be unhappy with their life, but will not change, because to choose to change is much more difficult than change being forced upon them. I have been pondering this for days now. Is it easier to change when change comes by force or by choice? Each of us knows when we are out of touch or not living our authentic lives. I knew. I needed to change and I was planning to change, but I was waiting until the right moment for everyone, not just myself. But the change came before I was ready. It was a matter of life and death. I just didn't know it then. I changed by force, and I don't wish that on anyone. I was ready and not ready at the same time. I describe what happened to me like someone in the middle of the night coming to the foot of my bed and ripping the covers off of my sleeping body, exposing me to the cold and the harsh realities of the world, leaving me naked and shivering.

Pinch me, is it really me? It wouldn't be me if I were back in Orlando trying to make a round peg fit into a square hole. It wouldn't be me if I had stayed with Warren and become the mother of two small children. It wouldn't be me if I weren't brave. The universe is always giving us signals of which direction to go, all we must do is be still enough to see the signs.

We must stop listening to our conscious voice, our head, the one society has taught us to listen to, the one that says make a plan and work the plan. *Work* being the key word here. I was taught that to get anywhere in life I must work hard, but the truth is just the opposite. Life is meant to be easy. When we start listening to our inner voice or our intuition, we become authentic. When we are on the right track, the whole world rises up to help us. We know what the right track is. It is not, Be-Do-Have, it is Be-Have. Our job is not to *do*, our job is to ask the universe and watch the *do* part happen right before our very eyes. Divine Intervention. The *do* for us is to be aware of the signs the universe is sending us, and to act when it feels right. Act out of love, not fear. Act out of *running to,* not *running from.*

Life has a funny way of allowing us to work ourselves into a corner, or to rephrase that in cosmic terms, we are all given free choice. We can choose anything we want. We can go for anything, but when we get it and it doesn't bring us the joy we were looking for, we know, somehow, it wasn't the right track. So choose again, but this is where we get stuck. We don't think we can choose again. Look how hard we worked. Look at what we have. We hold to what we have because we *should* be grateful. This is what society has taught us. Following our true, authentic self brings joy and success. When we radiate joy and happiness, we attract all good to us. When we get off the track, we are no longer radiating joy. We are just going through the motions. We are doing what we *think* we are supposed to do, not what *feels* right.

In my old life, I had every minute of the day planned and packed full. There was no time for divine intervention. I was too busy, and my motto was help me or get out of the way because I have things to do. There was no time to stop and smell the roses. It wasn't roses I was supposed to be smelling, but what *happens* when I slow down long enough to let serendipity happen. It is about slowing down enough to enjoy a breezy stroll into a shop, to chat with the girl and to learn she is looking for a place to rent, and I am looking for someone to rent an apartment I have available. All I have to do is ask, slow down enough to let the universe do its thing, and get out of my own way. I don't control it, the universe's plan is so much greater than mine.

Besides, busy-ness is a trick of the ego. It is false importance. It keeps you running, distracted, and thinking that these *things* and *you* are so important. I can assure you that these things would all be taken care of should you disappear one day. Your child's spot on the soccer team would be replaced by a child sitting on the bench, and your seat on the board would be replaced by someone who may a have a better or different vision for your organization. At any rate, the world moves on. Stop everything. Stillness is the answer.

I think that my personality was so strong that the universe had to blow up my whole life as I knew it, in order for me to change. I had to have Tom go, Brittany go, my job go. I had to *lose* everything in order to create a space for something new. That new thing being what I was praying for, begging for on the porch back in the tree house.

In hindsight now, I know I got exactly what I wanted, I just wish I had been a little flexible and that it didn't need to hurt so much. Or maybe that is just how hard I was clinging to the wrong tree, and God had to cut down the tree because there was no other way to make me let go. I always had free choice. I was praying and begging for change and I got it.

Did I really *do* anything to meet Giuseppe? I put out a group email to my friends to tell them I had arrived safely in Italy, most of whom didn't even know I was planning to come here. My friend, Susan, casually mentioned I Selvatici Winery in an email. I could have written it off as being too far away, I don't have a car, or I don't want to go alone, but for some reason, I didn't. And the day I went, I was carefree, full of sunshine and radiating joy; I couldn't have planned or stopped the outcome. The universe was doing its thing in the most beautiful, perfect way. The only way it knows.

Giuseppe is in the kitchen cooking dinner. I am the luckiest girl in the whole wide world. *Thank you.* I stroll over to the edge of the terrace and lean on the railing. I look out over the sea, draw a deep breath and take it all in. I am living my dream. I am in Italy, looking at the most beautiful view of the seaside, drinking a fabulous glass of wine and in love with the man who made it. I am swept away with emotion. "In a week, I am going back. All this will be over. Now what?" Tears slide down my cheeks.

Giuseppe comes up behind me and wraps his arms around me and places his cheek against mine. He pulls his face away and looks at me with surprise and concern.

"You are wet. What's happened?" he asks.

"Oh Love, I am so happy here with you, but this is all going to be over soon. I have to go back in a week."

"Why do you go back?" he asks, looking directly in my eyes.

"Good question," I whisper, looking down, barely getting the words out. A huge lump forms in my throat. I squirm, not wanting to look at him. He holds my face gently in his hands and makes me look at him. "The truth is I don't have anywhere to go," I croak.

"Then stay," he says. "Come home with me. Come back to the winery."

"Giuseppe, you live with your family. It's not for you to decide."

"Babee, I have already spoken with them. It is okay with them for you to come and stay."

"Really, you have already spoken to them!" I answer in complete surprise.

"Come home with me and help pick the grapes," he says.

"Oh Love," I exclaim jumping up and down, hugging him and kissing him all over his face.

"Call right now and change your flight," he instructs.

"Right now?" I answer surprised.

"Yes, Babee, right now."

"International Reservations, may I help you?" the agent answers.

"Yes, this is Barbara Singer. I am scheduled to fly with you on September 1st and I want to change my flight."

# Author Biography:

Barbara grew up in rural Lancaster County Pennsylvania. After graduating from Penn State, she moved to Orlando, Florida. She has one daughter. Being a life-long student of self-help and motivation, she has walked on fire with Tony Robins, finds great joy in traveling, meeting people from around the world, reading and listening to eclectic music. She is a three-time marathon finisher and two-time Ironman tri-athlete. As a dynamic speaker, her greatest passion is inspiring others to wake up and start living. Visit www.BarbaraElaineSinger.com for photo gallery, information about on-line coaching and speaking engagements.

# Post Script

*How did I really do it?*

I am not a trust fund baby or independently wealthy, and at any given time during the trips, I generally didn't have more than $10,000 in the bank. I had no debt other than mortgages, which were covered by my renters. My fall back plan was my 401K, which I didn't need to tap into. I lived on about $1000 a month. Each room I rented was not more than $500 and I kept other living expenses, such as food and transportation under $500 a month. After the harvest, Giuseppe and I spent the winter in Aspen where I worked as the hotel nanny and returned to Tuscany the following spring.

Go to my website www.BarbaraElaineSinger.com to find more specific details about "How to Quit Your Life and Start Living Without Reservations." Here you will find more information on topics like health insurance, security, responsibilities, working, liquidating and living anywhere in the world.

How to
Quit Your
Life and
Start Living

*a 12 step practical
guide to living
mobile.*

Barbara Elaine Singer

www.BarbaraElaineSinger.com

LaVergne, TN USA
15 March 2011
220229LV00003B/131/P

9 780984 325405